D1234132

# Speech Evaluation in Psychiatry

### Principal Scientific Consultant

Michael H. L. Hecker, Ph.D.
Senior Research Consultant
SRI International
Menlo Park, California

### Scientific Consultants

**Gavin Andrews, M.D.**
Associate Professor of Psychiatry
University of New South Wales
Prince Henry Hospital
Sydney N.S.W., Australia

**Harry Hollien, Ph.D.**
Professor and Director
Institute for Advanced Study of Communication Processes
University of Florida
Gainesville, Florida

**Peter F. Ostwald, M.D.**
Professor of Psychiatry
University of California Medical School
San Francisco, California

**Thomas Shipp, Ph.D.**
Chief
Speech Research Lab
Veterans Administration Medical Center
San Francisco, California

# Speech Evaluation in Psychiatry

Edited by

## John K. Darby, M.D.

*Teaching Faculty*
*San Mateo Mental Health Center*
*San Mateo, California*

## Grune & Stratton, Inc.

*A Subsidiary of Harcourt Brace Jovanovich, Publishers*
New York      London      Toronto      Sydney      San Francisco

**Library of Congress Cataloging in Publication Data**

Main entry under title:

Speech evaluation in psychiatry.

    Bibliography.
    Includes index.
      1.  Mentally ill—Language—Evaluation.
2.  Speech, Disorders of—Evaluation.    I.  Darby,
John K.
RC455.4.P78S66       616.85′5      80-24133
ISBN 0-8089-1315-8

**Grune & Stratton, Inc.**
**111 Fifth Avenue**
**New York, New York 10003**

**Distributed in the United Kingdom by**
**Academic Press Inc. (London) Ltd.**
**24/28 Oval Road, London NW 1**

Library of Congress Catalog Number 80-24133
International Standard Book Number 0-8089-1315-8

Printed in the United States of America

# Contents

**Preface**                                                                xi

Part I

**SPEECH BEHAVIOR AND METHODS OF EVALUATION**

I. **Speech Science**

1  **Speech Behavior as a Communication Process**     5
The sounds of speech; linguistic phonetics; prosodic and paralinguistic features; speech production and perception; the nonlinguistic domain; patterns of meaning; the communication process.
*Diana Van Lancker, Ph.D.*

2  **The Nonlinguistic Components of Speech**     39
The carrier nature of speech; inherent information; voluntary modifications of the voice.
*John J. Ohala, Ph.D.*

3  **Describing the Normal Voice**     51
Preliminary analytic concepts; problems in the standardization of voice terminology; the description of phonetic settings in voice quality; the relation between phonetic description and organic factors; conclusion.
*John Laver, Ph.D.*
*Robert Hanson, Ph.D.*

4  **Analog Instrumentation for Acoustic Speech Analysis   79**
Instrumental approaches; fundamental frequency analysis; vocal jitter; wave composition-spectrography; intensity analysis; temporal measures; computers.
*Harry Hollien, Ph.D.*

5  **Acoustic Analysis and Computer Systems   105**
Digitization of speech; digital filtering; spectral analysis; linear prediction; other speech analysis techniques; conclusion.
*Jared J. Wolf, Ph.D.*

## Part II
## SPEECH EVALUATION IN PSYCHIATRY

II.  **Speech Behavior Associated with Normal Personality**

6  **Speech Behavior and Personality   115**
Basic theoretical assumptions; the nature and measurement of major speech cues; empirical results on personality correlates of speech; voice and speech markers of extraversion; conclusion.
*Klaus R. Scherer, Ph.D.*
*Ursula Scherer, Dipl.-Volksw.soz.wiss. Richtg.*

7  **The Fährman Inventory of Speech Characteristics (FISC)   137**
Background; administration and scoring of the FISC; dimensions of the FISC; distributions of ratings and interlistener agreement; potential applications.
*Michael H.L. Hecker, Ph.D.*

8  **Vocal Style and the Process of Psychotherapy   151**
Research program at the University of Chicago; the client vocal quality classification system; research on client vocal quality; clinical applications; vocal cues, speech production, and cognitive processing; future directions.
*Laura N. Rice, Ph.D.*
*Conrad J. Koke, Ph.D.*

III.  **Speech Variability and Emotion**

9  **Vocal Indicators of Stress   171**
The effects of stress on speech production; empirical studies

on vocal correlates of stress; evidence on vocal indicators of stress; conclusion.
*Klaus R. Scherer, Ph.D.*

10 **Speech and Emotional States    189**
The nature and functions of emotion; the components of emotional states; affect vocalizations in animals and man; review of findings on acoustic correlates of emotion in speech; recognition of emotion from speech; conclusion.
*Klaus R. Scherer, Ph.D.*

11 **Vocal Correlates of Emotional States    221**
Some physiological considerations; review of selected studies; conclusion.
*Carl E. Williams, Ph.D.*
*Kenneth N. Stevens, D.Sc.*

IV. **Speech Behavior Associated with Character Disturbances and Neuroses**

12 **The Relevance of Voice in Forensic Psychiatric Evaluations    243**
Differential diagnosis; speech behavior and psychopathology; conclusion.
*Bernard L. Diamond, M.D.*

V. **Speech Behavior Associated with Psychotic Disturbances**

13 **Speech and Voice Studies in Psychiatric Populations    253**
Psychiatry and speech science; childhood psychosis; schizophrenia; affective disorders; mixed population studies; comparative studies; conclusion.
*John K. Darby, M.D.*

14 **Disorders of Language in Childhood Psychosis: Current Concepts and Approaches    285**
Approaches to the study of speech and language disturbances in childhood psychosis; abilities and abnormalities of interest in the context of language; conclusion.
*Christiane A.M. Baltaxe, Ph.D.*
*James Q. Simmons, III, M.D.*

15 **Speech and Schizophrenia    329**
History and definitions of schizophrenia; primary and secondary disturbances in schizophrenia; schizophrenia and

communication; acquisition of pathological speech; the inner
speech of schizophrenia; conclusion.
*Peter F. Ostwald, M.D.*

16  **Spoerri's Descriptions of Psychotic Speech    349**
Editor's preface; Spoerri's methods and concepts; case studies: language destruction; case studies: language reduction;
case studies: neoformation of language; case studies: unique
linguistic phenomena; characteristic features of Spoerri's
research.
*Hemmo Müller-Suur, M.D.*

17  **Speech and Disturbances of Affect    359**
Definition of clinical terms; acoustical features of voice; encoding of emotional arousal; encoding of flat affect; mechanisms of "normal" emphasis; flat affect and depression;
encoding of moods; conclusion.
*Murray Alpert, Ph.D.*

18  **Speech and Psychopharmacology    369**
Site and action of psychoactive drugs; effects of psychoactive
drugs on speech; possible directions of further research.
*Stanley Feldstein, Ph.D.*
*Herbert Weingartner, Ph.D.*

**Index    397**

# Contributors

**Murray Alpert, Ph.D.**
Professor of Psychology
New York University
Medical Center
New York, New York

**Christiane A.M. Baltaxe, Ph.D.**
Assistant Professor of
  Psychiatry
University of California
Los Angeles, California

**John K. Darby, M.D.**
Teaching Faculty
San Mateo Mental Health
  Center
San Mateo, California

**Bernard L. Diamond, M.D.**
Professor of Law, Emeritus
University of California
Berkeley, California;
Clinical Professor of Psychiatry
University of California,
San Francisco, California

**Stanley Feldstein, Ph.D.**
Professor of Psychology
University of Maryland
Baltimore County, Maryland

**Robert J. Hanson, Ph.D.**
Assistant Professor of Speech
  Science
University of California
Santa Barbara, California

**Michael H. L. Hecker, Ph.D.**
Senior Research Engineer
SRI International
Menlo Park, California

**Harry Hollien, Ph.D.**
Professor and Director
Institute for Advanced Study of
  Communication Processes
University of Florida
Gainesville, Florida

**Conrad J. Koke, Ph.D.**
Counseling and Development
  Center

York University
Ontario, Canada

**Diana Van Lancker, Ph.D.**
Postdoctoral Fellow
Department of Communication
  Disorders
Northwestern University
Evanston, Illinois

**John Laver, Ph.D.**
Director of the Phonetics
  Laboratory
University of Edinburgh
Edinburgh, Scotland

**Hemmo Müller-Suur, M.D.**
Professor of Psychiatry
Göttingen, West Germany

**John J. Ohala, Ph.D.**
Professor of Linguistics
University of California
Berkeley, California

**Peter F. Ostwald, M.D.**
Professor of Psychiatry
University of California
San Francisco, California

**Laura N. Rice, Ph.D.**
Professor of Psychology
York University
Ontario, Canada

**Klaus R. Scherer, Ph.D.**
Professor of Psychology
University of Giessen
West Germany

**Ursula Scherer, Dipl.-
  Volksw. soz. wiss. Richtg.**
Department of Psychology
University of Giessen
West Germany

**James Q. Simmons, III, M.D.**
Professor of Psychiatry
University of California
Los Angeles, California

**Kenneth N. Stevens**
Professor of Electrical
  Engineering and Computer
  Science
Massachusetts Institute of
  Technology
Cambridge, Massachusetts

**Herbert Weingartner, Ph.D.**
Laboratory of Psychology and
  Psychopathology
National Institutes of Mental
  Health
Adjunct Professor of
  Psychology
University of Maryland
Baltimore County, Maryland

**Carl E. Williams, Ph.D.**
Chief, Acoustical Sciences
  Division
Naval Aerospace Medical
  Research Laboratory
Pensacola, Florida

**Jared J. Wolf, Ph.D.**
Senior Scientist
Bolt Beranek and Newman Inc.
Cambridge, Massachusetts

# Preface

This book and its companion volume, *Speech Evaluation in Medicine,* are the outgrowths of two panel discussions on speech behaviors observed in certain psychiatric conditions and disease states. These panel discussions were conducted during the 1977 meeting of the International Phonetics Society in Miami, Florida.

Originally, a simple transcription of the presentations seemed adequate; however, it became apparent that the material was of such complexity that it required a thorough format of development and review. These volumes illustrate how the study of speech behavior in normal and pathological states requires extensive interdisciplinary knowledge from the fields of medicine, psychiatry, psychology, speech pathology, speech science, computer science, engineering, and physics. In organizing the material included in these volumes, an effort was made to provide a clear exposition of current knowledge and a foundation for further research. Each chapter is written by a recognized authority in a particular field, and it typically provides a key bibliography.

The use of the term "speech evaluation" in the titles of these volumes is intended to indicate a shift from the study of language toward the study of speech; specifically, toward the assessment of speech behavior. This orientation emphasizes: (1) the organs of speech production; (2) psychological and physiological factors which affect speech production; (3) quantitative measurement of speech properties; and (4) the relationship of speech properties to normal and pathological states.

*Speech Evaluation in Psychiatry* is divided into five sections. The first section reviews basic knowledge about speech behavior and methods of speech evaluation. These chapters describe normal speech production, the communication process, problems in auditory assessment, acoustic correlates of articulatory events, physical parameters of speech sounds, and methods of measurement.

The second section concerns relationships between personality traits and speech behavior. The third section reviews studies that relate emotional states, such as stress, fear, and anger, to speech production. The fourth and fifth sections address more traditional concerns of psychiatry, with particular emphasis on speech behaviors seen in the psychoses. These chapters include material on differential diagnosis, childhood psychoses, schizophrenia, affect disturbances, and psychopharmacology.

I am indebted to many people for their assistance in planning and carrying out this project. A grant from the Commonwealth Fund made the endeavor possible. Michael H. L. Hecker, the principal scientific consultant, provided valuable counsel throughout the project. The other scientific consultants made important suggestions concerning the selection of authors and topics and provided beneficial commentary. Patricia Bashaw edited the submitted manuscripts; her capable assistance is deeply appreciated. I am also grateful for the help of many people who reviewed specific chapters: Peter F. Ostwald, Dwight Bolinger, Harry Hollien, Klaus R. Scherer, Arnold E. Aronson, Nina Simmons, Thomas Shipp, Bruno Repp, David Wexler, Jack Vogenson, and many others.

# PART I
# Speech Behavior and Methods of Evaluation

# I. Speech Science

Diana Van Lancker

# 1

# Speech Behavior as a Communication Process

Speech behavior is made up of talking and listening, both highly complex skills. Individual intention and interpersonal interaction are cardinal properties of communication: messages are formulated (by the speaker) and interpreted (by the listener). For the communication process to occur, it is obviously necessary for the participants to share knowledge of many kinds, including knowledge about phonology, syntax, and semantics. But the attributes that make up the knowledge that underlies communicative ability are not a fixed repertory; instead, they are constituted so that a potentially infinite variety of messages can be communicated by means of them. On the one hand, it is true that the knowledge that each speaker has (which makes it possible to create those new messages) must have been drawn from the unique experience of that individual, and is therefore personal, subjective, and private. The fact that communication *can* occur, however, indicates that much of the knowledge about how to organize messages is shared. Therefore, if we can determine what kinds of

---

*This chapter, which benefitted from the thoughtful suggestions of Gerald J. Canter, Michael T. Shipley, John Lamendella, and Edward Carney, as well as from the research assistance of Paul Hardee and the voices of Harold Clumeck and Gerald J. Canter, was prepared during a postdoctoral fellowship in Speech and Language Pathology at Northwestern University, funded by Training Grant # NS-07100 from the National Institute of Neurological Diseases and Stroke. I am also grateful for the general encouragement and aid from members of the Department of Communicative Disorders at Northwestern University and for assistance from Peter Ladefoged at the University of California, Los Angeles.

5

knowledge are stored and what kinds are shared—both of which make language behavior possible—we may gain some understanding of the communication process.

It must be the case that particular kinds of knowledge about *sounds* and *meanings* are stored and shared by speakers of a language. Human language has been classically defined by linguists as a systematic pairing of sound and meaning. This is puzzling from the particular point of view that sounds and meanings are very different phenomena, in ways reminiscent of the "mind/brain problem" (see Dennett, 1978, for review). Sounds have physical properties that can be recorded, measured, labeled, and analyzed in many ways. Meanings or messages are abstract and can be investigated only indirectly. Yet a domain or "level" of *sound* correlates systematically with another "level" we can call *meaning*.

To investigate speech performance, it is useful to think of a number of levels relating sound and meaning. A brief overview may serve to introduce some terms and to orient the reader to the discussion that follows.

*Acoustic* descriptions of the speech signal involve measurements of frequency, intensity, and duration, i.e., properties of sound waves and sound spectra. Any utterance can be recorded in a number of ways and analyzed for its acoustic properties. *Linguistic phonetics* includes both *acoustic* and *articulatory* features, focusing on those that are significant in speech production and perception. In articulatory phonetics, the movements and positions of the human vocal tract are observed and measured during production of particular speech sounds. The purpose of linguistic phonetics is to establish the features of the sound level in speech perception and production that are significant in communicative behavior. *Phonetic features* combine to form phonological units on a *phonemic* level. *Phonemes* are the distinctive phonological units that make up the sound pattern of a language. For example, in English, the medial /t/ of *conductor* is aspirated, whereas the medial /t/ of *flutist* usually is not, and yet these sounds are interpreted as the same sound-types (both as /t/). These sound-types are called phonemes. A phoneme is an abstraction, a class of phonetic features or sounds that are interpreted as making up one of the repertory of phonological units in a given language.

The next level relating sound and meaning is the *morpheme,* which is made up of phonemes combined according to the phonological rules in a language. For example, the morphemes *pat* and *bat* are each made up of three phonemic segments. The initial segments *b* and *p* are two different phonemes, contrasted by one phonetic feature, the feature of voicing. Voicing is a distinctive feature in English. The final segment /t/ can be pronounced with or without aspiration, and still be heard as the same sound-type (or phoneme), since, again, aspiration is not a distinctive feature in English. The *phonology* of a language refers to the sound patterns that result from morphemes combining to form words. For example, changes in the stress pattern and the vowels in the words *sýmphony* and *symphónic* are predicted by regular phonological changes. *Sym-* and *-phon-* and *-y* can all be considered morphemes—minimal units of meaning. Affixes (such as *trans-*, *re-*, and *-tion*), which are attached to word stems (such as in trans*form*, re*form*, in*form*ation), grammatical categories (such as tense and number), and words themselves comprise the morphemes of a language. Words are morphemes and combinations of morphemes that make up the *lexicon* (or basic dictionary) of a language. *Syntax* means the ways words are put together to achieve a meaning. For example, sentence (1) differs in meaning from sentence (2)—namely, which player has the spotlight—only in the arrangement of words.

1. The cellist accompanied the bassoon player.
2. The bassoon player accompanied the cellist.

To a certain extent, syntactic patterns can be distinguished from *semantic patterns*. Sentences (3) and (4) challenge our ordinary sense of regular semantic patterns in English.

3. The bassoon elapsed.
4. The symphony slept furiously through the green concert.

In summary, phonetic features make up phonemic segments which combine to form morphemes and words. Morphemes and words also combine, according to syntactic rules and semantic patterns, to form phrases, sentences, paragraphs, and discourse.

## THE SOUNDS OF SPEECH

It is well known that the sounds of speech come from vibrations set off by moving a column of air from the lungs, past the larynx, and out through the oral (and, intermittently, the nasal) cavity. The particular settings of the vocal folds, positioning of the velum, and movements of the tongue and lips all contribute to the pattern of the airborne acoustic wave (see Figure 1-1). These vibrations impinge on the ear, where receptors convey coded patterns of nerve impulses along the auditory pathway in the brain to the auditory parts of the cerebral cortex (see Gulick, 1971). Somehow this neuronal activity is interpreted and used to extract messages.

We do not know exactly how the communicative process is accomplished through the many complex stages of a bidirectional transduc-

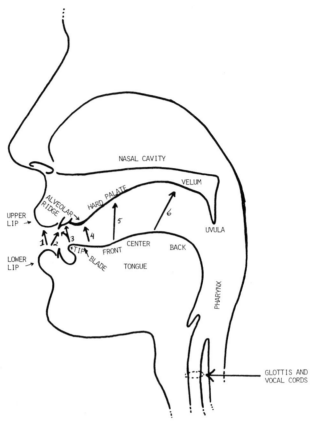

Fig. 1-1.   Diagram of the vocal organs, naming the parts commonly involved in the production of consonants and vowels. Numbered arrows indicate primary places of articulatory approximation or closure. (1) Bilabial; (2) Labiodental; (3) Dental and interdental; (4) Alveolar; (5) Palatal; (6) Velar.

tion, wherein a message is converted to sounds (by a speaker) and sounds are converted to a message (by a listener):

$$\text{message} \longrightarrow \text{sound} \Longrightarrow \text{sound} \longrightarrow \text{message}.$$

We are faced with the mystery of how physical events (in acoustic vibrations and neuronal firings) have such an intimate and repeatable association with mental activities. Some details of this process are understood, however. The objective of this chapter is to describe some established facts about speech production and perception and to infer from them certain general perspectives on the kinds of knowledge that speakers have stored and shared to enable them to engage in communicative behavior.

## LINGUISTIC PHONETICS

Descriptive articulatory phonetics has provided a good deal of information about how speech sounds are formed by gestures of the tongue, the velum, and the lips playing on the air column in synchrony with the phonatory activities of the larynx (see Figure 1-1). (Abercrombie, 1967; Ladefoged, 1971, 1975). These various anatomical structures contribute to speech production in varying degrees. Flexibility within the system allows for compensatory strategies such that even a tongueless person can sometimes learn to produce intelligible speech.

Speech is made up of temporal events that may occur at rates up to over 300 words per minute (Goldstein, 1940); artificially accelerated speech can be understood at rates of over 400 words per minute (Orr, Friedman, and Williams, 1965). And each rapidly-decaying moment is dense with acoustic data. The raw material of the acoustic signal *simultaneously* provides cues for many kinds of information in domains roughly classified as *linguistic* and *nonlinguistic*. The boundaries between these classes are vague. Linguistic domains traditionally include structured design features of human language found at levels called phonology (sound patterns), morphology (units of meaning), syntax (patterns of phrase and sentence structure), and semantics (patterns of meaning). Nonlinguistic domains include attitudes, emotions, personality traits, and social (regional accent, socioeconomic status) and biological (sex, height) information carried in the linguistic signal.

Not all the raw acoustic material is essential to the linguistic message, and some of it seems to be irrelevant to any aspect of the message. This comes from the fact that speech "surfaces" have the potential to vary infinitely. This is easily shown by asking someone to say something repeatedly, recording the utterances, and making an acoustic record of the series of utterances on a sound spectrograph. The resulting spectrogram is a visible two dimensional record of patterns of acoustic energy in time (Figure 1-2). Even a single word repeated and recorded spectrographically, such as the word *pint* [paint], will show measurable differences in vowel length, in the point at which the voicing for the vowel begins before release of the initial consonant [p], in the length of the aspiration during the release of the final consonant [t], and so on, depending on how minutely one measures. Yet the productions of this word "sound like" the "same" word. This point is important in understanding that *phonetic transcription* (the use of written symbols, such as the International Phonetic Alphabet, to represent sounds) occurs along a continuum from *broad* to *fine,* depending on how much articulatory detail—aspiration,

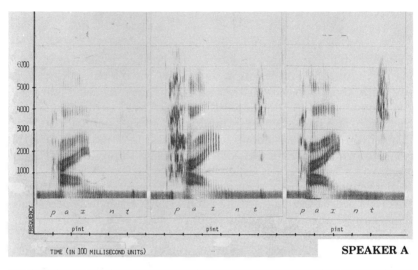

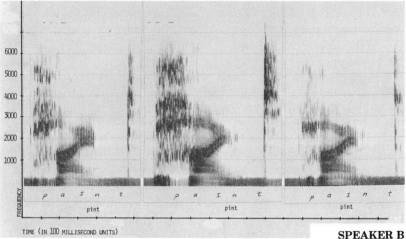

Fig. 1-2. Acoustic record in the form of a spectrogram. On the spectrogram, the different amounts of acoustic energy at different frequencies scaled along the vertical axis are seen as dark markings over time scaled on the horizontal axis. When the energy is concentrated into broad bands, as is usually the case in vowels, the dark markings on the spectrogram are called formants. The spectrograms here show repetitions in the word *pint* [paint] by two speakers, A and B. There are small differences at several points in the tokens of the word *pint* produced by one speaker and by both speakers compared. (By convention, phonetic units are enclosed in brackets, whereas phonemic units are bounded by slashes.)

length, pitch variation, precision of manner and place of articulation, etc.—is included in the transcribed record. The upper limit of "fineness" is a function of one's skill, perceptual ability, and patience.

Now, add to our example (of differing acoustic records of the "same" word) individual speaker differences, talking while tired or while eating a sandwich, dialect variation, fast and slow speech within and across speakers, mood changes reflected in the speech pattern, and noisy environments—add these to what has been called an intrinsically "poor" (low energy) signal to gain a sense of the variance in the speech signal. Speech scientists have been pursuing questions about the underlying patterns that must exist. In other words, what is it that is "shared" that enables speakers of a language to recognize recurrent phonological "sames" in a physical signal with so much variation?

The matter of *variant surfaces* perceived as *recurrent sames* is still further complicated by another fact of perception: the stream of sound, itself more or less continuously varying, is perceived as being made up of discontinuous segments, such as consonants and vowels, or "phonemes." Furthermore, many of the segments perceived as the same have acoustic patterns which regularly differ in different phonetic contexts. Because of both inertia and higher level programming of gestures, nearby articulatory positions influence each other or can be expected to show *coarticulation*. For example, /k/ before the vowel *i* is produced at a point along the palate more forward (resulting in a palatal /k/) than /k/ before /u/ (a velar /k/). This is because the vowel *i* is produced with the tongue raised toward the front of the mouth, whereas the vowel /u/ is produced with the tongue raised toward the back of the mouth; the ideal target position of the vowel influences the articulation of the consonant (Figure 1-3). These articulatory differences are reflected in the acoustic record. Figure 1-4 shows contrasts in the patterns of acoustic energy (formants) for the two pronunciations of /k/.

These facts about articulatory and acoustic phonetics are summed up in the notion of *encodedness* (Liberman, Cooper, Shankweiler et al. 1967). Encodedness in the speech signal refers to the sense in which part of the acoustic information for a particular perceived sound-type can occur at a point before and/or after the one perceived. The effects of coarticulation can spread over several articulatory gestures. The listener extracts an impression of individual segments from a signal in which information is smeared along the way in the stream of acoustic events.

The extracting must be done on the basis of something in the acoustic signal. Considerable work has been aimed at determining

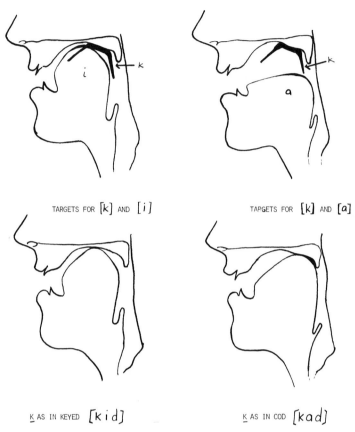

TARGETS FOR [k] AND [i]            TARGETS FOR [k] AND [a]

K̲ AS IN KEYED [k i d]            K̲ AS IN COD [k ɑ d]

Fig. 1-3. Drawing of vocal tract, showing the relation between ideal (target) articulatory positions and actual positions for the production of /k/. A palatalized or fronted [k] occurs in the phonetic environment of a front vowel [i]. A velarized or back [k] occurs adjacent to a back vowel [a]. (Compare with Ladefoged, 1975, pp. 50–51.)

which properties of the speech wave are associated with what kinds of processes residing in the human mind/brain that makes speech perception possible. The spectrogram can also be seen as a mixture of continuous elements (e.g., voiced consonants /b, d, g/ as coarticulated or "encoded" into contiguous vowels) and discontinuous elements (vowels and fricatives such as /f, v/) (see figure 1-5). Even in cases in which the formants corresponding to a particular speech sound are in fast transition to the succeeding sound, it is possible that discrete points or "loci" in their configuration (Delattre, Lieberman, and Cooper, 1955) or the shape of the energy pattern or the spectral "envelope" (Blumstein and Stevens, 1979) provide a primary cue to identification of the

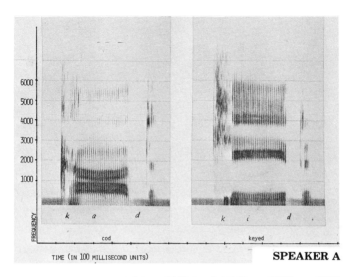

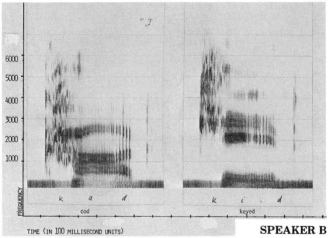

Fig. 1-4.   Spectrographic record of the pronunciation of /k/ before different vowels, in the words *keyed* [kid] and *cod* [kad] for two speakers, A and B. This shows the formant transition differences for [k] in two phonetic environments.

sound-type. There continue to be differing views about the relative roles of encoded versus invariant acoustic cues in the speech stream (see also Cole, 1977; Cole and Scott, 1975; Cutting and Eimas, 1975; Fant, 1967; Winitz, Scheib, and Reeds, 1972; Shoup and Pfeiffer, 1976; Stevens and Klatt, 1974).

Patterns of acoustic energy in the speech signal are processed by

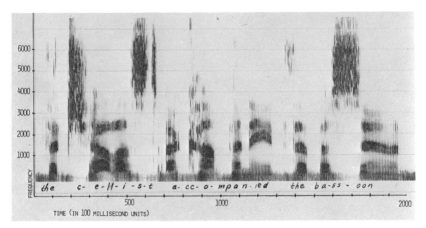

Fig. 1-5. Spectrographic record of continuous speech showing the utterance: *The cellist accompanied the bassoon.*

auditory systems in various ways, resulting in internally coded categories called *phonetic features*. It is in this sense that phonetic features can be said to exist at an abstract level, a level removed from the acoustic properties of the raw speech signal. The feature *voicing,* for example, is correlated with temporal phenomena (the onset of voicing, see Figure 1-8), fundamental frequency, harmonic overtones of the fundamental, and spectral characteristics of the high frequency burst. Under different circumstances, one of these acoustic events, or several in combination, might serve to cue the presence or absence of the phonetic feature *voicing.*

Of all the many possible kinds of phonetic features, only a subset provide linguistically significant contrasts in a given language. For example, in English, an aspirated [pʰ] as in *pit* differs phonetically from the unaspirated [p] in *spit;* but the acoustic difference between those two phones is never used to distinguish different morphemes, although the phonetic difference between the initial sounds in *pat* and *bat,* the feature of voicing, is used to distinguish different words in English. In other languages, such as Thai, aspiration *does* serve to distinguish between consonantal sound-types.

Phonetic descriptions have been traditionally based mainly on articulatory parameters, although more recently researchers have investigated the acoustic parameters that underlie perceived phonetic categories. In speech perception, some phonetic elements, particularly those comprising consonants, seem based primarily in articulatory phenomena; others, mainly vowels, seem ordered according to acoustic parameters (Ladefoged, 1971). A recent development in speech perception has led to a proposal for a special human speech processor, perhaps employing "hard-wire" neural mechanisms, which may be sensitive to particular phonetic features (as distinguished from raw acoustic events) (Abbs and Sussman, 1971; W. Cooper, 1975).

## Consonants and Vowels

In articulatory terms, vowels can best be described in terms of tongue position on the vertical and horizontal axis. Consonants are specified by *place* and *manner:* the place of the articulators that come together to produce the sound, and the manner of their approach—whether they make full contact and shut off the air stream or only come very close resulting in a noisy passage of air. Acoustically, vowels are characterized by relatively stable bands of energy at certain frequencies (formants). Some consonants are correlated with transient, shifting energy bands, others with none at all (during closure, for example, in the voiceless consonants /p,t,k/), and still others with stable energy in certain domains of the sound spectrum (fricatives such as /f, v, s, z/ (see Figure 1-5). For purposes of linguistic phonetics, vowels can be described in terms of two basic parameters: height and front-back position of the tongue (Figure 1-6A). Try pronouncing the vowel /i/ (pronounced "ee") and then the vowel /u/ ("oo") and note how the tongue moves from a position high in the front of the oral cavity (for /i/) to a high-back position (for /u/) (Figure 1-6B). A third parameter, rounding or spreading of the lips, is often included in vowel descriptions. Consonants can be minimally specified by *voicing, place* and *manner* of articulation (Figure 1-7). This traditional descriptive system has recently been expanded in theories of distinctive features.

## Distinctive Features

To explain how a small class of sound-types, or phonemic segments, is extracted from the variety of actually occurring speech signals, there has been proposed a system of distinctive phonetic features—that is, features that distinguish one sound-type, or phonemic segment, from another. Distinctive features are parameters which sufficiently specify all the consonants and vowels in a particular language. The earliest such proposal was for features as terms in binary opposition such as presence or absence of voicing or polar opposites in a category, such as tense versus lax (Jakobson and Halle, 1956). Additional systems have been developed using features based both on acoustic and articulatory properties (Van den Broecke, 1976). Some theoreticians continue to posit binary features underlying the phonetic or phonological units of their model, while others prefer to include multivalued features for some phonetic types (vowels, for example, being described along a scale from high to low). Some systems permit features which are "explanatory"—i.e., not based on any physical parameters (Chomsky and Halle, 1968), whereas another point of view holds that it is a sound theoretical practice to base distinctive features on observed phonetic behaviors (Fant, 1974; Ladefoged, 1971).

### Phoneme

The theoretical entity called the phoneme came as an answer to the feeling that segments, or sound-types, are interpreted from the continuously changing speech stream, wherein they are partially encoded. The phonemic notion can be illustrated by considering the fol-

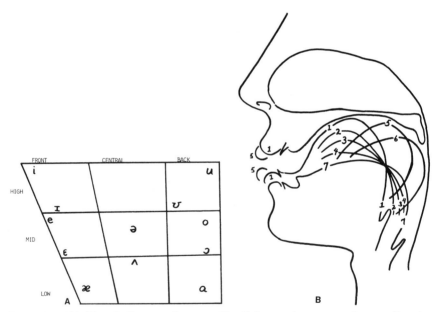

Fig. 1-6.   (A): Vowel diagram for most English vowels, arranged according to the parameters front-back and high-low. (B): Typical tongue positions during production of English vowels. Examples of English vowels are as follows:

i: beet, key, heed (1); ɪ: bit, kid, hid (2); e: bait, cake; ɛ: bet, head (3); æ: bat, had (4); ʌ: bud, cud; u: boot, cooed, food (5); ʊ: book, could (6); o: boat, hoed; ɔ :bawd, cawed; ɑ: hot, cod, father (7); ə : ("reduced" vowel of unstressed syllables such as information).

*Note:* Numbers in parentheses correspond to those in Figure 1-6 (B).

lowing words in which the phoneme /t/ is pronounced differently in each case because of the differing "phonetic environment."

*t*rench = palatized /t/
*t*ease = alveolar, aspirated /t/
s*t*ing = alveolar, unaspirated /t/
bu*t*ter = tongue–retracted, tapped /t/

The phonetic environment determines the specific actualizations, called allophones or conditioned variants, of the phoneme in these cases. These are all perceived as the sound-type, or phoneme, /t/.

Jakobson (1978) in his 1942–1943 lectures developed the idea that the phoneme is the functional vehicle by which meaning is carried on "meaningless" sound. Viewed in this way, the phoneme provides a sort of conceptual link between the "level" of sound and the "level"

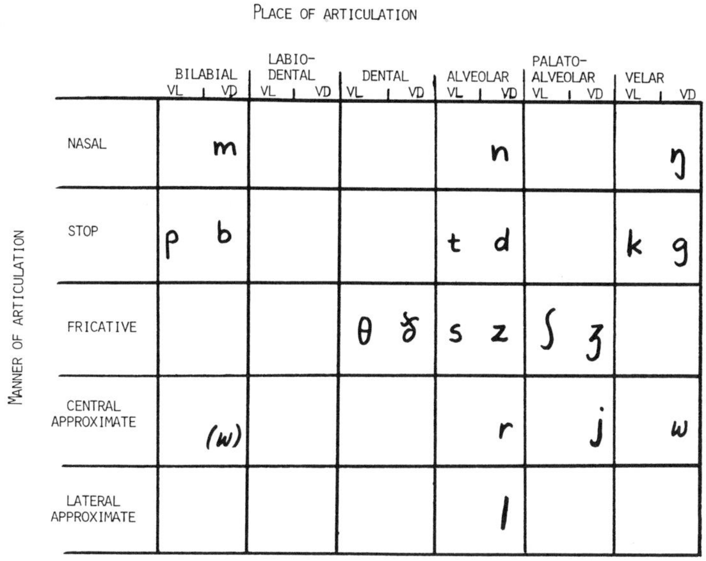

PLACE OF ARTICULATION

| | BILABIAL | | LABIO-DENTAL | | DENTAL | | ALVEOLAR | | PALATO-ALVEOLAR | | VELAR | |
|---|---|---|---|---|---|---|---|---|---|---|---|---|
| MANNER OF ARTICULATION | VL | VD | VL | VD | VL | VD | VL | VD | VL | VD | VL | VD |
| NASAL | m | | | | | | n | | | | | ŋ |
| STOP | p | b | | | | | t | d | | | k | g |
| FRICATIVE | | | | | θ | ð | s | z | ʃ | ʒ | | |
| CENTRAL APPROXIMATE | (w) | | | | | | | r | | j | | w |
| LATERAL APPROXIMATE | | | | | | | l | | | | | |

Fig. 1-7.   Chart of English Consonants. *Place of articulation* is indicated at the top from left-to-right; *manner of articulation* from top to bottom. *Voice-voiceless* distinctions are shown in each cell (the voiced member of the pair is on the right). Examples of English consonants are as follows:

m: ta*m*; n: ta*n*; ŋ: ta*ng*; p: *p*at; b: *b*at; t: *t*ip; d: *d*ip; k: *k*it; g: *g*ap; f: *f*oul; v: *v*owel; θ: *th*igh; ζ: *th*y; s: *f*ussy; z: fu*z-zy*; ʃ: *f*ission; ξ: *v*ision; w: *w*et; r: *r*ip; j: *y*ip; l: *l*ip.

The affricates tʃ (chin) and dξ (gin) are combinations of a stop and a fricative. *Note:* w is articulated in two places: bilabial and velar.

VL stands for *voiceless;* VD stands for *voiced.*

of meaning that constitutes spoken language. Phonemes themselves do not have meaning, but function to make distinctions between entities that do (morphemes).

The notion of underlying, abstract segments being part of a speaker's linguistic knowledge has inspired the discipline of phonology which attempts to work out a logical structure of these basic units and how they are related to a level of representation close to the actual speech stream itself (see review in Chomsky and Halle, 1968; Fischer-Jørgenson, 1975; Schane, 1973).

### Syllable

Vowels and consonants differ in both the articulatory and the acoustic domains. This can be seen in the ways the *syllable* is constructed. Phonetically, the syllable is made up of a releasing articulation (usually a consonant), a nucleus (usually a vowel), and an arresting articulation (usually a consonant). (For a discussion of how phonetic units actually fall along a continuum from consonantal to vocalic, see Pike, 1943.) The archetypal syllable is made up of a stop-consonant and a vowel—hence the term "cv" (consonant-vowel), often used in speech science to refer to the syllables used as stimuli in research. Many variants of this basic structure, however, still qualify as syllables, if they contain one and only one "syllabic nucleus." The problem is that the syllable is difficult to define rigorously. Suffice it to say here that the syllable is a unit which is useful in describing the physiology and phonetics of speech. The main point is that together consonants and vowels are organized into—or carried on—the syllable in speech performance. Although both carry linguistic and nonlinguistic information, vowels and consonants are patterned differently enough to lead to the generalization that consonants contribute more to linguistic information, while the vowel mainly carries nonlinguistic information (Studdert-Kennedy, 1975). This is no doubt largely true, although the role of consonants in nonlinguistic communication is often underestimated (see Fudge, 1970; Key, 1975; Stankiewicz, 1964).

The syllable is a functional unit in organizing motor speech production, but its physiological bases have not been established (Ladefoged, 1967). It is within the syllable that articulatory movements show the most overlapping and the most cohesion (Kent, 1976; Liberman, Cooper, Harris, et al., 1967). Although the syllable serves as a carrier of phonetic information, it is difficult to make use of as a unit in phonological theory (Studdert-Kennedy, 1975). Perhaps the syllable provides an "interface" between neuromotor and linguistic decisions (Kent, 1976).

## PROSODIC AND PARALINGUISTIC FEATURES

Both stress and intonation are made up of interactions of duration, intensity (amplitude), pitch (fundamental frequency), and basic acoustic parameters that function both to cue linguistic contrasts and to communicate information not traditionally included in models of linguistic structures. Stress and intonation have been called *suprasegmental* phenomena because they can occupy domains over more than one phonological segment (see Lehiste, 1970). The difference between segmental and suprasegmental becomes obvious when the contour seems inappropriate to the segmental information (i.e., that which is constituted by the phonemes) of the utterance, as in the following example from a novel by P. G. Wodehouse, when Bertie, a British aristocrat, criticizes his butler for exactly this sort of incongruity:

> Jeeves, ... don't keep saying 'Indeed, sir?' No doubt nothing is further from your mind than to convey such a suggestion, but you have a way of stressing the 'in' and coming down with a thud on the 'deed' which makes it virtually tantamount to 'Oh, yeah?' Correct this, Jeeves (Wodehouse, 1934).

The terms segmental (i.e. phonemic) and suprasegmental (also sometimes called *prosodic, paralinguistic,* or *nonlinguistic*), however, are merely convenient labels which do not reliably reflect acoustic detail nor do they correspond to differences in communicative function. We have discussed *encodedness,* the fact that acoustic cues for phonetic features may extend across several segments. Conversely, prosodic and paralinguistic features themselves fall along a continuum of discreteness and systematicness (Bolinger, 1961; Crystal, 1969). Stress and intonation, for example, carry many kinds of loads of communication, such as linguistic contrasts as well as nonlinguistic information. In English, stress provides the minimal cue to contrast the verb *impórt* with the noun *ímport,* a linguistic contrast. But the paralinguistic domain stress also indicates emphasis and helps to establish which idea is the new one and which is presupposed in the discourse (Gunter, 1972; Clark and Haviland, 1977), as illustrated by sentences 5–7:

5.  I gave *John* the book. (... not Jim)
6.  I gave John the *book.* (... not the violin)
7.  I *gave* John the Book. (I didn't sell it to him.)

The intonation contour, or rising and falling pitch level of the voice (indicated by lines drawn over sentences 8 and 9), signals basic syntactic differences, such as *statement* (sentence 8) versus *question* (sentence 9):

8.  You're going downtown.

9.  You're going downtown?

and nonrestrictive clause (in sentence 10) versus restrictive clause (in sentence 11) (Wang, 1971).

10.  The worker, who never shirks, sleeps well.
      (The worker, who *by the way* never shirks. . . .)
11.  The worker who never shirks sleeps well.
      (The other one has insomnia.)

Studies show that pitch changes (in the intonation contour) are important in cuing phrases and sentence structure (Collier and t'Hart, 1975; Lea, 1973, 1975; Lehiste, 1976; Wingfield, 1975; Wingfield and Klein, 1971). The role of the basic prosodic parameters of duration, intensity, and fundamental frequency (and of their combinants in stress and intonation) in communicating attitude and emotion is well accepted, although much remains to be understood both in detail and in theory. The point here is that acoustic cues perform multiple roles in the communication process.

Some idea of the multiple function of one of these parameters is given by the work on duration by Klatt (1976). This work shows that features of duration provide a variety of cues. Duration often provides the primary perceptual cue in the distinctions between sound-types (such as long versus short vowels, voiced versus voiceless fricatives), syntactic structure (because syllables at the ends of phrases are longer than comparable syllables elsewhere in the phrase), and the presence or absence of emphasis. Furthermore, not only do duration patterns reflect speaking rate, but also the speaker's mood (Klatt, 1976).

## SPEECH PRODUCTION AND PERCEPTION

Research in speech production and perception has aimed at uncovering structures or processes which underlie speech performance (see MacNeilage, 1978; Valian, 1977). For production, evidence from speech errors suggests that phonetic features, phonemic segments, and syllables all exist as programmed integral units in the speech production process. However, the search for invariance (i.e., a one-to-one relationship) between feature, segment or syllable, *and* neurophysiological correlate has proven inconclusive (F. Cooper, 1972; MacNeilage and Ladefoged, 1976).

In addition to the obvious unit sizes constituted by morphemes and words, there is considerable evidence that phrase-size units are utilized in speech production. Measurements of temporal precision in syntactic utterances, when contrasted with word lists, suggest that the presence of syntactic structure "facilitates the production of speech by increasing the size and complexity of the control patterns that are used to mobilize the vocal apparatus" (Lackner and Levine, 1975, p. 112). Similarly, evidence from speech errors (Fromkin, 1971), articulatory measurements (Lieberman, 1968), and temporal patterning in phrases and sentences (Kozhevnikov and Chistovich, 1966; Martin, 1972) suggests that such larger units (variously called intonation contour, breath-group, syntagma, or rhythmic unit) function in organizing speech production. Studies of speech errors, intonational patterning, and speech segment durations indicate that anticipatory stretches of up to seven words are planned ahead in speech production (Nooteboom and Cohen, 1975).

Research in speech perception has investigated the kinds of units, structures, and processes that figure in the listener's ability to relate a physical signal to an abstract meaning. Here, too, it has frequently been said that the clause is a primary perceptual unit (e.g., Bever, Garrett, and Hurtig, 1973). Although the speech stream is serial and occurs sequentially in time, however, there is evidence that speech perception is a hierarchical structure/process during which considerable exchange and comparing of information across levels occurs online. Acoustic features provide cues for interpretation at parallel levels (phonetic and phonological) and these interpretations, in turn, draw on information simultaneously taken from knowledge about syllables, morphemes, syntactic structure, prosody, and semantic patterns (Darwin, 1976; Pisoni, 1978; Pisoni and Sawusch, 1975; Wingfield, 1975). For example, experimental evidence shows that information from these several levels provided by the context enhances perception of individual words (Cole, 1973; Lieberman, 1963; Pollack and Pickett, 1963). Being deprived of the constraints contributed by the other levels—the rest of the linguistic messages—results in verbal transformations in which subjects hear various illusory changes when presented with repetitions of a single word with no linguistic context (Warren, 1976). Studies of shadowing, a task in which subjects attempt to approach simultaneous echoing of ongoing speech, suggests that sentence perception is best viewed as a "fully interactive parallel process," wherein each word enters simultaneously into phonetic, lexical, syntactic, and semantic levels to be analyzed in terms of whatever information is relevant at each level (Marslen-Wilson, 1975). Another series of studies asking subjects to look out for a target pho-

neme or a target syllable occurring at different linguistic "levels" led
to the conclusion that a search for *the* unit of speech perception at a
particular level is not a valid one. Subjects's performances depend on
the "level" their attention was directed to.

Thus speech perception is best modeled as a hierarchy or a network of processing stages over which attention can be distributed in
different ways (McNeill and Lindig, 1973). There is probably a gradation of potential conscious awareness at the acoustic/auditory, phonetic, phonological, and syllable phases for each of which training can
bring greater awareness (Darwin, 1976). This view is compatible with
Koestler's notion of consciousness, or awareness, being multidimensional, graded, and occurring in degrees in all acquired human skills
(Koestler, 1964, p. 154 and *passim*). Neisser (1967), too, has suggested
that there is no fixed perceptual unit, but that to understand speech
perception, researchers must look to such inner cognitive processes as
awareness and attention. McNeill and Repp (1973) give evidence for
the role of "autonomous internal processes," even at the initial point
of perception and acoustic analysis; the acoustic signal provides a brief
trigger, but "perceptual organization of speech is almost totally dependent on internal processes" (p. 1325). Another relevant finding is
the phonemic restoration effect, wherein people naturally "restore"
(perceive and identify) the correct missing speech sound while listening to recorded utterances from which that particular piece of sound
has been removed. This reliable finding suggests that perceptions are
inferred by reference to inner processes of recognition and identification of a larger pattern (Warren, 1976). More simply, the listening
process is active and constructive—even reconstructive, as developed
by Bartlett in his interpretation of remembering (Bartlett, 1932).

The process of communication involves a dynamic interaction of
acoustic, phonetic, phonological, lexical, syntactic, and semantic
stages or levels that are interdependent. Yet it is interesting to note
that speech perception and production can proceed in the absence of
one or another of these stages. For example, shadowing (repeating ongoing speech), reading aloud, or reciting memorized material can occur without apparent recourse to syntactic analysis or processing for
meaning. Conversely, Lackner and Garrett (1972) found that subjects
were unaware of having heard one of two messages presented (the one
at low intensity), although their responses showed that those meanings had been perceived. Production and perception of idioms and
"formulaic" expressions (greetings, sayings, prepackaged phrases),
which are highly familiar and learned as a whole chunk, probably do
not engage stages of lexical and syntactic analysis, which are usually

conceived of as intermediate between phonetic and semantic processing (Bolinger, 1976; Van Lancker, 1973).

This brief survey of the structures and processes posited to underlie communicative behavior reveals a rich and redundant functional system. The system is overdetermined, in the sense that all of the available systems work together but that various combinations of subsections of the whole can suffice to produce a version of the desired message (Wanner, 1973). Communicative behavior has been described as a "mosaic" of structures, skills, and knowledge (Dingwall, 1978). Accordingly, it is appropriate to focus more on the notion of *strategies* than the notion of *rules* or *fixed operations* underlying the process; or, perhaps, to postulate an interdigitation of fixed rules *and* flexible strategies (see Koestler, 1967, Pp. 42, 105, and *passim*) or of *rules* integrated with *schemata* (Tyler, 1979). Much of speech science research is compatible with this idea and recalls the relevance of earlier work on the role of attention (Broadbent and Gregory, 1967; Lieberman, 1963) and of "motives" such as expectation and preference (Neisser, 1967). More recently, studies have pointed out the contribution of set (Carey, Mehler, and Bever, 1970), and attention (Conrad, 1978; McNeill and Lindig, 1973). There is now considerable interest in the role of memory at all stages of speech perception (Bransford and Franks, 1971; Darwin and Baddeley, 1974; Liberman, Mattingly, and Turvey, 1972; Massaro and Cohen, 1975; Pisoni and Sawusch, 1975; Posner and Warren, 1972). Much of this work emphasizes the reconstructive role of memory processes at various levels of information processing.

## THE NONLINGUISTIC DOMAIN

Interwoven into the information that the speaker sends and the listener receives about the phonology, syntax, and semantic structures are "nonlinguistic" attributes such as attitudes, affect, social status, mood, implied meanings, and other factors that are too vague even to label but are potent and important aspects of communication. There is no clear division between linguistic and nonlinguistic features in the acoustic signal, although such a line can be drawn as a heuristic. In fact, an acoustic cue can give dual information simultaneously. Duration differences, for example, function as cues to segment type, word meaning, mood, and attitude of the speaker (Klatt, 1976; Lehiste, 1976). Similarly, pitch cues range in function from providing phonemic contrasts as in the tone languages, through lexical and syntactical kinds of contrasts, to indications of personal emotional states. In conversation, pitch height (in combination with intensity extremes and quantity) provides signals for "turn taking" (when one talker is prepared to give the other a "turn" to talk) (Duncan, 1974), and for "paragraph" organization in discourse (Lehiste, 1975). Acoustic cues that serve to make phonetic contrasts also contribute nonlinguistic content. For example, the onset of voicing (vocal fold vibration) for a vowel that follows a voiced consonant comes sooner than for a vowel that follows a voiceless consonant (Figure 1-8). A still later release, however, creating a longer gap and more aspiration before the vowel onset, can serve a nonlinguistic function such as that of dialect or idiolect (individual speech pattern) identification; it can serve to communicate emphasis, an attitude of irony, or the emotion of disgust; and the length of the gap/aspiration phase can correspond to the degree of the emphasis, attitude, or emotion expressed.

If the linguistic domain encompasses the phonological, syntactic, and semantic patterns in the language, then it is true to say that all components of the speech signal potentially carry nonlinguistic infor-

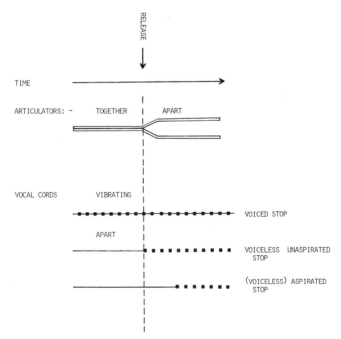

Fig. 1-8. The onset of voicing (vibration of the vocal cords) as related to the timing of articulatory movements. Aspiration occurs when the vocal cords remain apart after the articulators have been released.

mation, in addition to carrying information about these linguistic levels of structural patterning. The uniqueness of the human voice is based on the configuration of these acoustic microfeatures as they are intrinsic to the individual speaker's style. It is astonishing that nearly everyone can recognize many individual voices on hearing but a few words even if that voice has not been heard for years. Information about the biology, psychology, and sociology of the individual speaker (Laver, 1968) is carried in cues underlying both segmental and suprasegmental domains. The physical properties on which this ability is based perceptually have not been well established (Hecker, 1971).

Intonation is a striking illustration of dual functioning in both linguistic and nonlinguistic domains. Besides giving linguistic cues to phrase structure and grammatical sentence-type, intonation serves—often in combination with voice quality—to communicate a subtle nonlinguistic universe of attitudes. The tone of an utterance communicates the speaker's attitude toward himself or herself, toward the form of the utterance, toward the listener, toward the message in the utterance. There is a large repertoire of attitudes, all occurring in gradation (more or less surprise, more or less disapproval, more or less doubt, etc.). (For a discussion, see Abercrombie, 1968; Bolinger, 1961; Crystal, 1975.) Intonation and tone can even override literal meaning-content completely, as in the ironic remark, when the speaker means something opposite from what is literally stated. Attitudes, in turn, shade into the realm of emotions.

Further light on this subject comes from research in judgments and perceptions of vocal parameters of personality (Addington, 1968; Scherer, 1972; Starkweather, 1964), of accent and dialect (Giles, 1973; Giles and Powesland, 1975; Lambert, 1967; Ryan, 1973), and of attitudes and emotions (see Crystal, 1969). In personality studies, there is often more agreement among ratings by different judges than between these and self-ratings by speakers, or between judges' ratings and objective measures. This suggests the existence of vocal stereotypes. Studies of accent and dialect show consistent effects of a speaker's style on evaluations of the speaker's content, and the power of dialect features to elicit cultural and socioeconomic stereotypes (Giles and Bourhis, 1973). The acoustic correlates of these and of the attitudes signaled in the speech signal are not well established. There are methodological difficulties in studying the perception of emotional attributes of the utterance. Should one, for example, use actors to produce the utterances and have them read, recite, or spontaneously produce the utterances? And how are the emotions to be identified, and how are they to be distinguished from meaning-content in the utterance? (See Dittman, 1972.) There have been reliable findings, howev-

er. A study using the alphabet, which is content-free material, reported that subjects were moderately successful at identifying feelings such as love, sadness, pride, and nervousness (Davitz and Davitz, 1974). Fairbanks and Hoaglin (1941) found that durational contrasts in actors' simulations of fear, anger, and indifference differed from durational patterns in contempt and grief. Subjects, who listened to synthesized tone sequences varying in pitch, amplitude, and tempo which had been previously rated on evaluation scales and given emotional labels, were able to attach the correct labels, relying mainly on tempo and pitch (Scherer, 1974). Williams and Stevens (1972) used speech material both from actors and from real-life recordings to investigate the acoustic correlates of sorrow, fear, anger, and "neutral situations" in the speech signal. They found that the fundamental frequency contour over time provided the clearest indication of emotional state, although changes in the sound spectrum, timing, voicing regularity, and precision of articulation also contributed.

This overview of speech production and perception from the point of view of the *sounds* of speech has inevitably discussed *meanings*. The communicative process is based on production and perception of meaningful sounds. Yet more than sounds are employed to do the job. Facial expressions are at least as important in communicating aspects of the message (Mehrabian and Ferris, 1967) and gesture and other kinds of kinesics (details of body movement) contribute a great deal. These topics are covered by other chapters in this volume.

## PATTERNS OF MEANING

The meanings that can be expressed in any language are potentially infinite. Descriptive linguistics has concentrated on developing logically consistent models for relating a finite set of sounds to meanings. In this kind of structural approach, the key object of description is the sentence. Morphemes (words and word-constituents) and grammatical categories which constitute the building blocks of the structure are subject to various kinds of operations or "rules." Most of these kinds of linguistic models attempt to relate meanings and sounds through structural patterns or syntactic rules. Recently, in generative transformational grammar, linguistic analysis has been accompanied by rigorous and penetrating inquiries about the nature of human language and its status as a mental or cognitive ability and as a special attribute of the human brain (Chomsky, 1975). Much interesting discussion has developed around these issues. The explicit objective in generative grammar, however, is to describe linguistic structure in a formal model of language *competence* as abstracted away from speech *performance*. Some of this work, nonetheless, does have relevance to actual communicative behaviors, and recent active efforts in speech and language research have begun to address more directly the issues of what individual speakers of a language know how to do that makes communication possible. These issues address the basic ones of what kinds of knowledge are stored and shared by native speakers. Investigations of the sound "level"—phonetics and phonology—have been reviewed earlier in this chapter. Psycholinguistic research has also focused on the domains of linguistic structure on the way to the meaning "level"—those of morphemes (meaningful units), syntax, and semantics.

The principles by which words are stored and processed in speech performance—the properties of the lexicon—have been investigated in various ways. One well known study exploited the common occurrence in normal language use of not quite being able to think of a certain word, but having the sensation of being very close to it (called the "tip of the tongue" phenomenon, Brown and McNeill, 1966). This study and others—one that tested people's abilities to produce word lists in a certain class (words that all end with a consonant, words that are all nouns, words that begin with a vowel, for example; Baker, 1974) and another that investigated malapropisms (Fay and Cutler, 1977)—indicate that the first sound, the number of syllables, the stress pattern and the grammatical form (i.e., noun, verb) are key parameters in lexical organization. People seem to "know" more about the first sound, the stress pattern, and the grammatical form of a lexical item (i.e., a word) than any other properties in the word. They can know these facts about a word before recalling the actual word. It seems that these properties serve as *addresses* to help recognize and retrieve words.

There are many studies on syntactic rule processing in speech performance (see Fodor, Bever, and Garrett, 1974; Greene, 1972, for review). Various interesting hypotheses about sentential syntactic structures and their properties—structural complexity, grammaticality, sentence relatedness, role of structural ambiguity—have been proposed and tested by devising psycholinguistic tasks (Flores d'Arcais and Levelt, 1970). Some of this approach to linguistic research, however, has been superceded by recent findings that plausible sentence meanings determine comprehension of sentences more strongly than do syntactic cues (Clark and Clark, 1977; Clark and Haviland, 1977; Sachs, 1967).

Only a limited set of kinds of meaning—for example, referential and literal—has been treated in the structural analyses of language.

Other modes of meaning are now receiving much deserved attention. For example, recent work emphasizes the importance of figurative language in normal communication, maintaining that metaphor is not to be viewed as "merely" poetic and peripheral, but that metaphoric processes are at the center of the everyday creative capacity of language (Pollio, Barlow, Fine, *et al*, 1977; Ricoeur, 1975). The role of social meanings in communication behavior receives insightful treatment in studies by Carswell and Rommetveit (1971). The relational nature of concepts and their close connection to social and cultural scenarios (Chafe, 1977) leads to a theory of linguistic frames, which correlate with scenes as conceptualized by the speaker (Fillmore, 1977). Other linguists have recognized an essential indeterminacy in meanings, demonstrating by examples that linguistic meanings are graded or "fuzzy" (Lakoff, 1972). Experimental studies in variability versus invariance within ranges of lexical meanings have been contributed by Labov (1973). Theories about "speech acts" have brought attention to an important dimension of communicative behavior, the pragmatic effects of utterances (Austin, 1962; Searle, 1970, 1975; Sadock, 1975), and the sense in which the whole speech act—form and content together—has a unitary meaning (Wallace, 1970). Related to this is work on presuppositions and implied meanings and on principles of cooperation in conversation (Grice, 1975; Wilson, 1975).

Another new area of interest with important implications for communicative behavior studies is that of individual differences in linguistic behavior (Hymes, 1973; Fillmore et al., 1979). Such differences cut across linguistic and nonlinguistic categories, involving matters both of grammar and of personal style. Linguistically, individuals differ in their use and comprehension of sentences (Fillmore, 1979; Greenberg, 1969; Gleitman and Gleitman, 1970). Furthermore, individuals vary in grammatical judgments, and the judgments of each person include a region of uncertainty (Ross, 1979). An idiolect (the speech pattern unique to an individual person) makes up a personal and social style, communicates a spectrum of personality characteristics, and contributes to the whole meaning of an utterance (Steiner, 1975).

Despite variability, indeterminacy, and individual differences at all levels in communicative behavior, private meanings *are* given public form, and communication results. When speech behavior is primarily providing a format for interpersonal contact, exchange of information is not important (Hays, 1973; Fry, 1977). When information is the issue, it is interesting to consider that meanings do not pass in a simple manner from person to person, but are reconstructed by a listener based on heterogeneous strategies and guesses (Reddy,

1979). These strategies include linguistic kinds of knowledge, of course. They also include nonlinguistic knowledge of cultural norms and situational context and of beliefs, as well as presuppositions about past history, knowledge about the world and about the speaker, and even knowledge about the speaker's knowledge of the listener (Rommetveit, 1974, 1979).

## THE COMMUNICATION PROCESS

The ideas reviewed in this chapter lead to a view of the communication process as an interactive hierarchy constituted by several levels of structure from sound to meaning. Acoustic cues serve to trigger reconstruction of information at higher levels, and general information at all levels is drawn upon to synthesize components of the message. Cognitive processes such as attention, memory, and planning are in intimate interplay with the linguistic components. Furthermore, nonlinguistic aspects of both signal and message are interwoven into linguistic aspects. The communicative process is richly endowed with redundantly specified information across linguistic and nonlinguistic domains, making possible alternate strategies for relaying messages.

## REFERENCES

Abbs, J. H., Sussman, H. M. Neurophysiological feature detectors and speech perception: A discussion of theoretical implications. *Journal of Speech and Hearing Research,* 1971, *14,* 23–26.

Abercrombie, D. *Elements of general phonetics.* Chicago: Aldine, 1967.

Abercrombie, D. Paralanguage. *British Journal of Disorders of Communication,* 1968, *3,* 55–59.

Addington, D. W. The relationship of selected vocal characteristics to personality perception. *Speech Monographs,* 1968, *25,* 492–503.

Austin, J. L. *How to do things with words.* Cambridge: Harvard University Press, 1962.

Baker, L. The lexicon: Some psycholinguistic evidence. *UCLA Working Papers in Phonetics,* 1974, *26.*

Bartlett, C. F. *Remembering.* Cambridge, England: Cambridge University Press, 1932.

Bever, T. G., Garrett, M. F., Hurtig, F. The interaction of perceptual processes and ambiguous sentences. *Memory and Cognition,* 1973, *1.3,* 277–286.

Blumstein, S. The use and theoretical implications of the dichotic technique for investigating distinctive features. *Brain and Language,* 1974, *1,* 337–350.

Blumstein, S. E., Stevens, K. N. Acoustic invariance in speech production: Evidence from measurements of the spectral characteristics of stop consonants. *Journal of the Acoustical Society of America,* 1979, *66.4* 1001–1018.

Bolinger, D. (Ed.) *Intonation.* Middlesex, England: Penguin Books, 1972.

Bolinger, D. Meaning and memory. *Forum Linguisticum,* 1976, *1.1,* 1–14.

Bolinger, D. *Generality, gradience, and the all-or-none.* Mouton: The Hague, 1961.

Bransford, J. D. Franks, J. The abstraction of linguistic ideas: A review. *Cognition,* 1971, *1,* 211–249.

Broadbent, D. E., Gregory, M. Perception of emotionally toned words. *Nature,* 1967, *215,* 581–584.

Broadbent, D. E. Attention and the perception of speech. *Scientific American,* 1962, *206,* 143–151.

Brown, R., McNeill, D. The "tip of the tongue" phenomenon. *Journal of Verbal Learning and Verbal Behavior,* 1966, *5,* 325–337.

Carey, P, Mehler, J., Bever, T. When do we compute all the interpretations of an ambiguous sentence? In G. B. Flores d'Arcais, W. J. M. Levelt (Eds.), *Advances in psycholinguistics.* Amsterdam: North-Holland Publishing Co., 1970.

Carswell, E. A., Rommetveit, R. (Eds.) *Social contexts of messages.* Oslo, Norway: Psykologisk Institut, 1971.

Carterette, Edward C., Friedman, Morton P. (Eds.) *Handbook of perception* (Vol. VII): *Language and speech.* New York: Academic Press, 1976.

Caton, C. E. Overview. In Danny D. Steinberg and Leon Jakobovits (Eds.), *Semantics: An interdisciplinary reader in philosophy, linguistics, and psychology.* London: Cambridge University Press, 1971.

Chafe, W. L. Creativity in verbalization and its implications for the nature of stored knowledge. In Roy O. Freedle (Ed.), *Discourse production and comprehension.* Norwood, New Jersey: Ablex, 1977.

Chomsky, N., Halle, M. *The sound pattern of English.* New York: Harper and Row, 1968.

Chomsky, N. *Reflections on language.* New York: Random House, 1975.

Clark, H., Clark, E. *Psychology and language.* New York: Harcourt, Brace, Jovanovich, 1977.

Clark, H. H., Haviland, S. E. Comprehension and the given-new contract. In Roy O. Freedle (Ed.), *Discourse production and comprehension.* Norwood, New Jersey: Ablex, 1977.

Cohen, A., Nooteboom, S. G. (Eds.) *Structure and process in speech perception: Proceedings of the symposium on dynamic aspects of speech perception.* New York: Springer-Verlag, 1975.

Cole, R. A., Scott, B. The phantom in the phoneme: Invariant clues for stop consonants. *Perception and Psychophysics,* 1975, *15,* 101–107.

Cole, R. A. Invariant features and feature detectors: Some developmental implications. In Sidney J. Segalowitz and F. A. Gruber (Eds.), *Language development and neurological theory,* 1977.

Cole, R. A. Listening for mispronunciations: A measure of what we hear during speech. *Perception and Psychophysics,* 1973, *13,* 153–156.

Cole, R. A., Scott, B. Toward a theory of speech perception. *Psychological Review*, 1974, *81*, 348–374.

Cole, R. (Ed.) *Current issues in linguistic theory*, Bloomington, Indiana: University Press, 1977.

Collier, K., t'Hart, J. The role of intonation in speech perception. In A. Cohen and S. G. Nooteboom (Eds.), *Structure and process in speech perception: Proceedings of the symposium on dynamic aspects of speech perception.* New York: Springer-Verlag, 1975.

Conrad, C. Factors in the recognition of words. In John W. Cotton and Roberta Klatzy (Eds.), *Semantic factors in cognition.* Hillsdale, N.J.: Laurence Erlbaum, 1978.

Cooper, F. S. How is language conveyed by speech? In James F. Kavanaugh and Ignatius G. Mattingly (Eds.), *Language by ear and eye.* Cambridge, MA: Massachusetts Institute of Technology Press, 1972.

Cooper, W. E. Selective adaptation to speech. In F. Restle, R. M. Shiffrin, N.J. Castellen, et al. (Eds.), *Cognitive theory.* New York: Halsted Press, 1975.

Cotton, J. W., Klatzky, R. *Semantic factors in cognition.* Hillsdale, N.J.: Laurence Erlbaun, 1978.

Crystal, D. *Prosodic systems and intonation in English.* Cambridge, England: The University Press, 1969.

Crystal, D. *The English tone of voice.* New York: St. Martin's Press, 1975.

Cutting, J. E., Eimas, P. D. Phonetic feature analyzers in the processing of speech by infants. In J. F. Kavanaugh and J. E. Cutting (Eds.), *The role of speech in language.* Cambridge, MA: Massachusetts Institute of Technology Press, 1975, 127–148.

Darwin, C. J. *The perception of speech.* In Edward C. Carterette and Morton P. Friedman (Eds.), *Handbook of perception* (Vol. VII): Language and speech. New York: Academic Press, 1976.

Darwin, C. J. On the dynamic use of prosody in speech perception. In A. Cohen and S. G. Nooteboom (Eds.), *Structure and process in speech perception: Proceedings of the symposium on dynamic aspects of speech perception.* New York: Springer-Verlag, 1975.

Darwin, C. J., Baddeley, A. D. Acoustic memory and the perception of speech. *Cognitive Psychology,* 1974, *6*, 41–60.

David, E. E., Denes, P. B. (Eds.) *Human communication: A unified view.* New York: McGraw-Hill, 1972.

Davitz, J. R., Davitz, L. D. The communication of feelings by content-free speech. In S. Weitz (Ed.) *Nonverbal communication.* New York: Oxford University Press, 1974.

Delattre, P. C., Liberman, A. M., Cooper, Franklin S. Acoustic loci and transitional cues for consonants. *Journal of the Acoustical Society of America,* 1955, *27*, 769–773. Reprinted in Dennis Fry (Ed.), *Acoustic Phonetics.* Cambridge: Cambridge University Press, 1976.

Dennett, D. C. Current issues in the philosophy of the mind. *American Philosophical Quarterly,* 1978, *15*, 249–261.

Dingwall, W. O. Human communicative behavior: A biological model. *Die Neueren Sprachen* Heft 314 Juli, 1978.

Dittman, A. T. *Interpersonal messages of emotion.* New York: Springer-Verlag, 1972.

Duncan, S. On the structure of speaker-auditor interaction during speaking turns. *Language in Society,* 1974, *3,* 161–180.

Duncan, S. Some signals and rules for taking speaking turns in conversation. *Journal of Personality and Social Psychology,* 1972, *23,* 283–292. Reprinted in S. Weitz, (Ed.), *Nonverbal communication.* New York: Oxford University Press, 1974.

Fairbanks, G., Hoaglin, L. W. An experimental study of the durational characteristics of the voice during the expression of emotion. *Speech Monograph,* 1941, *8,* 85–90.

Fant, G. Auditory patterns in speech. In W. Walten-Dunn, (Ed.), *Models for the perception of speech and visual form.* Cambridge, MA: Massachusetts Institute of Technology Press, 1967.

Fant, G. *Speech sounds and features.* Cambridge, MA: Massachusetts Institute of Technology Press, 1974.

Fay, D., Cutler, A. Malapropisms and the lexicon. *Linguistic Inquiry,* 1977, *8,* 505–520.

Fillmore, C. On fluency. In C. J. Fillmore, D. Kempler, and S-Y. Wang (Eds.), *Individual differences in language ability and language behavior.* New York: Academic Press, 1979.

Fillmore, C. Topics of lexical semantics. In R. W. Cole (Ed.), *Current issues in linguistic theory.* Bloomington, Indiana: Indiana University Press, 1977.

Fischer-Jørgensen, E. *Trends in phonological theory: A historical introduction.* Copenhagen: Akademisk Forlag, 1975.

Flores d'Arcais, G. B. and Levelt, W. J. M. (Eds.) *Advances in psycholinguistics.* Amsterdam: North-Holland Publishing Company, 1970.

Fodor, J. A., Bever, T. G., and Garrett, M. F. *The psychology of language.* New York: McGraw-Hill, 1974.

Freedle, Roy O. (Ed.) *Discourse production and comprehension* (Vol. 1). Norwood, New Jersey: Ablex, 1977.

Fry, D. *Homo loquens: Man as a talking animal.* Cambridge, England: Cambridge University Press, 1977.

Fromkin, V. A. (Ed.) *Speech errors as linguistic evidence.* Mouton: The Hague, 1973.

Fromkin, V. A. The nonanomalous nature of anomalous utterances. *Language,* 1971, *47,* 27–52.

Fry, D. B. (Ed.) *Acoustic phonetics.* Cambridge: Cambridge University Press, 1976.

Fudge, E. Phonological features and "expressiveness." *Journal of Linguistics,* 1970, *6,* 161–188.

Giles, H., Bourhis, R. Y. Dialect perception revisited. *Quarterly Journal of Speech,* 1973, *59,* 337–342.

Giles, H., Powesland, P. *Speech style and social evaluation.* New York: Academic Press, 1975.

Giles, H. Communicative effectiveness as a function of accepted speech. *Speech Monographs,* 1973, *40,* 330–331.

Gleitman, L., Gleitman, H. *Phrase and paraphrase*. New York: Norton and Company, 1970.

Goldstein, H. Reading and listening comprehension at various controlled rates. *Teachers College Contributions to Education*, 1940, No. 821.

Greene, J. *Psycholinguistics*. Middlesex, England: Penguin, 1972.

Greenberg, S. R. Experimental study of certain intonation contrasts in American English. *UCLA Working Papers in Phonetics*, 1969, *13*.

Grice, H. P. Logic and conversation. In P. C. and J. Morgan (Eds.), *Syntax and semantics* (Vol. 3): *Speech acts*. New York: Academic Press, 1975.

Gulick, W. *Hearing: Physiology and psychophysics*. Toronto: Oxford University Press, 1971.

Gunter, R. Intonation and relevance. In Dwight Bolinger (Ed.), *Intonation*. Middlesex, England: Penguin Books, 1972.

Hays, D. G. Language and interpersonal relationships. *Daedalus*, Summer 1973.

Hecker, M. H. L. *Speaker recognition: An interpretative survey of the literature*. ASHA Monographs Number 16. Washington, D.C.: American Speech and Hearing Association, 1971.

Hymes, D. On the origins and foundations of inequality among speakers. *Daedalus*, Summer 1973.

Jakobson, R. *Six lectures on sound and meaning*. Cambridge, MA: Massachusetts Institute of Technology Press, 1978.

Jakobson, R. Verbal communication. *Scientific American*, September, 1972.

Jakobson, R., Halle, M. *Fundamentals of language*. Mouton: The Hague, 1956.

Kavanaugh, J., Cutting, J. (Eds.) *The role of speech in language*. Cambridge, MA: Massachusetts Institute of Technology Press, 1975.

Kavanagh, J. F. and Mattingly, Ignatius G. (Eds.) *Language by ear and eye: The relationship between speech and reading*. Cambridge, MA: Massachusetts Institute of Technology Press, 1972.

Kent, R. D. Models of speech production. In N. Lass (Ed.), *Contemporary issues in experimental phonetics*. New York, Academic Press, 1976.

Key, M. R. *Paralanguage and kinesics*. Metuchen, NJ: The Scarecrow Press, 1975.

Klatt, D. H. Linguistic uses of segmental duration in English: Acoustic and perceptual evidence. *Journal of the Acoustical Society of America*, 1976, *59*, 1208–1221.

Koestler, A. *The act of creation*. New York: The Macmillan Co., 1964.

Koestler, A. *The ghost in the machine*. Chicago: Henry Regnery Co., 1967.

Kozhevnikov, V. A., Chistovich, L. A. *Speech: Articulation and perception*. Washington DC: Clearinghouse for Federal and Scientific Information. Joint Publications Research Service 1966: 30, 543.

Kramer, E. Judgment of personal characteristics and emotions from nonverbal properties of speech. *Psychological Bulletin*, 1963, *61*, 408–420.

Labov, W. The boundaries of words and their meanings. In C.-J. N. Bailey and R. Shuy (Eds.), *New ways of analyzing variation in English*. Georgetown University Press, 1973.

Lackner, J. R. and Levine, K. B. Speech production: Evidence for syntactically and phonologically determined units. *Perception and Psychophysics,* 1975, *17.* 107–113.

Lackner, J. R., Garrett, M. F. Resolving ambiguity: Effects of biasing context in the unattended ear. *Cognition,* 1972, *1,* 359–372.

Ladefoged, P. *A course in phonetics.* New York: Harcourt, Brace, Jovanovich, Inc., 1975.

Ladefoged, P. *Preliminaries to linguistic phonetics.* Chicago: University of Chicago Press, 1971.

Ladefoged, P. *Three areas of experimental phonetics.* London, Oxford, 1967.

Lakoff, G. P. Hedges: A study in meaning criteria and the logic of fuzzy concepts. In *Papers from the 8th Regional Meeting,* Chicago Linguistic Society, University of Chicago, Department of Linguistics, 1972.

Lambert, W. A social psychology of bilingualism. *Journal of Social Issues,* 1967, *23,* 2. (Reprinted in A. S. Dil (Ed.), *Language, psychology and culture.* Palo Alto: Stanford University Press, 1972, pp. 212–235.)

Lass, N. J. (Ed.) *Contemporary issues in experimental phonetics.* New York: Academic Press, 1976.

Laver, J. Voice quality and indexical information. *British Journal of Disorders of Communication,* 1968, *3,* 43–54.

Lea, W. Use of prosodic features to segment continuous speech into sentences and phrases. PX 10058. Sperry/Univac, 1973.

Lea, W. An approach to syntactic recognition without phonemics. *IEEE Transactions on Audio and Electroacoustics,* 1973, *21,* No. 3, 249–258.

Lehiste, I. Suprasegmental features of speech. In N. Lass (Ed.), *Contemporary issues in experimental phonetics.* New York: Academic Press, 1976.

Lehiste, I. *Suprasegmentals.* Cambridge, MA: Massachusetts Institute of Technology Press, 1970.

Lehiste, I. The phonetic structure of paragraphs. In A. Cohen and S. G. Nooteboom (Eds.), *Structure and process in speech perception: Proceedings of the symposium on dynamic aspects of speech perception.* New York, Heidelberg: Springer-Verlag, 1975.

Liberman, A. M., Cooper, F. S., Harris, K. S., et al. Some observations on a model for speech perception. In W. Wathen-Dunn (Ed.), *Models for the perception of speech and visual form.* Cambridge, MA: Massachusetts Institute of Technology Press, 1967.

Liberman, A. M., Cooper, F. S., Shankweiler, D. P., et al. Perception of the speech code. *Psychological Review,* 1967, *74,* 431–461.

Liberman, A. M., Mattingly, I. G., Turvey, M. T. Language codes and memory codes. In A. W. Melton and E. Martin (Eds.), *Coding processes in human memory.* New York: John Wiley and Sons, 1972.

Lieberman, P. Intonation, perception, and language. Cambridge, MA: Massachusetts Institute of Technology Press, 1968.

Lieberman, P. Some effects of semantic and grammatical context on the production and perception of speech. *Language and Speech,* 1963, *6,* 172–187.

MacNeilage, P. Is the speaker-hearer a special hearer? In Herbert I. Pick and Elliot Saltzman (Eds.), *Modes of perceiving and processing information.* Hillsdale, NJ: Lawrence Erlbaum, 1978.

MacNeilage, P., Ladefoged, P. The production of speech and language. In E. C. Carterette and M. P. Friedman (Eds.), *Handbook of perception* (Vol. VII): *Language and Speech*. New York: Academic Press, 1976.

Marslen-Wilson, William D. Sentence perception as an interactive parallel process. *Science,* 1975, *189*.

Martin, J. G. Rhythmic (hierarchical) versus serial structure in speech and other behavior. *Psychological Review,* 1972, *79*, 487–509.

Martinet, A. *Elements of general linguistics*. London: Faber and Faber, 1964.

Massaro, D. W., Cohen, M. M. Preperceptual auditory storage in speech recognition. In A. Cohen and S. G. Nooteboom (Eds.), *Structure and process in speech perception: Proceedings of the symposium on dynamic aspects of speech perception*. New York: Springer-Verlag, 1975.

Massaro, D. W. (Ed.) *Understanding language: An information-processing analysis of speech perception, reading, and psycholinguistics.* New York: Academic Press, 1975.

McNeill, D., Lindig, K. The perceptual reality of phonemes, syllables, words, and sentences. *Journal of Verbal Learning and Verbal Behavior,* 1973, *12*, 419–430.

McNeill, D., Repp, B. Internal processes in speech perception. *Journal of the Acoustical Society of America,* 1973, *53*, 1320–1326.

Mehrabian, A. and Ferris, S. R. Inference of attitudes from nonverbal communication in two channels. *Journal of Consulting Psychology,* 1967, *31*, 248–252. Reprinted in S. Weitz (ed.), *Nonverbal communication*. New York: Oxford University Press, 1974.

Melton, A. W., and Martin, E. (Eds.) *Coding processes in human memory.* New York: Wiley, 1972.

Neisser, U. *Cognitive psychology.* New York: Appleton, 1967.

Nooteboom, S. F., Cohen, A. Anticipation in speech production and its implications for perception. In A. Cohen and S. G. Nooteboom (Eds.), *Structure and process in speech perception: Proceedings of the symposium on dynamic aspects of speech perception*. New York: Springer-Verlag, 1975.

Orr, D. B., Friedman, H. L., & Williams, J. C. C. Trainability of listening comprehension of speeded discourse. *Journal of Educational Psychology,* 1965, *56*, 148–156.

Pick, H. I. and Saltzmann, E. (Eds.) *Modes of perceiving and processing information*. Hillsdale, NJ: Lawrence Erlbaum, 1978.

Pike, K. L. *Phonetics*. Ann Arbor: The University of Michigan Press, 1943.

Pisoni, D. B., Sawusch, J. R. Some stages of processing in speech perception. In A. Cohen and S. G. Nooteboom (Eds.), *Structure and process in speech perception: Proceedings of the symposium on dynamic aspects of speech perception*. New York: Springer-Verlag, 1975.

Pisoni, D. B. Speech perception. In W. K. Estes (Ed.), *Handbook of learning and cognitive processes,* Vol. 6. *Linguistic functions in cognitive theory*. Hillsdale, NJ: Lawrence Erlbaum, 1978.

Pollack, I. Pickett, J. M. The intelligibility of excerpts from conversation. *Language and Speech,* 1963, *6*, 165–171.

Pollio, H.R., Barlow, J.M., Fine, H.J., et al. *Psychology and the poetics of growth.* Hillsdale, N.J.: Erlbaum, 1977.

Posner, M. I., Warren, R. E. Traces, concepts and conscious constructions. In Arthur W. Melton and Edwin Martin (Eds.), *Coding processes in human memory.* New York: John Wiley, 1972.

Reddy, M. The conduit metaphor—A case of frame conflict in our language about language. Presented at the Conference on Metaphor and Thought. National Institute of Education, University of Illinois, Champaign-Urbana, September, 1977. In Andrew Ortoney (Ed.), *Metaphor and thought.* Cambridge, England: The Cambridge University Press, 1979.

Restle, F., Shiffrin, R. M., Castellan, N. J., et al., (Eds.) *Cognitive theory.* Vol. 1. New York: Halsted Press, 1975.

Ricoeur, P. *The rule of metaphor.* Toronto: University of Toronto Press, 1975.

Rommetveit, R. *On message structure: A framework for the study of language and communication.* New York: John Wiley, 1974.

Rommetveit, R. "On the meanings of acts and what is meant by what is said," or "On the dawning of different aspects of life in a pluralistic social world." Lecture presented at Northwestern University, May 30, 1979.

Ross, J. R. Where's English? In C. L. Fillmore, D. Kempler, and W. S-Y. Wang (Eds.), *Individual differences in language ability and language behavior.* New York: Academic Press, 1979.

Ryan, E. G. Subjective reactions toward accented speech. In R. W. Shuy and R. W. Fasold (Eds.), *Language attitudes: Current trends and prospects.* Washington: Georgetown University Press, 1973.

Sachs, J. Recognition memory for syntactic and semantic aspects of connected discourse. *Perception and Psychophysics,* 1976, *2,* 437–442.

Sadock, J. *Toward a linguistic theory of speech acts.* New York: Academic Press, 1975.

Searle, J. R. *Speech acts.* Cambridge: The Cambridge University Press, 1970.

Searle, J. R. Indirect speech acts. In J. Morgan and P. Cole (Eds.), *Studies in syntax and semantics (Vol. 3): Speech Acts.* New York: Academic Press, 1975.

Schane, S. *Generative phonology.* Englewood Cliffs, NJ: Prentice-Hall, 1973.

Scherer, K. R. Judging personality from voice: A cross-cultural approach to an old issue of interpersonal perception. *Journal of Personality,* 1972, *40,* 191–210.

Scherer, K. R. Acoustic concomitants of emotional dimensions: Judging affect from synthesized tone sequences. In S. Weitz (Ed.), *Nonverbal communication.* New York: Oxford University Press, 1974.

Shoup, J. E. and Pfeiffer, L. L. Acoustic characteristics of speech sounds. In N. Lass (Ed.), *Contemporary issues in experimental phonetics.* New York: Academic Press, 1976.

Stankiewicz, E. Problems of emotive language. In T. A. Sebeok, A. S. Hayes, and M. C. Bateson (Eds.), *Approaches to semiotics.* The Hague: Mouton, 1964.

Starkweather, J. A. Variations in vocal behavior. In *Disorders of communication.* Proceedings of the Association for Research in Nervous and Mental Disease, 1964.

Steiner, G. *After Babel.* London: Oxford University Press, 1975.

Stevens, K. The quantal nature of speech: Evidence from articulatory acoustic data. In E. E. David and P. B. Denes (Eds.), *Human communication: A unified view.* New York: McGraw-Hill, 1972.

Stevens, K. and Klatt, D. H. Role of formant transitions in the voiced-voiceless distinction for stops. *Journal of the Acoustical Society of America,* 1974, *55,* 653–659.

Studdert-Kennedy, M. The nature and function of phonetic categories. In F. Restle, R. M. Shiffrin, J. N. Castellan, et al. (Eds.), *Cognitive theory.* New York: Halsted Press, 1975.

Studdert-Kennedy, M. From continual signal to discrete message: Syllable to phoneme. In J. F. Kavanagh and J. E. Cutting (Eds.), *The role of speech in language.* Cambridge, MA: The Massachusetts Institute of Technology Press, 1975.

Turner, E. A., Rommetveit, R. The effects of focus of attention on storing and retrieving of active and passive voice sentences. *Journal of Verbal Learning and Verbal Behavior,* 1968, *7,* 543–548.

Tyler, S. *The said and the unsaid.* New York: Academic Press, 1979.

Valian, V. Talk, talk, talk: A selective critical review of theories of speech production. In Roy O. Freedle (Ed.), *Discourse production and comprehension.* Vol. 1. Norwood, NJ: Ablex Publishing Company, 1977.

Van den Broecke, M. P. K. *Hierarchies and rank orders in distinctive features.* Assen: Van Gorcum, 1976.

Van Lancker, D. Language lateralization and grammars. In John Kimball (Ed.), *Studies in syntax and semantics.* Vol. 2. New York: Academic Press, 1973.

Vetter, H. J. *Language behavior and communication.* Itasca, IL: F. E. Peacock, 1969.

Wallace, K. R. Speech act and the unit of conversation. *Philosophy and Rhetoric,* 1970, *3:3,* 74–81.

Wang, W. S-Y. The basis of speech. In Carroll Reed (Ed.), *The learning of language.* New York: Appleby-Asturg-Crawford, 1971.

Wanner, E. Do we understand sentences from the outside-in or from the inside-out? *Daedalus,* Summer 1973.

Warren, R. M. Auditory temporal discrimination by trained listeners. *Cognitive Psychology,* 1974, *6,* 237–256.

Warren, R. M. Auditory illusions and perceptual processes. In N. J. Lass (Ed.), *Contemporary issues in experimental phonetics.* New York: Academic Press, 1976.

Wathen-Dunn, W. (Ed.) *Models for the perception of speech and visual form.* Cambridge, MA: Massachusetts Institute of Technology Press, 1967.

Wilson, D. *Presuppositions and non-truth-conditional semantics.* New York: Academic Press, 1975.

Weitz, S. (Ed.) *Nonverbal communication.* New York: Oxford University Press, 1974.

Williams, C., Stevens, K. Emotions and speech: Some acoustical correlates. *Journal of the Acoustical Society of America,* 1972, *52,* 1238–1249.

Wingfield, A., Klein, J. Syntactic structure and acoustic pattern in speech perception. *Perception and Psychophysics,* 1971, *9,* 23–28.

Wingfield, A. The intonation-syntax interaction: Prosodic features in perceptual processing of sentences. In A. Cohen and S. G. Nooteboom (Eds.), *Structure and process in speech perception: Proceedings of the symposium on dynamic aspects of speech perception.* New York: Springer-Verlag, 1975.

Winitz, H., Scheib, M. E., Reeds, J. A. Identification of stops and vowels for the burst portion of /p,t,k/ isolated from conversational speech. *Journal of the Acoustical Society of America,* 1972, *51,* 1309–1317.

Wodehouse, P. G. *Brinkley Manor.* Boston, MA: Little, Brown, and Co., 1934.

(3) *Dental and interdental* (4) *Alveolar* (5) *Palatal* (6) *Velar.*

John J. Ohala

# 2

# The Nonlinguistic Components of Speech

When we hear someone speak we can often obtain a great deal of information about the speaker besides what is conveyed by the linguistic content of the message. (As a first approximation, the "linguistic" content of an utterance can be characterized by that which would be conveyed by its written transcript.) For example, we may be able to deduce the speaker's sex, approximate age, approximate physical size, emotional state, state of physical health, attitude towards the listener (e.g., respectful, condescending), attitude towards the content of the message (e.g., his or her certainty or uncertainty about the truth of the statement), social or ethnic class, regional origin, and personal identity. That such information is packaged in speech is common knowledge and accounts for the special pains writers have to take to convey this information via the written word:

"Sit down," he said, *threateningly.*
"Don't mind if I do," Patterson replied, *coolly.*

*How* this information is packaged into speech is not common knowledge and, in fact, speech scientists so far have only succeeded in decoding some aspects of the nonlinguistic components of speech. One index of the lack of success in this area is the rather modest results obtained so far in the areas of *speaker identification* from voice (stripping away all information except that which characterizes the individual speaker) and *speech recognition* (stripping away all information except that which conveys the linguistic components). (See Hecker, 1971; Klatt, 1977; Bolt, 1979; Tosi, 1979; Lea, [in press].)

This chapter will provide a brief introduction to some of the theoretical and practical concepts necessary for an understanding of the origin of within-speaker and between-speaker variation in speech.

## THE CARRIER NATURE OF SPEECH

An interesting and insightful view of speech likens it to a carrier signal with the message-bearing modulations superimposed on it much like AM, FM, or PCM transmissions (Dudley, 1940). Adapting this view to our purposes, we may conveniently divide the nonlinguistic elements of speech into those which are *inherent* to the speech signal, i.e., part of the "carrier" signal, and those which have to be encoded in the speech signal, i.e., part of the message-bearing modulations. The former are assumed not to be under voluntary control by the speaker (or at least can be minimally influenced by him at the moment of speaking) whereas the latter are more or less variable and under voluntary, though not necessarily conscious, control of the speaker.

## INHERENT INFORMATION

The acoustic speech signal is a function of two basic elements: a sound *source* and a *filter*. The primary source is the complex siren-like, harmonic-rich sound produced by the vibrating vocal cords as they "chop up" the air stream issuing from the lungs. A secondary source is the audible noise created from the air turbulence which comes from forcing air through any one of several constrictions which can be made within the vocal tract. In the absence of a larynx, a close approximation to the laryngeal sound may be provided by the vibration of the flaps at the opening to the esophagus; this is the so-called "belch" or esophageal voice. The *filter* is the vocal tract which, due to its various shapes, selectively passes certain favored frequencies—the frequencies of *resonance*—and attenuates the other frequencies. (On *sound spectrograms* or "*voiceprints*" of speech the resonances of the voice are manifested as dark horizontal bars called *formants*). (See Chapter 4 of this volume.)

### What the Vocal Cords Reveal about Their Owner

The rate of vibration of the vocal cords is determined by their effective mass (the mass free to vibrate), the tension or elasticity, and the aerodynamic force. During the years of growth ($\leq$ 16 to 18 years of age) the mass of the vocal cords is generally positively correlated with overall body mass (Negus 1949, p. 177ff.). The adult male vocal cords are, however, disproportionately longer and more massive than those of the adult female by virtue of the more forward projection of the male's thyroid cartilage ("Adam's apple") to which the vocal cords are anchored (Broad, 1973). Thus the average pitch of voice, or at least the range of pitch used by a speaker, can reveal in a general way the age and size as well as the speaker's sex (Lass & Davis, 1976; Lass, Hughes, Bowyer, Waters, and Bourne, 1976). Zemlin (1968, p. 182) reports that the modal pitch of young adult males is about 130 HZ and of young adult females about 260 Hz. Children's modal pitch decreases as they grow older but generally ranges between 300 and 400 Hz. Boys' pitch of voice undergoes a sudden decrease at puberty. There is evidence that with advancing age ( > 65) the modal pitch of males again becomes slightly higher (Mysak, 1959). There is, however, considerable overlap in the total pitch ranges of males and females, and of adults and children, so that it might be thought that the pitch of voice would be an ambiguous cue to age, size, or sex. It is true that listeners may often make mistakes in interpreting these cues, but nevertheless there is suggestive evidence that listeners can somehow determine whether a given sample of voice is above or below the speaker's "natural" or modal pitch, i.e., the pitch level most often used by a given speaker. In this way the ambiguity is reduced.

There are also age and sex-related variations in the *shape* of the glottal pulse. These are reflected in the speech signal by variations in the overall spectral contours of the voice. A generally sharper glottal pulse, which is characteristic of adult males, will have relatively more energy in the higher harmonics, and a smoother pulse (with "rounded corners"), which is characteristic of females, will have relatively less energy in the higher harmonics (Monsen & Engebretson, 1977). See Figure 2-1.

Some of the same acoustic cues—i.e., modal pitch and spectral contours of the voice, in addition to the presence of aperiodicity and/ or added noise in the speaker's voice, as well as various dynamic parameters of voice—can often reveal whether the speaker is well or not. First, and most obviously, any pathological condition in the larynx itself will be reflected in the voice. Tumors, polyps, or a swelling on the vocal cords will give rise to aperiodic vibration. Inability to completely adduct the cords, due to paralysis, swelling, etc., will give rise to noise from air turbulence (Isshiki and von Leden 1964; Isshiki, Yanagihara, and Morimoto, 1966). Paralysis or disease affecting the nerves may also limit the range over which pitch can be varied (Critchley & Kubik, 1925; Sonninen, 1956). A considerable amount of

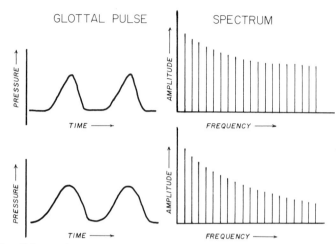

Fig. 2-1.  Schematic representation of the relation between two glottal pulse shapes and their respective spectra. *Top:* Pulse with sharp "corners" has higher harmonics with relatively higher amplitude; *Bottom:* Pulse with rounded "corners" has higher harmonics with relatively lower amplitude.

ongoing research is aimed at finding reliable, measurable acoustic correlates of these and other pathological states, especially neurological disorders (see Dordain and Chevrie-Muller, 1977; Logemann, Fisher, Boshes, and Blonsky, 1978; Davis, 1979).

Of considerable recent interest are changes in the voice induced by stress or extreme emotions including, especially, those which supposedly accompany lying or other vocally expressed deception (Papçun and Disner, [in press]). Everyone is familiar with some of the physiological changes which occur during high emotional states and which affect or might affect the voice:

1) Dryness in the mouth or larynx
2) Accelerated breathing rate
3) Muscle tremor

The first two factors probably contribute to the "huskiness" or momentary hoarseness of the voice of an emotionally excited speaker. The third is responsible for the often noted "quaver" in the voice of a nervous or tense speaker. This tremor is evident, for example, in the pitch of voice of the radio announcer describing the crash of the zeppelin *Hindenburgh* (Williams & Stevens 1972, p. 1246, Fig. 8). (The stuttering and stammering of speakers under stress may also be related to this muscle tremor, but it could as well be a function of a disarrangement of higher cortical processes leading to a disruption of the motor commands issued by the brain to the speech muscles. In this line, Goldman-Eisler (1968) has provided extensive evidence on the relation between hesitation pauses in speech and the intensity of cognitive processing.) Most investigators have concluded, nevertheless, that the vocal correlates of emotional state are highly speaker-specific (Hecker, Stevens, von Bismarck, and Williams, 1968; Scherer, 1979).

### Information Present in the Filter

Ordinary speech involves continuous changes in the shape of the vocal tract and, consequently, in the resonances of the vocal tract. Systematic variations in the lowest three resonances provide the listener cues to the identity of the specific vowels and consonants strung together in speech. Nevertheless, there is one aspect of the vocal tract configuration which cannot be changed very much, namely, its length. Roughly speaking, the shorter the speaker's vocal tract, the higher the resonant frequencies (Peterson and Barney, 1952; Fant, 1973). At least some of the cues to speaker size, sex, and identity are derived from an auditory analysis of the absolute and relative resonant frequencies (Garvin and Ladefoged, 1963; Ladefoged, 1967, p. 115ff.). These sex-specific characteristics of vocal tract dimensions are present even in preadolescents, although many of the cues listeners use to differentiate boys' and girls' voices are socially dictated patterns of use of pitch, timing, etc. (Bennett and Weinberg, 1979).

Other long-term characteristics of individual voices that are reflected in their resonances are: persistent nasalization, constricted pharynx, and raised larynx. This latter gesture is employed by Mel Blanc, the well known voice caricaturist, to produce the voice of the cartoon character "Bugs Bunny."

Some of these characteristics may be large enough that they are actually due to or constitute a pathological condition. Thus, excessive nasality in the voice may point to insufficient velopharyngeal closure on those speech sounds normally requiring it, e.g., plosives (p, t, k, b, d, g), close vowels such as [i] beet and [u] boot. Such a condition could arise from a cleft palate, swollen adenoids, or paralysis of one or more of the muscles controlling the position of the soft palate.

Missing teeth (especially the upper incisors) and malocclusions of the teeth (especially those forms causing an abnormally wide separation between upper and lower teeth) affect speech by distorting the spectral characteristics of dental fricatives, [s] (sin), [z] (Zen), [θ] (thin), [ð] (then).

In fact, we know of numerous ways the anatomy of the vocal tract can vary between individuals, the sexes, and races, and this is not surprising considering the many variations in the external anatomy which differentiate individuals, the sexes, and races. Variations in the contours of the palatal vault, the contours of the dental arch in the upper mandible, the shape of the nasal cavity, and even the presence or absence or the degree of development of certain muscles involved in the production of speech are all known to exist (Catford, 1977, pp. 21 ff.).

## VOLUNTARY MODIFICATIONS OF THE VOICE

Nonlinguistic elements can be transmitted in speech along with linguistic elements by two principle means: selection of variants and parallel or superimposed transmission.

### Variation in Speech

Everyone is aware of pronunciation variants for words or phrases, e.g., *ask* as [æsk] or [æks], *farm* as [farm] or [fɑːm], *going to* as ['gowɪŋ tʰu] or ['gʌnə], *government* as ['gʌvɚnmɛnt] or ['gʌmːɪnt]. Use of one or the other of these variants in speech allows listeners to draw some conclusion about where the speaker was raised, his ethnic and social background, the degree of intimacy or solidarity he wishes to establish with his listeners, etc.

Some variation in pronunciation arises due to purely inertial constraints of the speech organs: the speaker may try to quickly execute a given sequence of vocal tract configurations but the articulators may not be able to keep up. Such "slurred" pronunciations may be picked up and repeated by others and become for them the "standard" pronunciation or at least an accepted variant. This new pronunciation may be copied in turn by others and eventually represent a pronunciation characteristic of a specific linguistic community. This is just one possible scenario for "sound change." Among other causes of sound change is mishearing, e.g., *with* [wɪθ] heard (and repeated) as [wɪf]. This latter process is aided by the fact that many acoustic speech signals can be produced or very closely approximated by more than one articulatory gesture; there is, thus, a "many-to-one" relation between vocal tract shape and the output sound.

Sound change is a very complex topic, and, although it has been intensively studied for almost 200 years, there is much that remains to be discovered about its causes (Ohala, 1974). Whatever its origins, it represents one of the primary sources of pronunciation variants, the use of which reveals so much about the speaker. Thus, a listener hearing a given speech sound may repeat it using a different articulation from that employed by others. Even if the substituted articulation succeeds in reproducing most of the acoustic characteristics of the target sound, it will still differ in some other characteristics. In this way the substitution that led from Early Tibetan /sna/ "nose" to Modern Burmese [nna] (with an initial voiceless nasal) maintains some of the primary acoustic traits of the word, i.e., both still begin with a voiceless segment which has high frequency noise, but the initial fricative is still different in that the [n̥] possesses noise that is less intense and is not as well defined spectrally as the [s].

Not coincidentally, this same sound change occasionally shows up in English-speaking children's substitutions for initial /sn/ clusters, e.g., "snack" becomes [nnæk] and "snip" [nnɪp]. Greenlee and Ohala (in press) argue that this and other such parallels between diachronic phonology (sound change) and children's sound substitutions indicate that they are both governed by the same universal physical constraints.

## The Many-to-One Relation between Articulation and Sound

The fact that a given speech sound may be produced or closely approximated by two or more vocal tract shapes has considerable importance in speech science. Speakers with anatomical anomalies of the speech organs can often find alternate ways of producing articulations they are incapable of, e.g., in the absence of a tongue, pharyngeal fricatives may be substituted for oral fricatives (Goldstein, 1940; Eskew and Shepard, 1949; Weinberg and Horii, 1975). Some compensatory articulations are more successful than others, and some anatomical deficits are more amenable to compensation than others: one might gather from the literature in this area that the absence of a tongue is less damaging to speech intelligibility than velopharyngeal incompetence.

In some sense, the obstacles that speakers with anatomical deficits have to overcome represent extreme points on a continuum of physical constraints which speakers have to master. Even the normal speaker faces constraints inherent in the vocal tract, e.g., the fact that the build-up of air pressure in the oral cavity during voiced stops can extinguish the voicing—unless the oral cavity is enlarged to absorb some of the glottal air flow. Even in this case there is evidence that different speakers use different articulatory strategies to accomplish this (Bell-Berti, 1975).

### Parallel Transmission

The speech signal which carries the acoustic modulations representing the linguistic components of the message can also carry nonlinguistic messages simultaneously through a parallel or superimposed transmission. The pitch and quality of voice, the relative duration of the speech sounds, and the intensity of voice can indicate the speaker's attitude towards what is said towards the listener, etc.

A sentence spoken in a soft voice or a whisper may signal that the speaker intends the message to be confidential or directed exclusively to the listener. Anger, surprise, excitement, etc. is generally expressed in a loud voice.

An overall slow rate of speaking, coupled with precise articulation, can indicate that the speaker is rendering a carefully considered observation or question which should therefore command the listener's serious attention. Slow speech with deliberately slurred articulation can convey the speaker's indifference.

A slowing down of speech rate at the end of utterances (the so-called phrase-final "drawl"), in addition to specific variations in pitch, is a signal that the utterance is finished and that an interruption can be accepted. It is similar to the use of "over" in two-way radio communications.

The parameters of voice which offer the greatest potential for nonlinguistic expression are the pitch and quality of voice. The same utterance can be turned into a question or a statement simply by use of different pitch contours. Rising pitch as a sign of deference is often found in telephone conversations when the social ranking of the two parties is clearly marked by vendor/client relationships (see Figure 2-2).

Another cue for signalling aggressiveness/deference is that of a rough, raspy voice ("growl") vs. a smoother, purer voice. Ohala (1970, in press) and Morton (1977) have pointed out that the correlation: low pitched, rough voice for assertiveness or aggressiveness and high pitched, pure voice for deference or questions as used by humans, has an obvious parallel in the vocalization of animals, e.g., dogs, lions, various birds—i.e., in an encounter between two animals, a growl is used to express aggression and a whine or high-pitched yelp expresses surrender. In the case of animals, the origins of this particular sound-meaning correlation can be guessed at: other things being equal, the bigger animal usually wins the battle, and, since the average pitch of the voice is inversely correlated with body size, the lower the pitch of the growl (and the sharper the pulses) the larger will the vocalizing animal appear to its adversary; the use of a high-pitched whine for

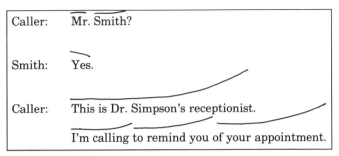

Fig. 2-2.  Hypothetical conversation showing use of rising pitch to signal deference. Pitch of voice is represented schematically by the curves above the text.

surrender or deference may be an attempt on the part of the capitulating animal to imitate the young of the species and to thereby elicit a paternal or helping response from the potential attacker. All of this need not be done consciously and is more likely instinctive. It is possible, then, that at least some of humans' use of their voice originates in the same way: as innately determined behavior.

In any case, humans are far more innovative in their use of the pitch of voice than animals. Fine nuances of emotion and attitude can be expressed by using any of a variety of stereotyped melodies, whose meanings may vary from one speech community to another. A thorough analysis and understanding of the meanings of the many melodies encountered in a given speech community is a task for the future.*

REFERENCES

Bell-Berti, F. The control of pharyngeal cavity size for English voiced and voiceless consonants. *J. Acous. Soc. Am.*, 1975, *57*, 456–461.

Bennett, S., Weinberg, B. Sexual characteristics of preadolescent children's voices. *J. Acous. Soc. Am.*, 1977, *65*, 179–189.

Bolt, R. H. On the theory and practice of voice identification. Committee on Evaluation of Sound Spectrograms. Washington, DC: National Academy of Sciences, 1979.

Broad, D. J. Phonation. In F. D. Minifie, T. J. Hixon, F. Williams (Eds.), *Normal aspects of speech, hearing, and language*. Englewood Cliffs: Prentice-Hall, Inc., 1973, pp. 127–167.

---

*See Pike, 1945, for a beginning.

Catford, J. C. *Fundamental problems in phonetics.* Bloomington: Indiana University Press, 1977.

Critchley, M., Kubik, C. S. The mechanism of speech and deglutition in progressive bulbar palsy. *Brain,* 1925, *48,* 492–534.

Davis, S. B. Acoustic characteristics of normal and pathological voices. In N. J. Lass (Ed.), *Speech and language: Advances in basic research and practice* (Vol. 1). New York: Academic Press, 1979, pp. 271–335.

Dordain, M., Chevrie-Muller, C. Voice and speech in Wilson's disease. *Folia Phoniatrica,* 1977, *29,* 217–232.

Dudley, H. The carrier nature of speech. *Bell System Technical J.,* 1940, *19,* 495–515.

Eskew, H. A., Shepard, E. Congenital aglossia. *American J. of Orthodontia,* 1949, *35,* 116–119.

Fant, G. A note on vocal tract size factors and nonuniform F-pattern scaling. In G. Fant, *Speech sounds and features.* Cambridge: M.I.T. Press, 1973, pp. 84–99.

Garvin, P. L., Ladefoged, P. Speaker identification and message identification in speech recognition. *Phonetica,* 1963, *9,* 193–199.

Goldman-Eisler, F. *Psycholinguistics. Experiments in spontaneous speech.* London: Academic Press, 1968.

Goldstein, M. New concepts of the function of the tongue. *Laryngoscope,* 1940, *50,* 164–188.

Greenlee, M., Ohala, J. J. Phonetically motivated parallels between child phonology and historical sound change. *Language Sciences,* in press.

Hecker, M. H. L. Speaker recognition. An interpretive survey of the literature. *Am. Speech and Hearing Assoc. Monographs,* 1971, No. 16.

Hecker, M. H. L., Stevens, K. N., von Bismarck, G., Williams, C. E. Manifestations of task-induced stress in the acoustic speech signal. *J. Acous. Soc. Am.,* 1968, *44,* 993–1001.

Isshiki, N., von Leden, H. Hoarseness: Aerodynamic studies. *Archives of Otolaryngology,* 1964, *80,* 206–213.

Isshiki, N., Yanagihara, N., Morimoto, M. Approach to the objective diagnosis of hoarseness. *Folia Phoniatrica,* 1966, *18,* 393–400.

Klatt, D. H. Review of the ARPA Speech Understanding Project. *J. Acous. Soc. Am.,* 1977, *62,* 1345–1366.

Ladefoged, P. *Three areas of experimental phonetics.* London: Oxford University Press, 1967.

Lass, N. J., Davis, M. An investigation of speaker height and weight identification. *J. Acous. Soc. Am.,* 1976, *60,* 700–703.

Lass, N. J., Hughes, K. R., Bowyer, M. D., Waters, L. T., Bourne, V. T. Speaker sex identification from voiced, whispered, and filtered isolated vowels. *J. Acous. Soc. Am.,* 1976, *59,* 675–678.

Lea, W. A. (Ed.) *Voice analysis on trial.* Springfield, Illinois: Charles Thomas, in press.

Logemann, J. A., Fisher, H. B., Boshes, B., Blonsky, E. R. Frequency and co-occurrence of vocal tract dysfunctions in the speech of a large sample of Parkinson patients. *J. Speech and Hearing Disorders,* 1978, *43,* 47–57.

Monsen, R. B., Engebretson, A. M. Study of variations in the male and female glottal wave. *J. Acous. Soc. Am.*, 1977, *62*, 981–993.

Morton, E. S. On the occurrence and significance of motivation-structural rules in some bird and mammal sounds. *The Am. Naturalist*, 1977, *111*, 855–869.

Mysak, E. D. Pitch and duration characteristics of older males. *J. Speech and Hearing Research*, 1959, *2*, 46–54.

Negus, V. E. *The comparative anatomy and physiology of the larynx*. New York: Grune & Stratton, 1949.

Ohala, J. J. Aspects of the control and production of speech. UCLA *Working Papers in Phonetics*, 1970, No. 15.

Ohala, J. J. Experimental historical phonology. In J. M. Anderson and C. Jones (Eds.), *Historical Linguistics* (Vol. 2). *Theory and description in phonology*. Amsterdam: North Holland Publishing Co., 1974, pp. 353–389.

Ohala, J. J. Discussion. In T. Myers, J. Laver, and J. Anderson (Eds.), *The cognitive representation of speech*. Amsterdam: North Holland Publishing Co., in press.

Papçun, G., Disner, S. Stress evaluation and voice lie detection: A review. In W. A. Lea (Ed.), *Voice analysis on trial*, in press.

Peterson, G. E., Barney, H. L. Control methods used in a study of the vowels. *J. Acous. Soc. Am.*, 1952, *24*, 175–184.

Pike, K. L. *The intonation of American English*. Ann Arbor: The University of Michigan Press, 1945.

Scherer, K. R. Nonlinguistic vocal indicators of emotion and psychopathology. In C. E. Izard (Ed.), *Emotions in personality and psychopathology*. New York: Plenum Press, 1979, pp. 495–529.

Sonninen, A. A. The role of the external laryngeal muscles in length adjustment of the vocal cords in singing. *Acta Oto-Laryngologica*, 1956, Supplement 130.

Tosi, O. *Voice identification. Theory and legal applications*. Baltimore: University Park Press, 1979.

Weinberg, B., Horii, Y. Acoustic features of pharyngeal /s/ fricatives produced by speakers with cleft palates. *Cleft Palate J.*, 1975, *12*, 12–16.

Williams, C. E., Stevens, K. N. Emotions and speech: Some acoustical correlates. *J. Acous. Soc. Am.*, 1972, *52*, 1238–1250.

Zemlin, W. R. *Speech and hearing science*. Englewood Cliffs: Prentice-Hall, Inc., 1968.

John Laver
Robert Hanson

# 3
# Describing the Normal Voice

As Ohala points out in the preceding chapter, in his example of listening to speech over the telephone (see Figure 2-2), listeners infer a vast amount of information about the characteristics of the speaker. This process of attribution often includes conclusions about physical aspects of the speaker's identity such as his or her sex, age, height, weight, physique and state of health, psychological aspects such as his or her personality and mood, and social aspects such as his or her regional origin and social status (Laver, 1968; Laver & Trudgill 1979). The capacity of speech to signal identity characteristics of the speaker is a vital part of communication in everyday spoken interaction. Furthermore, in medicine and psychiatry, this capacity can become vital in a more directly literal sense, when the voice is taken to furnish evidence of pathological conditions in the speaker. Both in everyday life and in the professional domains of medicine and psychiatry, the experienced ear helps us to make remarkably skillful subjective evaluations of speakers from the speech they produce.

One of the difficulties inhibiting our scientific understanding of the objective basis of this skilled attributional process, however, is that we lack a comprehensive system for describing the vocal phenomena, both normal and abnormal, which act as imputed evidence for

*Preparation of this chapter was funded by a Medical Research Council project on "Vocal Profiles of Speech Disorders" (Grant # G987/1192/N), in the Phonetics Laboratory of the University of Edinburgh. Robert Hanson is a Visiting Senior Scientist on the project, and we are grateful to Sheila Wirz, Janet Mackenzie and John Fisher, our project colleagues, for advice and comment.

51

the attributions. A comprehensive system of this sort, in which the description of the normal and the abnormal voice is unified, can be regarded as an ideal eventual goal; attainment of this goal is some way off in the future, at least as far as incorporation of the description of the abnormal voice into a unified theory is concerned. This is partly because any adequate attempt to define the nature and range of vocal abnormality necessarily presupposes an understanding of the nature and range of the normal voice. It is one of the multidisciplinary tasks of phonetic and allied sciences to provide an explicit descriptive theory of the normal voice, and it has to be said that this task is some way from completion. It is true that very substantial progress has been made towards this objective over the last fifteen years, especially in research on the normal mode of laryngeal vibration in the work, for example, of Baer (1975), Crystal (1966), Hirano (1975, 1977), Ishizaka & Flanagan (1972), Matsushita (1969, 1975), Titze (1973, 1974) and Titze and Strong (1975). But there are some major gaps in the theory. There are two areas in particular where more research is needed before we can hope for a properly adequate understanding of the resources of the normal voice. The first is the range of auditory qualities potentially available to the normal voice as a consequence of long-term muscular adjustments by the speaker. The second is the contribution that individual anatomy makes to a speaker's voice. The purpose of this chapter, which should be read in conjunction with those by Ohala, Darby, and Scherer (this volume), and Hirano, Davis, and Beadle (Darby, in press), is to offer some comments on the nature and range of the normal voice (particularly in the two areas just mentioned) and to explore some of the problems inherent in the attempt to provide an adequately comprehensive descriptive system for the normal voice.

## PRELIMINARY ANALYTIC CONCEPTS

It will be helpful to preface the discussion of the normal voice with a brief commentary on some initial analytic concepts.

We can consider first the notion of a time-base, as it affects different types of vocal features. Speech is often divided into three types of features—linguistic features, paralinguistic features of *tone of voice,* and extralinguistic features that make up the speaker's habitual *voice* (Laver and Trudgill, 1979, p. 6). These three aspects of vocal performance can be thought of as being organized on three broadly different types of time-base. Linguistic aspects of vocal performance characteristically exploit muscular activities on a relatively short time-base, with segmental and syllabic actions making up rapidly changing states of the larynx and the supralaryngeal vocal tract. Paralinguistic aspects of vocal performance, which are conventional signals of affective states such as anger, amusement, contempt and confidentiality, typically involve activities on a more medium-term time-base, where the muscular actions can be seen as exercising a constraint, or bias, on the shorter term muscular realizations of the linguistic elements.

Paralinguistic constraints of this sort usually color a whole utterance in everyday conversation. An example would be the raising of a speaker's pitch-range throughout an entire utterance as a paralinguistic signal of anger. Finally, there are those extralinguistic, long-term aspects of vocal performance which, being neither linguistic nor paralinguistic, serve only to individuate the speaker. They constitute the speaker's *voice,* as reflected in phrases like *voice recognition.*

It is the voice features that are the focus of this chapter. Acoustically, the voice features emerge as the long-term aspects cumulating through the more momentary and sporadic linguistic and paralinguistic acoustic events of vocal performance. Two different facets of linguistic and paralinguistic performance are reflected in the long-term voice features: firstly, the acoustic nature of each of the realizations of the different elements in the linguistic and paralinguistic systems in the speaker's accent; and secondly, the frequency of occurrence of each of these items in the habitual patterns of his speech. From an auditory point of view, the voice features can be envisaged as a background against which the linguistic and paralinguistic actions gain their perceptual clarity. If the voice features are the *carrier* for the rest of speech, they set the base-line values from which linguistic and paralinguistic realizations achieve their characterizing deviation.

By definition, voice features are the least variable of all the factors in a speaker's vocal performance. It is precisely for this reason that the voice features, as the long-term laryngeal and supralaryngeal output, constitute a suitable candidate for speaker characterization, either auditorily or by machine analysis.

There is a practical problem of determining the minimum sample duration that will allow the long-term aspects to emerge from the shorter-term perturbations of the linguistic and paralinguistic events. If the speech sample is free from a biasing paralinguistic tone of voice, as in unemotional reading, then text independence seems to be reached fairly successfully between 45 seconds (Frøkjaer-Jensen and Prytz, 1976, p. 6) and 70 seconds (Markel, Oshika & Gray, 1977, p. 330). With a sample of this length, the characteristics of the voice as a carrier for the rest of speech are available for assessment.

The second analytic concept to be considered is the distinction between *organic* and *phonetic* factors in a speaker's voice (Laver 1980, p. 9). Organic factors are derived from the nature of the speaker's individual apparatus, and the phonetic factors from the use to which he or she habitually puts the apparatus. Organic factors are the aspects of the voice that reflect the dimensions and geometry of a speaker's vocal organs, including the nasal and oral structures, the pharynx, larynx and respiratory system. Phonetic factors, whose description will make up the major part of the remainder of this chapter, reflect the habitual, long-term muscular biases that the individual speaker imposes on his vocal performance of linguistic and paralinguistic elements. Examples would be habitual tendency to maintain the lips in a protruded position throughout speech or the quasi-permanent use of a breathy mode of phonation or the characteristic adoption of a nasal quality of voice. Muscularly constraining biases of this sort have been called *settings* (Honikman, 1964), and this term will be adopted here.

In a machine analogy, organic aspects of the vocal apparatus relate to the notion of an *effector* component of a mechanical system, and the phonetic aspects to the *control* component. Phonetic theory has traditionally concerned itself primarily with control considerations, idealizing the effector component. Inter-speaker differences of anatomy within the normal distribution have been largely ignored. While this might be adequate when the focus of analytic attention is on linguistic performance, it becomes less helpful when voice features are being considered. To highlight the relevance of incorporating both control and effector components in a descriptive model of vocal performance, we can examine the analysis of pitch in a situation where a listener is hearing a particular speaker for the first time. The absolute values of fundamental frequency that the listener hears will be the product in the speaker of a number of factors, some relevant to the analysis of voice and some to the analysis of speech as a linguistic and paralinguistic medium. From the point of view of the speaker, his or her choice of the actual fundamental frequency will be constrained by two voice factors, one organic (effector) and one phonetic (control). In organic terms, the geometry, size and mass of his or her laryngeal structures will set the outer limits to the maximum range of fundamental frequency of which the speaker is physically capable. Within that maximum range set by effector limits, the speaker will have developed, as part of his or her phonetic control, a habitual span, or setting, of fundamental frequency within which he or she feels comfortable. On any given occasion, a speaker will normally choose a yet more limited range of fundamental frequency as appropriate for the paralinguistic communication of the particular mood of the moment—anger, amusement, sarcasm, or whatever. Finally, within the appropriate paralinguistic range of fundamental frequency, the speaker will select the actual contours which contribute to linguistic aspects of intonation. Now, it is clear that of all these factors which determine the details of fundamental frequency used by the speaker, only the first factor—the organic, effector limitations of the larynx— results in a constraint on the absolute values of fundamental frequency. All the other factors concern relative values and derive from a hierarchical set of control decisions, all of them perhaps outside conscious awareness on the part of the speaker. In order to evaluate the communicative status of any one of these factors, the listener has to be able to perceive the pitch details correlated with that factor as a figure against the perceptual ground of the pitch details correlated with the other factors. Thus, in order to be able to decide whether a particular intonation level is to count as a high pitch or a low pitch, the listener has to know something about the voice factors. For example, do organic factors constrain the speaker's voice to a naturally high range of pitch? Similarly, within the organic limits of his voice, does the speaker habitually opt for a low pitch-setting? The listener also needs, in order to interpret the linguistic value of a particular intonation level, to know something about the paralinguistic context of the utterance. Within the organic and voice-setting limits, is the speaker currently using a raised paralinguistic pitch-range, as in anger, or a low one, as in consolation?

The final analytic concept that needs briefly to be mentioned in this preliminary section is a distinction between some different acoustic aspects of the speech signal. One distinction has already been discussed in the preceding chapter by Ohala: that between the laryngeal *source* of sound energy and the vocal tract *filter* system. The distinction to which appeal is made in this chapter crosscuts the source-filter distinction; it is the distinction between spectral aspects of acoustic quality and the dynamic features of fundamental frequency and amplitude. It will be convenient to use the terms *voice quality* and *voice dynamics*. Voice quality will be used to refer to the spectral correlates of the organic and phonetic setting features, and voice dynamics to their fundamental frequency and amplitude correlates. There exist other long-term vocal features that characterize speakers, such as rate or tempo, continuity, rhythmicality, and breath support, but these can be considered to be features of temporal organization on a rather different principle.

Within voice quality and voice dynamics as defined, Markel, Oshika and Gray (1977, p. 337) have shown that, at least within their data, spectral parameters are the most successful in discriminating between speakers, then fundamental frequency parameters, and then amplitude parameters. Most of the commentary below will be devoted to a discussion of voice quality. But before embarking on that discussion, it is necessary to say a little about problems of terminology and its standardization.

## PROBLEMS IN THE STANDARDIZATION
## OF VOICE TERMINOLOGY

The question of an appropriate terminology for the description of voice features, both in the normal and the abnormal areas, is inherently problematic . The ideal solution would be one in which a given single label were taken universally to refer to a given vocal phenomenon. This is certainly not the present situation. As an example, we will use two current British otolaryngological textbooks. One book, Ballantine and Groves (1971), uses the terms *slight hoarseness* and *persistent huskiness* to discuss contact ulcers of the vocal fold, while the other, Hall and Coleman (1971), uses the terms *hoarse* and *rough* to discuss vocal fold lesions. In the absence of objective, acoustically based measures, it is not possible to be sure whether the term "hoarse" in these two textbooks refers to the same perceptual quality or not. In addition, it is not clear whether *hoarse* and *rough,* as used by Hall and Coleman, are intended as synonyms for the same quality or as descriptors of different perceptual components in the overall quality to which reference is being made. In short, the situation that exists is one where a single label has multiple potential referents, and a single phenomenon has multiple potential labels. The only practicable way of escaping from such vicious ambiguity, short of arranging for an audible demonstration every time reference was made to a given quality, would be to adopt a standardized terminology. Given that this is not easily achieved over a short period, perhaps the best that we can hope for is an awareness of the communicative problems involved in labeling vocal features, while working slowly towards progressive standardization.

The problem is compounded by the fact that labels for voices are of two different semiotic types (Laver, 1974). The first type of label, which we can call a *descriptive* label, refers to the sound-quality produced by the speaker. The second type of label, which can be called an *indexical* label, is one which is taken to indicate a characteristic of the speaker producing the voice. *A husky voice* would thus be an example of a descriptive label, and *an authoritative voice* an example of an indexical label. The majority of descriptive labels used in everyday life are subjective and impressionistic, relying for effective communication on our everyday understanding of metaphorical association. *A sepulchral voice,* for example, can only have metaphorical validity.

Descriptive labels become scientific only to the extent that they have an objective basis, where the physical characteristics of the sound-quality being labelled are capable of being verified by techniques of physical measurement.

It seems a basic argument that descriptive labels should be used in any account of normal voice quality and voice dynamics. They should also be used for symptomatic description in discussion of the abnormal voice, provided standardized terminology is available. But indexical labels have a crucial part to play in discussion of the abnormal voice, in the diagnosis of the causes underlying particular vocal effects. Present practice in speech pathology often combines description of symptoms with an indication of their etiology within a single label. Examples would be *myopathic dysphonia,* in which the symptom of dysphonia is attributed to a myopathic cause, and *hysterical falsetto,* in which a psychogenic cause is suggested for the vocal sympton of falsetto. Terminology of this sort furnishes a very convenient short-hand, as it were, for postdiagnosis discussion, but the danger in using such a vocabulary for the initial description of symptoms is that it amalgamates prejudicial, indexical aspects of etiological diagnosis with the symptomatic description.

With the range of possible descriptive labels for voices, many subjective and objective systems are conceivable. Some objective, scientific system is clearly preferable to an impressionistic, subjective method. But whatever objective system is preferred, it will be necessary to have a set of established auditory correlates for routine professional use. This chapter presents the outline of one such system, based on articulatory and acoustic criteria, which is described in greater detail in Laver (1980). The auditory correlates of the system, which attempts to describe only the phonetic possibilities of the normal voice, are illustrated on a tape recording accompanying that book. Readers who are interested in descriptive and indexical aspects of research on voice quality and voice dynamics are referred to Laver (1979), which is a bibliography of some 1300 items classified into 100 topics.

## THE DESCRIPTION OF PHONETIC SETTINGS IN VOICE QUALITY

This section offers a summary account of a phonetic model for the description of the long-term muscular adjustments, or settings, that can form part of the production of the normal voice. The model is couched in phonetic, articulatory terms and specifies correlations with auditory, acoustic, and muscular characteristics. The discussion presented here will concern chiefly the articulatory and acoustic levels of description: the other levels are discussed more fully in Laver (1980).

The contribution of individual anatomy to the overall quality of a voice can often be very marked, but for convenience of exposition the assumption will be made that all the settings to be described are performed on a standard vocal apparatus. This assumption, however, is merely convenient, since it preserves the generality of the descriptive model; but the inadequacy of the assumption will be further explored after the presentation of the model.

The analysis of each type of setting will be described in isolation. Once again this is a convenient approach only, because the vocal apparatus, though treated descriptively as if it were a chain of relatively independent muscle systems, is in fact a complex of interlinked, synergistically interdependent systems that are so highly interactive that virtually no activity can take place anywhere in the apparatus without repercussions of varying degrees elsewhere. This is also true to some extent at the acoustic level. Not all settings, however, can co-occur in a given voice. Certain settings have conflicting muscular or perceptual requirements. There is thus a *compatibility* principle, based upon muscular and acoustic criteria that governs the potential combinability of settings.

A second important principle, which derives from the compatibility principle, is that of segmental *susceptibility* to the biasing effect of a given setting. Depending on their articulatory and acoustic characteristics, individual consonant and vowel segments will vary in their susceptibility (Laver, 1978). When a speaker uses a velarizing setting, which tends to keep the body of the tongue in a raised position towards the back of the mouth, as in a Brooklyn accent, vowels which are normally performed close to that area will be less affected than those performed furthest away. Similarly, when a speaker habitually maintains his lips in a rounded posture, vowels and consonants whose necessary linguistic performance requires lip-rounding will be less affected than those with linguistically unspecified lip-position. Conversely, in some cases segments over-ride the effect of a given setting, as in the case of nasal consonants in the speech of a speaker who uses a nasality setting as part of his habitual voice quality. The most obvious example of differential susceptibility is that any phonatory setting of the internal laryngeal musculature will affect only voiced segments, with voiceless segments being largely unaffected.

The most convenient way to describe the individual settings is to compare them with a standard, *neutral* setting of the vocal apparatus. This neutral setting is acoustically defined and has the status only of a reference point. There are no implications of *normality*, nor is any suggestion of a *representative rest-position* of the vocal organs intended.

The neutral setting of the vocal apparatus can be defined as the one which, if we take a vocal tract representative of an average, adult male speaker, will produce the following long-term-average acoustic characteristics:

- The frequencies of the higher formants are odd multiples of that of the first formant. When the formant frequencies are in this ratio of $1 : 3 : 5 \ldots$, the average configuration of the vocal tract will be the one in which it is most nearly in equal cross-section along its full length (Stevens and House, 1961). In the case of a 17 cm vocal tract $F_1$ will be 500 Hz, $F_2$ 1500 Hz and $F_3$ 2500 Hz.
- The frequency ranges for the first three formants are $F_1$, 150–850 Hz, $F_2$ 500–2500 Hz and $F_3$ 1700–3500 Hz (Fant, 1956).
- The bandwidths of the first three formants are 100 Hz (Stevens and House, 1961).
- There is no acoustic coupling of the nasal tract to the rest of the vocal tract, except when necessary for nasal segments as linguistically required.
- The range of fundamental frequency is from 60–240 Hz (Fant, 1956).
- The larynx pulse shape is approximately triangular, regular in amplitude and frequency, with maximum excitation of the resonatory system of the supralaryngeal vocal tract occurring during the closing phase of the glottal cycle (Miller, 1959).
- The closing phase lasts for approximately 33 percent of the glottal cycle (Monsen and Engebretson, 1977).
  Phonation is at moderate effort and in this condition the spectral slope of the glottal waveform is – 12dB per octave above 250 Hz and closer to – 10dB per octave at frequencies below 250 Hz (Flanagan, 1958; Stevens and House, 1961).
- The larynx pulse has only a limited range of frequency jitter and amplitude shimmer. The distribution of these perturbations is normal, with the standard deviation 2 percent or less of the mean (Hanson, 1978). There is no aperiodic noise in the glottal waveform.

To achieve this constellation of acoustic characteristics, the vocal apparatus has to conform on a long-term-average articulatory basis to the following requirements:

- The longitudinal axis of the vocal tract must be undistorted, in that the lips must not be protruded, and the larynx must be neither raised nor lowered.
- The latitudinal axis of the vocal tract must be undistorted, in that

no local constrictions by the lips, tongue, jaw, faucal pillars, or pharynx must disturb the long-term tendency of the tract to equality of cross-section along its length.

- Front oral articulations must be performed by the blade of the tongue.

- The velopharyngeal system must cause audible nasality only where necessary for linguistic purposes.

- The vibration of the true vocal folds must be "regularly periodic, efficient in air use, without audible friction, with the folds in full glottal vibration under moderate longitudinal tension, moderate adductive tension and moderate medial compression" (Laver, 1980, p. 14).

- Muscle tension through the vocal apparatus must be neither unduly high nor unduly low.

Each of the individual settings can be described as departing from at least one of these acoustic and articulatory requirements of the neutral setting. The settings will be discussed in five groups, corresponding to settings of the longitudinal axis of the vocal tract, those of the latitudinal axis, velopharyngeal settings, phonatory settings, and overall muscle-tension settings.

### Longitudinal Settings of the Vocal Tract

The longitudinal axis of the vocal tract can be distorted by muscular adjustments at either end. A short section can be added to the length of the tract at the lips by the action of protruding them forwards. *Labial protrusion* of this sort is usually a concomitant of a lip-rounded setting, and in this condition has the acoustic effect of lowering all formant frequencies, relative to the values for the neutral setting. In absolute terms, the higher formants are more affected (Lindblom and Sundberg, 1971, p. 1176).

The vocal tract can also be elongated by lowering the larynx from its neutral position, by contraction of the infrahyoid musculature. The acoustic effect of this setting is broadly similar to that of labial protrusion, in that all formant values are lowered, but in this case the lower formants are more affected (Fant, 1960, p. 64). Lindblom and Sundberg (1971) suggest that for most vowel segments $F_1$ is reduced by approximately 5 percent, $F_2$ lowers by 8 percent for close front vowels but less for others, and $F_3$ is relatively insensitive.

The longitudinal axis of the vocal tract can be shortened in two ways: firstly, by adopting a *labiodentalized* setting, where the lower lip is drawn inwards and upwards, and held close to the upper front teeth and, secondly, by raising the larynx. The acoustic effect of habitual labiodentalization is not unlike that of labial protrusion in that the higher formant frequencies are lowered.

These three settings: labial protrusion (with rounding), labiodentalization, and a *lowered larynx* position have acoustic correlates which all rely broadly on lowering formant frequencies. But we have seen that a lowered larynx position can be distinguished from the two labial settings by the fact that the former affects the lower formants more markedly, while the latter affects chiefly the higher formants. The audible distinction between the lowered larynx setting and the labial settings is also clear when the effect of the settings on individual susceptible segments is considered. The labial settings will constrain the detailed articulatory performance of labial segments, particularly in their onset and offset, in ways which are quite unlike the corresponding effects in lowered larynx voice. The performance of individual susceptible segments also distinguishes the audible characteristics of each of the labial settings. Both labial settings alter the apparent pitch of front oral fricatives. Both lower the pitch of alveolar fricatives, as in the consonantal beginning the the word *sin,* but to different degrees. But while labial protrusion with rounding also lowers the pitch of dental fricatives, as at the beginning of the word *thin,* labiodentalization raises it. This example of the way in which the audible clues to the identity of settings have to be gathered from the characteristics of ephemeral and intermittently occurring susceptible segments serves as a paradigm for the perception of phonetic aspects of voice quality.

Shortening the vocal tract by raising the larynx using the suprahyoid musculature has an acoustic effect which is quite different from that of all the settings so far mentioned. With this setting, all formant frequencies rise. Sundberg and Nördstrom (1976, pp. 38–39) show that $F_3$ rises as the larynx rises and that $F_2$ rises substantially for close front vowels but without a comparable rise in $F_1$, while $F_1$ and $F_2$ both rise in open vowels.

Because of the interactive nature of the muscle systems involved, adjustments of vertical larynx position are very often associated with dynamic changes in the frequency of vibration of the vocal folds. *Raised larynx voice* is often accompanied by a raised range of fundamental frequency, and lowered larynx voice by a lowered range. The mode of vibration of the vocal folds is also usually affected and raised larynx voice normally sounds rather tense, as in the voice of a would-be tenor singer who has to strain to achieve the necessary high pitch-range. In the case of lowered larynx voice, the mode of phonation is often rather lax and breathy in quality.

It is not that the adjustments of fundamental frequency which tend to accompany vertical changes of larynx position are mechanically inevitable. Appropriate muscular compensations can readjust the frequency-range. But it is a reflection of the interactive nature of the vocal apparatus that such compensations have to be specifically adopted. The interactivity of muscle systems thus results in the observable tendency for certain voice quality settings to co-occur in constellations.

### Latitudinal Settings of the Vocal Tract

Latitudinal settings result in a long-term tendency to constrict (or to expand) the cross-sectional area of the supralaryngeal vocal tract at some point along its length. This can be achieved by the action of the lips, the tongue, or the jaw. Additional possibilities such as settings of the faucal pillars, the pharynx, and the root of the tongue will not be discussed here.

Latitudinal labial settings manipulate the interlabial space in the vertical and transverse dimensions of the coronal plane of the lips. If analysis is restricted merely to expansion and constriction of these two dimensions compared with the neutral values, then eight different, non-neutral, latitudinal settings of the lips can be distinguished. For most practical purposes, however, it is probably sufficient to limit the non-neutral categories to just three. These are, firstly, the (goldfish-like) position of *open rounding,* which consists of vertical expansion of the interlabial space with lateral constriction, normally with labial protrusion. Secondly, *close rounding,* which is sometimes given the lay description of a *pursed-lips* position and which is made by vertical and lateral constriction of the interlabial space, normally with slight protrusion. Thirdly, *lip-spreading,* as in smiling, which is produced by lateral expansion of the interlabial space, normally without either vertical adjustment or protrusion.

Rounding has the acoustic effect noted above of lowering the formants with a greater influence on the higher formants, while lip-spreading results in a raising of formant frequencies (Fant 1957, p. 19). Labial settings have a mutually enabling interaction with mandibular settings, as do lingual settings.

The muscle systems of the tongue have such a complex interplay that many different types of settings could potentially be described. Discussion here will be limited to settings of the body of the tongue and of the tip and blade of the tongue.

The tip and blade of the tongue can be regarded as an articulatory system which is only partially independent of the actions of the body of the tongue. Just as the movements of the body of the tongue have to be facilitated by appropriate adjustments of the jaw, so also are articulatory activities of the tip and blade of the tongue enabled by accommodation of the tongue-body. The neutral setting of the tip/blade system is one where front oral lingual articulations, as in the consonants in *sun, dot, lose* and *rush,* are performed by the blade rather than by the tip. This can be achieved with the tongue-body in a variety of positions. But when the tip/blade system is in a *retroflex* setting, with the tip (or in more extreme cases the underside of the tip) being presented to the palato-alveolar region of the front of the hard palate, then there is more constraint on the range of settings open to the body of the tongue. A raised tongue-body setting, for example, would be incompatible with a retroflex setting of the tip/blade system.

It would be possible to distinguish many different categories of tongue-body settings. Once again, however, it is probably sufficient for practical purposes to limit the delicacy of description to a small number of settings, and we can consider these as long-term adjustments of the gross positioning of the tongue in the mouth in two dimensions of the sagittal plane, vertical and horizontal. Distinctions can be drawn between a *raised* versus a *lowered* position, relative to the neutral setting, and between a *fronted* versus a *retracted* position. A retracted, lowered setting, for instance, would be one where the long-term-average posture of the tongue was low and back in the mouth, constricting the lower part of the pharynx and expanding the front oral cavity. As a consequence of this setting, front oral articulations of the tip/blade would be correspondingly retracted.

In contrast, a raised, fronted tongue-body would constrict the front oral cavity and expand the pharynx. Raising and fronting of the tongue-body are the articulatory basis for our imitations of *little girl* voices in Western culture. Such adjustments in effect copy the smaller vocal tract whose auditory quality they are imitating and are not infrequently exploited for the projection of infantile or vulnerable personality traits. Marilyn Monroe, for example, used this setting.

Finer analysis could resort to traditional phonetic labels of place of articulation and could use such terms as *laryngopharyngalized voice* (for lowering and retraction), *pharyngalized voice* (retraction), *velarized voice* (retraction and raising), *palatalized voice* (raising), *palato-alveolarized voice* (raising and fronting) and *dentalized voice* (for fronting).

Acoustically, there is an interaction between the results of fronting and raising the body of the tongue, such that in palatalization (raising only) $F_2$ is very high, is close to $F_3$ (Fant, 1962, p. 14), and drops progressively as the tongue moves through palato-alveolarization (raising and fronting) to dentalization (fronting only). $F_3$ remains relatively high throughout. In settings with a backing component, there is an $F_1$–$F_2$ proximity, with $F_1$ higher and $F_2$ lower than in the neutral setting.

It is more difficult to specify acoustic characteristics of tip/blade settings, because of the acoustic contamination by the enabling tongue-body setting. But the retroflex setting has an accessible acoustic profile, in that in slight retroflexion $F_4$ lowers towards $F_3$, and in extreme retroflexion $F_3$ lowers to close to $F_2$ (Fant, 1962, p. 14). The film actor James Stewart characteristically uses a retroflex setting.

Mandibular contributions to speech tend to be overlooked in most phonetic discussion. Yet the lower jaw has a very important influence on articulatory performance in general in that it constrains the operational baseline for the activities of all the other supralaryngeal structures. To the extent that the mandible is the carrier of the lower lip, it necessarily participates as a working partner in the achievement of all labial settings (Sussman, MacNeilage, and Hanson, 1973). The mandible coexists in an even more intimate working relationship with the tongue. Every lingual setting has to be performed within the mechanical context set by the jaw. Furthermore, since the tongue is muscularly linked to the velopharyngeal system by the paired palatoglossus muscle and to the pharyngeal system by the pharyngeal constrictors, the mandible can be seen as exercising an indirect influence even on the articulatory operation of these systems.

The articulatory versatility of the jaw, even though this is best reflected in long-term settings rather than short-term movements, arises from its four dimensions of movement—vertical, horizontal, lateral, and rotational. All four are exploited in voice quality settings, but the laterally offset and asymmetrically rotated settings seem much rarer than the vertical settings of an *open* or a *close jaw position,* which are the most frequent, and the horizontally *protruded* or *retracted* position which one sees from time to time. The extremes of vertical settings are the slack-jawed, open position and the clenched-teeth position. A retracted jaw setting is sometimes seen as a concomitant of habitual labiodentalization.

In acoustic terms, all formants rise as the jaw opening becomes larger. Lindblom and Sundberg (1971, p. 1174) have shown that when all other articulatory parameters are held stable, movement of the jaw alone causes considerable changes in $F_1$. Higher formants are less sensitive. In a close jaw position, not only does the value of $F_1$ decrease, but its range is diminished (Lindblom and Sundberg, 1969).

## Velopharyngeal Settings

'Nasality' is a cover term for a very wide range of phenomena. It will be treated here as essentially an auditory concept, correlated with particular articulatory characteristics and with side-branch resonance induced by acoustic coupling of the nasal cavity to the rest of the vocal tract by velic opening. This is not to say that velic opening as such is a sufficient condition for nasality in speech. A crucial factor in inducing side-branch resonance in the nasal cavity is the ratio of two cross-sectional areas—the area of the oral entry from the pharynx to the mouth, and the area of the nasal port at the pharyngeal entry to the nasal cavity. This ratio has to surpass a critical level before audible nasal resonance is produced. This means that velic openings of subcritical proportions can exist in speech without audible nasality.

The velum is in constant movement during speech, and so of course is the tongue. The position of the velum will tend to be correlated with the type of segment being performed (Condax, Acson, Miki and Sakoda, 1976), and this can be used to reach a definition of nasality. Cagliari (1978, p. 159–166), drawing together findings on nasality from endoscopic, fiberoptic, cineradiographic, electromyographic, and aerodynamic techniques, proposes a *neutral velic scale* based on the covariation of velic height with segment type. Within a scale from highest in blowing to lowest in the respiratory position, velic height drops progressively in the following hierarchy of segment type: voiceless then voiced stops; voiceless then voiced fricatives; close then open oral vowels; close then open nasalized vowels; and nasal consonants. Earlier in this chapter, the neutral velopharyngeal setting was described as one where the velopharyngeal system produced audible nasality only as linguistically required. For the voice quality to change from neutral to *nasal,* Cagliari specifies that at least some segments must show a drop in velic height from their neutral value. Conversely, a *denasal* quality will derive from a rise in velic height for some segments relative to the neutral scale (Laver, 1980, pp. 87–88). A nasal setting thus produces more nasality than can be accounted for by the neutral setting and a denasal setting produces less.

The acoustic characteristics of nasality are multiple and are summarized in Laver (1980, pp. 91–92). Briefly, nasal formants and antiresonances are introduced into the spectrum. The most prominent nasal formant in average male speakers is between 200 and 300 Hz, with a bandwidth of approximately 300 Hz: higher frequency nasal formants have bandwidths that increase in width with frequency, reaching 1000 Hz for frequencies near 2500 Hz (House, 1957). The introduction of antiresonances results in an overall attentuation of power

(Dickson, 1962), particularly in the higher frequencies. All formant bandwidths are broadened and spectral peaks flattened.

The acoustic characteristics of a denasal setting consist of the minimization of these features on susceptible segments.

### Phonatory Settings of the Larynx

The theory of vocal fold vibration that is assumed in this account of modes of phonation is the standard aerodynamic-myoelastic theory as proposed by Müller (1837), Smith (1954), Faaborg-Andersen (1957), van den Berg (1958) and others.

It was suggested earlier that in the neutral mode of phonation, the vibration of the true vocal folds was "regularly periodic, efficient in air use, without audible friction, with the folds in full glottal vibration under moderate longitudinal tension, moderate adductive tension and moderate medial compression" (Laver, 1980, p. 14). This is the mode of phonation that Hollien (1974) calls the *modal register*, because of its overwhelmingly wide distribution. *Modal voice* in the definition offered contrasts with five other major phonatory settings, some of which can co-occur, while others cannot. Their combinability is in part tentatively explained in terms of the different specifications of the phonatory settings on the three muscular parameters of longitudinal tension, adductive tension and medial compression. These are parameters suggested by van den Berg (1968) and, in a slightly modified form, can be described as follows. *Longitudinal tension* is muscular tension in the vocalis and/or the cricothyroid muscles, and is a major determinant of fundamental frequency; *adductive tension* is the muscular tension of the interarytenoid muscles. In contraction, these approximate the arytenoid cartilages, thus closing the cartilaginous and the ligamental glottis. *Medial compression* is the force exercised on the vocal processes of the arytenoid cartilages by the lateral cricoarytenoid muscles, in collaboration with tension in the lateral parts of the thyroarytenoid muscles. Medial compression closes the ligamental glottis, but whether the cartilaginous glottis also closes will depend on the adductive tension exerted by the interarytenoid musculature.

Specification of the six phonation types in terms of these three myoelastic parameters is advanced as an explanatory hypothesis based on a wide range of published work on the larynx. But it should be emphasized that further research is necessary to test the hypothesis.

The five phonatory settings to be compared with the neutral, modal setting are *falsetto, whisper, creak, harshness* and *breathiness*.

The laryngeal mechanisms for falsetto are fairly well understood. In contrast with the moderate values in modal voice of the three laryngeal parameters, falsetto has high values. The cross-section of the vocal folds is thin and triangular. Subglottal pressure is low (Kunze, 1964) and air use frugal (Van Riper and Irwin, 1958). The range of fundamental frequency is raised but still overlaps that of modal voice (Hollien and Michel, 1968). The control of fundamental frequency is different from that of modal voice, in that in falsetto the vocalis muscles remain relaxed and the characteristic high longitudinal tension is the product of vigorous contraction of the cricothyroid system, putting the vocal ligaments under strong tension (van den Berg, 1968). Contraction of the lateral parts of the thyroarytenoid muscles keeps the mass of each vocal fold stiff and relatively immobile, limiting vibratory movement chiefly to the thin glottal edges of the folds.

Because of the high fundamental frequency, harmonics are more widely spaced in the spectrum, and falsetto has in consequence a somewhat thin auditory quality. The spectral slope of the laryngeal waveform, falling at about $-20$ dB per octave (Monsen and Engebretson, 1977), is steeper than in modal voice, whose spectral slope falls at approximately $-12$ dB per octave.

The physiology of the whisper setting is also comparatively well understood. In strong whisper, the ligamental glottis is closed and the cartilaginous glottis open. Flowing copiously through this narrow constriction in a high-velocity jet into the pharynx at flow-rates of up to 500 cl/sec, the transglottal airflow becomes turbulent (Catford, 1964), and the eddies generated by this friction give rise to the characteristic auditory quality of whisper (van den Berg, 1968). The Y shape of the glottis is achieved by weak adductive and longitudinal tension, but moderate to high medial compression caused by the action of the lateral cricoarytenoid muscles pivoting the vocal processes of the arytenoid cartilages together (Zemlin, 1964).

Creak, which in American terminology is more often called *vocal fry* or *glottal fry,* is less well understood. The auditory effect is familiar, however, resembling "a rapid series of taps, like a stick being run along a railing" (Catford, 1964, p. 32). Fundamental frequency is very low, with a range in adult males of 24–52 Hz (Michel & Hollien, 1968), with both transglottal airflow (Murry, 1969) and subglottal pressure (Murry and Brown, 1971) less than for modal voice. Neither length nor thickness of the thick, slack vocal folds vary with fundamental frequency (Hollien and Michel, 1968), suggesting that the control of pitch is managed by aerodynamic means. Fundamental frequency is also irregular on a cycle-to-cycle basis (Monsen and Engebretson, 1977).

Wendahl, Moore, and Hollien (1963) suggest that the auditory effect of discrete, low frequency taps in creak is criterial, and that this effect is due to an unusually high degree of damping of the vocal tract. Coleman (1963) established that creak is perceived when the soundwave decays by approximately 43 dB between excitation pulses. Damping of laryngeal pulses may also be produced mechanically by the tendency, observed by Hollien, Moore, Wendahl, and Michel (1966), of the ventricular folds to compress the laryngeal ventricle, and, coming into contact with the upper surfaces of the true vocal folds, to vibrate together as damped, composite structures.

Ladefoged (1971, pp. 14–15) suggests that in creak the "arytenoid cartilages are pressed inward so that the posterior portions of the vocal cords are held together and only the (ligamental) portions are able to vibrate." This would indicate that creak is made with strong adductive tension and strong or moderate medial compression, but with only weak longitudinal tension.

Harshness is not a voice quality that can exist by itself: it can only modify other types of phonation. It will be described here as a modification applied to modal voice, giving *harsh voice*. It is characterized by irregular perturbations of fundamental frequency (jitter) and of intensity (shimmer), together with spectral noise. The mean fundamental frequency is similar to that of modal voice. Muscularly, harshness is the product of laryngeal hypertension, and in extreme harshness the ventricular folds also participate in vibration (Aronson, Peterson, and Litin, 1964). *Ventricular voice* of this sort, according to Plotkin (1964), "once heard is never forgotten," and the "characteristic deep, hoarse voice, alike in male and female, causes an almost sympathetic tightening of the listener's throat." It may be that such extreme tension produces a quality that speech pathology would class as dysphonic. The point being made here is that it is capable of being produced by the normal vocal apparatus, and therefore offers a useful indication of the very wide-ranging potential repertoire of the organically nonpathological voice.

The muscular hypertension in harsh voice is thus likely to be extreme medial compression and extreme adductive tension, but with longitudinal tension remaining moderate.

Breathiness is also a quality that can only modulate other types of phonation. It is the inverse of harshness, in that it is the result of extreme relaxation of muscle tension in the larynx. In combination with modal voice, when giving *breathy voice,* adductive tension is low and medial compression and longitudinal tension are weak. In consequence, the vocal folds vibrate inefficiently, not always meeting at the midline. Airflow rates are high (Catford, 1977), giving a *sighing* quality to the voice, and intensity is low (Fairbanks, 1960), with flattened spectral peaks and broad bandwidths.

In the analysis offered here, breathiness in fact combines only with modal voice. In all other cases, the requisite values of at least one of the three laryngeal parameters are mandatorily higher than permissible for a breathy quality.

### Compound Phonatory Settings

In suggesting that harshness and breathiness are unlike other phonation types in that they cannot stand alone, appeal is being made to a distinction between simple and compound types of phonation (Laver, 1980, p. 111). Simple phonation types can occur alone and compound types are made up of combinations of phonatory settings. Modal voice, falsetto, whisper, and creak are all examples of simple phonation types, but they fall into two categories as far as their behavior in compound phonations is concerned. In the first category, modal voice and falsetto can each occur alone and can combine with whisper and creak in compound phonations, giving *whispery voice, whispery falsetto, creaky voice,* and *creaky falsetto.* Modal voice and falsetto, because they compete for use of the same laryngeal apparatus in mutually pre-emptive ways, cannot combine in a compound phonation with each other.

In the second category, whisper and creak can not only occur alone as simple types and as compound types with modal voice and falsetto, but, because they do not compete for the same laryngeal apparatus, can occur together in the compound phonation *whispery creak.* They also form triple compound phonations with modal voice and falsetto, giving *whispery creaky voice* and *whispery creaky falsetto.*

Lastly, as a third category, harshness and breathiness can only participate in compound phonations. As mentioned, breathiness is restricted to combination with modal voice in breathy voice. Harshness, however, has wider latitude. It combines with modal voice and falsetto to give *harsh voice* and *harsh falsetto,* and it figures in triple compounds such as *harsh whispery voice, harsh creaky voice, harsh whispery falsetto,* and *harsh creaky falsetto.* Finally, harshness participates in quadruple compound phonation types: in *harsh whispery creaky voice* and *harsh whispery creaky falsetto.*

*Harsh whisper* and *harsh creak* are missing from these listings not for reasons of physiological incompatibility, but because their components are acoustically mutually redundant. Harshness shares a necessary irregularity with both whisper and creak.

## Settings of Overall Muscular Tension

There is one final category of types of phonetic setting to discuss. Some voices differ in the overall level of muscular tension exerted throughout the vocal system. Such adjustments will find their manifestation at many different locations in the vocal apparatus, and tension settings could alternatively be described as constellations of co-

**Table 3-1**
Listing of Labels for Phonetic Settings in Normal Voice Quality

| SUPRALARYNGEAL SETTINGS | | LARYNGEAL SETTINGS |
|---|---|---|
| *longitudinal axis settings* | | *simple phonation types* |
| labial | labial protrusion | modal voice |
| | labiodentalization | falsetto |
| laryngeal | raised larynx | whisper |
| | lowered larynx | creak |
| *latitudinal axis settings* | | *compound phonation types* |
| labial | close rounding | whispery voice |
| | open rounding | whispery falsetoo |
| | lip-spreading | creaky voice |
| lingual tip/ | tip articulation | creaky falsetto |
| blade | blade articulation | whispery creak |
| | retroflex articulation | whispery creaky voice |
| | | whispery creaky falsetto |
| tongue-body | dentalized | breathy voice |
| | palato-alveolarized | harsh voice |
| | palatalized | harsh falsetto |
| | velarized | harsh whispery voice |
| | pharyngalized | harsh whispery falsetto |
| | laryngopharyngalized | harsh creaky voice |
| | | harsh creaky falsetto |
| mandibular | close jaw position | harsh whispery creaky voice |
| | open jaw position | harsh whispery creaky falsetto |
| | protruded jaw | |
| | position | |
| | retracted jaw | OVERALL MUSCULAR |
| | position | TENSION SETTINGS |
| | | tense voice |
| *velopharyngeal settings* | | lax voice |
| | nasal | |
| | denasal | |

occurring local settings. However, because their production is explainable in terms of a single underlying tendency to boost or drop muscular tension levels throughout the vocal apparatus, it seems preferable to categorize these *overall* settings more globally. An overall increase in muscular tension, compared to that of the neutral setting, is therefore called *tense voice,* and an overall decrease is called *lax voice.*

The local components of tense voice will tend to include the following characteristics: loud, high-pitched, tense or harsh phonation with higher subglottal air pressure and slightly raised larynx; constriction of the upper larynx and lower pharynx (and possibly of the faucal pillars); a tensed velum; vigorous and extensive radial movements of the convex-surfaced tongue in segmental articulation; and vigorous labial and mandibular activity (Laver, 1980, pp. 154–55).

A lax voice will tend to involve contrasting characteristics: soft, low-pitched, lax, breathy phonation with lower subglottal air pressure and slightly lowered larynx; a relaxed pharynx; moderate nasality; inhibited, minimized radial movements of the flat-surfaced tongue in segmental articulation; and minimal labial and mandibular activity (Laver, 1980, p. 155).

A summary list of all the settings included in the descriptive system outlined above is given in Table 3-1.

## THE RELATION BETWEEN PHONETIC DESCRIPTION
## AND ORGANIC FACTORS

In order to reach a proper understanding of the normal voice, future research will have to establish the theoretical and empirical basis for the union of phonetic and organic factors in the voice of the individual speaker. This applies even more strongly to the abnormal voice.

By exploiting the convenient assumption of a standard vocal apparatus, a largely phonetic model of the normal voice has a certain demonstrable measure of descriptive success. Interpersonal organic differences can to some extent be minimized by taking relative rather than absolute measures. Thus Nolan (1980) was able to show in an acoustic comparison of two phoneticians' performance of the same nine phonetic settings on readings of a standard passage that a good match between the two sets of performances was found provided that the ratios of formant frequencies were used rather than absolute frequency values. Another technique for normalizing the effects of interpersonal differences in vocal tract length has been proposed by Wakita (1977). In this study, he transformed actual formant frequency values obtained from the vowel productions of 14 male and 12 female speakers to values for the same articulatory configuration in a vocal tract of reference length. The resulting normalized formant frequency values had much more compact distributions than the measured values, indicating that differences in vocal tract length can account for a substantial portion of the interspeaker variability. Other techniques for defining relative measurements, based on aspects of interpersonal organic differences other than vocal tract length, are also important and are the object of current research (Wakita and Fant, 1978).

A relative measurement approach allows comparative statements about the phonetic performance of speakers to be made; but these statements are strictly only reliable when the speakers are taken from an organically reasonably homogeneous group, and where organic proportions are comparable. The problem is that the human population forms at least two different groups, in terms of proportional organic dimensions. One group is made up of adult male speakers, of whom the acoustic specifications offered in this chapter are representative. The other group consists of adult female speakers and of children of both sexes, of whom the acoustic assumptions are not necessarily representative. One major difference between the two groups is that the ratio of mouth cavity length to pharynx length is different. Adult male vocal tracts are thus not merely larger-scale versions of adult female and child tracts. A consequence of this is that male-female comparisons have normally to be calculated on a different basis for different articulatory zones of segmental performance (Fant, 1966, p. 22).

Even within comparisons of speakers from one of these groups, there are problems of phonetic interpretation that arise from organic factors. A given acoustic output reflects a given configuration of the vocal tract, within certain limits. But there are two ways in which a given configuration can occur. The first is by phonetic adjustment. The second is by the accident of individual anatomy. For example, labiodentalization as a long-term articulatory tendency can be the result either of phonetic control or of a naturally undershot jaw. Similarly, palatalization can be the consequence of phonetic action or of a large tongue and a small palate. Another example of long-term articulatory compensation for anatomical abnormalities can be found in speakers with cleft lip and palate. In a study of two speakers, Hanson and D'Antonio (1979) found that the immobility of the upper lip was compensated by unusually large and rapid movements of the normal lower lip. A more general example would be the difficulty of deciding whether a particular speaker is a natural tenor with a short vocal tract and a comparatively small larynx, or a larger speaker with a raised larynx setting and a raised range of fundamental frequency.

Abercrombie, whose phonetic description of voice quality furnished the point of departure for the model offered here, expresses the range of this problem succinctly:

The relative importance of the learnt and the unlearnt in voice quality is difficult to assess ... It is ... possible to neutralize, by means of muscular adjustments, the components in voice quality which are anatomically derived—at least to some extent, and perhaps even, given enough skill, entirely. There are many professional mimics on stage, radio and television who are able to give convincing imitations of their fellow actors and of public figures, imitations in which the performer's own voice-quality characteristics are effectively submerged ... The extreme of virtuosity, probably, was reached by a certain music hall performer, a large middle-aged man, who had learnt to produce, completely convincingly, the voice-quality of a seven-year-old girl, showing that it is possible to compensate, by muscular adjustments, for extreme anatomical differences. (Abercrombie, 1967, p. 94)

There is a wide range of organic research on vocal anatomy that needs to be done on a correlational basis, linking vocal anatomy to other general anatomical characteristics. When we hear a low-pitched voice on the telephone, with low formant ranges, we confidently expect the speaker to be a tall, adult male. But we do not yet know, on an objective basis, the detailed correlation between vocal tract length and a speaker's height. Objective data of this sort would be useful, to take one application, in the investigation of correlations between genetic disorders and a speaker's voice-type. In genetic disorders with an influence on general anatomy, it is not unreasonable to expect this to be reflected in characteristic vocal anatomy as well. Thus the tendency to greater-than-average height in speakers of, say, an XYY genotype (Slater and Cowie, 1971, p. 301), or the tendency to short stature in XO genotype speakers with Turner's syndrome (Slater and Cowie, 1971, p. 303), might be found to correlate with bigger-than-average vocal tracts and larynges versus smaller-than-average vocal tracts and larynges respectively, with consequent acoustic effects. More subtly, in the case of XXY genotype the voice of speakers with Klinefelter's syndrome may reflect this, to the extent that the syndrome is marked by the tendency towards anatomically or hormonally female characteristics. There is usually a close resemblance between the phenotypes of patients with a given chromosomal aberration (Pashayan, 1975, p. 154). It would be interesting to establish whether this resemblance extends to include voice features. In this application, the interest would lie not so much in the diagnostic role of such characterizing voice-types, since diagnosis is essentially carried out on quite other criteria, but rather in completing the symptomatic mosaic of the disorders concerned.

CONCLUSION

The description of the normal voice is far from being a finished task. One important area of improvement would be the comprehensive statement of the susceptibility relation between all types of segmental articulations and individual settings. Another would be the development of more detailed acoustic statements about each of the settings and the implementation of automatic computer-based voice-analysis programs which could factor out the acoustic contributions of the settings. Most important of all for the overall development of a descriptive theory for the normal voice are the two areas mentioned at the beginning of this chapter: firstly, establishing the range of auditory qualities potentially available to the normal voice on a phonetic basis, and secondly, incorporating an adequate organic component to take account of interspeaker differences of anatomy and their acoustic correlates.

Underlying the discussion in this chapter has been the attitude that it should be possible to aim towards a unified model for the description of the normal and the abnormal voice. The two areas will probably never entirely overlap, because of the different assumptions that have to come into play when the nature of the speech apparatus itself changes in pathological conditions. But there are many areas of the abnormal voice, particularly in the control aspects of functional disorders, and possibly in the control aspects of organic pathology, where it would be thoroughly profitable to explore commonalities between the normal and the abnormal. If it becomes possible to develop an adequately powerful descriptive theory for the range of variations potentially found in the normal voice, then it is at least plausible that some aspects of abnormal vocal performance could usefully be seen as extensions of some of the dimensionalities of normal performance, as explored, for example, in Davis (1976). The benefit of establishing continuities between the normal and the abnormal is that such an approach facilitates both measures of distance between the two for diagnostic use and measures of progress towards the normal in rehabilitative therapy.

The exploration of such continuities cannot be properly achieved by any single discipline: it should be the focus of multidisciplinary effort by the range of professions represented in this volume.

REFERENCES

Abercrombie, D. *Elements of general phonetics.* Edinburgh, Scotland: Edinburgh University Press, 1967.

Aronson, A. E., Peterson, H. W., Litin, E. M. Voice symptomatology in functional dysphonia and aphonia, *Journal of Speech and Hearing Disorders*, 1964, 29:367–380.

Baer, T. Investigation of phonation using excised larynxes. Unpublished Ph.D. dissertation, Massachusetts Institute of Technology, 1975. 1975.

Ballantine, J., Groves, J. *Diseases of the Ear, Nose and Throat*, (Vol. 4): *The Throat*. London: Butterworth, 1971.

Berg, J. van den. Myoelastic-aerodynamic theory of voice production, *Journal of Speech and Hearing Research*, 1958, 1:227–244.

Berg, J. van den. Mechanisms of the larynx and the laryngeal vibrations. In B. Malmberg, (Ed.), *Manual of Phonetics*. London: North-Holland, 1968, pp. 278–308.

Cagliari, L. C. An experimental study of nasality with particular reference to Brazilian Portuguese. Ph.D. dissertation, Edinburgh, Scotland: University of Edinburgh, 1978.

Catford, J. C. Phonation types: The Classification of some laryngeal components of speech production. In D. Abercrombie, D. B. Fry, P. A. D. MacCarthy, et al. (Eds.), In *In honour of Daniel Jones*. London: Longmans, 1964.

Catford, J. C. (1977) *Fundamental problems in phonetics*. Edinburgh, Scotland: Edinburgh University Press, 1977.

Coleman, R. F. Decay characteristics of vocal fry. *Folia Phoniatrica*, 1963, 15:256–263.

Condax, I. D., Acson, V., Miki, C. C., et al. A technique for monitoring velic action by means of a photo-electric nasal probe: Application to French. *Journal of Phonetics*, 1976, 4:173–181.

Crystal, T. H. (1966) A model of laryngeal activity during phonation. Unpublished Ph.D. dissertation, Massachusetts Institute of Technology, 1966.

Davis, S. B. *Computer evaluation of laryngeal pathology based on inverse filtering of speech* (monograph no. 13). Santa Barbara, CA: Speech Communication Research Laboratory, 1976.

Dickson, D. R. An acoustic study of nasality. *Journal of Speech and Hearing Research*, 1962, 5:103–111.

Faaborg-Andersen, K. Electromyographic investigation of intrinsic laryngeal muscles in humans. *Acta Physiologica Scandinavica*, 1957, Supplement No. 140:1–149.

Fairbanks, G. *Voice and articulation drill-book* (Ed 2). New York: Harper & Row, 1960.

Fant, G. On the predictability of formant levels and spectrum envelopes from formant frequencies. In M. Halle, H. Lunt, and H. MacLean, (Eds.), *For Roman Jakobson*. The Hague: Mouton, 1956, pp. 109–120.

Fant, G. Modern instruments and methods for acoustic studies of speech. *Proceedings of the 8th International Congress of Linguists*. Oslo: 1957, pp. 282–388. Also in *Acta Polytechnica Scandinavica*, 1958 1:1–81.

Fant, G. *Acoustic theory of speech production*, The Hague: Mouton, 1960.

Fant, G. Descriptive analysis of the acoustic aspects of speech. *Logos*, 1962, 5:3–17.

Fant, G. A note on vocal tract size factors and non-uniform f-pattern scalings. *Quarterly Progress and Status Report*, Speech Transmission Laboratory, Royal Institute of Technology, Stockholm, 1966, 4:22–30.

Flanagan, J. L. Some properties of the glottal sound source. *Journal of Speech and Hearing Research*, 1958, 1:99–116.

Frøkjaer-Jensen, B., Prytz, S. Registration of voice quality. *Bruel and Kjaer Technical Review*, 1976, 3:3–17.

Hall, I. S., Coleman, B. H. *Diseases of the Nose, Throat and Ear.* Edinburgh, Scotland: Livingstone, 1975.

Hanson, R. J. A two-state model of $F_0$ control. *Journal of the Acoustical Society of America*, 1978, 64:1, 543–544.

Hanson, R. J. and D'Antonio, L. L. Long term compensation for upper lip immobility. *Journal of the Acoustical Society of America*, 1979, 65:1, 526. Also in Wolf, J. J. and Klatt, D. H. (Eds.). *Speech communication papers presented at the 97th Meeting of the Acoustical Society of America*, Acoustical Society of America, 1979.

Hirano, M. Phonosurgery: Basic and clinical investigations, *Otologia* (Fukuoka), 1975, 21:239–440 [in Japanese].

Hirano, M. Structure and vibratory behavior of the vocal folds. In M. Sawashima, and F. S. Cooper, (Eds.), *Dynamic aspects of speech production.* Tokyo: University of Tokyo Press, 1977, pp. 13–27.

Hollien, H. On vocal registers. *Journal of Phonetics*, 1974, 2:125–43.

Hollien, H., Michel, J. F. Vocal fry as a phonational register. *Journal of Speech and Hearing Research*, 1968, 11:600–604.

Hollien, H., Moore, P., Wendahl, R. W., et al. On the nature of vocal fry. *Journal of Speech and Hearing Research*, 1966, 9:245–247.

Honikman, B. Articulatory settings. In D. Abercrombie, D. B. Fry, P. A. D. MacCarthy, et al (Eds.), In *In honour of Daniel Jones.* London: Longmans, 1964, pp. 73–84.

House, A. S. Analog studies of nasal consonants. *Journal of Speech and Hearing Disorders*, 1957, 22:190–204.

Ishizaka, K., Flanagan, J. L. Synthesis of voiced sounds from a two-mass model of the vocal cords. *Bell System Technical Journal*, 1972, 51:1233–68.

Kunze, L. H. Evaluation of methods of estimating subglottal air pressure. *Journal of Speech and Hearing Research*, 1964, 7:151–64.

Ladefoged, P. *Preliminaries to linguistic phonetics.* Chicago: University of Chicago Press, 1971.

Laver, J. Voice quality and indexical information. *British Journal of Disorders of Communication*, 1968, 3:43–54.

Laver, J. Labels for voices. *Journal of the International Phonetic Association*, 1974, 4:62–75.

Laver, J. The concept of articulatory settings: An historical survey. *Historiographia Linguistica*, 1978, 5:1–14.

Laver, J. *Voice quality: A classified bibliography.* Amsterdam: John Benjamins, 1979.

Laver, J. *The phonetic description of voice quality.* Cambridge, England: Cambridge University Press, 1980.

Laver, J., Trudgill, P. Phonetic and linguistic markers in speech. In K. R. Scherer, and H. Giles, (Eds.) (1979) pp. 1–32. *Social markers in speech.* Cambridge, England: Cambridge University Press, 1979.

Lindblom, B., Sundberg, J. A quantitative model of vowel production and the distinctive features of Swedish vowels. *Quarterly Progress and Status Report.* Speech Transmission Laboratory, Royal Institute of Technology, Stockholm, 1969, 1:14–32.

Lindblom, B. E. F., Sundberg, J. Acoustical consequencies of lip, tongue, jaw, and larynmovement. *Journal of the Acoustical Society of America,* 1971, 50:1166–1179.

Markel, J. D., Oshika, B. T., Gray, A. H. Long-term feature averaging for speaker recognition. *IEEE Transactions on Acoustics, Speech, and Signal Processing,* 1979, ASSP-25, No. 4:330–337.

Matsushita, H. Vocal cord vibration of excised larynges: A study with ultrahigh-speed cinematography. *Otologia* (Fukuoka), 1969, 15, No. 2:127–142 [in Japanese].

Matsushita, H. The vibratory mode of the vocal folds in the excised larynx. *Folia Phoniatrica,* 1975, 27:7–18.

Michel, J. F., Hollien, H. Perceptual differentiation in vocal fry and harshness. *Journal of Speech and Hearing Research,* 1968, 11:439–443.

Miller, R. L. Nature of the vocal cord wave. *Journal of the Acoustical Society of America,* 1959, 31:667–77.

Monsen, R. B., Engebretson, A. M. Study of variations in the male and female glottal wave. *Journal of the Acoustical Society of America,* 1977, 62:981–93.

Müller, J. *Handbuch der Physiologie des Menschen,* Vol. 2. Coblenz: Holscher, 1837.

Murry, T. Subglottal pressure measures during vocal fry phonation. Ph.D. dissertation, University of Florida, 1969.

Murry, T., Brown, W. S. Subglottal air pressure during two types of vocal activity: Vocal fry and modal phonation. *Folia Phoniatrica,* 23:440–9.

Nolan, F. The phonetic bases of speaker recognition. Ph.D. dissertation, University of Cambridge, 1980.

Pashayan, H. M. The basic concepts of medical genetics. *Journal of Speech and Hearing Disorders,* 1975, 40:147–163.

Plotkin, W. H. Ventricular phonation: A clinical discussion of etiology, symptoms and therapy. *American Speech and Hearing Association Convention Abstracts,* 1964, 6:409.

Scherer, K. R., Giles, H. (Eds.). *Social markers in speech.* Cambridge, England: Cambridge University Press, 1979.

Slater, E., Cowie, V. *The Genetics of Mental Disorders.* London: Oxford University Press, 1971.

Smith, S. Remarks on the physiology of the vibrations of the vocal cord. *Folia Phoniatrica,* 1954, 6:166–78.

Sundberg, J., Nordström, P. E. Raised and lowered larynx: The effect on vowel formant frequencies. *Quarterly Progress and Status Report,* Speech Transmission Laboratory, Royal Institute of Technology, Stockholm, 1976, 2-3:35–39.

Sussman, H. M., MacNeilage, P. F., Hanson, R. J. Labial and mandibular dynamics during the production of bilabial consonants: Preliminary observations. *Journal of Speech and Hearing Research*, 1973, 16:397–420.

Titze, I. R. The human vocal cords: A mathematical model (Part I). *Phonetica*, 1973, 28:129–170.

Titze, I. R. The human vocal cords: A mathematical model (Part II). *Phonetica*, 1974, 29:1–21.

Titze, I. R., Strong, W. J. Normal modes in vocal cord tissues. *Journal of the Acoustical Society of America*, 1975, 57:736–744.

Trojan, F. Experimentelle Untersuchunger uber den Zusammenhang zwischen dem Ausdruck der Sprechstimme und dem vegetativen Nervensystem. *Folia Phoniatrica*, 1952, 4:65–92.

Van Riper, C., Irwin, J. W. *Voice and articulation*. Englewood Cliffs: Prentice-Hall, 1958.

Wakita, H. Normalization of vowels by vocal-track length and its application 18 vowel identification. *IEEE Transactions on Acoustics, Speech, and Signal Processing*, 1977, ASSP-25:2, 183–192.

Wakita, H. Normalization of vowels by vocal-tract length and its application to vowel identification. *IEEE Transactions on Acoustics, Speech, and Signal Processing*, 1977, ASSP-25:2, 183–192.

Wendahl, R. W., Moore, P., Hollien, H. Comments on vocal fry. *Folia Phoniatrica*, 1963, 15:251–255.

Wolf, J. J. and Klatt, D. H. (Eds.). *Speech communication papers presented at the 97th Meeting of the Acoustical Society of America*, Acoustical Society of America, 1979.

Zemlin, W. R. *Speech and hearing science*. Champaign, ILL: Stipes, 1964.

Harry Hollien

# 4

# Analog Instrumentation for Acoustic Speech Analysis

There are many acoustical measurement techniques that permit the study of voice, speech, and language. The approaches utilized may be based on a deductive form of model construction from either a verbal or mathematical explanation,or on empirical testing by means of electronic processing systems. Collectively, the available approaches permit a great variety of postulates to be studied by a plethora of analysis techniques.

Instrumentation and techniques used in such research may be organized in a number of ways. One particularly useful approach is to divide the appropriate subareas into sets, each with a particular focus: 1) auditory approaches; 2) analog instrumentation approaches; and 3) digital instrumentation (computer approaches). The focus of this presentation will be on analog instrumentation for analyzing the acoustical properties of speech.

One problem encountered in the instrumental analysis of speech and voice occurs with the difficulty of properly matching the equipment to the hypotheses under test. Indeed, in some instances excellent experiments are structured and carried out but the resulting data have little relevance to the questions asked because the appropriate instrumentation either was not available or was unknown to the investigator.

*The author wishes to recognize the assistance provided by Drs. E. Thomas Doherty, Thomas Shipp, John Darby, and by Mrs. Patricia Hollien in the development of this manuscript.

The bulk of this chapter focuses on descriptions of relatively so-phisticated analysis equipment and some of the principles governing its use. It is assumed that the reader has a working knowledge of basic instrumentation such as AM and FM tape recorders, microphone char-acteristics, and filters.

## INSTRUMENTAL APPROACHES

This chapter is organized to provide information about some of the equipment and approaches that permit a reasonable analysis of a person's speech. The basic features of speech and voice include: 1) speaking fundamental frequency (SFF or $f_o$); 2) speech spectra; 3) voice/speech intensity information; and 4) the temporal features of speech. In each instance, attempts will be made to demonstrate how a feature can be analyzed so that the appropriate relationships may be quantified for study. In most instances, the apparatus that permits easy analysis of large quantities of data will be described in greatest detail. While intensive study of a single patient can be meritorious—especially when clinical information about that individual is to be communicated from one physician to another—this approach is one that provides only minimal information about the nature of the dis-order itself. Hence, in order to understand the dimensions and mod-ifiable characteristics of a psychopathological entity, such as schizophrenia, it is necessary to determine how it affects not just one individual, but rather the entire population experiencing it. Finally, it is recognized that, while the systems described below are reasonably robust, they are somewhat primitive when contrasted with currently developing technology and future potentials.

## FUNDAMENTAL FREQUENCY ANALYSIS

The perception of the *pitch* of a signal is a common, everyday ex-perience; for example, the pitch of a given phonatory event may be perceived as high or low. The term pitch refers to the human psycho-physical response to the acoustic signal and is difficult to quantify. On the other hand, the physical basis of pitch, i.e., the fundamental fre-quency ($f_o$) of a periodic tone, is relatively easy to quantify and mea-sure. Fundamental frequency may be best understood by reference to Figure 4-1 where both simple and complex waveforms are presented, as well as two schemes for $f_o$ measurement (axis crossing and peak picking). The perception of pitch and the measurement of speaking fundamental frequency (SFF) are based on the systematic opening and

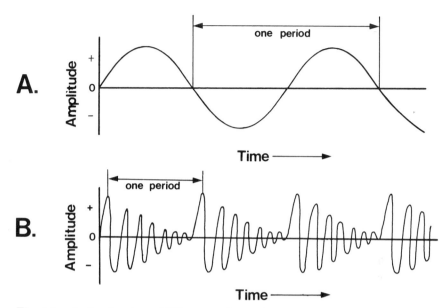

Fig. 4-1. A simple, sinusoidlike, waveform (A) and a waveform (B) of a more complex nature (similar to one resulting from phonation). Measurement of wave A is by the axis crossing method; of B by a peak picking technique.

closing of the vocal folds during the production of voiced speech signals. Indeed, when SFF is measured acoustically, the process is actually to count these openings and closings by some method (see again Figure 4-1). Both mean level and patterns of voice frequency change are important in assessing the vocal behaviors of experimental and control groups since they enable the general effects of a disease or its progress upon the individual to be studied. Several approaches to such study, and the metrics common to the area, will be discussed below.

*1. Oscillographs: Oscilloscopes.* Devices of this type have long been used to extract fundamental frequency ($f_0$) information from an acoustical signal. They work on the principle that a beam of light, or an electron beam, can be varied in exactly the same pattern as the stored electronic analog of a speech signal—and that this trace can be permanently recorded in some manner. Although very time-consuming to use, many devices of this type have been successfully utilized in the study of $f_0$ and SFF. Since operation of all devices of this type is based on relatively similar principles, the description of a single light-writing oscillograph should provide an understanding of most systems of this class.

The optical oscillograph takes a voice signal played back from a tape recorder and converts the signal's electrical analog to movements of a mirror mounted on a galvanometer (converting electrical energy to mechanical movement). A light beam directed at this mirror is deflected in accordance with the mirror's vibration. This light image of the vocal signal is directed onto a moving, light-sensitive paper producing a permanent visible trace similar to the one shown in Figure 4-2. By measuring between similar points on successive soundwaves or a group of waves, the frequency of voice is determined.

There are numerous problems associated with oscillographs in analysis of SFF. The first of these involves the conversion of the measured traces to frequency, preferably using a parallel measurement of a time signal (of known frequency), which also is placed on the record. Accurate measurement of these signals is difficult and time-consuming; if accuracy is not maintained, the resulting errors are not trivial. Measurement problems can arise if any of the devices's drive mechanisms vary in speed, a condition that commonly occurs in sprocket driven oscillographs or motion picture cameras. The most serious problem with procedures of this type, however, is the inefficient and time-consuming measurement procedures that must be applied. Measurement-time ratios often are as great as 2000 to 1.

*2. Electronic Approaches to $f_o$ Measurement.* Automatic or semi-automatic analysis of the voice period is desirable if this parameter is to be efficiently studied. Many attempts have been made to design and fabricate such systems. In 1965, McKinney described over 100 attempts of this nature; he concluded that none of them operated with satisfactory efficiency and/or validity. Why is it so difficult to design and develop a fundamental frequency tracking system? The answer to this question lies in the nature of the speech wave. First, the signal is quite complex, with a large and varying number of partials; it has abrupt on-off characteristics from silence to a sudden burst of substan-

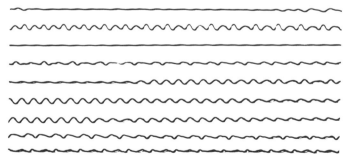

Fig. 4-2.   A strip of unmeasured phonellograph traces.

tial intensity. Further, very rapid and extensive fluctuations in both vocal intensity and SFF occur—and there are many aperiodic, or noise, components within the voice/speech signal. Finally, most recordings are made at the lips after the effects of the vocal tract have been added to the glottal signal, resulting in artifacts being added continually to the laryngeal tone. These effects result from variation in the vocal tract due to articulatory activity, variation in phase, effects of the overt behaviors of the speaker, and so on. Indeed, many factors can operate to obscure the boundaries of a phonated wave and make frequency analysis difficult. Recently, however, investigators have had some success in developing computer-aided solutions to this problem.

*3. A Fundamental Frequency Analysis System.* A device that automatically extracts $f_o$ is the Fundamental Frequency Indicator (FFI-8) (Hollien and Harrington, 1977).

*General:* The Fundamental Frequency Indicator is a hardware/software system which continuously extracts SFF from tape recorded speech input and performs statistical analyses on these frequency data. The "hardware" portion of the system processes the speech by continually extracting the fundamental; the "software" portion computes a mean and standard deviation of these data over the duration of the speech sample. Subroutines permit extraction of other information including frequency contours, histograms of the frequency distributions, and digital displays. The software also provides for print-out of the statistical procedures carried out.

*Processing Hardware:* Figure 4-3 provides a functional schematic of FFI-8 extraction electronics; this portion of the system is referred to as the Fundamental Extraction Subsystem (FES). Speech is played into eight sharp-cutoff (75 dB per octave), low-pass filters with 3dB roll-off frequencies fixed approximately 0.5 octave apart. For any speech sample, any one filter may contain no spectral components while another will contain the fundamental frequency, another the fundamental plus the first harmonic partial, while another the fundamental plus the first and second harmonic partials, etc. Digital electronics in the form of a parallel, 8-channel A/D converter (shown within the Figure 4-3 dashed line) monitors the output of all eight filters and determines which filter contains only the fundamental frequency. This information is presented in 8–bit digital form to the "Analog Switching Section" where, based on this sequence, only the filter containing the fundamental is coupled to the output. Between the switch and the system output is a Schmitt trigger circuit which converts the SFF sinusoids to pulses as can be seen in Figure 4-4. This

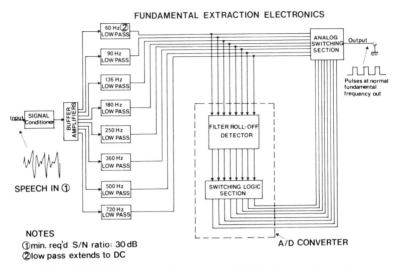

FUNDAMENTAL EXTRACTION ELECTRONICS

NOTES
① min. req'd S/N ratio: 30 dB
② low pass extends to DC

Fig. 4-3. The FFI-8 filter extraction system (FES). The logic section permits the output to be coupled to the lowest filter containing energy (i.e., the $f_o$).

section is necessary to compensate for the characteristic of tape recorders to be less sensitive to very low fundamental frequencies.

*Processing Steps:* Figure 4-5 provides a graphic summary of the steps involved in the software data reduction of the $f_o$ pulses; note that Figure 4-3 is included as the block labeled FES. A "conditioned" tape of the original speech sample is first produced. "Conditioning" entails filtering any noise or hum from the original sample and providing a minimum 10-second silent interval between speech samples (required for subsequent processing steps below). The first step shown by Figure 4-5 involves fundamental frequency extraction. The fundamental is marked and timed and stored on computer tape. Timing of the interval between successive pulses is accomplished by the computer's real-time clock. In step 2, the period measures are recalled from the computer tape in the mass storage and the statistical analyses performed. Finally, the results of these analyses are printed. A typical output may be seen in Figure 4-6. Much of the information is in the nature of the experiment/subject identification, internal validity evaluation, and so on. The materials of interest may be seen by reference to Figure 4-6, parts A: mean SFF, both Hertz and semitone levels; B: standard deviation of the distribution in tones; c: the semitone interval distribution table; and D: a frequency histogram.

As can be seen, the FFI system is one that is designed to provide

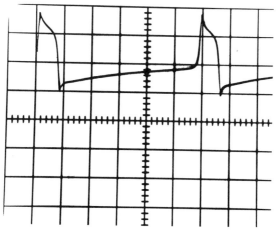

Fig. 4-4.   Photograph of a FFI-8 output pulse.

## FFI  Data  Reduction  Section

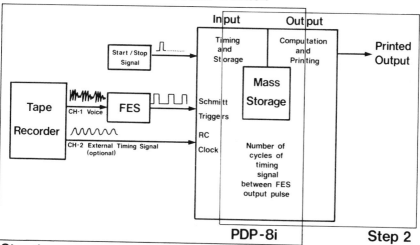

Fig. 4-5.   Block diagram of the entire FFI system. In Step 1, the complex wave is processed and stored; Step 2 permits descriptive statistical procedures to be carried out on these (stored) values.

FFI   DEMONSTRATION

LIMITS:  LOW FREQ = 50   HI FREQ = 300   CAST = 6.00

| RUN:<br>NO. | RUN IDENTIFICATION | HI R<br>%TIM | LO R<br>%TIM | | GOOD<br>%TIM | TOTAL<br>TIME | **A**<br>MEAN<br>(ST) | MEAN<br>(Hz) | **B**<br>SDV<br>(TO) |
|---|---|---|---|---|---|---|---|---|---|
| 2 SUB # 2 H.R. | | 1.4 | 21.8 | | 52.9 | 0926 | 33.0 | 110.2 | 1.9 |

| | | | | |
|---|---|---|---|---|
| HR: | 142., | 0.3572 SECS | 23.9 | 5.6414 SECS |
| LR: | 75,, | | | |
| CST: | 736., | 6.1899 SECS | INV: | 953,, | 12.1885 SECS |
| VAL: | 1545., | 13.6924 SECS | THT: | 2498,, | 25.8803 SECS |

**C** DISTRIBUTION TABLE

| ST | HZ | # | SECS | % |
|---|---|---|---|---|
| 23 | 61.7 | 1. | 0.0 | 0.1 |
| 24 | 65.4 | 6. | 0.1 | 0.7 |
| 25 | 69.3 | 16. | 0.2 | 1.7 |
| 26 | 73.4 | 13. | 0.2 | 1.3 |
| 27 | 77.8 | 24. | 0.3 | 2.2 |
| 28 | 82.4 | 41. | 0.5 | 3.6 |
| 29 | 87.3 | 66. | 0.8 | 5.5 |
| 30 | 92.5 | 102. | 1.1 | 8.1 |
| 31 | 98.0 | 137. | 1.4 | 10.2 |
| 32 | 103.8 | 149. | 1.4 | 10.5 |
| 33 | 110.0 | 167. | 1.5 | 11.1 |
| 34 | 116.5 | 211. | 1.8 | 13.3 |
| 35 | 123.5 | 197. | 1.6 | 11.7 |
| 36 | 130.8 | 108. | 0.8 | 6.0 |
| 37 | 138.6 | 72. | 0.5 | 3.8 |
| 38 | 146.8 | 71. | 0.5 | 3.6 |
| 39 | 155.6 | 40. | 0.3 | 1.9 |

| | | | | |
|---|---|---|---|---|
| 40 | 164.8 | 20. | 0.1 | 0.9 |
| 41 | 174.6 | 15. | 0.1 | 0.6 |
| 42 | 185.0 | 25. | 0.1 | 1.0 |
| 43 | 196.0 | 25. | 0.1 | 0.9 |
| 44 | 207.7 | 17. | 0.1 | 0.6 |
| 45 | 220.0 | 5. | 0.0 | 0.2 |
| 46 | 233.1 | 12. | 0.1 | 0.4 |
| 47 | 246.9 | 4. | 0.0 | 0.1 |
| 49 | 277.2 | 1. | 0.0 | 0.0 |

**D** HISTOGRAM

```
      13                  *
      12                  * *
      11                 ** *
      10               **** *
       9               **** *
       8             * **** *
    % 7              * **** *
       6          *  * **** * *
       5          *  * **** * *
       4         **  * **** * ***
       3         **  * **** * ***
       2     *  ***  * **** * ****
       1   * * ****  * **** * ****  * ****
        +----+----+----+----+----+----+----+----+----+(---+----+
ST:     15   20   25   30   35   40   45   50   55   60   65
HZ:     39   52   69   92  123  165  220  294  392  523  698
```

Fig. 4-6. A copy of the printed FFI-8 readout. Included are the mean SFF (A) in Hz and st; the standard deviation of the distribution in tones (B), the distribution organized into semitone intervals (C) and a histogram of the distribution (D).

SFF information for large groups of subjects and extensive corpora of speech materials, quickly and efficiently. It does not operate particularly well on very short utterances (less than 5 seconds in length), on voice signals mixed with noise, or on hoarse or harsh voices.

There are a number of other $f_0$ extraction procedures/systems now available. Some are designed for the processing of general SFF information, others for specialized purposes. Several devices of note include the "Purdue Pitch Meter" (Dempsey 1955; Dempsey, et al., 1950), multistage hardware that has been utilized for some years (Mysak, 1958), and a system developed by Boë and Rakotofiringa (1971) that has been used in support of a number of research projects (Boë, 1975; Boë and Rakotofiringa, 1975; Boë, Contini, and Rakotofiringa, 1975). In both instances, the device utilized was developed to permit analysis of reasonably large groups of subjects for the purpose of describing SFF usage in normally speaking individuals. While the validity of these systems has been established, data reduction can be somewhat lengthy. Another approach, best typified by the work of Frøkjaer-Jensen, or by the Kay Elemetrics Visi-Pitch 6087, attempts to provide a visual display of the phonation produced by individuals who exhibit either normal or pathological voices. Even though both of these devices have digital capability, they are best used in teaching or in clinical evaluations of voice disorders. Analysis of quantitative materials for large groups of subjects is cumbersome when these units are utilized in SFF research.

An area of extensive activity in SFF/$f_0$ processing is that involving hardware/software, or software only, computer approaches. The research being carried out in this area is typified by the work of Gold (1962), Gold and Rabiner (1969), Harris and Weiss (1963), Markel (1972), McGonegal, Rabiner and Rosenberg (1975), Rabiner, Cheng, Rosenberg, et al., (1976), and Sondhi (1968). The thrust of these approaches ranges from the development of "voices" for vocoders to analysis of single "pitch periods"; from the analysis of large corpora of research materials to the evaluation of mathematical models of laryngeal function. In any case, much of the work carried out in these areas relates in some manner to telephone communication systems. Some of these techniques require extensive processing time (factors of up to 100:1); others approach real-time in speed; most require powerful computing facilities.

In summary, it may be seen that a variety of procedures currently are available for the SFF/$f_0$ analysis of speech. These systems include devices that: 1) can provide visual information (with little or no time delay) for clinical purposes or for cues which can lead to more highly structured investigations; 2) will permit a small group of subjects to be analyzed quickly; and 3) can permit large and complex experiments to be carried out.

## VOCAL JITTER

Closely related to speaking fundamental frequency is vocal jitter, a laryngeal phenomenon defined as the cycle-to-cycle variation found within successive periods of a laryngeal vibratory pattern. Since jitter is well accepted as a common occurrence in normal phonation, virtually all vocal signals must be considered to be "quasiperiodic" in nature (Flanagan, 1958; Fant, 1960; Stevens and House, 1971; Peterson and Shoup, 1966). The laryngeal phenomenon of vocal jitter has been found to exist under a variety of phonatory conditions: 1) in sustained phonation (Beckett, 1979; Hollien, Michel and Doherty, 1973; Horii, 1979); 2) in connected speech (Lieberman, 1961, 1963); and 3) as related to unusual laryngeal conditions and voice pathologies (Beckett, 1979; Denber, 1978; Hecker and Kruel, 1971; Kioke, 1967, 1973; Lieberman, 1963; Moore and Thompson, 1965; Murry and Doherty, 1980; Smith, Weinberg, Feth, et al. 1978).

Traditionally, two basic measurement techniques have been applied to the study of vocal jitter. Data have been extracted either from high-speed motion pictures of the waveform (Lieberman, 1963; Moore and Thompson, 1965) or from similar photographs of the acoustic signal displayed on an oscilloscope (Hecker and Kruel, 1977; Hollien, Michel, and Doherty, 1973). Beckett (1969) utilized an approach which is, in principle, similar to the latter one except that the measurements were made from oscillographic records rather than films.

The procedure proposed by Hollien, Michel, and Doherty, (1973) is a simple one—and is representative of the three techniques cited above. It can be best understood by reference to Figure 4-7. The signal produced by a human voice is recorded on a dual channel tape recorder simultaneously with a reference frequency; both are then transferred to a cathode ray oscilloscope. The two signals appear on the face of the oscilloscope and are photographed by an ultra high-speed camera with its regular lens capped. While this procedure is simple, its measurement phase unfortunately is extremely time-consuming. Thus, little research has been carried out on vocal jitter that utilizes any of these three cited techniques.

More recently, computer based jitter extraction systems have been implemented (Anderson, Deller, and Stone, 1976; Davis, 1976;

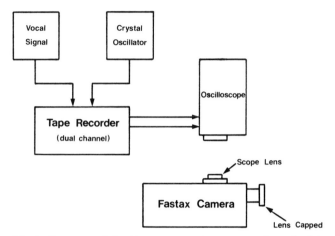

Fig. 4-7. Block diagram of the jitter extraction system described in the text. In this case, measurements must be made by hand.

Horii, 1975, 1979). In these cases algorithms underlying the computational process are applied to the digitized representation of either the acoustic waveforms or its residues. The procedures utilized are based on some method of "peak picking" or on autocorrelation techniques. For example, Horii (1975) measured jitter by selecting peaks in the waveform on the basis of the second order maxima while Davis (1976) described a method that seeks the highest correlation between the two sets of points which define first one period and then the next. Most recently, Doherty (1977) has proposed a system based on modified use of the Fundamental Frequency Indicator (FFI-8). In the Doherty approach, software has been developed that permits a computer to measure continuously a series of the waves as specified; statistical comparisons are made between all adjacent waves, and a jitter metric is developed. This technique has the advantage of being faster than the other computer approaches cited; yet it is just as accurate.

### WAVE COMPOSITION - SPECTROGRAPHY

The area of spectrography is complex. There are scores of spectrometers—most of which measure events other than acoustic waves. In the acoustic domain, there are a variety of approaches that attempt to measure various characteristics of a given spectra. Problems facing the scientist who is interested in determining the wave composition of a signal can be seen in Figure 4-8. This figure shows an *instantaneous* spectrogram with a fundamental frequency of 100 Hz and 14 harmonic partials. Inharmonic partials (i.e., energy at frequencies other than integral multiples of the fundamental) are not shown, as they would introduce noise into the signal or change it into an aperiodic tone. In any case, this type of spectrogram provides information about the composition of an acoustic wave. It specifies the frequencies present, the energy at each frequency, the resonance regions, and the overall energy present in the wave. What *cannot* be determined by this form of spectrogram are the spectral changes that take place over time. Moreover, the signal must remain unchanged from periods of from 500 milliseconds to as much as 4 sec. (depending upon the equipment used) in order that a spectrum of this type can be generated.

### "Instantaneous" Spectrometers and Wave Analyzers

The most basic type of spectrometer in this class can be typified by the General Radio, model 1900-A, Wave analyzer which has a maximum frequency response of 20–54,000 Hz and a choice of three filter bandwidths (3, 10, and 50 Hz). It sweeps the continuously repeated signal and provides a spectrum (not precisely instantaneous) that por-

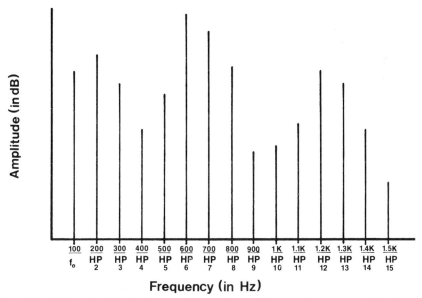

Fig. 4-8. A line (or "instantaneous") spectrum of a complex wave with a fundamental frequency of 100 Hz and 14 harmonic overtones (partials).

trays the energy found within the entire period of the wave. Since, ordinarily, an individual cannot sustain phonation with an exact $f_o$ and spectrum, the typical product of a wave analyzer usually will appear as in Figure 4-9 rather than as the spectrum seen in Figure 4-8. Nevertheless, reasonable calculations of steady state tones (or at least, quasiperiodic phonation) can be analyzed by this method. Current units usually provide interface electronics so that the output of the wave analyzer can be fed directly to a digital computer and processed quantitatively. Observation of graphic displays, such as those seen in Figures 4-8 and 4-9, can be interesting and can lead to structured research. They are by nature subjective, however, and, if the observations made are not confirmed by external evidence, they can be misleading.

A somewhat more versatile unit of the "instantaneous" spectrum class is the Bruel and Kjaer, model 2110, Audio Frequency Spectrometer. The B&K 2110 has 30 one-third-octave filters with center frequencies ranging from 40 Hz to 3.15 kHz. By linking and time-aligning this unit to a graphic level recorder, a display similar to that produced by the GR-1900A may be obtained. The B&K 2100 also has the capability (in modified configurations) to provide digital readout and long term spectra.

A third type of device within this class are the "real-time" spectrometers. The Princeton Applied Research model 4512 FFT Real-Time Spectrum Analyzer typifies this class and uses a Fast Fourier Transform (FFT) technique to determine the spectral content of a signal. As with many of the "real-time" class of analyzers, this unit has the capability of producing "line" (instantaneous) or long-term spectra

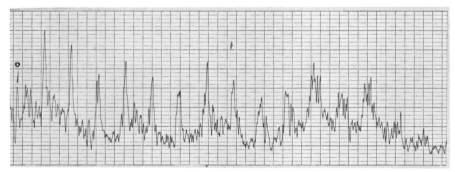

Fig. 4-9. An example of a wave analyzed for fundamental frequency and overtones (partials). Note that the individual who produced this signal exhibits some jitter or vibrato as the higher partials have a substantial "bandwidth."

either for direct observation on the face of an oscilloscope or as hard copy. Perhaps the greatest advantage of these devices is that they can be interfaced easily to a computer in a hardware/software configuration; hence, they provide a method of carrying out a great deal of processing with minimum time expenditures. An analyzer such as the PAR 4512 is a little difficult to describe, since it has many capabilities and modes of operation. Basically, it has a frequency range of from 10 Hz to 41 kHz with a real-time bandwidth of 15.5 kHz, a sampling frequency of up to nearly 82 kHz, and input windows varying from 0.0125–50 sec. Input signals are sampled by a 12 bit A/D converter and stored in input memory. The contents of the memory then are transferred to "calculate memory," where the spectral components are computed by means of the FFT algorithm. Since this processing can take as little as 33 milliseconds, continuous spectral displays can be provided or fed into a computer for statistical analysis. Finally, it is now possible to carry out various forms of spectrometry by means of software only.

## Long-Term Spectral Analysis

The speech spectrum is a representation of the frequency-intensity relationships of the individual partials within the acoustic wave. In the immediately preceding section, spectrometers were described that attempted to provide information about the particular partials and the specific intensities (of these partials) that occur at an "instant" in time. Spectral data, however, can be organized in many other ways—and for a variety of purposes.

An understanding of LTS can best be gained by reference to Figure 4-10, which provides information about this type of spectral display. (An excellent description of LTS also can be found in Denes and Pinson, 1970). The LTS process is one where the relative intensities of all frequencies occurring during the entire speech sample are measured and analyzed. As can be seen by the figure, the amount of energy occurring at any given frequency is displayed. Analyzed sample length typically ranges from 10 seconds to 2 minutes. The curve produced provides a profile for an individual or a composite profile for a group.

The General Radio Spectrum Analyzer Model 1921 is an example of a device that produces LTS. This device has a number of "channels," each consisting of a one-third-octave filter band; 23 of these channels are commonly utilized for speech analysis; they cover a range of 80–12,500 Hz. A tape recorded speech sample is fed into the GR unit, and the amount of energy within each channel is computed

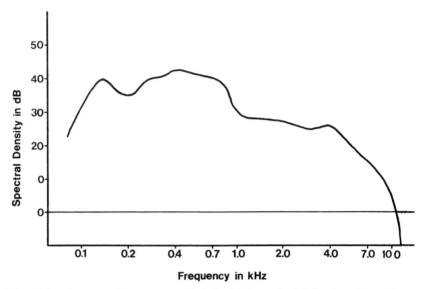

Fig. 4-10. A composite spectrum (of the LTS type) of 2.5 min. of speech produced by 50 adult males (From Majewski, Rothman, and Hollien, 1977. Reprinted with permission.) The line represents a summation over time of that proportion of the total energy contributed by each frequency.

simultaneously for the entire duration of the sample. Since the maximum integration time for the GR 1921 analyzer is 32 seconds, longer samples must be processed in segments and the several data sets averaged by a later operation. In any case, the output is an array of 23 measurements that can be fed into a digital computer for analysis. For example, Euclidean distances may be calculated in order to permit development of a vector useful in determining the identity of the speaker (Hollien and Majewski, 1977), or in contrasting languages (Majewski, Rothman, and Hollien, 1977).

The GR 1921 is not the only averaging spectrum analyzer available, as many others can be found that provide similar data. For example, the Princeton Applied Research Model 4512 analyzer (previously cited) has a provision for spectrum averaging. Once the interface to a computer of appropriate power is accomplished, statistical analysis of the LTS can be carried out efficiently.

### Time-Frequency-Amplitude Spectrometry.

Without question the most commonly used type of sound spectrometry for speech/voice research is that involving time-frequency-amplitude (T-F-A) displays. First developed at Bell Telephone

Laboratories, they were described by inhouse publications and by Potter (1945) and Potter, Kopp and Green (1947).

When the T-F-A spectrometer was made commercially available by the Kay Company, it provided phoneticians, linguists, and speech scientists with a powerful tool for the acoustic analysis of connected speech. Joos (1948) was perhaps the first to see its value, followed closely by Potter and Steinberg (1950) and Peterson and Barney (1952) in their specification of vowel formants. This approach has been used as the basis of thousands of experiments on speech.

Figure 4-11 depicts a typical spectrometer: a Kay Elemetrics Corp., model 6061B Sona-Graph. This system is one of a class with similar devices available from Spectraphonics, Inc. (their unit also features a useful TV display) and Voice Identification, Inc. Each of the systems manufactured by these three firms are produced in various configurations; however, only the basic characteristics of this class of

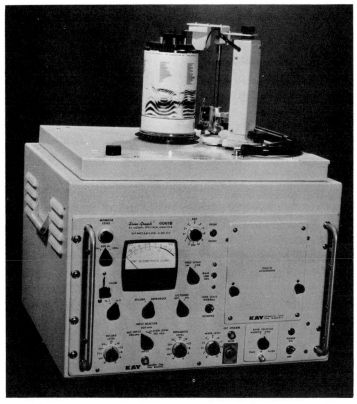

Fig. 4-11.   A photograph of a time-by-frequency-by-amplitude (t-f-a) spectrometer. The unit is seen prior to removal of a t-f-a spectrogram.

spectrometers will be described. Specifically, the Kay 6061B has frequency ranges of 80–8000 Hz and 160–16,000 Hz with two filter bandwidths of 45 Hz (narrow) and 300 Hz (broad). The bandwidths are doubled when the device is used in the 160–16,000 Hz mode—and total sample time is halved from 2.4 seconds to 1.2 seconds. Operating procedures involve inputting a sample of speech 2.4 seconds in length; the sample is stored and then continuously replayed while the filters "sweep" the entire frequency range. The product of this type of spectrometer may be seen illustrated in Figure 4-12. In this case, time is on the abcissa and frequency on the ordinate; the horizontal lines are 1,000 Hz division indicators. The density (blackness) of the traces shows where energy exists; the darker the trace, the greater the energy. As with all of the systems described in this chapter, the Sona-Graph 6061B must be calibrated if it is to be used for research purposes. As would be expected, the accuracy of the time measurements made from these spectrograms is the best, accuracy of frequency second, and amplitude accuracy a distant third. Frequency measurements may be made by hand or by means of digital data provided by auxiliary equipment; amplitude often can be estimated by an associated sectioner or similar auxiliary device.

As Fant pointed out as early as 1958, Sona-Graph records of an utterance provide the investigator with an array of interesting information about speech, some of which can be appreciated after only a short learning period. Thus these devices are excellent for teaching, for clinical evaluations, for viewing the dynamics of speech over time—even for rapid pattern analysis of the type that can lead to the development of more precise experiments. On the other hand, with the exception of the highly sophisticated 51 channel analyzer developed by Fant and his associates (Liljencrants, 1968), highly accurate quantitative data are difficult to extract via this technique, as it is structured to provide visual displays rather than digital readout.

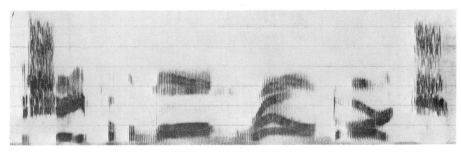

Fig. 4-12.  A t-f-a spectrogram of an individual producing the words "shape of a long round arch."

## INTENSITY ANALYSIS

While speaking intensity level and variability are fruitful areas for research, intensity is difficult to measure. In order to determine *absolute* intensity levels accurately, the equipment must be precisely calibrated, the exact characteristics of the input microphone must be known, and the talker must be positioned in very specific relationship to the microphone. The third variable cited is perhaps the most difficult of the three to control. If the microphone is to be kept in precise relationship to the lips of the talker, either a bulky apparatus must be worn on the head or the position of the talkers's head must be severely limited. In either case, an artificial speaking situation occurs. If absolute intensity is denied the investigator as an experimental variable, only relative intensity measures remain.

Intensity is an energy phenomenon and is difficult to measure directly. Sound *pressure,* however, is directly proportional to sound intensity on the basis that $I \approx P^2$. Both utilize the same basic ratio scale; one Bel "intensity" is a 10:1 ratio, and one Bel "pressure" is a 20:1 ratio. Pressure is not so difficult to measure, and levels can be determined in relationship to a standard (such as 0.0002 dynes/cm² or 1 microbar). Thus, changes or variations in the patterns of sound pressure level (SPL) can be obtained to study speech samples. If the subject-to-microphone distance can be controlled, absolute pressure levels can be established and compared.

A basic device used to provide a readout of pressure (intensity) is the graphic level recorder. One such recorder is the GR 1521B cited above; another is the Brüel and Kjaer model 2305. A graphic level recorder can provide a running trace of the amplitude of a speech signal that will permit the measurement of *relative* speech intensity. A typical trace can be seen in Figure 4-13. Here, the base, or ambient, noise level can be seen extending across the bottom of the trace, and emerging from it vertically are the speech bursts. If this system is properly calibrated, differences in level, extent of the slopes, and other such features can be calculated in decibels. Finally, several of the T-F-A spectrometers have the capability of providing a graphic trace of the intensity (pressure) level of the 2.4 seconds of speech stored for spectral analysis. These displays are especially useful for the measurement of the consonant–vowel ratios found in an utterance.

The procedure described constitutes a laborious task that relies heavily on human judgment, as the investigator must physically make the measures. Accordingly, a number of investigators have attempted to automate the process by developing computer-aided procedures. While there are several excellent schemes of this type, the one select-

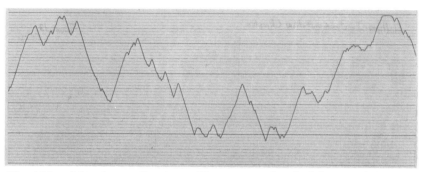

Fig. 4-13.  A level recording trace. The pressure level of the speech bursts (in dB) may be seen portrayed as a function of time.


ed for discussion is that developed by Hicks (1979). This approach permits the investigator to make a large number of analyses of a subject's intensity levels and patterns. One of the most useful displays (whether visual, hard copy, or digital) is the subject's intensity distribution, in decibel steps, with the levels calculated as proportions of the total energy produced. Analysis of these distributions permits calculation of peak pressure, the range of pressures utilized, and pressure "configurations."

The envelope of the speech signal is obtained by means of a rectifier/integrator circuit coupled via an A/D converter to a computer. Specially developed software controls the storage, processing, and analysis of the energy dimensions of the recorded utterance. The software is designed to permit the investigator to preselect various parameters such as sampling rate and the length of the sample to be analyzed. A typical sampling rate/length would involve 50 samples per second and a duration of 120 seconds, respectively. The output lists the minimum and maximum values as well as the number of sample points and the corresponding percentage of the total data for each. It also includes the total pressure of the utterance, the intensity range utilized, mean intensity (pressure) level, the standard deviation of the distribution, and all levels of the entire distribution and their associated statistics.


## TEMPORAL MEASURES

The simple measure of "total time" elapsed has been applied to spoken utterances for many centuries and for many purposes. There are several other measures that can be applied to a sample of speech for the purposes of determining the temporal characteristics. Some of the more useful parameters include: 1) sample duration; 2) speaking rate and rate patterns; 3) phonationtime (P/T) ratios and speech-time (S/T) ratios; 4) pauses: number/length/patterns; 5) speech bursts: number/length/patterns; and 6) vectors of combined factors.

In many instances the parameters in question are measured with equipment as simple as a stopwatch or they are hand calculated. Information about speech pauses or bursts often is obtained from measurements of the traces provided by level recorders; P/T ratios can be obtained from SFF tracking devices as one of the FFI software subroutines provides this information.

Recently, a number of algorithms have been proposed that extract various temporal parameters from the speech signal either directly or as a consequence of some other related process. One of these approaches is the "TED" vector developed by Johnson (1978). This approach is a relatively complex one, based on sectional time-by-energy measurements. It can best be understood by reference to Figure 4-14.

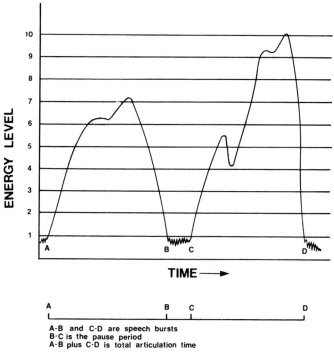

A-B and C-D are speech bursts
B-C is the pause period
A-B plus C-D is total articulation time

Fig. 4-14.   A schematic representation of a typical energy envelope as generated by means of the TED technique.

An r/c circuit is used to generate an energy envelope of the speech signal. The signal is "digitized" by an A/D converter coupled to a minicomputer. The digital sequence then is analyzed for duration relative to ten levels by means of a special software package. The digitized envelope is partitioned functionally into ten linearly equal energy levels initiating with the peak level. Figure 4-14 provides a graphic representation of a typical envelope as partitioned; the number and duration of the speech bursts and pause periods, as well as the means and standard deviation for both, are then calculated as a function of the ten levels. Thus, a temporal vector consisting of a total of 40 features can be obtained. The TED approach is just one of a number of temporal analysis schemes that currently are available to the investigator.

## COMPUTERS

Many references have been made to computers throughout this chapter. In some cases, the measurement techniques have been comprised totally of software, in other cases the system described was hybrid (hardware/software), and in other instances the processing described was carried out by application of a specific piece of equipment—with computer analysis reserved only for statistical treatment of the data. In modern science it is difficult to avoid the use of computers even if one would want to do so. The modern digital computer is advancing in sophistication at a pace that is difficult to comprehend. Two relationships must be kept in mind, however.

First, a digital computer is simply a tool. Accordingly, research and assessment considerations should not be adjusted to fit the computer; rather computer capability—and associated software—should be developed to serve the needs of the experiments specified by the design protocols.

Additionally, it should be remembered that *control* computers as yet have only a limited usefulness for most types of speech and voice research. It is possible for investigators in psychoacoustics to design research that is amenable to protocols where the computer controls the experiment and then processes the subject's responses. In the case of many of the instrumental techniques described in this chapter, however, an approach of that type is not possible. Indeed, much of the work that attempts to relate various speech/voice parameters to behavioral states consists of exploratory ventures and/or the assessment of relationships not directly under experimenter control.

These cautions should not be construed to suggest that computers are not powerful tools among the instrumental repertoire of the scientist interested in the issues relating speech behavior to psychological states. The modern digital computer permits the efficient storage and processing of data as well as allowing the investigator to be privy to the results of the procedures applied within a very short period of time. Computers are now permitting us to mathematically study behaviors that were not approachable *in situ*—and to construct theoretical models of complex systems. In short, the general impact of computers upon science and technology is substantial; new advances (such as the Josephson Junction) will further increase their effect. An intelligent and judicious use of such devices should greatly enhance the research being conducted in those areas represented by this book.

REFERENCES

Anderson, D. J., Deller, J. R., Jr., Stone, R. E., Jr. Computer analysis of jitter in vowel sounds. *Record of IEEE 1976 Inter. Conf. on Acoustics, Speech, and Signal Processing.* New York: Inst. Electrical and Electronics Eng., 1976, 340–342.

Beckett, R. L. Pitch perturbation as a function of subjective vocal constriction. *Folia Phoniat.,* 1969, *21,* 416–425.

Boë, L-J., Rakotofiringa, H. Exigences, réalisation et limites d'un appareillage destiné à l'études de l'intensité et de la hauteur d'un signal acoustique. *Rev. d'Acoust.,* 1971, *4,* 104–113.

Boë, L-J. Quelques remarques et precisions concernant l'étude statistique de la fréquence laryngienne. *Bull. de l'Instit. Phonet. de Grenoble,* 1975, *4,* 67–84.

Boë, L-J, and Rakotofiringa, H. A statistical analysis of laryngeal frequency: Its relationship to intensity, level and duration. *Lang. Speech,* 1975, *18,* 1–13.

Boë, L-J., Contini, M., Rakotofiringa, H. Etude statistique de la fréquence laryngienne, application à l'analyse et à la synthése des faits prosodiques du Francais. *Phonetica,* 1975, *32,* 1–23.

Davis, S. Computer evaluation of laryngeal pathology based on inverse filtering of speech. *SCRL Mono # 13,* 1976, 247.

Dempsey, M. E. Design and evaluation of a fundamental frequency recorder for complex sounds. Unpublished Ph. D. dissertation, Purdue University, 1955.

Dempsey, M. E., Draegert, G. L., Siakind, R. P., et al. The Purdue pitch meter—A direct-reading fundamental frequency analyzer. *J. Speech Hear. Dis.,* 1950, *15,* 135–141.

Denber, M. J. A. Sound spectrum analysis of the mentally ill. Unpublished Masters thesis, University of Rochester, 1978.

Denes, P. B., Pinson, E.N. *The speech chain.* New Jersey: Bell Telephone Laboratories, 1970.

Doherty, E. T. Preliminary report on jitter extraction system. *Occasionally,* 1977, *2,* 7–8.

Fant, G. Modern instruments and methods for acoustic studies of speech. *Acta Polytech Scan.,* 1958, 1–81.

Fant, G. *Acoustic theory of speech production.* Mouton and Co., The Hague, 'S-Gravenhage, 1960.

Flanagan, J. Some properties of the glottal sound source. *J. Speech Hear. Res.,* 1958, *1,* 99–116.

Gold, B. Computer program for pitch extraction. *J. Acoust. Soc. Amer.,* 1962, *34,* 916–921.

Gold, B., Rabiner, L. R. Parallel processing techniques for estimating pitch period of speech in the time domain. *J. Acoust. Soc. Amer.,* 1969, *46,* 442–448.

Harris, C. M., Weiss, M. R. Pitch extraction by computer processing of high-resolution Fourier analysis data. *J. Acoust. Soc. Amer.,* 1963, *35,* 339–343.

Hecker, M. H. L., Kreul, E. J. Descriptions of the speech of patients with cancer of the vocal folds. Part 1: Measurements of fundamental frequency. *J. Acoust. Soc. Amer.,* 1971, *49,* 1275–1282.

Hicks, J. W., Jr. An acoustical/temporal analysis of emotional stress in speech. Unpublished Ph.D. dissertation, University of Florida, 1979.

Hollien, H., Malcik, B., Hollien, B. Adolescent voice change in southern white males. *Speech Mono.,* 1965, *32,* 87–90.

Hollien, H., Michel, J., Doherty, E. T. A method for analyzing vocal jitter in sustained phonation. *J. Phonetics,* 1973, *1,* 85–91.

Hollien, H., Majewski, W. Speaker identification by long-term spectra under normal and distorted speech conditions. *J. Acoust. Soc. Amer.,* 1977, *62,* 975–980.

Hollien, H., Harrington, W. Fundamental frequency indicator (FFI). *Occasionally,* 1977, *2,* 4–6.

Horii, Y. Some statistical characteristics of voice fundamental frequency. *J. Speech Hear. Res.,* 1975, *18,* 192–201.

Horii, Y. Fundamental frequency perturbation observed in sustained phonation. *J. Speech Hear. Res.,* 1979, *22,* 5–19.

Johnson, C. C. Temporal parameters within the speech signal applied to speaker identification. Unpublished Ph. D. dissertation, University of Florida, 1978.

Joos, M. Acoustic Phonetics. *Lang.,* 1948, *24,* 1–136.

Koike, Y. Experimental studies on vocal attack. *Pract. Otolary,* 1967, *60,* 663–668.

Koike, Y. Application of some acoustic measures for the evaluation of laryngeal dysfunction. *Stud. Phonolog.,* 1973, *7,* 17–23.

Lieberman, P. Perturbations in vocal pitch. *J. Acoust. Soc. Amer.,* 1961, *33,* 597–603.

Lieberman, P. Some acoustic measures of the fundamental periodicity of normal and pathological larynges. *J. Acoust. Soc. Amer.,* 1963, *35,* 344–353.

Liljencrants, J. A filter bank speech spectrum analyzer. *Technical Report, Speech Transmission Laboratory.* Stockholm: Royal Institute of Technology, (Jan. 15), 1968, 37.

Majewski, W., Rothman, H. B., Hollien, H. Acoustic comparisons of American English and Polish. *J. Phonetics,* 1977, *5,* 247–251.

Markel, J. D. The SIFT algorithm for fundamental frequency estimation. *IEEE Trans. Audio Electroacoust.,* 1972, *20,* 367–377.

McGonegal, C. A., Rabiner, L. R., Rosenberg, A. E. A semi-automatic pitch detector (SAPD). *IEEE Trans. Acoust., Speech, Signal Proc.,* 1975, *23,* 570–574.

McKinney, N. P. Laryngeal frequency analysis for linguistic research. *Rep. No. 14: Nonr 1224–22,* Communication Sciences Laboratory, University of Michigan, 1965.

Moore, G. P., Thompson, C.L. Comments on the physiology of hoarseness. *Arch. Otolaryn.,* 1965, *81,* 97–102.

Murry, T., Doherty, .E. T. Selected acoustic characteristics of pathologic and normal speakers. *J. Speech Hear. Res.,* (in press).

Mysak, E. D. Pitch and duration characteristics of older males. *J. Speech Hear. Res.,* 1958, *2,* 46–54.

Peterson, G. E., Barney, H.L. Control methods used in the study of vowels. *J. Acoust. Soc. Amer.,* 1952, *24,* 175–184.

Peterson, G., Shoup, J. A physiological theory of phonetics. *J. Speech Hear. Res.,* 1966, *9,* 5–67.

Potter, R. K. Visible patterns of sound. *Science,* November, 1945.

Potter, R. K., Steinberg, J.C. Toward the specification of speech. *J. Acoust. Soc. Amer.,* 1950, *22,* 807–820.

Potter, R. K., Kopp, A. G., Green, H. C. *Visible speech.* New York: Van Norstrand, 1947.

Rabiner, L. R., Cheng, M. J., Rosenberg, A. E., et al. A comparative performance study of several pitch detection algorithms. *IEEE Trans. Acoust., Speech, Signal Proc.,* 1976, *24,* 399–417.

Smith, B. E., Weinberg, B., Feth, L. L., et al. Vocal roughness and jitter characteristics of vowels produced by esophageal speakers. *J. Speech Hear. Res.* 1978, *21,* 240–249.

Sondhi, M. M. New methods of pitch extraction. *IEEE Trans. Audio Electroacoust.,* 1968, *16,* 262–266.

Stevens, K., House, A. An acoustic theory of vowel production and some of its implications. *J. Speech Hear. Res.,* 1961, *4,* 303–320.

Tiffin, J. Phonophotograph apparatus. *University Iowa Studies Psych. Music,* 1932, *1,* 118–133.

Wendahl, R. W. Laryngeal analog synthesis for jitter and shimmer: The auditory parameter of harshness. *Folia Phoniat.,* 1966, *18,* 98–108.

Jared J. Wolf

# 5
# Acoustic Analysis and Computer Systems

During the past fifteen years it has become increasingly attractive to perform signal processing and analysis of audio signals, such as speech, by using a digital computer instead of conventional instrumentation. Part of the reason for this is the increasing availability of computers in laboratories and hospitals, as well as the growth of our understanding of how to do acoustic analysis by digital means. Today digital signal processing is a research area in its own right, but it is also accessible to researchers for application to their own fields of endeavor. It is the purpose of this chapter to introduce these new methods of analyzing speech.

Conventional (analog) instrumentation requires investment in special-purpose electronic equipment, which, although frequently modular, is somewhat inflexible and furthermore requires periodic calibration and adjustment. Digital signal analysis, which forms another kind of "instrumentation," can be performed on a general purpose digital computer, the existence or availability of which may almost be taken for granted these days. Such digital instrumentation is very flexible. Programming turns the computer into a custom-designed instrument; the characteristics of the instrument may be changed or even redesigned without recourse to a soldering iron or supply cabinet, and there is nothing to go out of calibration. Furthermore, many of the techniques now available digitally are simply not realizable in the analog domain. Perhaps the most notable drawback is that while analog instrumentation is inherently real-time, it is not always possible for digital techniques to be performed in real-time.

This is counterbalanced by the potentially far greater functionality of digital techniques. The same technological advances that have made computers faster and cheaper have done the same for digital processing techniques, and we may expect this tendency to accelerate.

Many texts on digital signal processing are now available, but there are several that deserve special note. The text by Rabiner and Schafer (1978) is entirely devoted to digital speech processing, and it is comprehensive in terms of techniques. Schafer and Markel (1979) have assembled into one volume reprints of fundamental articles on speech analysis, and the Digital Signal Processing (DSP) Committee (1979) has assembled a unique collection of computer programs, which is also available on magnetic tape. Markel and Gray (1976), while treating the subject of linear prediction of speech, also include many example computer programs.

## DIGITIZATION OF SPEECH

For a signal to be analyzed digitally, it must first be converted from the form of a continuous signal (the acoustic pressure wave or its electrical analog) to a digital signal. A digital signal is discrete in two ways: it consists of measurements of the speech signal amplitude at discrete, regularly spaced instants of time, and each of these *samples* has been *quantized* to a certain number of bits of precision. This transformation from a continuous waveform to a list of digital numbers is performed by an *analog-to-digital converter*. Nyquist's sampling theorem (Rabiner and Schafer, 1978, p. 24) tells us that in order to capture the information contained in a bandwidth of B Hz, we must sample at a rate of at least 2B samples per second, and furthermore, if the signal contains energy at frequencies higher than B Hz, the result will be distorted unless we first low-pass filter the signal at or below B Hz. Therefore, an application in which the 0–5 kHz band is of interest may call for low-pass filtering at or below 5 kHz and sampling at 10,000 samples per second, with each sample represented by a 12 bit number.

## DIGITAL FILTERING

The stream of numbers that forms a digitized signal is as valid a representation of that signal as the continuous waveform from which it was derived, and there are computational procedures on this stream that are analogous to the filtering operations that can be performed on electrical signals. (As an example, we can see that a running average taken of several adjacent samples of the signal tends to smooth out rapid [high-frequency] variations. This averaging operation is one form of low-pass filtering, and we can calculate the frequency response of such a filter; the more samples that are averaged together, the greater is the attenuation of high frequencies.)

The analogies between conventional filtering and digital filtering mean that techniques for designing conventional filters have counterparts in the digital domain. Therefore, the usual filtering operations such as low- and high-pass, band-pass, notch, and slope filtering are all realizable with digital signals and filters, and digital filters may also be used in ways not realizable with analog hardware.

## SPECTRAL ANALYSIS

The properties of the speech signal change as the vocal tract moves from one sound to the next, and for many purposes it is necessary to follow these changes in time. This requires the use of "short-time" processing, in which short segments of the speech signal are isolated and processed as if they had come from a steady sound with fixed properties. The analysis is repeated as often as desired, usually at regular intervals, so that the sequence of results follows the time-course of the changing speech signal. Analysis window widths of 10 to 30 milliseconds and repetitions of 50 to 200 per second are commonly used; successive analysis windows may overlap.

The spectral content of a digital signal may be analyzed by computing the discrete Fourier transform (DFT) of the signal. The Fast Fourier Transform (FFT), an efficient algorithm for computing the DFT, is a simple yet efficient way to do this. (For example, Oppenheim and Schafer [1975].) The short-time spectrum of voiced speech has both a fine structure due to the harmonics of the periodic voice source and a gross structure due to the resonances of the vocal tract. For most purposes it is desirable to suppress the effects of the voice source so as to display the resonance structure of the spectrum. The methods of cepstral smoothing (Oppenheim and Schafer, 1975) and linear prediction are the most effective. Formant frequencies may be estimated from the local maxima of the smoothed spectrum.

## LINEAR PREDICTION

One of the most powerful techniques of digital speech processing is that of linear predictive analysis (Markel and Gray, 1976; Rabiner and Schafer, 1978). It has become the predominant method for esti-

mating the basic parameters of the speech signal (formants, fundamental frequency, vocal tract area function, and spectra), and it lies
behind other powerful methods of speech processing, such as low bit-
rate transmission of speech and inverse filtering of speech for the detection of laryngeal pathology (Davis, in press).

The basic mathematical idea behind linear prediction is that a
(digital) speech signal may be approximated as a linear combination
of past values of the signal, but, for our purposes, this is less important
than the fact that linear prediction permits us to approximate a
speech spectrum with an *all-pole model*. This is important because our
most useful acoustical model of the vocal tract also takes the same
form (Flanagan, 1972), and thus from the speech signal itself we can
calculate a model that approximates the relevant parameters of the
vocal tract.

As with spectral analysis, we apply linear predictive analysis to
the speech signal on a short-time basis and thus capture the short-
time behavior of the vocal tract as it moves to form successive speech
sounds. The parameters of the linear prediction model may be manip-
ulated to yield excellent estimates of formant frequencies; they may
be transformed via the DFT to yield a smoothed spectrum that emphasizes the vocal tract frequency response; and they may also be manip-
ulated so as to portray a vocal tract shape in the form of an area
function (although it must be mentioned that there can be problems
in interpreting this area function).

## OTHER SPEECH ANALYSIS TECHNIQUES

The estimation of fundamental frequency contours of speech is
important for investigations of linguistic and nonlinguistic behavior.
This is a difficult problem, and several digital techniques have been
developed for doing this automatically, such as autocorrelation, average magnitude difference function, linear prediction inverse filtering,
cepstral analysis, and others. No single technique is best for all applications. Schafer and Markel (1979) contains an excellent collection of
articles on this subject, including one (Rabiner, Cheng, Rosenberg, et
al., 1976) that describes a comparative study of several of these methods.

The estimation of vocal tract parameters, such as formant frequencies and bandwidths, is another important application area. This
was mentioned under linear prediction, but there are other useful
techniques as well. Schafer and Markel (1979) also contains useful articles on this problem.

## CONCLUSION

The techniques of digital speech analysis briefly discussed above are algorithms, realizable as computer programs. Many of these computer programs are available verbatim in the literature; others require implementation by a programmer. Certain general purpose algorithms, such as FFT spectral analysis, are available in special purpose hardware, such as spectral analyzers, oscilloscope plug-in units, and signal processing oscilloscopes. These instruments, however, while useful for many applications, do not offer the flexibility or sophistication available through application-specific programming.

A single computer program may be designed to contain a number of different speech analysis algorithms, effectively operating in parallel to extract different aspects of the speech signal. An additional attractiveness of digital techniques for speech analysis is the fact that they can be performed on the same computer (and as part of the same program), as may be used for subsequent higher level analyses. Quite powerful programs can thus be built up to carry analysis all the way from digital speech signals to statistical summaries of their properties with respect to a problem of interest.

It has not been the intent of this short chapter to do more than introduce the substance of digital speech analysis and the concept of customized application-specific instrumentation realized through programming of a general purpose computer. The techniques of digital signal processing are uniquely powerful and almost infinitely flexible. They are a new pair of shoulders on which to stand as we reach for better understanding of the speech signal and the organism that produces it.

## REFERENCES

Davis, S. Acoustic Characteristics of Laryngeal Pathology. In J. Darby (Ed.), *Speech evaluation in medicine.* New York: Grune & Stratton (in press).
Digital Signal Processing Committee, IEEE acoustics, speech, and signal processing society (Eds.). *Programs for digital signal processing.* New York: IEEE Press, 1979.
Flanagan, J. L. *Speech analysis synthesis and perception.* (2nd ed.) New York: Springer-Verlag, 1972.
Markel, J. D., Gray, A. H., Jr. *Linear prediction of speech.* New York: Springer-Verlag, 1976.
Oppenheim, A. V., Schafer, R. W. *Digital signal processing.* Englewood Cliffs, NJ: Prentice-Hall, 1975.

Rabiner, L. R., Cheng, M. J., Rosenberg, A. E., et al. A comparative performance study of several pitch detection algorithms. *IEEE* Trans. Acoust., Speech, Signal Proc., 1976, *ASSP-24*, 399–417.

Rabiner, L. R., Schafer, R. W. *Digital processing of speech signals.* Englewood Cliffs, NJ: Prentice-Hall, 1978.

Schafer, R. W., Markel, J. D. (Eds.) *Speech analysis.* New York: Inst. Electrical and Electronics Eng., 1979.

# PART II
# Speech Evaluation
# in Psychiatry

# II. Speech Behavior Associated with Normal Personality

Klaus R. Scherer
Ursula Scherer

# 6
# Speech Behavior and Personality

## BASIC THEORETICAL ASSUMPTIONS

### The Concept of Personality

To almost all individuals engaged in everyday social interaction it is self-evident that partners differ consistently and predictably in different aspects of their behavior. These differences are usually attributed to fundamental dispositions called character or personality. We all tend to categorize others on the basis of their behavior as sociable versus withdrawn, cautious versus reckless, stable versus neurotic, and so on. To laypersons this seems a rather natural procedure and, although they may not use the term "personality" in the same way as it is used by psychologists, in essence they use the term to mean something rather similar.

Psychologists, however, in trying to define personality—to conceptualize it in terms of underlying constructs and to find concomitant behavioral differences—have not been quite as successful as the pervasiveness of the notion would lead us to believe (Mischel, 1971). The basic difficulty is that "personality" represents a hypothetical construct derived from theory and is empirically testable only in its behavioral manifestations or in self-reports. Consequently, definitions

---

*This chapter draws heavily from a recent report for a different audience (Scherer, 1979b), as there has been little of substance published in this area of research since that date.

of personality vary widely according to the theoretical position of the respective psychologists (from the Freudian viewpoint of subconscious processes to a notion of learned stimulus-response associations). In addition, there are enormous differences in conceptions of the structure of personality (from the interplay of "ego," "id," and "super-ego" and various field forces to notions of systems of needs or traits varying in number and comprehensiveness) and in conceptions of its origins (from personality dispositions being partly inherited to being almost totally a product of past experiences). (For reviews of the various personality theories, see Hall and Lindzey [1970], Maddi [1968], or Pervin [1970].) In empirical, experimental research on personality, however, it is generally assumed that "personality" can be conceived of as a number of traits or dispositions. These are either described as clusters of apparently related behaviors (e.g., dominance–submissiveness) or as cognitive information processing patterns (e.g., cognitive complexity) or as underlying psychophysiological mechanisms resulting in specific behavior dispositions (e.g., extraversion–introversion). (See Borgatta and Lambert [1968], Eysenck and Eysenck [1969], London and Exner [1979].)

Since we cannot do justice to the complexities of the personality concept in theory and research, we propose the following eclectic definition of personality. It is reasonable to assume that there are stable individual differences in terms of the nature and frequency of the occurrence of particular combinations of cognitive and motivational states which jointly determine behavioral outcomes. For example, people may differ in terms of the frequency with which they will slow down their car upon seeing a uniformed policeman. This may be the result of a cognitive evaluation of the significance and the possible consequences of the policeman's appearance and of a particular motivational/emotional state such as fear of being stopped or of general anxiety in the presence of authority figures. The specific nature of these cognitive and motivational processes (leading to preferred reaction patterns) is probably the result of a continuous interaction between an individual's physical characteristics and the results of his or her experiences in adjusting to environmental demands in the course of socialization. Thus, an anxious response to a police uniform may be a typical cognitive/motivational reaction pattern of a person with high emotional reactivity and a history of aversive experiences with authority figures. It should be noted that individual differences may exist for both types of processing (i.e., cognitive complexity or emotional reactivity), as well as for the contents that dominate a particular system (i.e., values, interests, or attitudes in cognition; needs and feelings in motivation and emotion). The recurrence of particular combinations of such cognitive and motivational states, coupled with a particular type of stimulus processing in one or both of these domains, is likely to produce relatively stable behavior tendencies or dispositions for an individual. Under appropriate eliciting conditions, this should lead to corresponding overt behavior unless precluded by situational constraints.

The present eclectic view of individual differences does not contradict any of the established personality theories which are seen as differing mainly in their emphasis on particular domains or processes. Obviously, the scientific analysis of these individual differences can focus on one particular aspect, such as the nature of the physiological response system, the development and organization of cognitive structures, the hierarchy of needs, or the response capability. In each case, the level of analysis and the resulting categories will be determined by the respective domain.

Empirical evidence for the influence of personality (in terms of specific personality traits as measured by paper and pencil tests) on behavior has been characteristically inconclusive (personality explaining generally about 10 percent of behavioral variance; Mischel, 1968). Consequently, some psychologists have been tempted to reject the concept of personality altogether and have maintained that behavior is basically a function of situational demands. In their view, the apparent consistency of behavior to the observer is due to attribution errors on the part of the observer, to the general tendency toward meaningful categorization of stimuli, and to attempts of the person observed to appear consistent in interactions with the observer. This "situationist" approach, however, has not fared much better in explaining behavioral variance (Argyle and Little, 1972).

Recently, an "interactionist" position has emerged whose proponents accept the notion of pervasive situational influences on behavior but maintain that to predict and explain behavior individual dispositions and situational factors have to be jointly taken into account. In studies in which both determinants of behavior have been investigated, substantial person-by-situation interactions emerged pointing to the fact that the interactionists' assumptions were justified (Endler and Magnusson, 1976). At the present time it is generally posited that research efforts should be directed away from the long-standing search for stable intrapersonal traits towards a search for dimensions by which situations can be described. According to this view, once a taxonomy of situations has been successfully established, it will be possible to identify various personality-situation links by way of which the prediction of behavior will be accomplished more satisfactorily.

### Personality and Behavior

Although there is a large body of literature on both personality and situations, the third unknown in the equation—the behavior itself—has received comparatively little attention. The first problem to be solved is the identification of behavior relevant to particular personality traits. If we want to find out whether extraversion, for example, reliably affects the behavior of persons labeled "extraverted" on the basis of personality tests, we have to define the relevant behavior. Which discrete and measurable acts, for instance, constitute impulsive behavior, impulsiveness being one component of extraversion?

In addition, we have to take into account that the expression of personality traits via certain kinds of behavior may be effectively controlled by situational demands or societal norms (Scherer and Scherer, 1977, pp. 241–243; 1980. pp. 316–317). Behavior is restricted externally to various degrees. It may very well be possible that the "impulsive" behavior we are looking for is not displayed by the individual we are studying, but rather is controlled because "impulsivity" is frowned upon in the respective society or group (at least in certain situations). There are, however, differences in the extent to which different kinds of behavior underlie external restrictions.

We have postulated three criteria on the basis of which a particular behavior can be identified as more or less prone to external restriction: 1) molarity; 2) goal-relevance; and 3) negotiability. By molarity we mean the spatial or temporal extent of behavior. Lengthy utterances or speech acts, for instance, can be viewed as molar, short speech pauses or interjections as molecular. Both the meaning and the occurrence of a behavior are "negotiable" in that a person can deny having emitted a certain behavior ("I certainly did not yawn") or can reinterpret its significance ("No, I'm not bored at all, I just went to bed very late last night"). It is very difficult to negotiate the meaning of *what* is said (i.e., the speech content), whereas it is rather easy to reinterpret the meaning of a speech pause, when it is interpreted as "hesitation" by the partner and when this interpretation is not desired. Goal relevance refers to the goals pursued by the participant in a given situation. Verbal utterances of a distinctive content are certainly relevant for goal attainment (e.g., an influence attempt), whereas the goal relevance of speech pauses is less easy to establish.

Molar, goal-relevant, and non-negotiable behavior underlying comparatively strong external restrictions should therefore be affected to a relatively small degree by personality dispositions. These influences, however, should be discernible to a much greater extent in those behaviors which are less externally restricted, namely, in molecular, negotiable and goal-irrelevant aspects of behavior. Since many nonlinguistic aspects of speech behavior fall into this category, it is to be expected that these are subject to the influence of personality differences.

The remainder of this chapter reviews the empirical evidence on the effects of personality differences on nonlinguistic aspects of voice and speech. Coverage will be restricted to "normal" personality dispositions. (For reviews of personality disturbance and psychopathology, see Darby and Sherk, 1979; Scherer, 1979a and Section V in this volume). In the following section we will briefly present an account of some of the mechanisms that may be responsible for the externalization of personality dispositions in behavior.

## Personality and Speech Behavior

As pointed out above, we assume that personality manifests itself mainly in those types of behavior which are subject to relatively little external restriction. According to this viewpoint, the verbal aspects of speech are relatively strongly restricted by external demands, as they are relatively molar, negotiable only under certain conditions, and highly relevant for interactional goals. Obviously, there are components of the verbal aspects of speech which could be viewed as relatively free of external restriction, such as stylistic choice of lexical items and syntactical structures. There is, however, neither consistent evidence from relevant studies on these aspects nor an established methodology for their objective assessment to warrant further attention to these variables in the present context (Scherer, 1979b). Consequently, we will limit our discussion to the so-called paralinguistic concomitants of speech, particularly to those that focus on vocal and fluency aspects of speech.

Before examining the relationships between personality dispositions and vocal and fluency aspects of speech, it seems profitable to explore the bases for the effects of such dispositions on behavior. To fully understand the nature of the personality-speech relationship, we need to know more about the biological, psychological, and cultural factors underlying speech production.

BIOPHYSICAL FACTORS

Speech production like other behavior is to some extent determined by biophysical characteristics of the individual. Empirical results on the nature and the extent of this determination, thus far, are rather scarce. Some factors, however, are more likely than others to affect speech production. These are bodily characteristics and emotional reactivity. Obviously, structural characteristics of an individual's body, especially of the vocal apparatus (e.g., size of the larynx, resonance characteristics of the vocal tract), should affect speech production. Some psychologists have tried to identify distinctive body types (Kretzschmer, 1921; Sheldon, 1954) and have postulated differences in temperament and psychological functioning. The evidence is still inconclusive (Hall and Lindzey, 1970). Whether these different body types are likely to result in different vocal characteristics remains largely unclear (Fährmann, 1967; Görlitz, 1972).

Emotional reactivity is thought to be reflected in stable interindividual differences in habitual muscle tone and other physiological processes (Goldstein, 1964, Gellhorn, 1967; cf. chapter 3.1 on vocal indicators of stress).

A complicating factor in the analysis of the relationship between physiological processes and aspects of speech and voice is the fact that these processes do not occur continuously. For instance, levels of arousal may differ from individual to individual depending on fundamental physiological differences (e.g., extraversion–introversion) and/or coping strategies (e.g., repression–sensitization). Without taking these moderator variables into account, studies on the effects of physiological processes may yield rather inconclusive or even invalid results (Scherer, 1979a).

PSYCHOLOGICAL FACTORS

Speech production is largely regulated by cognitive processes. Consequently, it is reasonable to assume a strong relationship between cognitive structure and speech behavior. This relationship is quite evident in severe disturbances of intellectual functioning, such as brain damage, which can lead to aphasia and other speech abnormalities (Lenneberg, 1967; Whitaker, 1976). While more psychologically relevant factors such as rigidity, cognitive complexity, or cognitive differentiation may exert a strong influence on speech production, their role has not been well established to date. While verbal behavior is used to measure certain aspects of intelligence, the relationship between intelligence and noncontent aspects of speech production (e.g., fluency, verbal productivity) has not yet been systematically investigated.

FUNCTIONAL EFFICIENCY

An individual may habitually show certain aspects of speech behavior, such as loudness, because in the past this behavior has facilitated the attainment of interactional goals (for instance, fending off the interlocutor's interruptions). Due to these rewards, individuals may have engaged habitually in behavior of this kind, either consciously or subconsciously. If the interactional goals attained by these behavioral aspects are strongly related to some underlying personality disposition, then the frequency of the occurence of a particular behavior should be maintained at a rather high level. It is conceivable, therefore, that more dominant persons may habitually speak in a louder voice than do submissive persons, as loudness of speaking has been instrumental in facilitating their attempt to monopolize interactions.

SELF-PRESENTATION

Closely related to the notion of functional efficiency in the externalization of personality is the strategy of self-presentation. Whereas functional efficiency refers to the attainment of interactional goals relevant to a certain personality-related need, self-presentation refers to the production of certain personality attributions in an observer that may or may not be related to underlying personality dispositions of the actor. The prerequisite for self-presentation is the existence of strong and culturally shared rules for the inference of personality from behavior, which need not necessarily be based on facts. If in a society there are a number of highly valued personality traits, such as extraversion, and if there are shared inference rules according to which extraverted people talk more and louder, a person trying to present himself or herself as extraverted is likely to talk a lot in a rather loud voice. Generally, it can be assumed that aspects of behavior, which in a given cultural context serve as valid and reliable bases of attribution for highly valued characteristics, may be displayed by actors in a conscious or unconscious attempt to generate these respective attributions.

SELF-FULFILLING PROPHECY

According to most personality theorists, personality dispositions are partly determined by inherited temperamental propensity and partly by the course of socialization (Mischel, 1968). An important part of the socialization process are the reactions of significant others in the social environment toward the person. These reactions are obviously determined to a large extent by the behavior of that person. Since the latter, however, is interpreted with the help of existing inference rules, it is conceivable that individuals who display an attribute or a behavior that is linked to some factor other than personality (e.g., a breathy voice due to problems of glottal control) may be reacted to according to these inference rules rather than according to her or his actual personality dispositions. As the self-concept is generally thought to be formed from the reactions of the significant others (Mead, 1934), an individual may attribute the corresponding personality trait to himself or herself, behave accordingly and consistently, and may in the long run develop personality dispositions corresponding to these inference rules.

It is very difficult to decide on the appropriateness of any one of these explanations for the effects of personality on speech. It is possible that all of the processes described may operate at the same time, reinforcing each other or working at cross purposes. The nature of the personality traits expected to underlie manifest behavior may sometimes be a cue as to which mechanism may be operative most strongly. Some personality theories postulate basic needs which motivate a person to behave in a certain way (Murray, 1971), whereas others try to link overt behavioral manifestations via trait descriptions to underlying physiological processes (Eysenck, 1967). In this case the first mechanism described would probably be responsible for the effects of personality on speech behavior, whereas the concept of functional efficiency can best be evoked to explain the effects of needs on behavior. The last mechanism described, self-fulfilling prophecy, can be employed to account for behavioral differences linked to differences in self concepts, the existence of which is acknowledged by almost all personality theorists. Psychological processes like cognitive functioning may cut across all of these mechanisms whereas self-presentation is a distinctly social-psychological concept, the operation of which may be independent of the mechanisms described before.

## THE NATURE AND MEASUREMENT OF MAJOR SPEECH CUES

### VOCAL ASPECTS OF SPEECH

Vocal aspects of speech are those aspects of human speech that are determined by the respiratory, phonatory, and articulatory processes of human sound production. Three major parameters of the acoustic speech signal described earlier in this volume are likely to be affected by personality variables: fundamental frequency (level and variability), vocal energy or intensity (level and variability), and energy distribution in the voice spectrum. These objectively measurable acoustic cues correspond to perceptual cues as experienced by observers, namely, pitch, loudness, and voice quality. There is, however, no perfect correlation between these parameters and their corresponding percepts, as a number of further variables seem to be related to these perceptual analogues (Scherer, 1974, 1979b).

In the studies on the relationship between certain personality dispositions and vocal aspects of speech, both objective acoustic measures and subjective ratings have been used. Therefore, the respective results often are not directly comparable, and differences in the results of studies purporting to investigate similar questions may be due to the fact that acoustic measures of objective cues and subjective ratings of their perceptual resentations may not be measures of the same phenomena.

FLUENCY ASPECTS OF SPEECH

Fluency aspects of speech such as pauses, tempo, tongue slips, sentence corrections, etc. seem to be straightforward phenomena and would appear to be relatively easy to assess. But, in fact, the assessment of these parameters has been more difficult than initially assumed. The definition of various types of pauses has been especially problematic. "Silent" pauses have to be distinguished from filled pauses such as "ah," "mhm," which is a fairly easy task. The "silent" pauses, however, have proven problematic to measure and categorize. "Juncture" pauses, short interruptions of the speech flow between syntactic units (thought to serve cognitive planning purposes), and nonjuncture or hesitation pauses (probably indicating encoding difficulties or psychological arousal) have to be distinguished.

This difference in function has become one of the major obstacles for automatic, computer-based extraction of sounds and silences (Matarazzo, 1965; Jaffe and Feldstein, 1970; Feldstein and Welkowitz, 1978). In view of this difficulty it seems appropriate to make a distinction between computer extracted *silent periods* (generally of more than 200 or 250 milliseconds in duration) and *silent hesitation pauses* (coded by human judges listening to recorded speech). The latter may have to be further categorized by length: Siegman (1978) proposed that pauses longer than 2 seconds may be determined by other cognitive and/or emotional processes than shorter silent pauses.

To generate measures yielding results comparable across speakers or across studies, the number and/or duration of silent pauses is usually set in relation to the length of utterances or to the total speaking time. Resulting ratios commonly used are: mean number of silent pauses per utterance; mean pause duration; and pausing time over total speaking time. One of the most frequently used measures is the so-called sound–silence ratio, computed by dividing the total vocalization time (pauses excluded) by the total duration of silent periods.

Speech tempo or speech rate is much easier to assess. Two measures are usually computed: "speech rate" is obtained by dividing the total speaking time, silent periods included, by the number of words or syllables uttered; and "articulation rate," which is obtained by dividing the total vocalization time, silent periods excluded, by an index for the number of linguistic units produced.

Disruptions of the speech flow such as filled pauses ("uhm," "hm"), speech intrusions, false starts, tongue slips, sentence corrections or changes, omissions and repetitions, etc. are generally considered to belong to one class of phenomena: speech discontinuities or disturbances. A "speech disturbance ratio" (sometimes including only "non-ah" disturbances) can be computed by dividing the number of speech disturbances by the total number of spoken words (Mahl, 1956).

## EMPIRICAL RESULTS ON PERSONALITY CORRELATES OF SPEECH

The inquiry into the relationship between personality and speech has a long tradition in psychology (see Laver, 1975; Sanford, 1942; for historical overviews). Most of the existing studies, however, do not satisfy our present day criteria for scientific research. In many cases they mostly consist of speculations on relationships between different aspects of voice and speech and many diverse personality traits (e.g., Moses, 1954; Fährmann, 1967; Rudert, 1965; Trojan, 1975), stemming from the German introspective "Ausdruckspsychologie" (psychology of expression) tradition. Although detailed and careful case observations are presented in most cases, from the empirical viewpoint these accounts have merely generated interesting hypotheses rather than acceptable evidence. For the present purposes we will concentrate on empirical studies in which standardized personality tests were used and aspects of speech behavior objectively measured.

Experimental research on voice and personality has been rather scarce. Many early researchers seem to have given up hope after a few inconclusive studies. They left the area before high-quality sound recording and digital speech analysis methods became available and improved the chances to obtain empirically valid results. As a consequence of the relative scarcity of empirical studies on voice and personality, we have to cite our own studies more extensively than usual. In particular, there are two studies which are directly related to the topic under discussion, the "juror" study, a cross-cultural study involving speech samples for 30 American and 30 German male speakers from simulated jury discussions (Scherer, 1970, 1972, 1974, 1978, 1979c), and the public official study involving speech samples for 39 male German public officials from interactions with a "standard client" in a simulated office encounter (Scherer and Scherer, 1977, 1980; Scherer, Scherer and Klink, 1979).

In this section we will briefly summarize the major empirical results on the relationship between the vocal and fluency aspects of speech and personality dispositions. (The reader interested in a more comprehensive review of the literature is referred to Diehl, 1960; Görlitz, 1972; Kramer, 1963; and Scherer, 1979b.) The final section is devoted to a more detailed review of the relationships between extraversion and speech, since this personality trait has been studied most extensively.

**Vocal Aspects of Speech**

FUNDAMENTAL FREQUENCY ($F_o$)

$F_o$ seems to be a reliable indicator of psychological arousal. This is not surprising given that the physiological aspects of voice production are significantly affected by changes in muscle tension—muscle tension being at least partly determined by habitual or transitory states of arousal (see Chapter 9 on vocal indicators of stress). A number of studies have yielded fairly consistent evidence concerning the relationship between arousal and heightened $F_o$, although there are strong individual differences (Scherer, 1979a).

While $F_o$ as an indicator of arousal *state* seems fairly established, the relationship between $F_o$ and more enduring personality *traits* or dispositions is much less clear, particularly since there may be strong sex differences as well as differences between speakers from different cultures. Mallory and Miller (1958) studied subjectively rated pitch in 372 female American students and found that pitch was lower for dominant and extraverted girls. Similarly, Scherer (1977) in a study of 31 female American nurse students found a negative correlation between computer extracted $F_o$ and the California Psychological Inventory (CPI) scales capacity for Status, Sociability, Social presence and Self-acceptance, which seems to confirm the earlier results. Male American speakers who rated themselves high on achievement, task ability, sociability, dominance, and aggressiveness (and were seen as being dominant and assertive by peers), however, spoke with higher $F_o$ in the juror study. Thus, relationships between $F_o$ and dominance or extraversion may be different for male and female speakers, although task differences in the studies reported have to be taken into account. (It could be that achievement oriented, dominant speakers got more involved in the jury discussions, raising their arousal level and thus their $F_o$.) The patterns for the male German speakers in the juror study are still different. Here speakers, who rate themselves highly on scales of adjustment, orderliness, and lack of autonomy (and are rated as dependable and likeable by peers), speak with significantly higher $F_o$. Scherer (1979b) has attempted to explain the different patterns of results in terms of habitually elevated arousal levels for different personality dispositions, depending on sex role and cultural factors.

VOCAL INTENSITY

Results on the relationship between vocal intensity (perceived as loudness) and personality dispositons are equally scarce but somewhat more consistent than results on $F_o$. The results of several studies indicate that there may be a positive relationship between extraversion and high vocal intensity (Mallory and Miller, 1958; Trimboli, 1973); in the juror study, however, a significant correlation was found for American speakers only (Scherer, 1978). In addition, ratings of "inadequate" loudness were found to be related to submissiveness (Mallory and Miller, 1958).

VOICE QUALITY

Voice quality or timbre may well be a good indicator for personality dispositions, but, as most other vocal aspects of speech, it is almost completely unresearched. The immense difficulties in defining voice qualities objectively may be largely responsible for this lack of research. Attempts have been made only recently to specify voice quality rigorously in articulatory-phonetic terms (Laver, 1975). Empirical results, however, are still very limited. In some early studies where expert ratings of voice quality were employed, breathy voices were found to be indicative of introversion, neurotic tendency, and anxiety (Moore, 1939; Diehl, White, and Burke, 1959) and, in the juror study, with German speakers of emotional instability. Harsh, metallic, and resonant voices may point to emotional stability, extraversion, and dominance in the respective speakers. (For a more detailed discussion of the topic, see Scherer, 1979b, Laver, 1975).

## Fluency Aspects of Speech

Research on fluency aspects of speech is much more common than research on vocal aspects, although the emphasis is often on state variables, and personality related determinants are often disregarded. Results on the relationship of specific cues to specific personality traits are fairly consistent, especially in the case of extraversion and emotional stability. Yet, slightly different measurement procedures in different studies make it difficult to compare findings.

SILENT PAUSES

A number of studies (Siegman and Pope, 1965; Ramsey, 1966; Scherer, 1979b) studied the effects of extraversion on silent pauses. In those studies where American speakers were used, there was a tendency for extraverts to speak with fewer pauses (fewer filled pauses, fewer pauses longer than 2 seconds, shorter periods of silence between sound bursts, and a smaller number of silent hesitation pauses). The German extraverts in the juror study, however, actually showed *more* silent pauses.

Many of the studies on silent pauses have been concerned with anxiety, both as a state and a trait. (For reviews, see Mahl and Schulze, 1964; Murray, 1971; Rochester, 1973; Siegman, 1978.) In these studies, anxious speakers were often found to show fewer short silent pauses (or generally shorter silent portions) but more frequent longer pauses in their speech. Siegman (1978) tried to account for this complex pattern of results by arguing that pausing decreases with an increase of anxiety induced arousal yielding a faster speech rate, and that highly anxious speakers with a very fast speech rate have to use more frequent longer silent pauses to accommodate cognitive planning. Scherer (1979b) has pointed out that the relationship between state and trait anxiety and pausing may be even more complex, since a number of social psychological factors, such as sensitivity to listener response, self-presentation strategies, and social skills have to be taken into account.

SPEECH DISCONTINUITIES

Although the analysis of speech disturbances, such as filled pauses, repetitions, etc., seemed to be rather fruitful several years ago, empirical results on their relationship to underlying personality variables are similar to those of studies dealing with other aspects of speech, namely, scarce and inconclusive. While the "non-ah" ratio seems significantly correlated with differences in situationally related anxiety (Harper, Wiens, and Matarazzo, 1978), their relationship to trait-anxiety (or emotional lability) is much less clear. One reviewer of relevant research (Rochester, 1973) concluded that highly anxious speakers not only exhibit fewer silent pauses, but fewer filled pauses as well. In the juror study, however, American and German speakers high on emotional lability showed significantly more filled pauses. Beekman (1975) also found more filled pauses in male American speakers with high scores on counseling readiness (similar to emotional lability), abasement, and lack of dominance. Clearly, the evidence is far from being consistent (see also Harper, Wiens, and Matarazzo, 1978, pp. 40–46).

## VOICE AND SPEECH MARKERS OF EXTRAVERSION

As the preceding section has shown, empirical results on the relationships of objectively measureable aspects of voice and speech to personality dispositions that can be assessed by using established assessment procedures are very rare on the one hand, and have proved to be rather inconclusive on the other. In this section we will focus on extraversion to explore the issue of speech-personality relationships further.

The personality dimension extraversion–introversion has long been used for the typology of persons (Wilson, 1978). The psychologist, H. J. Eysenck has studied this disposition most intensively. He and his collaborators have developed an inventory (Maudsley Personality Inventory, Eysenck and Eysenck, 1964, 1969) that is used to distinguish various degrees of extraversion in the respondents. The following description of the typical persons located at the endpoints of this dimension is suggested by Eysenck and his collaborators.

Typical extroverts are sociable, like parties, have many friends, need to have people to talk to, and do not like reading or studying by themselves. They crave excitement, take chances, often stick their neck out, act on the spur of the moment, and are generally impulsive. They are fond of practical jokes, always have a ready answer, and generally like change; they are carefree, easygoing, optimistic, and like to 'laugh and be merry.' They prefer to keep moving and doing things, tend to be aggressive and lose their temper quickly; altogether their feelings are not kept under tight control, and they are not always reliable persons.

Typical introverts are quiet, retiring persons, introspective, fond of books rather than people; they are reserved and distant except to intimate friends; they tend to plan ahead, 'look before they leap,' and distrust the impulse of the moment. They do not like excitement, take matters of everyday life with proper seriousness, and like a well-ordered mode of life. They keep their feelings under close control, seldom behave in an aggressive manner, and do not lose their temper easily. They are reliable, somewhat pessimistic and place great value on ethical standards (Eysenck and Eysenck, 1964).

Numerous studies have shown that introversion–extraversion is a consistent dimension of personality. Eysenck's theory, contrary to other personality theories, is explanatory rather than descriptive in nature. Thus, an attempt is made to explain differences between extraverted and introverted individuals in terms of underlying psychophysiological factors. According to Eysenck the extraversion–introversion differences correspond to differences in the habitual level of arousal induced by stimuli impinging on the organism. Given the same stimulus, introverts are more aroused than extraverts. To reduce arousal they tend to avoid stimulation by withdrawl or by restriction of responses. Extraverts on the other hand are so little aroused by stimulation of the same degree that they have to actively seek it and to expose themselves to it to maintain a level high enough for their subjective feeling of well being. This explanation has received considerable support in a wide range of experimental studies (Wilson, 1978).

It is easily conceivable that a personality disposition as stable and as interactionally relevant as extraversion–introversion should manifest itself in speech behavior and should be inferred by observers partly from those cues. Although the number of studies concerned with this relationship is too small to allow any definite conclusions, it seems as if extraverted speakers speak louder (Mallory and Miller, 1958; Trimboli, 1973; Scherer, 1978, 1979b) with fewer silent pauses (Siegman and Pope, 1965; Ramsay, 1966; Scherer, 1979b). Some doubt is cast on the generality of these findings, however, by conflicting results obtained with German speakers. In the juror study extraverted speakers did not speak with louder voices, but actually spoke with more silent hesitation pauses than introverts. In the public officials study there was a tendency for extraverted speakers to use more frequently pauses longer than 2 seconds. Moreover, the results reported should not be interpreted as indicating a configuration of cues, as no such configurations were ever measured.

It is a general weakness among the studies on personality and speech that the attribution or inference aspect usually is disregarded. There are only very few studies on attributions of extraversion from speech cues by naive listeners. The results available show that higher $F_0$ (Scherer, 1979b, juror study), higher variability of $F_0$ (for males only, Aronovitch, 1976; Addington, 1968), higher intensity (Scherer, 1978, juror study), fewer pauses (for females only, Aronovitch, 1976), and higher speech rate (Aronovitch, 1976) may all lead to attributions of extraversion to the speaker. As the results by Aronovitch show, there may be important sex differences in the attributions of personality traits from speech. As in the externalization domain there probably are rather strong cross-cultural differences in the attribution domain as well. The juror study showed a relationship between high $F_0$ as well as high vocal intensity and attributions of extraversion for American speakers only. In the public officials study German speakers with higher $F_0$ were in fact rated as less likeable, less friendly, and more aggressive (Scherer et al., 1979), characteristics blatantly contradicting attributions of extraversion.

As the earlier discussion of the origins of speech/personality relationships has shown, it is quite possible that self-presentation and self-fulfilling prophecy processes combined with cultural stereotypes about voice and personality may be among the determinants of observable correlations between voice and speech cues on the one hand and personality dispositions on the other. Thus, it would seem desirable to study jointly the expression of personality in voice with the impression listeners get from voice and speech in terms of personality. Scherer (1978, 1979b) has proposed the Brunswikian lens model as a promising paradigm for research in this area. According to this model, criteria, such as personality traits, are "externalized" via "distal cues" (i.e., observable and objectively measurable parameters in the behavior of the speaker). These objective distal cues are perceived by naive observers and yield "proximal cues" or subjective percepts of distal cues. Finally, cognitive inference processes (which are usually culturally shared) are used to arrive at an attribution based on those proximal cues.

Figure 6-1 (based on results from the juror study and reproduced from Scherer, 1978) shows such a lens model for the case of extraversion. This model shows why American listeners can accurately identify extraversion of a speaker (but not emotional stability, for

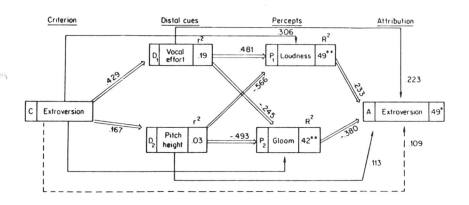

Fig. 6-1. Two-dimensional path analysis model for the extroversion inference. (From Personality inference from voice quality: The loud voice of extroversion. *European Journal of Social Psychology*, 1978, vol. 8, 467–487. Reprinted with permission of John Wiley and Sons.)

$^*p < .05$      $^{**}p < .01$

†The dashed line represents the direct path, the double line the postulated indirect paths, and the single lines the indirect paths compatible with the model. Coefficients shown are standardized coefficients except for $r_{CD_1}$ and $r_{CD_2}$ which are Pearson $rs$ (the direction shown is theoretically postulated). $R^2$s based on all predictors from which paths lead to the variable.

example) on the basis of content masked voice samples alone and why this is not true for German speakers (Scherer, 1972). The model allows to specify whether the lack of accurate judgment is due to a nonexistent externalization link between a personality trait and voice and speech cues, or to the failure of human listeners to correctly perceive the distal cues which may be related to a trait or to faulty inference rules of the listeners in attributing particular traits on the basis of voice cues. Path analysis models can be used to evaluate the success of the model quantitatively and to suggest improvements in terms of the voice and speech cues measured and used in the model (Scherer, 1975, 1978).

## CONCLUSION

Despite the scarcity of research and the considerable amount of conflicting evidence, there can be little doubt that the voice of a speaker and his speech behavior are related to his personality dispositions. Just which traits determine speech behavior most strongly and exactly how they influence the different voice and speech cues is largely unknown. Judging from the evidence provided by the empirical studies available in the literature, the relationship between extraversion and speech behavior seems to be well established. Extraverts, particularly in the United States, seem to speak with a louder voice and fewer hesitation pauses (to name but two cues for which there are data from several independent studies). Furthermore, extraversion seems to be one of the few traits that can be accurately judged by naive listeners on the basis of voice and speech cues alone (Scherer, 1979b; Siegman, 1978). It is possible that the reason for this association between extraversion and various speech cues is due not only to factors internal to the person but also to social, psychological, and cultural factors that guide the speech behavior of a person during social interaction. This may also be true for dominance, a behavior disposition which is equally relevant for interactive behavior. There is no consistent evidence so far, however, for this trait. Trait anxiety is another personality dimension which may be strongly manifested in speech behavior. Here, more internal, biophysical factors having to do with habitual arousal and excitability may be at the root of the speech/personality relationship. Even as far as anxiety is concerned, however, one cannot exclude social factors as possible determinants of the speech/personality relationship. Given the strong probability that social factors are involved, the lack of studies in which speech/personality correlations are studied under different situations is all the more deplorable. Given the conflicting evidence from many studies, it seems highly likely that situational constraints may strongly modify or even alter speech/personality relationships. Furthermore, the present evidence suggests that there may be strong sex differences as well as strong differences between speakers in different cultures.

Consequently, in addition to a need for improved methodological sophistication of voice and personality studies, new research paradigms are urgently needed. Scherer has stated:

> ... significant advances of our knowledge on personality marking in speech cannot be obtained by one shot single-culture studies with small groups of college undergraduates in rigged 'waiting room' encounters. In order to assess both the existence and power and the origins and functions of personality markers in speech, we have to embark on long term intercultural research programs utilizing natural speech samples from different social situations. ... such research programs should be guided by hypotheses based on theoretical considerations concerning both the externalization of personality dispositions as well as the inferential utilization of speech cues within an integrative model of marking. (Scherer, 1979b, p. 202)

One promising research paradigm is the Brunswikian lens model, as discussed in the last section. Obviously, studies utilizing this model are much more demanding and expensive than simple correlational studies. On the other hand, isolated and inconsistent results, as they are now found in the field, are of little use for either the accumulation of scientific knowledge or for applications in psychiatry and medicine.

REFERENCES

Addington, D. W. The relationship of selected vocal characteristics to personality perception. *Speech Monographs,* 1968, *35,* 492–503.

Argyle, M., Little, B. R. Do personality traits apply to social behavior? *Journal for the Theory of Social Behavior,* 1972, *2,* 1–35.

Aronovitch, C. D. The voice of personality: Stereotyped judgments and their relation to voice quality and sex of speaker. *Journal of Social Psychology,* 1976, *99,* 207–220.

Beekman, S. J. Sex differences in nonverbal behavior. Paper presented at the meeting of the American Psychological Association. Chicago, 1975.

Borgatta, E. F., Lambert, W. W. *Handbook of personality theory and research.* Chicago: Rand McNally, 1968.

Diehl, C. F. Voice and personality: An evaluation. In D. A. Barbara (Ed.), Psychological and psychiatric aspects of speech and hearing. Springfield, Ill.: C.C. Thomas, 1960.

Diehl, C. F., White, R., Burk, K. W. Voice quality and anxiety. *Journal of Speech and Hearing Research,* 1959, *2,* 282–285.

Endler, N. S., Magnusson, D. (Eds.). *Interactional psychology and personality.* Washington: Hemisphere Publ., 1976.

Eysenck, H. J. *The biological basis of personality.* Springfield, Ill.: Charles C. Thomas, 1967.

Eysenck, H. J., Eysenck, S. B. G. *Manual of the Eysenck Personality Inventory.* London: University of London Press, 1964.

Eysenck, H. J., Eysenck, S. B. G. *Personality structure and measurement.* London: Routledge & Kegan Paul, 1969.

Fährmann, R. Die Deutung des Sprechausdrucks. *Studien zur Einführung in die Praxis der charakterologischen Stimm- und Sprechanalyse.* Bonn: Bouvier & Co., 1960 (2 ed., 1967).

Feldstein, S., Welkowitz, J. A chronography of conversation: In defense of an objective approach. In A. W. Siegman and S. Feldstein (Eds.), *Nonverbal behavior and communication.* Hillsdale, N.J.: Erlbaum, 1978, pp. 329–378.

Gellhorn, E. The tuning of the nervous system: Physiological foundations and implications for behavior. *Perspectives in Biology and Medicine,* 1967, *10,* 559–591.

Görlitz, D. *Ergebnisse und Probleme der ausdruckspsychologischen Sprechstimmforschung.* Meisenheim: Hain, 1972.

Goldstein, I. B. Role of muscle tension in personality theory. *Psychological Bulletin,* 1964, *61,* 413–425.

Hall, C. S., Lindzey, G. *Theories of personality* (ed. 2). New York: John Wiley and Sons, 1970.

Harper, R. G., Wiens, A. N., Matarazzo, J. D. *Nonverbal communication: The state of the art.* New York: John Wiley and Sons, 1978.

Jaffe, J., Feldstein, S. *Rhythms of dialogue.* New York: Academic Press, 1970.

Kramer, E. Judgment of personal characteristics and emotions from nonverbal properties of speech. *Psychological Bulletin,* 1963, *60,* 408–420.

Kretschmer, E. Körperbau und Charakter. Berlin: Springer, 1921.

Laver, J. Individual features in voice quality. Unpublished Ph.D. thesis, University of Edinburgh, 1975.

Lenneberg, E. *Biological foundations of language.* New York: John Wiley and Sons, 1967.

London, H., Exner, J. E. *Dimensions of personality.* New York: John Wiley & Sons, 1978.

Maddi, S. R. *Personality theories: A comparative analysis.* Homewood, Ill.: Dorsey Press, 1968.

Mahl, G. F. Disturbances and silences in the patient's speech in psychotherapy. *Journal of Abnormal and Social Psychology,* 1956, *53,* 1–15.

Mallory E., Miller, V. A possible basis for the association of voice characteristics and personality traits. *Speech Monographs,* 1958, *25,* 255–260.

Matarazzo, J. D. The interview. In B. B. Wolman (Ed.), *Handbook of clinical psychology.* New York: McGraw-Hill, 1965, pp. 403–450.

Mead, G. H. *Mind, self, and society.* Chicago: University of Chicago Press, 1934.

Mischel, W. *Personality and assessment.* New York: John Wiley and Sons, 1968.

Mischel, W. *Introduction to personality.* New York: Holt, Rinehart & Winston, 1971.

Moore, G. E. Personality traits and voice quality deficiencies. *Journal of Speech Disorders,* 1939, *4,* 33–36.

Moses, P. J. *The voice of neurosis.* New York: Grune & Stratton, 1954.

Murray, D. C. Talk, silence, and anxiety. *Psychological Bulletin,* 1971, *75,* 244–260.

Murray, H. A. *Explorations in personality.* New York: Oxford University Press, 1938.

Pervin, L. A. *Personality: Theory, assessment and research.* New York: John Wiley and Sons, 1970.

Ramsay, R. W. Personality and speech. *Journal of Personality and Social Psychology,* 1966, *4,* 116–118.

Rochester, S. R. The significance of pauses in spontaneous speech. *Journal of Psycholinguistic Research,* 1973, *2,* 51–81.

Rudert, J. Vom Ausdruck der Sprechstimme. In R. Kirchhoff (Ed.), *Ausdruckspsychologie* (Vol. 5), *Handbuch der Psychologie,* Göttingen: Hogrefe 1965, pp. 422–468.

Sanford, F. H. Speech and personality. *Psychological Bulletin,* 1942, *39,* 811–845.

Scherer, K. R. Attribution of personality from voice: A cross-cultural study on dynamics of interpersonal perception. Unpublished Ph.D. thesis, Harvard University, 1970.

Scherer, K. R. Judging personality from voice: A cross-cultural approach to an old issue in interpersonal perception. *Journal of Personality,* 1972, *40,* 191–210.

Scherer, K. R. Persönlichkeit, Stimmqualität und Persönlichkeitsattribution: Pfadanalytische Untersuchungen zu nonverbalen Kommunikationsprozessen. In L. H. Eckensberger & U.S. Eckensberger (Eds.), *Bericht über den 28. Kongress der Deutschen Gesellschaft für Psychologie, Bd. 3.* Göttingen: Hogrefe, 1974, 61–73. (a)

Scherer, K. R. Voice quality analysis of American and German speakers. *Journal of Psycholinguistic Research,* 1974, *3,* 281–290. (b)

Scherer, K. R. The effect of stress on the fundamental frequency of the voice. Paper presented at the Acoustical Society of America Meeting, Miami, 1977. *Journal of the Acoustical Society of America,* 1977, *62,* Supplement No. 1, 25–26 (abstract).

Scherer, K. R. Inference rules in personality attribution from voice quality: The loud voice of extraversion. *European Journal of Social Psychology,* 1978, *8,* 467–487.

Scherer, K. R. Nonlinguistic vocal indicators of emotion and psychopathology. In C. E. Izard (Ed.), *Emotions in personality and psychopathology.* New York: Plenum, 1979, pp. 493–529. (a)

Scherer, K. R. Personality markers in speech. In K. R. Scherer and H. Giles

(Eds.), *Social markers in speech.* Cambridge: Cambridge University Press, 1979, pp. 147–209. (b)

Scherer, K. R. Voice and speech correlates of perceived social influence. In H. Giles and R. St. Clair (Eds.), *The social psychology of language.* London: Blackwell, 1979, pp. 88–120. (c)

Scherer, U., Scherer, K. R. Bürgernähe im Publikumsverkehr: Die Rolle des menschlichen Faktors in der Sozialplanung. In F. X. Kaufmann (Ed.), *Bürgernahe Gestaltung der sozialen Umwelt: Probleme und theoretische Perspektiven.* Meisenheim: Hain, 1977, pp. 237–272.

Scherer, K. R., Scherer, U., Klink, M. Determinanten des Verhaltens öffentlich Bediensteter im Publikumsverkehr. In F. X. Kaufmann (Ed.), *Bürgernahe Sozialpolitik.* Frankfurt: Campus Verlag, 1979, pp. 408–451.

Scherer, U., Scherer, K. R. Psychological factors in bureaucratic encounters: Determinants and effects of interactions between officials and clients. In W. T. Singleton, P. Spurgeon, and R. B. Stammers (Eds.), *The analysis of social skill.* New York: Plenum, 1980, pp. 315–328.

Sheldon, W. H. *Atlas of men: A guide for somatotyping the adult male at all ages.* New York: Harper and Row, 1954.

Siegman, A. W. The telltale voice: Nonverbal messages of verbal communication. In A. W. Siegman and S. Feldstein (Eds.), *Nonverbal behavior and communication.* Hillsdale, N.J.: Erlbaum, 1978, pp. 183–243.

Siegman, A. W., Pope, B. Effects of question specificity and anxiety producing messages on verbal fluency in the initial interview. *Journal of Personality and Social Psychology,* 1965, *2,* 522–530.

Trimboli, F. Changes in voice characteristics as a function of trait and state personality variables. *Dissertation Abstracts International,* 1973, *33* (8-B).

Trojan, F. *Biophonetik.* Zürich: Bibliographisches Institut, 1975.

Whitaker, H. H. Neurobiology of language. In E. C. Carterette and M. P. Friedman (Eds.), *Handbook of perception* (Vol. 3): *Language and speech.* New York: Academic Press, 1976, pp. 121–144.

Michael H. L. Hecker

# 7

# The Fährmann Inventory of Speech Characteristics (FISC)

The purpose of this chapter is to stimulate further research on a speech-assessment procedure that is largely unknown outside of Europe. Developed by Fährmann (1960) as an instrument of characterology, the procedure has been used for many years by European psychologists to make inferences about personality traits of speakers. Because the procedure is a general method of speech analysis, it is likely to have other important applications. In the field of behavioral medicine, for example, it may be valuable in diagnosing a behavior pattern that is associated with heart disease.

For convenience, the speech-assessment procedure will be referred to as the Fährmann Inventory of Speech Characteristics (FISC). Using the FISC involves only two persons, a subject and a trained listener. The subject speaks about a personal experience during a recorded informal interview. The listener rates the recorded speech sample in terms of 26 dimensions that are more or less independent of the spoken words. To perform this task correctly, the listener must be thoroughly familiar with the perceptual criteria that pertain to each dimension. The completed rating form provides a detailed description of the subject's speech characteristics.

The FISC may be compared with other auditory methods of speech analysis. Crystal and Quirk (1964) created a framework for studying the prosodic and paralinguistic features of speech. They regarded these features as having a personal component, which was physiologically determined for each speaker, and a conventional component, which had a communicative function. The personal component was of only peripheral interest. For the conventional component, 15 independent systems of feature classification were devised and illustrated. This method is most suitable for linguistic studies that are not concerned with speaker differences.

Voiers (1979) developed a method for exploring the perceptual dimensions used in discriminating among speakers. On the basis of an experimental screening of a large inventory of potential speech descriptors, 48 bipolar and 27 monopolar rating scales were selected. The bipolar scales were labeled at their endpoints with adjectives of opposite meaning. A group of listeners rated the speech of 80 adult males, and a factor analysis of the ratings indicated the presence of eight orthogonal dimensions. This finding has implications for measuring the degree to which speakers can be recognized over communication systems.

McDermott, Scagliola, and Goodman (1978) reported a similar method for describing the perceptual characteristics of processed speech. All speech samples were presented in pairs, and the listeners were asked to express the difference between the members of each pair with reference to a single rating scale. A multidimensional scaling technique was used to analyze the difference ratings. For the particular type of speech processing studied, the results revealed three perceptual characteristics that could be related to the coding parameters. This approach is especially valuable in designing new speech-processing systems.

## BACKGROUND

The design of the FISC evolved from a theory of expression formulated by Klages (1936). According to this theory, each movement of the body expresses some aspect of the personality of the individual. The interpretation of a complex movement, such as writing or speaking, depends on an evaluation of its rhythmic qualities. To facilitate this evaluation, the product of a complex movement, such as a written document or a speech recording, is described in terms of many dimensions. If a measurement of the product suggests that the underlying movement was restrained or forced, the measurement is classified as an indicator of contraction; if a measurement suggests that the underlying movement was spontaneous or free, the measurement is classified as an indicator of release. For example, one of the many dimensions used in the analysis of handwriting is the size of the writing. Small writing is an indication of a contraction tendency, while large writing is an indication of a release tendency.

Lewinson and Zubin (1942) extended this theory of expression by introducing a more detailed classification procedure. Instead of dichotomizing a measurement, these investigators classified it with reference to a 7-point scale. They used three levels of contraction, three levels of release, and an intermediate level of rhythmic balance that indicated neither contraction nor release tendencies. To increase the reliability of classifications, they provided specific criteria for each level of each dimension. This procedure was originally devised for a method of handwriting analysis. Later, it appeared in other characterological systems, including a method of speech analysis developed by Fährmann (1960).

Fährmann defined 33 perceptual dimensions of extemporaneous speech. Most of these dimensions were independent of the contents of a speech sample (e.g., *Loudness of Voice*); other dimensions required that the listener have some knowledge of the language being spoken (e.g., *Sentence Complexity*). For each dimension, the speech sample was rated on a 9-point scale that spanned the range from extreme contraction to extreme release. Reference recordings were provided to illustrate several points on this scale. The profile of ratings thus obtained was interpreted with the aid of a set of tables. Each speech pattern could be mapped into a unique personality configuration.

The FISC is an excerpt from the method of speech analysis developed by Fährmann. In the interest of a more compact procedure, this author excluded all dimensions that require an evaluation of the linguistic structure of an utterance. The criteria given for these dimensions seemed to depend on conventions of the German language, and their applicability to spoken English was therefore questioned. The interpretive tables were also excluded, because they have never been validated in carefully controlled experiments. What remains is the most valuable component of the method: a practical and efficient instrument for describing the speech characteristics of an individual.

## ADMINISTRATION AND SCORING OF THE FISC

An informal interview is the most convenient vehicle for obtaining a high-quality speech recording of a particular subject. The interview should have a secondary purpose that can be used to draw the subject's attention away from the microphone and tape recorder. While the topic to be discussed is a matter of choice, the style of the interviewer should be relaxed and emotionally supportive. After the subject has answered a number of preliminary questions, he or she is asked to relate a personal experience that would illustrate an earlier statement. For example, a male subject who says that he enjoys traveling with his family might be asked to describe his most joyful trip. After the subject begins, the interviewer comments only as is necessary to provide a speech sample of about five minutes duration.

The recording equipment should be of professional quality. An electret condensor microphone that can be fastened to the subject's clothing is recommended; this type of microphone has excellent response characteristics, and it is unobtrusive. Either an open-reel or a cassette tape recorder can be used, but the machine should allow manual control of the record level. The automatic gain control circuits built into many cassette tape recorders produce undesirable level changes, especially when the speech is not fluent.

To evaluate a recorded speech sample, the tape should be played back over a high-fidelity loudspeaker system. A good location for the loudspeaker system is a corner of a quiet room. The listener, who sits approximately ten feet in front of the loudspeaker system, gradually increases the playback level until he or she has the auditory impression that the recorded subject is physically present. Earphones are not recommended, because they produce a sound image in the center of the head; there is no perception of the distance that normally separates a listener from a speaker.

The training of the listener is a critical factor in the evaluation process. It is not sufficient for the listener to know the definition of each dimension of the FISC and to understand the underlying theoretical considerations. He or she must also be versant in using the perceptual criteria that apply to each dimension. The listener's ability to classify a speech characteristic with reference to a graded continuum can be developed through instruction and practice. In training this author, Fährmann evaluated several speech recordings that have since been used to train other listeners. Training should be continued until independent ratings by the teacher and the student are highly correlated.

During the playback of a recording, the listener rates the subject's speech in terms of the 26 dimensions of the FISC. The rating form used for this purpose is shown in Figure 7-1. Sixteen dimensions are rated with reference to a 9-point scale that extends from A4 (left-hand margin) through 0 (center) to B4 (right-hand margin). The endpoints of this scale represent extreme levels of contraction and release, and the midpoint represents a level of rhythmic balance. Ten dimensions are rated with reference to a 5-point scale that extends either from A4 to 0 or from 0 to B4. In these cases, A2 and B2 represent levels of rhythmic balance. The names of the dimensions and their designations on the rating form are given in Table 7-1.

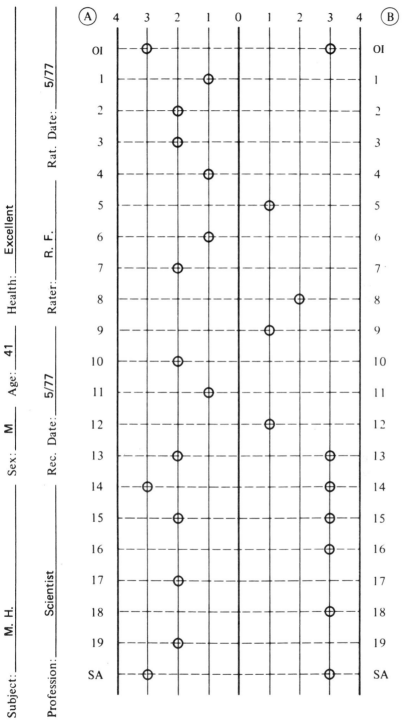

Fig. 7-1. A completed rating form describing the speech of Subject M. H.

141

**Table 7-1.**
Names and designations of the 26 dimensions of the FISC.

| Name of Dimension | Designation |
|---|---|
| Overall Impression | |
| *Expressive Strength* | OI/A |
| *Verbal Urgency* | OI/B |
| | |
| *Vocal Pitch* | 1 |
| *Loudness of Voice* | 2 |
| *Volume of Voice* | 3 |
| | |
| Timbre: *Dark-Light* | 4 |
| Timbre: *Colorful-Dull* | 5 |
| Timbre: *Warm-Cold* | 6 |
| Timbre: *Delicate-Empty* | 7 |
| | |
| *Syllabic Rate* | 8 |
| | |
| Rhythmics: *Regularity* | 9 |
| Rhythmics: *Flow* | 10 |
| Rhythmics: *Phase* | 11 |
| Rhythmics: *Tension* | 12 |
| | |
| Accentuation: *Intonation* | |
| *Range of Variability* | 13/A |
| *Frequency of Occurrence* | 13/B |
| Accentuation: *Variation in Loudness* | |
| *Range of Variability* | 14/A |
| *Frequency of Occurrence* | 14/B |
| Accentuation: *Variation in Syllabic Rate* | |
| *Range of Variability* | 15/A |
| *Frequency of Occurrence* | 15/B |
| | |
| Articulation: *Precision* | 16 |
| Articulation: *Vocalic-Consonantal* | 17 |
| | |
| Style: *Emotional-Intellectual* | 18 |
| Style: *Dialogical-Monological* | 19 |
| | |
| Summary Assessment | |
| *Speech Dynamics* | SA/A |
| *Total Quality Level* | SA/B |

## DIMENSIONS OF THE FISC

The following descriptions of the 26 dimensions of the FISC are intended solely to orient the reader. Without suitable reference recordings that illustrate the dimensions perceptually, these descriptions cannot be used to train listeners.

Two dimensions preserve the listener's overall impression of the speech sample. *Expressive Strength* is primarily a measure of the subject's rhetorical skill and confidence, but it also takes into account other factors such as the fullness of the subject's voice. *Verbal Urgency* is a measure of how much the subject is driven to be active as a speaker. Inhibited subjects speak only when absolutely necessary; talkative subjects are compelled to speak even if they have little or nothing to say.

Two dimensions are basic measures of phonation. *Vocal Pitch* is the lowest pitch of the subject's natural speaking voice. It is most easily assessed near the end of a sentence, where the pitch drops to a unique resting level. This dimension is sometimes specified with reference to the musical scale. *Loudness of Voice* can be assessed even if the level at which the speech sample is played back is not exactly the same as the level at which the subject spoke during the interview. The listener relies on certain voice qualities that are associated with loudness in the face-to-face situation. Very loud voices tend to sound forceful and strained, while very soft voices tend to sound weak and fragile.

One dimension gauges the fullness and carrying power of the subject's voice. *Volume of Voice* depends on the degree to which the subject's body reinforces the acoustic signal generated in the larynx. Large voices, also called chest voices, sound full and can be heard over great distances. Small voices, also called head voices, sound thin and do not carry well.

Four dimensions are measures of the timbre or coloration of the subject's voice. *Dark-Light* depends on how long the glottis is closed during each period of vocal-fold vibration. Incomplete or momentary glottal closure is observed in voices that are deficient in high-frequency energy; such voices sound dark or muffled. Extended glottal closure is observed in voices that are rich in high-frequency energy; such voices sound light or crisp. *Colorful-Dull* presumably reflects the habitual state of contraction of the muscles supporting the larynx. Voices produced with minimal muscular contraction sound colorful, bright, or clear. Voices produced with maximal muscular contraction sound dull, rough, covered, or veiled. *Warm-Cold* makes a distinction between voices that sound warm, soft, or melodious and voices that sound cold, hard, sharp, shrill, or cutting. Many physiological factors are associated with this measure. *Delicate-Empty* applies primarily to voices that have a small volume. Some of these voices sound delicate or loosened, while others sound empty, withered, wiry, or pointed.

One dimension is used to specify how rapidly the subject is speaking. *Syllabic Rate* is an estimate of the average number of syllables produced per minute. Such an estimate can be obtained in several ways. Fährmann recommends counting the syllables spoken in five 1-minute segments that are free of major pauses and dividing the sum by five.

Four dimensions concern the rhythm of the subject's speech. *Regularity* is influenced by the subject's memory and thought patterns. Rigidly timed speech has a uniform temporal quality; it sounds as though the subject were reading from a script. Poorly timed speech contains many pauses where the subject searches for a proper word or thinks about the next sentence. *Flow* is influenced by the subject's emotional disposition. Lively, uninhibited speech appears to be always in motion, even if the syllabic rate is low. Lifeless, inhibited speech contains many interruptions where the subject is overcome by anxiety or other emotions. *Phase* is primarily a measure of how much speech the subject produces on a single breath. In long-phased speech, the typical breath group consists of a complete phrase or sentence. In short-phased speech, the typical breath group consists of a few words. *Tension* reflects the subject's compliance with the conventions of syllabic stress. In relaxed speech, each multisyllabic word carries the prescribed stress pattern; some syllables are stressed while others are clearly unstressed. In tense speech, all syllables appear to be stressed equally.

The listener must consider three kinds of accentuation or selective emphasis in the speech sample: *Intonation* (variation in pitch), *Variation in Loudness,* and *Variation in Syllabic Rate.* For each kind of accentuation, the perceived changes are described in terms of two dimensions. *Range of Variability* is used to indicate the magnitude of the largest changes, and *Frequency of Occurrence* is used to indicate how often large changes occur. *Intonation* includes all temporary departures from the average pitch of the subject's voice. Speech with large pitch changes sounds melodious and lively, especially if the changes occur relatively often, while speech with small pitch changes sounds monotone. *Variation in Loudness* can be a gradual phenomenon (e.g., the subject neglects the final words of a sentence) or a sudden event (e.g., the subject explosively emphasizes a single word). Speech with large loudness changes sounds dynamic, while speech with small loudness changes sounds flat. *Variation in Syllabic Rate* includes all temporary departures from the average speaking rate of the subject. Speech with large and frequent changes in syllabic rate sounds somewhat like a roller coaster.

Two dimensions relate to the articulation or pronunciation of the subject. *Precision* depends on how much control the subject exercises in varying the shape of the vocal tract during speech production. Neglected speech is often hard to understand, while distinct speech is highly intelligible. *Vocalic-Consonantal* refers to the relative emphasis of vowels and consonants in the subject's speech. Vocalic speech is characterized by its prolonged vowels; it has a legato quality. Consonantal speech is characterized by its reduced vowels and exaggerated consonants; it has a staccato quality.

Two dimensions are measures of the speaking style of the subject. *Emotional-Intellectual* reflects the extent to which the subject is in touch with his or her feelings. Emotional speech gives the impression that the subject is reliving the personal experience rather than just describing it. Intellectual speech gives the impression that the subject is detached from any feelings. *Dialogical-Monological* focuses on the communicative function of the subject's speech. Dialogical speech gives the impression that the subject is reaching out to engage the interest of another person, the interviewer. Monological speech gives the impression that the subject is speaking only to himself or herself.

Two dimensions describe the listener's summary assessment of the speech sample. *Speech Dynamics* is a weighted measure of the volume and loudness of the subject's voice, the strength of each kind of accentuation, and the precision of the articulation. *Total Quality Level* combines *Speech Dynamics* with estimates of the genuineness and individuality of the subject's speech.

## DISTRIBUTIONS OF RATINGS
## AND INTERLISTENER AGREEMENT

The FISC has been used in a preliminary study of the relationship between speech behavior and personality variables. This study provided an opportunity to examine frequency distributions of ratings obtained with the FISC and measurements of interlistener agreement. The author and a research assistant, who was being trained by the author, served as listeners. To facilitate learning, the listeners first collaborated on a restricted evaluation of the speech of 100 subjects. Eight dimensions of the FISC were randomly selected for this task: *Verbal Urgency, Loudness of Voice, Warm-Cold, Syllabic Rate, Regularity, Flow, Precision,* and *Dialogical-Monological.* For each speech sample, the listeners discussed their perceptions regarding these dimensions and agreed on eight joint ratings.

Later, the listeners worked independently. They evaluated the speech of 36 additional subjects in terms of the same dimensions. However, the author no longer rated speech samples with respect to *Syllabic Rate*. This dimension was assessed by means of a well-defined procedure that had already been mastered by the research assistant. The procedure entailed marking off twenty 6-second intervals of continuous speech, transcribing the words spoken in each interval, and computing the average speaking rate in syllables per minute.

The eight frequency distributions of the joint ratings are shown in Figure 7-2. *Verbal Urgency* was rated with reference to a 9-point scale that extended from 0 to B4; the other dimensions were rated with reference to a 17-point scale that extended from A4 to B4. In gen-

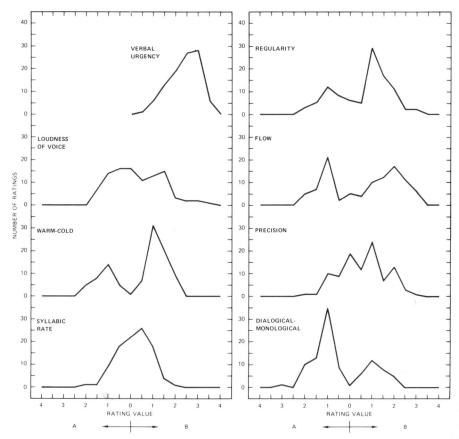

Fig. 7–2. Frequency distributions of ratings for eight dimensions of the FISC

eral, considering that each dimension is assumed to be a normally distributed variable and that 100 subjects cannot represent all possible speech characteristics, the distributions of the joint ratings do not appear to be unreasonable. For *Verbal Urgency, Loudness of Voice, Syllabic Rate,* and *Precision,* the distributions exhibit a major peak near the midpoint of the scale, as is expected. For *Warm-Cold, Regularity, Flow,* and *Dialogical-Monological,* the distributions are more bimodal, which suggests that the author may have overemphasized the dichotomous nature of these dimensions.

To measure interlistener agreement, Pearson product-moment correlation coefficients were computed from the independent ratings (Hays, 1963). No correlation coefficient could be computed for *Syllabic Rate* because the author did not use this dimension in evaluating the speech of the last 36 subjects. The highest level of interlistener agreement, 0.80, was obtained for *Verbal Urgency.* Apparently, the perceptual criteria underlying this dimension are relatively easy to convey in a training program. For the other dimensions, the following levels of interlistener agreement were obtained: *Loudness of Voice,* 0.62; *Warm-Cold,* 0.67; *Regularity,* 0.43; *Flow,* 0.53; *Precision,* 0.57; and *Dialogical-Monological,* 0.37. These six dimensions clearly require more intensive training than was provided in this study.

In a training situation, if the teacher is experienced in using the FISC, poor interlistener agreement means that the student must receive further instruction. Being a subjective instrument, the FISC has an upper limit with respect to interlistener agreement, but most of the results presented here are considered to fall short of this limit. The achievement of uniformly high levels of interlistener agreement is a prerequisite for any comparison between related studies involving different listeners.

## POTENTIAL APPLICATIONS

The FISC has potential applications in speech science, psychology, behavioral medicine, psychiatry, and many other fields. There is much speculation about possible relationships between speech behavior and various measurable criteria, including personality traits, emotional states, vocal deception, occupational stress, organic diseases, and psychopathologies. Because the FISC was designed to provide a comprehensive description of speech behavior, it may be suitable for examining such relationships in experimental studies.

Most applications envisioned for the FISC are composed of two consecutive steps. The first step is exploratory in nature; the FISC is used to determine which aspects of speech behavior are related to the criterion variable. Many speech samples representing at least two levels of the criterion variable are evaluated with respect to all 26 dimensions. The second step is diagnostic in nature; the FISC is used to predict the level of the criterion variable from the speech behavior of a single subject. Here, one speech sample is evaluated with respect to a few dimensions that are known to have predictive strength.

As mentioned earlier, the author has studied the relationship between speech behavior and personality traits. Speech samples obtained from 100 subjects were evaluated with respect to eight dimensions of the FISC. All subjects took a standard intelligence test, which was used to implement a personality model described by Winne and Gittinger (1973); a subject scored either high or low on each of ten personality dimensions. Each speech dimension was divided into a lower segment, a middle segment, and an upper segment. For each segment, a search was made for personality patterns that differentiated the subjects included in the segment from the remaining subjects. The proportion of subjects included in the segment was calculated and graphed for various combinations of these personality patterns.

This study produced inconclusive results because of the small number of subjects involved. It would be inappropriate to describe the results in detail, but a few general comments may be of value to investigators who wish to design a more definitive study. The relationship between a given speech dimension and a given personality dimension typically depended on the levels of at least two other personality dimensions. For example, *Verbal Urgency* and *Activity Level* (a personality dimension) were directly related for subjects who scored high on both *Externalized-Internalized* and *Flexible-Regulated,* but they were inversely related for subjects who scored low on either *Externalized-Internalized* or *Flexible-Regulated.* To examine relationships of this kind more thoroughly, speech and personality data from several thousand subjects must be available for analysis.

Another potential application of the FISC is in the assessment of coronary-prone behavior. So-called Type A behavior is characterized by excessive amounts of ambition, competitiveness, hostility, and impatience, which are evoked by environmental circumstances; Type B behavior is characterized by the relative absence of these features. In a major prospective epidemiologic study, Type A behavior was found to be a significant risk factor for coronary heart disease (Rosenman, Brand, Sholtz, et al., 1976). The assessment of Type A behavior involves a structured interview in which the subject is asked many challenging questions. On the basis of an integrated impression of the various behaviors reported and exhibited by the subject during the interview, a judge assigns the subject to one of five classes. The criteria underlying these global assessments are not well defined, and inter-judge agreement tends to be poor.

One objective of current research in this area is a more systematic procedure for assessing the subject's behavior in the interview. Concentrating on the subject's speech behavior appears to be a promising approach. Schucker and Jacobs (1977) demonstrated that simple measures of loudness, dynamic emphasis, and speaking rate account for much of the variance in global assessments. Other investigators studying different aspects of the subject's speech behavior obtained similar results. To provide a unified assessment procedure, the author developed a speech-rating method that included six dimensions of the FISC: *Loudness of Voice, Variation in Loudness, Syllabic Rate, Variation in Syllabic Rate, Vocalic-Consonantal,* and *Warm-Cold.* The method was used to describe the speech behavior of 84 subjects who had received global assessments from three judges.

A linear discriminant analysis of these data is in progress. For each subject, the speech ratings pertaining to the different dimensions are weighted and combined into a single discriminant score. If most subjects are classified correctly on the basis of their discriminant scores, it can be argued that speech ratings should replace global assessments as measures of coronary-prone behavior.

## REFERENCES

Crystal, D., and Quirk, R., *Systems of prosodic and paralinguistic features in english.* The Hague: Mouton & Co., 1964.

Fährmann, R., *Die Deutung des Sprechausdrucks.* Bonn: Bouvier u. Co., 1960, 2nd ed., 1967.

Hays, W. L., *Statistics for psychologists.* New York: Holt, Rinehart and Winston, 1963.

Klages, L., *Grundlegung der Wissenschaft vom Ausdruck.* Leipzig: Barth, 1936.

Lewinson, T. S., and Zubin, J., *Handwriting analysis.* New York: King's Crown Press, 1942.

McDermott, B., Scagliola, C., and Goodman, D., Perceptual and objective evaluation of speech processed by adaptive differential PCM. *Bell System Tech. J.,* 1978, *57,* No. 5, 1597–1618.

Rosenman, R. H., Brand, R. J., Sholtz, R. I., et al., Multivariate prediction of coronary heart disease during 8.5 year follow-up in the Western Collaborative Group Study. *Am. J. Cardiology,* 1976, *37,* 903–910.

Schucker, B., and Jacobs, Jr., D. R., Assessment of behavioral risk for coronary disease by voice characteristics. *Psychosomatic Medicine,* 1977, *39,* No. 4, 219–228.

Voiers, W. D., Toward the development of practical methods of evaluating speaker recognizability. *Record of 1979 IEEE Intern. Conf. on Acoustics, Speech, and Signal Processing.* New York: Inst. Electrical and Electronics Eng., 1979.

Winne, J. F., and Gittinger, J. W., An introduction to the Personality Assessment System. *J. Clinical Psychology,* 1973, Monograph Suppl. No. 38.

Laura N. Rice
Conrad J. Koke

# 8
# Vocal Style and the Process
# of Psychotherapy

Experienced and innovative clinicians have long been aware of the significance of voice in the therapeutic process. Sullivan, for example, described himself as an "aural" therapist and was convinced that by listening to vocal cues alone he could "hear" all of the potentially significant information in a therapeutic interview. Attending to the vocal but nonverbal aspects of a patient's communication appeared to serve at least two purposes for Sullivan. First of all such attention served a diagnostic function. It allowed Sullivan to make formulations of his patients' characteristic interpersonal styles and problem behaviors in a relatively short period of time (Sullivan, 1954). Secondly, Sullivan viewed vocal cues as indicating possible intervention points for the therapist. He noted that, "tonal variations in the voice . . . are frequently wonderfully dependable clues to shifts in the communicative situation" (Sullivan, 1954, pp. 6,7).

Moses in *The Voice of Neurosis* argued that "voice is the primary experession of the individual, and even through voice alone the neurotic patterns can be discovered" (1954, p.1). Moses described what he considered to be the primary dimensions of voice (as revealed by acoustical research) and then attempted to use these dimensions to analyze both normal and neurotic voice. Unfortunately, although Moses provided some important hypotheses concerning the relationship between personality, voice, and psychotherapy, the impact of his ideas on therapists in general has been rather limited.

Another clinician who was particularly interested in the relationship between vocal phenomena and therapy was the noted analyst

Frieda Fromm-Reichmann. She spent the last year of her life at the Center for Advanced Study in the Behavioral Sciences and was instrumental in the development and application to therapy of two areas of communication analysis previously neglected by linguists and psychiatrists alike: paralinguistics and kinesics. Bateson (1958) vividly describes Fromm-Reichmann's search for the actual nonverbal cues underlying her own clinical sensitivity.

Skilled clinicians have clearly recognized their own reliance on vocal cues in both diagnosis and intervention, have generated a number of provocative hypotheses, and have initiated the process of systematic investigation. For the past 20 years investigators from a number of different disciplines, using a variety of different approaches, have continued the task of making accurate descriptions of vocal phenomena and have attempted to verify scientifically their significance in the context of psychotherapy. The present chapter will discuss the approach used in one such research program, will describe in some detail the Client Vocal Quality Classification System (CVQ), and will report the findings from the System's use in a variety of psychotherapy research investigations.

## RESEARCH PROGRAM AT THE
## UNIVERSITY OF CHICAGO

In 1960 Butler, Rice, and Wagstaff, at the University of Chicago Counseling and Psychotherapy Research Center, began a series of studies designed to identify significant patterns of client and therapist process in client-centered therapy and to link these patterns to pretherapy measures of prognosis and post-therapy measures of outcome.* Underlying the design of this research program were some assumptions about the active ingredients in psychotherapy. The primary assumption was that the impact of therapy could probably be best understood not by studying the specific topics discussed or affects experienced, but by studying the style of participation of client and therapist. It was hypothesized that clients who could readily turn, inward (thus getting in touch with the edges of their own inner experience) would have a good prognosis for psychotherapy. Poor prognosis clients, on the other hand, would be those who engaged in the therapy process in ways that would constrict their own inner experiencing. Futhermore this constricted client process would probably have a dampening effect on the therapist's own style, making him or her less

*Their work was supported by Research Grant MH 4609 from the National Institute of Mental Health, U. S. Public Health Service.

expressive, thus further constricting the client's style. Therefore it was concluded that an attempt should be made to construct classification systems that would be maximally sensitive to stylistic variations in the therapeutic interchanges.

As Rice and Wagstaff began constructing category systems for classifying and quantifying some of the stylistic aspects of client and therapist process, they realized immediately that, in order to capture the essential aspects of therapeutic interchanges, they would have to assess vocal phenomena as well as the purely lexical aspects of speech. Consequently they constructed the Client Vocal Quality system (to be reviewed in this chapter), as well as a parallel but different therapist system (as described in Rice, 1965). They also made four strategy decisions in an attempt to achieve simplification, objectivity, and quantification, without loss of clinical significance.

First, in keeping with the basic assumptions of the study, the decision was made to focus on style rather than content. The question asked was not *what* is being said, but *how* is it being said and *how* is the client engaged in the process? This strategy is in contrast to the frequently used approach of selecting some clinically significant affective state, such as depression (Feldstein, 1964; Pope, Blass, Siegman, et al., 1970; Aronson and Weintraub, 1972) or anxiety (Mahl, 1956, 1961; Siegman, 1978), and attempting to specify the relevant vocal correlates by asking the question: "How do we recognize this affect from the voice?" This shift in focus allows us to simplify the enormous complexity of constructing a vocal taxonomy of different feelings, meanings, and interpersonal acts. If one can select a limited number of styles on the basis of some clinically meaningful criteria, the resulting classification should achieve simplification without undue loss of clinical significance. With a limited number of subclasses (styles) one can move beyond the purely descriptive level and quantify the findings by using the number (or proportion) of client responses in a given segment that fall within each subclass.

The second strategy decision was that each style (subclass) should be described by means of *patterns* of vocal behavior rather than by single aspects. Studies of separate speech features, such as filled and unfilled pauses, speech latency, and pitch contours, have provided some provocative findings. However, since a specific vocal sign can have quite different significance in different contexts, the assigning of clinical meaning to such signs usually involves questionable inferential leaps. As Labov and Fanshel have pointed out: "There is still no agreement on the categorization of paralinguistic cues, and linguists still find it difficult to deal with the multiple ambiguity these signals show in isolation." (1977, p.29). The basic advantage of using patterns defined by the joint occurrence of a number of vocal aspects is that the meaning of any one sign, such as a pitch contour, is evaluated in the context of the other features defining this particular pattern.

The third strategy decision involved the assumption that the vocal channel is a particularly sensitive index of the manner in which attentional energy is being regulated and deployed at any given time. It is generally agreed that the voice is a vehicle for expressing extra-linguistic interpersonal messages. A number of studies in speech production, however, have suggested that the vocal channel may also reflect the nature of the cognitive processes in which the individual is engaged at that point. It seems evident that productive psychotherapy involves not only appropriate interpersonal processes but also such intrapersonal processes as scanning one's own inner awareness, attempting to symbolize it accurately in words, and making relevant differentiations and integrations among inner states. Thus, vocal patterns in therapy may be sensitive indicators of the way in which energy and attention are being deployed in cognitive, affective, and interpersonal tasks.

The fourth strategy decision was to make use of expert clinical judgment at the very beginning of the research process, in locating what seemed to be meaningful patterns and then in describing these patterns in terms of objectively discernible features. This is the reverse of the strategy used by Pittinger, Hockett, and Danehy (1960), who started with detailed microscopic linguistic and paralinguistic transcription, from which they then made interpretations involving high levels of clinical inference.

Experienced therapists were asked to tape record interviews, or parts of interviews, and to characterize each segment in such general terms as "good session," "poor session," "difficult client," "frustrating client," "productive work," and so forth. Then these segments were intensively listened to by the investigators in order to isolate the vocal patterns that seemed to characterize "good" or "poor" segments. Once tentatively isolated, these vocal patterns were then broken down into the discriminable aspects that seemed to characterize them most clearly. Further tests were then applied to ensure that these patterns could be reliably rated by independent raters.

## THE CLIENT VOCAL QUALITY
## CLASSIFICATION SYSTEM

The Client Vocal Quality System (CVQ) contains four mutually exclusive classes that form a nominal (not ordinal) measure. Any client utterance of a few words or more can be identified as fitting one of the four patterns. The raters typically use audio tapes without transcripts. Content is not removed by filtering, or any other method of removing intelligibility, because the system depends on judging vocal patterns in relation to the usual accentual patterns for a given syntax. Raters are instructed to ignore content, however, and it is typically found that experienced raters are unable to remember content from moment to moment. In order to orient the reader, general descriptions of the four patterns are given here. Raters are *not* given these descriptions, but are trained to rate on the basis of six aspects that can be discriminated with reasonable objectivity.

### Clinical Descriptions

1. *Focused.* This vocal style seems to involve a turning inward of attentional energy, deployed toward tracking inner experience and finding a way to symbolize it in words. The effort to symbolize seems to be as much for oneself as for the listener, with little energy being directed outward toward the listener. There is often a quality of groping and hesitation. This is different from the nonfluency of thought disruption, since it has the pondering quality of moving into new territory, of generating new facets of experience.

2. *Externalizing.* This vocal style seems to involve a deployment of attentional energy outward in an effort to produce some effect in the outside world. The vocal pattern has a pre-monitored quality, suggesting that energy is being invested in recounting, rather than in exploration, and that the content is *not* being newly experienced and symbolized. Although the high energy and wide pitch range may give an impression of color and expressiveness, the rhythmic intonation pattern conveys a "talking at" quality.

3. *Limited.* This vocal pattern seems to involve the holding back or withdrawal of energy. There is a thin, "walking-on-eggs" quality, a distance from what is being said and probably from what is being experienced.

4. *Emotional.* The main distinguishing feature of this pattern is a disruption of the speech pattern. Different emotions take different forms, but the utterance is not placed in this class unless the overflow of emotion distorts or disrupts the ongoing pattern.

### The Six Discriminable Aspects of Vocal Patterns

The raters learn to discriminate patterns on the basis of the following six aspects (features). The aspects are not wholly independent, and not all of them are relevant to each pattern.

1. *Production of Accents.* Accentuation is usually produced by some combination of three shifts: increase in loudness, rise in pitch, and lengthening of the syllable (drawl). Raters should note whether accents are achieved primarily by pitch rise or primarily by increased loudness with some drawl.
2. *Accentuation Patterns.* In some utterances one can notice a regular emphasis pattern. This is not usually pronounced enough to distort the intended meaning, but it does give a subtle effect of a regular beat or cadence. In other utterances the emphasis pattern may be even more irregular than is usual for English, with two or more heavily accented syllables in a single clause, sometimes even on adjoining syllables.
3. *Regularity of Pace.* The pace of speech may be slow or fast, but in either case there may be considerable variation within a given utterance, with one group of words spoken slowly followed by a few spoken faster, and so on. This variation may be caused by the speed with which the actual words are spoken and/or by the pauses between words.
4. *Terminal Contours.* On the last syllable of a clause the pitch can rise, drop, remain level, slide from high to low, or form a U shape. These contours are often used to modify the import of what is being said or to mark off and emphasize the syntactical structure. It is difficult to state precise rules for judging this because of varying structure. The important judgment to make, however, is whether the contours tend to accentuate the meaning or structure of the clause in a speech-making way or whether they tend to give the intonation pattern a more ragged and unexpected sound.
5. *Perceived Energy.** Judgment of this aspect involves more than simple loudness. This is a complex judgment involving at least two decisions. First it is necessary to decide whether the voice in a particular utterance sounds reasonably full or whether the impression is one of thinness, with the voice not resting on its own natural platform. The second decision is related to this and involves a judgment of the "push" or force in the voice. Thus, an utterance that is somewhat above the natural platform will sound *Limited* if there is little push in the voice, while more push will take it out of the limited category. On the other hand, when the voice is resting on its own platform, it can be quite soft and still have adequate perceived energy.

---

*"Perceived Energy" is probably questionable terminology from the standpoint of acoustic phonetics. We are attempting to avoid the terminological confusion surrounding such concepts as timbre, voice quality, etc. (Crystal, 1969), by using descriptive terms that would be meaningful to relatively inexperienced raters.

6. *Disruption of Speech Pattern.* The decision to make is whether or not the regular speech pattern is being disrupted or seriously distorted by emotional overflow. If the pattern is not disrupted, the segment is not rated emotional.

### The Four Vocal Patterns

Figure 8-1 summarizes the aspects that distinguish the four patterns. The raters are given a training manual, containing detailed specifications with taped examples of the different patterns, and a summary chart of the distinguishing features. (Rice, Koke, Greenberg, et al., 1979).

### Interrater Reliability

Rank order correlations between pairs of raters for interview segments are approximately .70 for *Focused*, .75 for *Externalizing*, and .79 for *Limited*. The appearance of *Emotional* in the samples used was too infrequent to permit adequate estimates of reliability. Reliability issues are discussed in detail in the CVQ Manual (Rice, Koke, Greenberg, et al., 1979).

### RESEARCH ON CLIENT VOCAL QUALITY

Research with the CVQ has taken three related but rather different directions. Findings in each of these areas are summarized briefly below.

### Vocal Style and Psychotherapy Outcome

The first line of research concerned relationships between the different vocal styles and the outcome of psychotherapy. Results of two studies involving client-centered (Rogerian) therapy have supported the idea that clients using the *Focused* style are engaged in a productive therapy process. The amount of *Focused* voice in first and second interviews was significantly related to favourableness of outcome, assessed from both client's and therapist's perspectives (Butler, Rice, and Wagstaff, 1962; Rice and Wagstaff, 1967). Studying predictors of therapist's outcome ratings in psychoanalytically oriented therapy, Sarnat (1976) found a positive correlation between the amount of *Focused* voice in the first interview and the therapist's outcome rating, but the correlation was significant only when the number of sessions was held constant. She concluded that *Focused* voice and number of sessions used together provided one of the best predictors of outcome.

**Table 8-1**
The Four Vocal Patterns

| Aspects | Focused | Externalizing | Limited | Emotional |
|---|---|---|---|---|
| Production of accents | Achieved with loudness and/or drawl more than pitch rise | Achieved with pitch more than loudness or drawl | Usual balance for English | Not applicable |
| Accentuation pattern | Irregular | Extremely regular | Usual pattern for English | Usually irregular |
| Regularity of pace | Uneven; usually slowed but may be speeded patches | Even pace | Neither markedly even nor uneven | Usually uneven |
| Terminal contours | Ragged and unexpected | Highly expected in relation to the structure of what is said. | Direction about as usual, but energy tends to peter out, yielding a breathy quality | Unexpected |
| Perceived energy | Moderate to high; voice may be soft but on platform | Moderate to high; may be a bit above platform but adequate push | Voice not resting on own platform; inadequate push | Not applicable |
| Disruption of speech pattern | No | No | No | Yes |

(Reproduced with permission from Laura N. Rice)

The *Externalizing* vocal style appears to be a relatively unproductive mode of engaging in client-centered therapy. Butler, Rice, and Wagstaff (1962) found a significant negative relationship between amount of *Externalizing* voice and outcome as rated by both client and therapist. In a later more detailed study on a much larger sample, Rice and Wagstaff (1967) divided the sample into five groups: (1) successful from both therapist's and client's perspective; (2) successful from therapist's perspective but not from the client's; (3) successful from client's perspective but not from the therapist's; (4) unsuccessful from both perspectives; and (5) early attrition. Groups 3 and 5 showed extremely high concentrations of *Externalizing* voice. In fact almost none of the clients' statements fell in the other three styles. There was some subjective but rather suggestive evidence that some of the clients' self-change ratings in Group 3 were defensively motivated. Nothing is yet known about relationships between *Externalizing* voice and other therapeutic orientations.

The *Limited* vocal style also appears to be an unproductive mode in client-centered therapy, but in a different way from *Externalizing*. In the study just described, the clients with high concentrations of *Limited* voice fell primarily into Group 4, the clearly unsuccessful group. In contrasting the *Externalizing* and *Limited* vocal styles, one could infer that clients using the former seem to cope actively with the pressures of the therapy situation, either by quitting after two or three sessions or by completing at least ten sessions and maintaining at the close of it that favorable change had taken place. The clients with a *Limited* style on the other hand remained in therapy, continued to see themselves in a rather unfavorable light, and were seen by their therapists as having changed very little.

The appearance of an *Emotional* voice in samples studied was too infrequent to permit statistical prediction of outcome; however, combining *Emotional* with *Focused* segments somewhat improved the prediction for *Focused*.

We conclude that the evidence for relationships between vocal style and therapeutic outcome in client-centered therapy is substantial. The evidence for relationships with outcome in psychoanalytically oriented therapy is suggestive but needs further confirmation. Inasmuch as we are making the assumption that different therapeutic orientations make somewhat different kinds of cognitive, affective and interpersonal demands on the client, it is important to investigate vocal styles in a variety of orientations. Studies are currently underway on a more extensive sample of psychoanalytically oriented therapy and also on samples from gestalt and primal therapy, for which outcome ratings are available.

### Individual Difference Research

A second line of research on CVQ is concerned with the nature of the processes manifested in these different vocal patterns, that is, do people manifesting these different styles show other relatively stable differences in their modes of functioning? In a study by Rice and Gay-

lin (1973) a number of pretherapy Rorschach scores significantly differentiated among clients using a preponderance of *Focused,*
*Externalizing,* or *Limited* vocal styles in early interviews in client-centered therapy. High *Focused* clients tended to approach the processing
demands of the Rorschach with high energy, a capacity for using inner awareness, and the ability to generate internal organizations of
considerable complexity. High *Externalizing* clients tended to show a
lack of internal imagery and relatively poor capacity for generating
new organizations of inner awareness. High *Limited* clients showed a
capacity for using inner awareness, but were not high in energy or organization. Sarnat (1976), using her sample of psychoanalytically oriented interviews, replicated two of the correlations between *Focused*
voice and Rorschach indices, but the relationships with the other vocal styles were more equivocal.

A study by Wexler (1974) in a nontherapy context lent further
support to the idea that *Focused* voice reflects an engagement in the
cognitive-affective operation of differentiating new facets of one's own
inner experience, thus creating new experience for oneself. Under-
graduate students were asked to spend four minutes describing their
feelings when they experienced the emotion of sadness. The transcripts of these taped sessions were independently rated on Wexler's
lexical measures: *Differentiation–Integration, Vividness,* and *Variety.*
Highly significant correlations were found between the proportion of
*Focused* voice used during the four minutes and all three lexical measures. Proportion of *Externalizing* voice yielded significant negative
correlations with all three lexical measures, while *Limited* voice yielded a significant negative correlation with *Vividness.* In a partial replication using different instructions (Spray, 1978), *Focused* voice was
found to be significantly correlated with *Differentiation–Integration*
and with *Variety,* but not with *Vividness. Externalizing* voice correlated negatively with these measures and significantly only with *Variety.*

Vognsen (1969) proposed that the need for new and varied experience might explain the relationship between vocal style and outcome in client-centered therapy. His assumption was that client-
centered therapy with its emphasis on generating new inner
experience would be intrinsically satisfying to people with a *Focused*
style, while an interview stressing shared exploration of external
events would be essentially unsatisfying. Just the reverse prediction
was made for people in the *Externalizing* group.* Using either a client-centered or external-sharing interview he employed a therapy

---

*Predictions were also made for the *Limited* style, but the results were too complex
to include here.

analogue and assessed the need for new experience immediately before and after the interview.

The first hypothesis received general confirmation, with a drop in need for new experience immediately after the client-centered interview and a rise in need for new experience after the external-sharing interview, thus confirming the idea that people with a *Focused* vocal style find satisfaction in internal exploration but not in external exploration. In addition to the analogue results, Vognsen reported comparisons of *High-Focused* with *Low-Focused* people on a variety of personality measures. *High-Focused* people tended to share an internally consistent group of attributes, with a high need for new internal experience, an interest in establishing close, accepting relationships with others, and high emotionality. They were markedly uninterested in structuring, manipulating, and understanding the outside world.

The hypothesis that *Externalizing* people would find the client centered interview unsatisfying and the external-sharing interview satisfying was not confirmed. Need for new experience did not change significantly after either kind of interview. This, together with some of the other studies reported above, suggests that *high-Externalizing* people may not seek newness from either external or internal sources. Certainly this fits the clinical impression that the *high-Externalizing* style represents in some sense a "closed system." Comparison of *high* and *low Externalizers* on the various personality measures, suggested that *high Externalizers* do not form an internally consistent group in terms of personality.

### Moment-to-Moment Variations in Vocal Style

Most of the research reported thus far has involved treating vocal style as a more or less stable characteristic of an individual. However, CVQ was originally designed as a state rather than a trait measure, that is, it was intended to assess the quality of a client's involvement in the therapy process at any given moment. Although the results reported clearly indicate a good deal of intrapersonal stability of vocal style over time, there is further evidence of considerable intrapersonal variability between interviews, and even within a single interview. Using Wexler's design but establishing experimental conditions of varying degrees of psychological comfort, Spray (1978) found that the proportion of *Focused* voice was significantly higher in the "high comfort condition" than it was for the "low comfort condition." Furthermore, the higher use of *Focused* voice was accompanied by significantly less preoccupation with the external requirements of the experimental situation.

Greenberg (1975; 1980) has studied certain key interventions in Gestalt therapy by examining their effects on client performance. The intervention, which he calls "the two chair experiment," is designed to enable clients to separate out and then bring into constructive dialogue two warring parts of the self. He found that the proportions of *Externalizing* and *Limited* voice dropped significantly at points indicating integration or resolution of the dialogue. This would suggest that vocal quality may prove to be a valuable tool for teaching and evaluating successive interventions over the course of a therapy hour.

As part of a pilot collaborative study, a number of brief therapy segments were rated on a variety of different process measures (Rice, Klein, Greenberg, et al., 1978). The segments had been chosen by various investigators from different orientations and were to contain some key transaction, viewed as extremely helpful by the client, the therapist, or both. The segments were rated independently on the different process systems by raters who were unaware of the location of the key transaction. The design of the pilot study did not permit statistical analysis, but the results were highly suggestive. Each of the key transactions was characterized by a shift toward a *Focused* voice, as well as shifts on several of the other process measures. One striking finding was that the shift on the lexical measures was often immediately preceded by the shift in CVQ, suggesting that the move into that style may be one precondition for insight or resolution. This moment-to-moment tracking of the ongoing interactions seems potentially even more interesting than the use of vocal style as a predictive measure.

## CLINICAL APPLICATIONS

Although much more research is needed, some immediate clinical applications appear justified. We have found awareness of vocal quality to be an especially useful tool in supervision. Trainees can be taught to listen for moments when a client's voice slows, softens, and becomes *Focused,* even if only for a few moments. Even though the content being discussed may be less than exciting, this is a sign that something here may be alive for the client, and if the therapist responds in a facilitative manner, productive work may follow. Secondly, trainees may become aware of changes in vocal style immediately after some of their therapeutic interventions. Has the voice become *Focused* for a moment? Has the energy and fullness suddenly gone out of the voice? Has the client become deflected into some long explanation delivered in an *Externalizing* tone? Trainee therapists can thus obtain immediate feedback on the effect of their own style of participation.

In addition to these moment-to-moment uses of vocal style, there is another function that might be called "process diagnosis." Clinicians commonly view the psychotherapy process as a series of motivated interpersonal acts, such as defence, manipulation, and so on. Therapists, in turn, often handle such acts by challenging or interpreting the defenses. From the viewpoint of processing style, on the other hand, one would be more concerned with habitual processing styles that are maladaptive in therapy. For instance, clients habitually using what might be called a "hard core" *Externalizing* style seem to be processing in a kind of closed system. They stay on well-worn tracks, with no room for newness to emerge. There is no space for pausing to grasp a new facet of an old experience or to get in touch with the edge of some new feeling or even to grope for words to express a new thought. The clinical challenge here is to find ways to help the client to jump the track, to focus fully on some new inner aspect—even if only briefly. Actively challenging defenses may be not only useless but even destructive to a client for whom no other style is readily available. Viewed from the perspective of processing style, the approach would be to attempt to use one's *own* style to shift the client's style. One could, for instance, make an extra effort to grasp fully the inner feel of what was being expressed and to ask the client to check it out inside. This would not only slow and break the client's rhythm, but, in groping for the exact flavor of the client's experience, the therapist would be modeling a whole different style of relating to one's own experience. Another process strategy would be to attempt to unfold the client's "packaged" experience further by responding, not in generalized or abstract terms, but with vivid, connotative language that would help to expand the client's own experience. Several such approaches have been proposed (Gendlin, 1974; Rice, 1974; Wexler, 1974), in each of which the strategy lies not in countering interpersonal acts, but in using one's own style to help the client to engage, at least momentarily, in a more productive style of participation.

## VOCAL CUES, SPEECH PRODUCTION, AND COGNITIVE PROCESSING

Discussing vocal quality in terms of the deployment of attentional energy raises the issue of the relationship between vocal styles and cognitive processing. Many studies of speech planning and production

have utilized paralinguistic behaviors as indicators of cognitive processing (Goldman-Eisler, 1968; Boomer, 1965), and there are some interesting parallels between these studies and some of the results from
the studies of vocal style.

For example, Goldman-Eisler studied hesitation phenomena in
subjects who were given tasks such as describing and/or explaining
magazine cartoons and found that: (1) in spontaneous speech much of
the pausing does not occur at grammatical junctures (as opposed to
reading prepared texts where pauses are almost entirely grammatical); (2) greater hesitancy was associated with increased amounts of information in the ensuing speech; and (3) unfilled pauses were
associated with more creative output than filled pauses. From her
studies, Goldman-Eisler recognized that: "One might therefore regard
pausing as an attribute of spontaneity in the creation of new verbal
constructions and structures, i.e., of verbal planning," and that "continuous and rapid vocalization on the other hand would be the result
of practice and thus occur in the use of well-learned word sequences" (1968, p. 26).

Duncan, Rice and Butler (1968) have found that certain paralinguistic behaviors (alone, and/or in specific patterns) are related to
"peak" and "poor" therapy hours. In particular this study found a
clear correlation between the use of unfilled pauses and "peak" hours
and filled pauses and "poor" hours. This relationship held for both
therapist and client (Duncan, 1965). These results are entirely consistent with Goldman-Eisler's finding of a relationship between unfilled
pauses and creative speech. Similarly, Goldman-Eisler's conclusion
that hesitation in spontaneous speech is related to new and complex
productions seems to concur with our previous discussion on *Focused*
voice, in which pace is irregular and the client gives the impression
of "looking inward." Furthermore, the regularity of pace of an *Externalizing* voice seems to be related to a lack of hesitation phenomena.

While these comparisons are interesting and provocative, the
reader should be warned that presently there is considerable controversy regarding studies of speech production in general and hesitation
phenomena in particular. The controversy regarding hesitation phenomena is well reviewed by Rochester (1973). There appears to be
clear methodological problems with aspects of the Goldman-Eisler research, and some other investigators have found conflicting results
(Boomer, 1965; Boomer, 1970). These inconsistencies and conflicting
results must be resolved by further research, but for the present purpose it is sufficient to point out the intriguing similarities between
some of these studies of speech production conducted in the laboratory
and the "naturalistic" studies of ongoing psychotherapy.

## FUTURE DIRECTIONS

In our opinion neither a preoccupation with traits and typologies nor an exclusive focus on momentary states evoked by the stimulus situation is an adequate strategy for investigating speech in psychotherapy. The model that seems to us to be potentially the most productive is that of "stylistic repertoire." This model assumes that each person has a number of different processing styles that can be differentially deployed, depending on one's perceptions of the demands and possibilities of the situation. The findings of the CVQ research are consistent with this model. Firstly, people clearly differ from each other in their dominant styles, and these differences remain relatively stable over time provided that the situation as construed is not markedly changed. Secondly, people differ in the breadth or variety of styles readily available to them. For instance, some clients used an *Externalizing* voice almost exclusively during the course of therapy, while others shifted from style to style even within a single hour. Although it is not within the scope of this chapter to elaborate upon the implications of this model, we will sketch out some of the research directions that follow from it.

One direction would be to test more directly our hypotheses concerning the cognitive-affective processes underlying the different vocal styles. One would first detail the dimensions on which the processing styles are presumed to vary. For instance, *Focused* in contrast to *Externalizing* probably involves new rather than habitual thoughts; an inner rather than an outer focus of attention; and directly experiencing inner states rather than analyzing or comparing them, while both involve a reasonable investment of energy. After each pattern had been thus spelled out, one could conduct experimental analogue studies in which the task demands would be systematically varied. By using groups of participants with different dominant styles in a repeated measures design, the resulting vocal output could be rigorously compared by means of multivariate designs.

The other two research directions, which are more directly related to psychotherapy, are currently being pursued. One of these builds on the relative stability of habitual processing styles, since it focuses on what kinds of cognitive-affective styles are likely to be most productive in different psychotherapeutic orientations. The eventual goal is to match clients with the therapeutic approach most likely to be congruent with their dominant styles. The research strategy here is to specify the styles that seem most relevant in the different therapeutic orientations and then to correlate the amount (or proportion) of this style used in the initial interview with posttherapy outcome measures. Studies are currently underway on samples of gestalt and primal therapy, as well as on a more extensive sample of psychoanalytically oriented therapy than was previously used. From these studies it has become apparent that additional stylistic patterns must be added to the existing four to do justice to the tasks presented by these different orientations. Thus, for example, a pattern tentatively entitled "Expressive Contact" is currently being studied in gestalt interviews.

The third research direction follows from the assumption that some stylistic variability is possible for most people under the right conditions. It is further assumed that such stylistic shifts will probably not result from direct instruction but can result, at least for brief periods, from certain kinds of therapist participation. The research strategy here is to make intensive analyses of a series of single cases, using sequential designs that make use of uncertainity analysis techniques (Hayes-Roth and Longabaugh, 1972; Neufeld, 1977). These designs enable one to compare the unconditional (base rate) probability of a particular client vocal style in a particular client–therapist dyad, with the probability of that vocal style appearing following certain key classes of therapist participation. One can thus differentiate in a clinically meaningful but quantitatively rigorous fashion the kinds of therapist participation that tend to maintain the client in unproductive styles from those that tend to shift the client into productive therapeutic work. Currently we are making intensive analyses of 10 clients who have had markedly poor therapeutic outcomes and 10 clients with markedly favorable outcomes in client-centered therapy.

The transactions between client and therapist, even during a single hour, are tremendously complex, and yet it is in the midst of this complexity that the therapeutic alliance is forged and the change process facilitated. The search for understanding of the vocal aspects of these transactions is one of the most promising frontiers in speech analysis and psychotherapy research.

REFERENCES

Aronson, E., Weintraub, W. Personal adaptation as reflected in verbal behavior. In A. W. Siegman and B. Pope (Eds.), *Studies in dyadic communication.* New York: Pergamon Press, 1972.

Bateson, G. Language and psychotherapy—Frieda Fromm-Reichmann's last project. *Psychiatry,* 1958, *21,* 96–100.

Boomer, D. S. Review of Psycholinguistics by F. Goldman-Eisler. *Lingua,* 1970, *25,* 152–164.

Boomer, D. S. Hesitation and grammatical encoding. *Language and Speech*, 1965, *8*, 148–158.

Butler, J. M., Rice, L. N., Wagstaff, A. K. On the naturalistic definition of variables: An analogue of clinical analysis. In H. Strupp and L. Luborsky (Eds.) *Research in psychotherapy*. Vol. 2. Washington, D.C.: American Psychological Association, 1962.

Crystal, D. *Prosodic systems and intonation in English*. Cambridge: University Press, 1969.

Duncan, S. D. Jr., *Paralinguistic behaviors in client-therapist communication in psychotherapy*. Unpublished Doctoral dissertation, University of Chicago, 1965.

Duncan, S. D. Jr., Rice, L. N., Butler, J. M. Therapists' paralanguage in peak and poor psychotherapy hours. *Journal of Abnormal Psychology*, 1968, *73*, 566–570.

Feldstein, S. Vocal patterning of emotional expression. In J. H. Masserman (Ed.), *Science and psychoanalysis*. Vol. 7. New York: Grune & Stratton, 1964.

Gendlin, E. T. Client-centered and experiential psychotherapy. In D.A. Wexler and L.N. Rice (Eds.), *Innovations in client-centered therapy*. New York: John Wiley and Sons, 1974.

Greenberg, L. S. *A task-analytic approach to the events of psychotherapy*. Unpublished Doctoral dissertation, York University, 1975.

Greenberg, L. S. The intensive analysis of recurring events from the practice of gestalt therapy. *Psychotherapy: Theory, Research and Practice*, 1980, *17*, 143–152.

Goldman-Eisler. F. *Psycholinguistics: Experiments in spontaneous speech*. New York: Academic Press, 1968.

Hayes-Roth, F., and Longabaugh, R. REACT: a tool for the analysis of complex transitional behavioral matrices. *Behavioral Science*, 1972, *17*, 384–394.

Labov, W., and Fanshel, D. *Therapeutic discourse*. New York: Academic Press, 1977.

Mahl, G. F. Disturbances and silences in the patient's speech in psychotherapy. *Journal of Abnormal Social Psychology*, 1956, 53, 1–15.

Mahl, G. F. Measures of two expressive aspects of a patient's speech in two psychotherapeutic interviews. In L. A. Gottschalk (Ed.), *Comparative psycholinguistic analysis of two psychotherapeutic interviews*. New York: International Universities Press, 1961.

Moses, P. J. *The voice of neurosis*. New York: Grune & Stratton, 1954.

Neufeld, R. W. J. *Clinical quantitative methods*. New York: Grune & Stratton, 1977.

Pittenger, R. E., Hockett, C. F., Danehy, J. J. *The first five minutes*. Ithaca: Paul Martineau, 1960.

Pope, B., Blass, T., Siegman, A. W., Raher, J. Anxiety and depression in speech. *Journal of Consulting and Clinical Psychology*. 1970, *35*, 128–133.

Rice, L. N. Therapist's style of participation and case outcome. *Journal of Consulting Psychology*, 1965, *29*, 155–160.

Rice, L. N. The evocative function of the therapist. In D. A. Wexler and L. N.

Rice (Eds.), *Innovations in client-centered therapy.* New York: John Wiley and Sons, 1974.

Rice, L. N., Gaylin, N. L. Personality processes reflected in client vocal style and Rorschach performance. *Journal of Consulting and Clinical Psychology,* 1973, *40,* 133–138.

Rice, L. N., Klein, M. K., Greenberg, L. S., Elliott, R., Whiteside, J., Benjamin, L. S., Hill, C. Comparison of process systems as descriptors of productive psychotherapy. Paper presented at the meeting of the Society for Psychotherapy Research, Toronto, June 1978.

Rice, L. N., Koke, C. J., Greenberg, L. S., Wagstaff, A. K. *Manual for the client vocal quality classification system.* York University Counselling and Development Centre, 1979.

Rice, L. N., Wagstaff, A. K. Client voice quality and expressive style as indexes of productive psychotherapy. *Journal of Consulting Psychology,* 1967, *31,* 557–563.

Rochester, S. The significance of pauses in spontaneous speech. *Journal of Psycholinguistic Research,* 1973, *2,* 51–81.

Sarnat, J. E. *A comparison of psychoanalytic and client-centered measures of initial in-therapy patient participation* (Doctoral dissertation, University of Michigan), Ann Arbor, Mich. University Microfilms, 1976, No. 76-9504.

Siegman, A. W. The telltale voice: Nonverbal messages of verbal communication. In A. W. Siegman and S. Feldstein (Eds.), *Nonverbal behavior and communication.* Hillsdale, N.J.: Lawrence Erlbaum, 1978.

Spray, M. B. *The effects of instructional variation on self-disclosing behavior.* Unpublished Doctoral dissertation, Waterloo University, 1978.

Sullivan, H. S. *The psychiatric interview.* New York: Norton, 1954.

Vognsen, J. P. *Need for new experience: An explanatory bridge between client vocal style and outcome of psychotherapy.* Unpublished Doctoral dissertation, University of Chicago, 1969.

Wexler, D. A. A cognitive theory of experiencing, self-actualization, and therapeutic process. In D.A. Wexler and L. N. Rice (Eds.), *Innovations in client-centered therapy.* New York: John Wiley and Sons, 1974.

Wexler, D. A. Self-actualization and cognitive processes. *Journal of Consulting and Clinical Psychology,* 1974, *42,* 47–53.

# III. Speech Variability and Emotion

Klaus R. Scherer

# 9
# Vocal Indicators of Stress

## THE EFFECTS OF STRESS ON SPEECH PRODUCTION

### The Nature of Stress

A steadily growing number of studies on stress in medicine, psychiatry, and psychology reflects the importance of this phenomenon for the process of coping with changing social and physical environments. This research is aimed at the investigation of the process underlying both normal adjustment to stimulation and failure to cope (possibly resulting in somatic or mental disease). One important part of these research efforts is the search for indicators of stress that can be used as diagnostic tools in monitoring coping processes. In this chapter, evidence concerning the potential use of voice and speech parameters as indicators of stress will be reviewed.

The wide use of the term "stress" has resulted in a multitude of different definitions as well as diverse theoretical notions concerning the underlying processes. While Selye (1956) defined stress as a pattern of endocrine and autonomic responses (the "general adaptation syndrome"), other researchers use the concept of stress to refer to the stimuli that provoke this response pattern or to denote the psychological evaluation and reaction to these stimuli. Furthermore, the stimuli or situations designated as stressors in different studies vary widely: physical or mental activity (e.g., exercising, arithmetic tasks), noxious stimulation (extreme temperature, shock, noise, drugs, sensory deprivation), aversive psychological stimulation (conflict, offense, social isolation), danger situations, and "life stresses," such as catastrophes, accidents, death of relatives, or other negative events.

Given the diversity of empirical approaches, it is impossible to offer a stringent definition of stress. There seems to be general consensus, however, that the concept involves external or internal stimulation of the organism, which upsets its internal balance requiring an adaptive coping response to restore it. The occurrence of such an adaption response is determined not only by the objective nature of the threatening stimulus or event, but also by psychological factors, such as the perceived significance, predictability, escapability, and controllability of the event (Lazarus, 1966; Miller, 1964; Kahn, 1970; Seligman, 1975; Ursin, Baade, and Levine, 1978).

Furthermore, there is agreement that stress involves a series of physiological and behavioral changes that prepare the organism for an appropriate coping response. It is evident that these changes are characterized by some degree of activation, arousal, or emotional tension of the organism, which insures that the body is ready for action (Cannon, 1915; Selye, 1956; Gellhorn, 1967; Malmo, 1975). There is, however, disagreement as to whether this arousal or activation is nonspecific or whether there are specific physiological response patterns. It is possible that discrete emotions involving specific physiological responses dominate the stress reaction, such as anger or fear (Grossman, 1967; Schachter, 1975; Strongman, 1973). The study of the nature of stress responses is complicated by a high degree of individual response specificity in the autonomic indicators studied so far (Lang, Rice, and Sternbach, 1972; Grossman, 1967; Lacey, 1967).

Apart from methodological difficulties in assessing endocrine and autonomic indicators of stress, all of the respective measurement procedures are highly obtrusive and cannot be used without the knowledge and cooperation of the person studied. The use of these assessment procedures is difficult if not impossible in many cases that require stress detection and/or continuous monitoring of stress levels (such as supervision of work stress, monitoring pilot or astronaut states, lie detection, evaluation of threatening phone calls, etc.). In these cases, stress detection and monitoring via vocal indicators would be highly useful as long as speech activity is present. These indicators can be assessed without the knowledge or even the presence of a speaker if an audiorecording of the speech activity in a stressful situation has been made.

The discussion of potential vocal indicators of stress will be preceded by a short review of the physiological correlates of stress and their possible effects on voice production. (See Scherer, 1979a, for a more detailed review.)

## Physiological Stress Correlates

The following discussion will deal primarily with sympathetic activation that characterizes many stress reactions. This does not imply, however, that the possibility of discriminable physiological reaction patterns for discrete emotions is placed in doubt (Izard, 1977). In this chapter, we cannot do justice to the complex pattern of findings on different physiological correlates of stress both in terms of endocrine functions and autonomic responses (Selye, 1956; Leshner, 1978; Levi, 1975; Ursin et al., 1978). We will restrict the discussion to those physiological responses which have been repeatedly observed to follow stress events and which can be expected to have an effect on speech production. (See also Chapter 11).

Sympathetic arousal, the emergency reaction of the organism to prepare the body for action (Cannon, 1915; Malmo, 1975; Gellhorn, 1967, 1970) is characterized by changes in cardiac activity, respiration patterns, and muscle tension. Of these, respiration and muscle tension can be expected to have a direct effect on voice and speech production. Respiration is likely to affect the subglottal pressure in phonation where general muscle tone will affect the operation of the extra- and intralaryngeal mechanisms involved in phonation, as well as the characteristics of the vocal tract resonance walls and the articulatory mechanisms. Furthermore, apart from general muscle tone, disturbances in the coordination of neural impulses which determine phonation and articulation activities may affect speech production.

Unfortunately, we know very little about the effect of emotional arousal on the physiology of the voice and speech production mechanisms. Apart from some speculations by clinically oriented researchers (Moses, 1954; Trojan, 1975), there is little published work on the effects of psychological arousal on objectively measurable physiological aspects of voice and speech production. Most of the relevant research in phonetics has been concerned with the physiological substratum of linguistically relevant changes in intensity or fundamental frequency (Lieberman, 1967, 1974; MacNeilage and Ladefoged, 1976; Harris, 1974; Sawashima, 1974). Scherer (1979a) has attempted to consolidate the evidence on the likely effects of increased muscle tension on phonation and articulation mechanisms. Given the importance of respiration and muscle activity in speech production and the special role of respiration and muscle tension changes under stress and emotion (Grossman, 1967; Malmo, 1975; von Eiff, 1976; Gellhorn, 1967, 1970), one would expect fairly strong effects of stress on voice and speech production yielding indicators that can be traced by acoustic analysis or auditory judgment of the speech signal.

One can even venture some cautious hypotheses on the relationships between stress, physiological response, and the speech signal. (see
also Chapter 11). Given the deepening of respiration and dilation of
the bronchi (Gray, 1971, p. 58) and the increase in muscle tone under
stress, one should expect higher intensity and higher fundamental frequency due to increased subglottal pressure and higher medial compression and tension of the vocal folds, as well as a shift of the energy
concentration in the spectrum to higher frequencies (Scherer, 1979a,
p. 449–504). In this chapter, we will review the scarce evidence furnished by empirical studies on vocal indicators of stress to date.

## EMPIRICAL STUDIES ON VOCAL CORRELATES
## OF STRESS

In the following section the relevant empirical studies available
to the author will be reviewed briefly. Unfortunately, it is extremely
difficult to gain access to a multitude of unpublished research reports,
often issued by private institutions or companies, which are presumably relevant to the issue. This is particularly true for studies employing the Psychological Stress Evaluator (PSE), a device which
supposedly measures the absence of microtremor as a stress indicator
(Holden, 1975; Hollien, 1979; Papcun & Dibner, 1979).[*] Those studies
that are published in very diverse journals sometimes lack the level
of detailed reporting of methodology which is usually considered normative for empirical sciences. Consequently, the author is more hes-
itant than usual to accept the findings reported at face value and to
draw conclusions from them. Studies involving real life stress and
studies using laboratory induction of stress are reviewed separately.

### Real Life Studies of Stress and Danger

In a number of studies, tape recordings of speech under realistic
stress conditions have been obtained and analyzed. Due to the difficulties involved in finding appropriate instances, these studies frequently
report individual cases rather than well designed experiments. Yet,
the advantage of studying stress in a realistic situation in which the
degree of arousal might attain levels which are not obtainable in the
laboratory, justifies such efforts. It must be kept in mind, however,

---

[*]As yet, no detailed and unequivocal published account of the principles underlying
PSE operation nor of the electro-acoustic measurement procedures and parameters has
become available to the author.

that the sources of uncontrolled error and individual characteristics of each case do not allow to generalize these results, unless they can be confirmed in more controlled experiments.

The most lifelike situations studied are air-to-ground communication in aviation and space flight under dangerous conditions. In most of the studies (Williams and Stevens, 1969; Niwa, 1970, 1971; Kuroda, Fujiwara, Okamura and Utsuki, 1976) an increase of fundamental frequency $(F_0)$ with increasing danger is reported. Williams and Stevens (1969) also suggest an increase of $F_0$-range and abrupt fluctuation of $F_0$-contour with increasing stress in the pilots they studied. In a Russian study (Popov, Simonov, Frolov, et al., 1971; Simonov and Frolov, 1973) the voices of astronauts are studied and changes in spectral energy distribution (spectral centroid moving up in the frequency range) is reported. Stronger energy components in the upper frequency ranges (above 500 Hz) are also suggested in an illustrative case of pilot communication under stress reported by Roessler and Lester (1979).

Hauser (1976) studied 10 patients who were presumably experiencing stress in a counseling session and found strong individual differences with a trend towards higher $F_0$ and $F_0$-range under stress. Scherer and his coworkers (Scherer, 1979a; Tolkmitt, Helfrich, Standke and Scherer, 1980) found that depressive patients speak with higher $F_0$ and higher proportion of energy above 500 Hz before therapy at admission to a psychiatric hospital (with the level of emotional tension probably at its peak) as compared to their levels of $F_0$ and spectral energy below 500 Hz at the time of discharge. They concluded that the high level of stress at the time of admission is reflected in these vocal indicators.

In all of the remaining studies in this section, the PSE has been used to assess: vocal effects of stress due to upcoming hospitalization (Brockway, Plummer, and Lowe, 1976), final exams (Brockway, 1979), drug application (Borgen and Goodman, 1976), or emotional disturbance (Wiggins, McCraine, and Bailey, 1975). While some success for stress detection with the PSE is claimed in these studies, the justification for these claims cannot be properly established, since important methodological details are either not reported or remain unclear. Furthermore, even if it were indeed possible to detect stress with the PSE, it remains unclear as to what are the relevant vocal indicators. The existence of microtremor in the musculature involved in voice production has not yet been scientifically demonstrated, nor have the resulting changes in the acoustic waveform been established. On the contrary, many of acoustic-phonetic experts have expressed doubt concerning the existence of microtremor or the possibility of detecting it in speech waves (Hollien, 1979; Papcun and Dibner, 1979; McGlone,

1976; Shipp and McGlone, 1973). Until it is known what exactly the PSE registers, it is difficult to specify what the vocal parameters measured with this device are and whether they are valid indicators of stress. Uncritical acceptance of the validity of the PSE as a stress detector may be dangerous if the device is used in the absence of any other external criteria for stress. It has been used, for example, to claim stress reactions in emotionally disturbed children (Wiggins et al., 1975) and for particular words in presidential speechs (Wiegele, 1978). Apart from scientific concerns with the validity of the research instruments used and the appropriate design of empirical studies, a number of legal and ethical issues involved in the use of the PSE have to be considered (Holden, 1975; Jones, 1974).

## Laboratory Induction of Stress

### NOXIOUS STIMULI AND UNPLEASANT SITUATIONS

In many laboratory studies, stress is induced by showing unpleasant or disgusting stimuli to subjects, such as slides or films with gory content, or by placing subjects in situations which produce unpleasant emotions, such as stage fright, fear of electric shock, or anxiety in threatening interactions with others. While the experimental manipulation allows a fairly high degree of control over the stimulus conditions, the reaction patterns of subjects are often difficult to determine. Depending on their habitual anxiety levels or squeamishness, they will react quite differently to expectation of electroshock or viewing of gory movies. Thus, the stress level induced may be minimal for some subjects, whereas it may be moderate or rather strong for others. Since it is often difficult to determine a definite external criterion for stress (even psychophysiological variables cannot always be expected to indicate the stress level of an individual consistently and validly,)* experimenters using laboratory stress induction can only hope that they have been able to induce a reasonable amount of stress in their subjects. These difficulties in predicting the reactions of different subjects make it hard to evaluate the strong individual differences that have been reported for most acoustic cues in most of these studies. It is unclear whether these individual differences in vocal reaction are due to the differential degree of stress induction or to dif-

---

*Hormonal changes may be more reliable and consistent indicators of stress (Leshner, 1978; Levi, 1975; Ursin, et al., 1978) but are somewhat more difficult to assess (particularly by researchers without medical training).

ferences in physiological or vocal reaction patterns. We shall return to this point later on.

Apart from these individual differences, some studies show trends toward greater intensity (Friedhoff, Alpert, and Kurtzberg, 1964; Hicks, 1979), increased fundamental frequency (Bonner, 1943; Hicks, 1979; Plaikner, 1970; Scherer, 1977; Streeter, Krauss, Geller, et al., 1977), and a stronger energy concentration above 500 Hz (Roessler and Lester, 1979; Helfrich and Scherer, 1977) under stress.

In some of the studies using the PSE to detect stress induced by laboratory methods (Lewis and Worth, n.d.; Brenner, 1974; van der Car, 1977; Johnson, Pinkham and Kerber, 1979; Smith, 1977; McGlone and Hollien, 1976) a modicum of success is claimed. Again, methodological concerns and the reservations concerning the validity of the PSE mentioned above make it difficult to use the results of these studies to draw conclusions concerning vocal indicators of stress.

DECEPTION STUDIES

One particular class of laboratory induced stress uses a deception paradigm, where subjects are requested to lie to the experimenter or to a third person. This, of course, is the type of experimental design that has most often been used with the PSE and similar devices, which are supposedly usable for lie detection. The design adopted most frequently in such studies, is the "guilty knowledge" technique, which requires the subject to answer incorrectly even though he has the correct information (Podlesny and Raskin, 1977). In almost all of these studies the PSE has been used, and in almost all of the studies it was found to operate at about chance level (Horvath, 1978; Kubis, 1973; Barland, 1973; Vagts, 1978; Brenner, Branscomb, and Schwartz, 1979). Hollien (1979) pointed out that, whatever the PSE measures, it might only correlate with strong stress levels and that the guilty knowledge technique may not lead to a sufficiently high level of stress. Even in studies with high risk lies or simulated theft (Kubis, 1973; Barland, 1973), however, the PSE accuracy did not exceed chance level. The practitioners utilizing the PSE or similar devices claim much greater success, of course, (Bennett, 1977; Heisse, 1976) but, until evidence based on carefully controlled empirical studies is presented, such claims cannot be used for scientific evaluation.

There are some other studies in which subjects were requested to lie using filter bank spectra (Friedhoff et al., 1964; Ciofu, 1974) or subjective ratings (Olechowski, 1967). However, there are either serious concerns about the methodology (Scherer, 1979a, p. 506) or the results are fairly inconclusive. Similarly, Almeida, Fleischmann, Heike, et al., (1975) did not find significant changes when requesting their subjects to lie. In the studies by Ekman, Friesen, and Scherer (1976; Scherer 1977; in prep.) and Streeter, Krauss, Geller, et al., (1977) deception was also used. In both of these cases, however, additional stress factors were present in the situation (gory movies in the Ekman et al. study, and lying to a peer with additional stressors involved in the Streeter et al. study). These additional factors may have led to the significant results in these studies rather than the deception aspect. Generally, the use of deception or lying paradigms in the laboratory does not seem to reliably produce stress levels which affect voice and speech parameters. This is not surprising since the stress concept as defined above requires that a particular situation is subjectively evaluated as dangerous by the organism. This may not be the case in many deception situations, particularly in the laboratory.

ACHIEVEMENT TASKS

It is surprising that there are very few experiments in which cognitive or other achievement tasks were used to induce stress. Tasks involving arithmetic computations, word association, counting, or many other types of mental or perceptual achievements are routinely used in stress research to produce stress levels that can be detected in psychophysiological reactions. As far as vocal indicators are concerned, a study by Hecker, Stevens, von Bismarck, et al. (1968) examined the verbal responses of subjects required to read off meters under stress. Case studies were presented which showed that task induced stress seemed to affect a large number of vocal parameters. At the same time, strong individual differences were noted.

The only other study on task stress was conducted by Brenner, Branscomb, and Schwartz (1979) using a standard arithmetic task. They used the PSE, and, contrary to the part of their study where they employed the guilty knowledge technique, they found differences in PSE scores between easy and difficult parts of the arithmetic task. However, their claim that there is a positive linear trend of the PSE scores with the difficulty levels of the task does not seem to be borne out by the mean PSE scores for all subjects and conditions shown in their report. The significance level they obtained seems to be based on the difference in PSE scores between numbers that did not have to be processed at all by the subjects (adding zero to numbers appearing on a screen) to those conditions in which they had to add 1, 3, or 4 to the numbers. Given the degree of experimental control and methodological rigor employed in the study, it is difficult to doubt that the PSE scores seem to be related to some aspects of the subjects' speech. As pointed out before, however, it remains unclear which speech parameters are involved. It is possible, for example, that the subjects always hesitated and prolonged their answers when giving numbers that were the results of an arithmetic operation as opposed to just having to read off numbers that they did not have to change. These aspects of the speech signal might remain visible after having passed through the PSE circuit and might allow the PSE scorer to detect systematic differences between numbers spoken that are read and numbers that are spoken after arithmetic operation.

## EVIDENCE ON VOCAL INDICATORS OF STRESS

In spite of a fairly large number of studies and a burst of recent interest, the evidence on vocal indicators of stress is still scant. The vocal parameters which seem most likely to qualify as indicators of stress are fundamental frequency and energy concentration between 500 and 1000 Hz, possibly due to tense voice (Scherer, 1979a). Intensity may qualify but this parameter has not yet been sufficiently studied (due to the difficulty in determining absolute amplitude levels). Prosodic and fluency aspects of speech may be indicative of stress but again, the few isolated results reported in the literature have not been systematically replicated. There are many vocal parameters that might possibly be indicators of psychological stress such as $F_0$ perturbation, formant structure, formant transitions, etc. (Williams and Stevens, 1972; Hecker, Stevens, von Bismarck, et al., 1968; Scherer and Tolkmitt, 1979; see also Chapter 11 in this volume; Scherer, in press). Until we have systematic evidence from carefully designed experimental studies, however, there is little use in discussing such parameters in detail. This is all the more true, since virtually all of the studies in this field have found very strong individual differences in terms of the number and kind of vocal parameters that seem to accompany stress.

The issue of individual differences is one of the most urgent concerns for future research. Unless we are able to determine the causes for such individual differences, stress detection based on vocal parameters will remain a rather dubious exercise. Progress in this respect depends on many factors. Procedures have to be developed to ensure that the stress level experienced by a person can be determined independent of the vocal measurement. As mentioned before, it is quite possible that, in a large number of studies, subjects were differentially stressed by the stressor to which they were exposed. If this is the case, it is not surprising that there will be strong individual differences in vocal reactivity, just as there will be in psychophysiological and behavioral reactivity. Thus, either stressors have to be used that are powerful enough to assure the appropriate effect on virtually all of the subjects (which may be ethically indefensible in experimental research) or procedures have to be developed to measure stress levels independent of vocal response to allow appropriate covariation. This will be very difficult, given the scarcity of reliable and easily obtainable criteria for the stress level of a subject. Hopefully, psychophysiological research on stress will eventually establish combinations of psychophysiological parameters that can be shown to consistently indicate arousal or activation. Until such measures have been devised, it will be difficult for researchers of vocal indicators of stress to avoid the problem of differential stress levels.

It is dubious, however, whether a stress level equal for all subjects can ever be achieved in an experiment. Not only will the psychological evaluation of a potentially stressful stimulus or event be different for subjects, their coping strategies (in terms of repression or other defense strategies) and/or their psychophysiological structures may be different and thus result in widely varying vocal response patterns. Furthermore, subjects may differ in terms of the degree of control they can exert as far as their vocal production under emotional arousal is concerned. This may effect the degree of internal feedback and the ability to finetune the vocal production apparatus. Also, the general concern with affect control and expressive behavior (due to self-concept or situational or cultural constraints) may play an important role. One of the reasons why more pronounced changes in vocal output are found under more severe stress is that vocal production becomes increasingly more difficult to control as stress increases and coping becomes more difficult and demanding.

While such individual differences can never be eliminated, we can attempt to come to grips with the sources of such individual differences. Knowing more about the bases of individual reactivity may enable us to predict differential vocal response to stress. For example, in the study by Ekman, Friesen, and Scherer (1976; Scherer, 1977; in prep.) it was possible to divide subjects into two groups on the basis of a personality test scale (*achievement via independence* from the California Psychological Inventory). As Figure 9-1 shows, the significant $F_0$ increase under stress was almost totally due to subjects high on *achievement* via *independence,* whereas there was no change for any subjects low on this scale. This suggests that it may be possible, using personality tests, to isolate types of subjects with particular response styles. If we are able to find the dimensions that are relevant for predicting vocal responses to stress, the problem of individual response specificity may be clarified further. Extensive empirical research will be necessary to determine what are some of the predictor

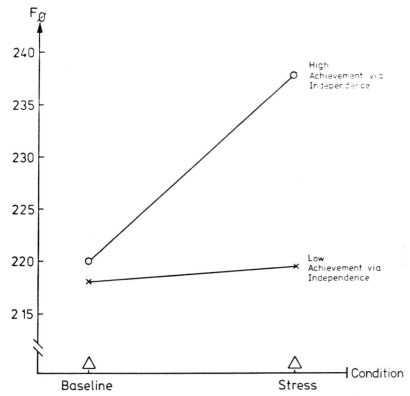

Fig. 9-1.   $F_0$ changes under stress in relation to personality differences

variables (in terms of personality tests or other assessment devices) for such response types. We are presently conducting a study at our laboratory in Giessen where we are using groups of repressers (who tend to verbally deny being stressed but generally show higher autonomic reactivity) and sensitizers (who verbalize their stress openly but show lower physiological reactivity) to determine whether this coping style is involved in vocal stress reactivity. (For the repression–sensitization dimension, see Byrne, 1964.) In a pilot study using slides of accidents we found that repressers responded with $F_0$ increase to stressful slides whereas sensitizers did not.

Apart from these individual differences in vocal responding, there may not be a general vocal response pattern for all kinds of stress. Researchers have repeatedly pointed out (e.g., Janis and Leventhal, 1968) that the type of arousal experienced in a situation labeled as stressful may be very different depending on whether the predominant emotion is anger or fear (which may in turn depend on whether or not the person feels able to cope with a threat; see Chapter 10). If this is the case, and if there are indeed specific physiological arousal patterns for different kinds of emotion (Ax, 1953), it would not be surprising to find different patterns of vocal responses for these different emotions.

Furthermore, even within one particular discrete emotion, there may be different modes of reaction, for example, hot anger versus cold anger. Clearly, one might expect that both the physiological processes and the related vocal changes are different for these two types of anger. Furthermore, Bonner (1943) pointed out that speakers may pass through different phases of stress, which may differentially affect their vocal production. Since such phases may have different length and sequential structures, it might be very difficult to make sure that one is obtaining speech samples for comparable stages from all subjects. Again, it would be important to be able to obtain independent criteria for stress on a continuous basis to allow investigation of this issue.

Finally, in order to assess vocal stress indicators in relation to individual differences in responding, it is important to study the same individual under different types of stress. Virtually all of the studies reported in this chapter have used only one stressor for a particular group of subjects. Consequently, it is impossible to determine whether speakers will show similar patterns of vocal response (even if these patterns are specific to an individual) for different types of stressors, such as mental stress due to an achievement task involving arithmetic operation or emotional stress resulting from being exposed to an unpleasant experience. In our present study with repressers and sensitizers we are using both an arithmetic task stressor and a gory movie stressor to assess similarities and differences in vocal response for these two different types of stressors for the same subjects. Preliminary results show that there are significant interaction effects between the type of stressor and the coping strategy of the speaker.

## CONCLUSION

After this review one is left with the impression that there is a strong likelihood that there are indeed vocal indicators of stress. Stress effects on respiration and muscle tension are most likely to affect phonation and articulation; hence it would certainly seem to pay to engage in systematic research to find hard evidence for the existence of acoustic parameters reflecting these vocal indicators of stress. Many of the studies presently available suffer from methodological shortcomings (either in design or in analysis, but generally in both), which may well account for the fact that most results are inconclusive. There is concrete evidence that, for fairly high levels of stress and for a majority of the subjects studied, fundamental frequency of the voice rises and the proportion of energy above 500 Hz in the spectrum increases. In addition, there are many other vocal parameters that appear promising as possible indicators of stress, but which have not yet been systematically investigated.

In the course of this review, it has also become apparent that the problem of vocal indicators of stress has to be seen within the larger topic of coping with stress. The problem of response specificity, both in terms of individual differences and differences in types of stress, cannot be solved unless the investigation is placed squarely within the systematic psychological study of stress and coping. This, however, requires cooperation and collaboration of researchers from many disciplines to ensure that all aspects of the problem are properly taken into account. Only after a lengthy series of carefully designed and well executed studies can we expect more reliable information about the nature of vocal indicators of stress.

## REFERENCES

Almeida, A., Fleischmann, G., Heike, G., Thormann, E. Short time statistics of the fundamental tone in verbal utterances under psychic stress. Paper read at the Eighth International Congress on Phonetic Sciences, Leeds, England, 1975.

Ax, A. F. The physiological differentiation of fear and anger in humans. *Psychosomatic Medicine*, 1953, *15*, 433–442.

Barland, G. Use of voice changes in detection of deception. Paper read at the meeting of the Acoustical Society of America, Los Angeles, 1973.

Bennett, R. H., Jr. *Hagoth: Fundamentals of voice stress analysis*. Hagoth Corp., Issaquah, WA, 1977.

Bonner, M. R. Changes in the speech pattern under emotional tension. *American Journal of Psychology*, 1943, *56*, 262–273.

Brenner, M. Stagefright and Stevens's law. Paper presented at the Eastern Psychological Association Convention, 1974.

Brenner, M., Branscomb, H. H., Schwartz, G. E. Psychological stress evaluator: Two tests of a vocal measure. *Psychophysiology*, 1979, *16*, 351–357.

Brockway, B. F. Situational stress and temporal changes in self-report and vocal measurements. *Nursing Research*, 1979, *28*, 20–24.

Brockway, B. F., Plummer, O. B., Lowe, B. M. The effects of two types of nursing reassurance upon patient vocal stress levels as measured by a new tool, the PSE. *Nursing Research*, 1976, *25*, 440–446.

Byrne, D. Repression–sensitization as a dimension of personality. In B. Maher (Ed.), *Progress in experimental personality research,* Vol. 1, New York: Academic Press, 1964, pp. 169–219.

Cannon, W. B. *Bodily changes in panic, hunger, fear, and rage.* New York: Appleton-Century-Crofts, 1915.

Ciofu, J. Audiospectral analysis in lie detection. *Archiv für Psychologie,* 1974, *126,* 170–180.

Eiff, A. W. v. (Ed.) *Seelische und körperliche Störungen durch Stress.* Stuttgart/New York: Gustav Fischer, 1976.

Ekman, P., Friesen, W. V., Scherer, K. R. Body movement and voice pitch in deceptive interaction. *Semiotica,* 1976, *16,* 23–27.

Friedhoff, A. J., Alpert, M., Kurtzberg, R. L. An electro-acoustic analysis of the effects of stress on voice. *Journal of Neuropsychiatry,* 1964, *5,* 266–272.

Gellhorn, E. The tuning of the nervous system: Physiological foundations and implications for behavior. *Perspectives in Biology and Medicine,* 1967, *10,* 559–591.

Gellhorn, E. The emotions and the ergotropic and trophotropic systems. *Psychologische Forschung,* 1970, *34,* 48–94.

Gray, J. A. *The psychology of fear and stress.* New York: McGraw-Hill, 1971.

Grossman, S. P. *Physiological psychology.* New York: John Wiley and Sons, 1967.

Harris, K. S. Physiological aspects of articulatory behavior. In T. A. Sebeok (Ed.), *Current trends in linguistics* (Vol. 12): *Linguistics and adjacent arts and sciences.* The Hague: Mouton, 1974, pp. 2282–2302.

Hauser, K. O. The use of acoustical analysis for identification of client stress within the counseling session. *Dissertation Abstracts International,* 1976, *36,* 5149–5150.

Hecker, M. H. L., Stevens, K. N., von Bismarck, G., Williams, C. E. Manifestations of task-induced stress in the acoustical speech signal. *Journal of the Acoustical Society of America,* 1968, *44,* 993–1001.

Heisse, J. W. Audio stress analysis—A validation and reliability study of the psychological stress evaluator (PSE). Proceedings, 1976 Carnahan Conference on Crime Countermeasures. Lexington, KY, 1976, 5–18.

Helfrich, H., Scherer, K. R. Experimental assessment of antidepressant drug effects using spectral analysis of voice. Paper presented at the Acoustical Society of America Meeting, Miami, 1977. *Journal of the Acoustical Society of America,* Supplement 1, 1977, *62,* 26 (Abstract).

Hicks, J. W. Jr. An acoustical/temporal analysis of emotional stress in speech. Unpublished Ph.D. dissertation, University of Florida, 1979.

Holden, C. Lie detectors: PSE gains audience despite critics' doubts. *Science,* 1975, *190,* 359–362.

Hollien, H. The case against stress evaluators and voice lie detection. Paper delivered at the AFACS Meeting, "Voice analysis on trial," Salt Lake City, November 1979.

Horvath, F. An experimental comparison of the psychological stress evaluator and the galvanic skin response in detection of deception. *Journal of Applied Psychology,* 1978, *63,* 338–344.

Izard, C. E. *Human emotions.* New York: Plenum, 1977.

Janis, I. L., Leventhal, H. Human reactions to stress. In E. F. Borgatta and W. W. Lambert (Eds.) *Handbook of personality theory and research.* Chicago: Rand McNally, 1968, pp. 1041–1085.

Johnson, J. B., Pinkham, J. R., Kerber, P. E. Stress reactions of various judging groups to the child dental patient. *Journal of Dental Research,* 1979, *58,* 1664–1671.

Jones, W. R. Evidence vel non. The non sense of voiceprint identification. *Kentucky Law Journal,* 1974, *62,* 301–326.

Kahn, R. L. Some propositions toward a researchable conceptualization of stress. In J. McGrath (Ed.) *Social and psychological factors in stress.* New York: Holt, Rinehart & Winston, 1970, pp. 97–103.

Kubis, J. F. Physiological and voice indices of stress in a simulated theft experiment. Paper presented at the 86th Meeting of the Acoustical Society of America, 1973.

Kuroda, I., Fujiwara, O., Okamura, N., Utsuki, N. Method for determining pilot stress through analysis of voice communication. *Aviation, Space, and Environmental Medicine,* 1976, *47,* 528–533.

Lacey, J. T. Somatic response patterning and stress: Some revisions of activation theory. In M. H. Appley and R. Trumbull (Eds.), *Psychological stress: Issues in research.* New York: Appleton-Century-Crofts, 1967, pp. 14–37.

Lang, P. J., Rice, D. G., Sternbach, R. A. The psychophysiology of emotion. In N. S. Greenfield and R. A. Sternbach (Eds.), *Handbook of psychophysiology.* New York: Holt, Rinehart & Winston, 1972, pp. 623–643.

Lazarus, R. S. *Psychological stress and the coping process.* New York: McGraw-Hill, 1966.

Leshner, A. I. *An introduction to behavioral endicronology.* New York: Oxford University Press, 1978.

Levi, L. (Ed.) *Emotions—Their parameters and measurement.* New York: Raven Press, 1975.

Lieberman, P. A study of prosodic features. In T. A. Sebeok (Ed.), *Current trends in linguistics* (Vol. 12): *Linguistics and adjacent arts and sciences.* The Hague: Mouton, 1974, pp. 2419–2449.

Lieberman, P. (ed.) *Intonation, perception, and language.* Cambridge, Mass.: M.I.T. Press, 1967.

MacNeilage, P., Ladefoged, P. The production of speech and language. In E. C. Carterette and M. P. Friedman (Eds.), *Handbook of perception* (Vol. VII): *Language and speech.* New York: Academic Press, 1976, pp. 75–120.

Malmo, R. B. *On emotions, needs, and our archaic brain.* New York: Holt, Rinehart & Winston, 1975.

McGlone, R. E. Tests of the psychological stress evaluator (PSE) as a lie and stress detector. Proceedings, 1975 Carnahan Conference on Crime Countermeasures. Lexington, KY, 1975, 83–86.

McGlone, R. E., Hollien, H. Partial analysis of the acoustic signal of stressed and unstressed speech. Proceedings, 1976 Carnahan Conference on Crime Countermeasures. Lexington, KY, 1976, 19–21.

Miller, J. G. A theorectical review of individual and group psychological reactions to stress. In Grosser, G. H., Wechsler, and Greenblatt (Eds.), The threat to impending disaster: Contributions to the psychology of stress. Cambridge, Mass.: MIT Press, 1964, pp. 11–33.

Moses, P. J. The voice of neurosis. New York: Grune & Stratton, 1954.

Niwa, S. Changes of voice characteristics in urgent situation (1). Reports of the Aeromedical Laboratory. Japan Air Self Defense Force, 1970, 11, 51–58.

Niwa, S. Changes of voice characteristics in urgent situation (2). Reports of the Aeromedical Laboratory. Japan Air Self Defense Force, 1971, 11, 246–251.

Olechowski, R. Experimente über den Stimm- und Sprechausdruck beim Lügen. Zeitschrift für Experimentelle und Angewandte Psychologie, 1967, 14, 474–482.

Papcun, G., Dibner, S. Stress evaluation and voice lie detection: A review. Paper delivered at the AFACS Meeting, "Voice analysis on trial," Salt Lake City, November 1979.

Plaikner, D. Die Veränderung der menschlichen Stimme unter dem Einfluss psychischer Belastung. Unpublished doctoral dissertation, Philosophische Fakultät der Universität Innsbruck, 1970.

Podlesny, J. A., Raskin, D. C. Physiological measures and the detection of deception. Psychological Bulletin, 1977, 84, 782–799.

Popov, V. A., Simonov, P. V., Frolov, M. V., Khachatur'iants, L. S. The frequency spectrum of speech as an indicator of the degree and character of emotional tension in man. Zhurnal Vysshei Nervnoi Deyatel nosti, 1971, 21, 104–109.

Roessler, R., Lester, J. W. Vocal patterns in anxiety. In W. E. Fann, A. D. Pokorny, I. Koracau, R. L. Williams (Eds.), Phenomenology and treatment of anxiety. New York: Spectrum, 1979.

Sawashima, M. Laryngeal research in experimental phonetics. In T. A. Sebeok (Ed.), Current trends in linguistics (Vol. 12): Linguistics and adjacent arts and sciences. The Hague: Mouton, 1974, pp. 2303–2348.

Schachter, S. Cognition and peripheralist–centralist controversies in motivation and emotion. In M. S. Gazzaniga and C. W. Blakemore (Eds.), Handbook of psychobiology. New York: Academic Press, 1975, pp. 529–564.

Scherer, K. R. The effect of stress on the fundamental frequency of the voice. Acoustical Society of America Meeting. Miami, 1977, Journal of the Acoustical Society of America, 1977, 62, Supplement No. 1, 25–26 (Abstract).

Scherer, K. R. Nonlinguistic vocal indicators of emotion and psychopathology. In C. E. Izard (Ed.), Emotions in personality and psychopathology. New York: Plenum, 1979, pp. 493–529.

Scherer, K. R. Methods of research on vocal communication: Paradigms and parameters. In K. R. Scherer and P. Ekman (Eds.), Handbook of methods in nonverbal behavior research. Cambridge: Cambridge Univ. Press, in press.

Scherer, K. R. Voice and speech changes following stress induction in a deceptive interaction. Unpublished manuscript, University of Giessen, in prep.

Scherer, K. R., Tolkmitt, F. The effect of stress and task variation on formant location. Paper presented at the Acoustical Society of America Meeting, Salt Lake City 1979. *Journal of the Acoustical Society of America*, Supplement 1, 1979, *66*, 512 (Abstract).

Seligman, M. E. P. *Helplessness: On depression, development and death.* San Francisco: W. H. Freeman, 1975.

Selye, H. *The stress of life.* New York: McGraw-Hill, 1956.

Shipp, T., McGlone, R. E. Physiologic correlates of acoustic correlates of psychological stress. *Journal of the Acoustical Society of America*, 1973, *53*, 63 (A).

Simonov, P. V., Frolov, M. V. Utilisation of human voice for estimation of man's emotional stress and state of attention. *Aerospace Medicine*, 1973, *44*, 256–258.

Smith, G. A. Voice analysis for the measurement of anxiety. British *Journal of Medical Psychology*, 1977, *50*, 367–373.

Streeter, L. A., Krauss, R. M., Geller, V., Olson, C., Apple W. Pitch changes during attempted deception. *Journal of Personality and Social Psychology*, 1977, *35*, 345–350.

Strongman, K. T. *The psychology of emotion.* London: John Wiley and Sons, 1973.

Tolkmitt, F., Helfrich, H., Standke, R., Scherer, K. R. Vocal indicators of psychiatric treatment effects in depressives and schizophrenics. Unpublished manuscript, University of Giessen, 1980.

Trojan, F. *Biophonetik.* Zürich: Bibliographisches Institut, 1975.

Ursin, H., Baade, E., Levine, S. (Eds.) *Psychobiology of stress.* New York: Academic Press, 1978.

Vagts, A. E. Validity of voice analysis of stress under low levels of mendacious anxiety. *Dissertation Abstracts International*, 1978, *38*, 5551.

VanderCar, D. H., Greaner, J., Hibler, N., Speelberger, C. D., Bloch, S. An analysis of the psychological stress evaluation as a tool for assessing emotional states. Paper presented at the Florida Academy of Sciences meeting, Gainesville, Florida, 1977.

Wiegele, T. The psychophysiology of elite stress in five international crises. *International Studies Quarterly*, 1978, *22*, 467–511.

Wiggins, S. L., McCraine, M. L., Bailey, P. Assessment of voice stress in children. *Journal of Nervous and Mental Disease*, 1975, *160*, 402–408.

Williams, C. E., Stevens, K. N. On determining the emotional state of pilots during flight: An exploratory study. *Aerospace Medicine*, 1969, *40*, 1369–1372.

Williams, C. E., Stevens, K. N. Emotions and speech: Some acoustical correlates. *Journal of the Acoustical Society of America*, 1972, *52*, 1238–1250.

Klaus R. Scherer

# 10
# Speech and Emotional States

Most laymen agree that there are discrete emotions, such as anger, fear, or joy, and they seem to agree on what it feels like to be angry, fearful, or joyous. Psychologists also recognize these discrete emotions, but find it difficult to define the theoretical construct and to reach a consensus about its relevant aspects and about the relationships of this construct to other psychological concepts. Thus, since no simple definition can be given, it is necessary to begin this review of the effects of emotional states on speech with an introductory overview on the nature and functions of emotion.

## THE NATURE AND FUNCTIONS OF EMOTION

Emotions serve as the organism's interface to the world outside. They are the mediators between the external stimuli constantly impinging upon the sense organs and the organism's responses to them. The major functions of the emotions in allowing the organism to cope with constantly changing situations can be described as follows:

They reflect the evaluation of the relevance and significance of particular stimuli or stimulus configurations in the situation in terms of the organism's needs, plans, and preferences (thereby playing a major role in learning).

They physiologically and psychologically prepare the organism for appropriate action.

They communicate the organism's state and behavioral intentions to other organisms in the surroundings, via various modalities of expression.

Systems that do not have the capacity for emotion, such as simple organisms or complex computers, can also process information from the environment and adjust their behavior accordingly. As compared to more complex organisms with a capacity for emotion, however, both the types of information obtained and the behavioral options available to these systems as responses are finite and highly restricted. Whereas both the amoeba and the highspeed computer operate under a predetermined "IF x GO TO z" decision rule, human decision makers are faced with an extraordinary gamut of different interpretations as to what x may mean to them, as well as with a wide variety of behavioral options available as possible responses. As we shall see, it is the capacity for emotion that allows this high degree of openness and flexibility in the interpretation of stimuli and situations, as well as in the choice of response.

A corollary to this openness of choice in complex organisms is the provisional nature of stimulus interpretation and the plasticity of behavioral responses. While neither the amoeba nor the computer can change an interpretation of a stimulus once made nor stop an action that has been initiated, complex organisms can reinterpret or reevaluate stimuli with or without new information. They show "intention movements," as in expressive displays, which serve as precursors to a specific course of action; and they can stop a behavior once initiated and replace it with a different course of behavior, depending on a reinterpretation of the original stimulus, novel information, or on feedback concerning the effects of the initiated action. The structure that makes this kind of flexibility possible is the emotion system. For different types of evaluations or appraisals of stimulus situations, emotions provide both motivational energy and appropriate action tendencies to deal adaptively with the environmental contingencies. Emotions set up potentials rather than rigid unchangeable behavior sequences. Furthermore, through their expressive components, which communicate the organism's state and action tendencies to others, emotions themselves provide the potential for rapid feedback on the probable consequences of an intended action.

All of the aspects of emotional processes mentioned above can be found in psychological theories of emotion. Many theorists, however, have concentrated on and emphasized subsets of these aspects, sometimes to the point of denying the existence or the importance of particular aspects. While an extensive review of existing psychological theories of emotion is beyond the scope of this chapter (see Strongman 1973, for a systematic review), some of the more important theories will be mentioned in passing in the following review of the components of emotional states.

## THE COMPONENTS OF EMOTIONAL STATES

### Emotion As a Reaction to Stimulus Appraisal

Different stimuli mean different things to different organisms. Thus, no emotion can ensue as a reaction to a particular stimulus unless the organism has first somehow evaluated its significance. Theories of emotion differ widely in terms of the psychological mechanisms, which they postulate as the basis of evaluation. One question of major importance is whether stimulus evaluation requires cognitive activity involving cortical structures or whether it can procede on a subcortical level, or at least without awareness. The latter view is maintained by several theorists. William James postulated a releaser mechanism in terms of a lock-key analogy (James, 1884, reprinted in Arnold, 1968, p. 20). Tomkins (1962) argues that different stimuli produce differential rates of neural firing resulting in differential emotions. Mandler (1975) stresses the role of the interruption of ongoing plans and actions as an evaluating mechanism for differential attendance to stimuli. The counterposition has been argued most vigorously by Arnold (1960, 1968) and Lazarus (1968), who have adopted a cognitive-phenomenological view of stimulus appraisal. Arnold focuses on the appraisal of the stimulus as beneficial or harmful (good or bad) by an organism (1960, p. 182), whereas Lazarus assumes that there is a specific pattern of appraisal for each emotion (Lazarus, Averill, and Opton, 1970). Both theorists stress the importance of the possibility for reappraisals in which the significance of a stimulus is reevaluated following cognitive interpretation or new information.

The relative merit of these assumptions is often difficult to assess, since many theorists are somewhat vague about the exact nature of the psychological processes which they assume. It is often not clear whether the distinction is to be sought in terms of neurological structures (e.g., cortical versus subcortical) or whether it is the role of attention or awareness that is at stake. In part this may be due to the fact that it is difficult to specify, at our present state of knowledge, just which psychological mechanisms are involved in the categorization and evaluation of stimuli.

The minimal dimensions required for adequate evaluation of the stimulus by the organism seem to be the following: Has the stimulus been expected? Is it good or bad? Will the organism be able to cope with it? The position of a stimulus on these three dimensions—novelty/expectedness, valence, and coping ability—seems to indicate roughly the emotion that will ensue. Thus, anger will follow an unexpected stimulus which is negatively evaluated but with which the organism can easily cope. Since this three dimensional scheme might be used to account for different types of emotional states in higher animals, an evaluation proceeding along these lines may not require complex cognitive processing. It is most likely, however, that stimulus appraisal in humans proceeds along many more dimensions, as might be suspected by the presence of verbal labels for a large number of rather subtly differentiated emotional states.

As a consequence of this stimulus appraisal function, emotion is centrally involved in the organism's learning of adaptive responses (Mowrer, 1960). A conditioned emotional response represents an evaluation of a stimulus configuration encountered in the past. Since the emotional response to a danger signal is in most cases much less intense than the experience of pain in the initial evaluation situation, such stored evaluations spare the organism an excessive amount of negative experiences in interacting with the environment.

### Preparing the Organism for Action

While it had been common to think of emotions as having a disruptive, disorganizing effect on human action, most theorists now seem convinced that emotions are constructive and serve important motivational purposes. The way in which the motivational effects of emotions are described in different theories varies widely from theory to theory. While some theorists (e.g., Leeper, 1970) stress the general motivational characteristics of emotions, others emphasize specific patterns. It seems possible to divide the motivational aspect into two categories: the physiological preparation of the organism for action (to be discussed in this section) and the instigation of specific action tendencies (to be described in the next section).

One of the most obvious characteristics of emotional states is a high degree of autonomic and somatic arousal or activation. Much of the empirical work of psychologists and physiologists has been devoted to studying the patterns of autonomic and somatic responses in different emotional states. One of the persistent problems in this area has been the failure to find empirical evidence for different patterns of autonomic and somatic arousal for different emotions (Grossman,

1967, p. 503–515). Since the issue is still unsettled, theories which claim that the autonomic arousal underlying emotions is nonspecific (Mandler, 1975; Schachter, 1970) or that the autonomic arousal is just an auxiliary system (Izard, 1978) are hard to refute.

Independent of the specificity problem, most theorists are convinced that the autonomic and somatic arousal accompanying emotional states serves to prepare the organism for action. While this notion can already be found in early work on emotion, the emergency theory proposed by Cannon (1915) had the most significant impact. Cannon argued that the sympathetic changes accompanying strong emotions serve to mobilize all energies of the organism for fight or flight. He assumed that the activation of the sympathetic nervous system served to increase the level of glucose in the blood stream, which in turn allowed more vigorous contractions of the muscles and prevented fatigue. While some of the physiological assumptions in this theory have been challenged (Grossman, 1967, p. 515), the notion that physiological changes occurring during emotion prepare the organism for appropriate action still seems viable. In recent years, Gellhorn (1968) has advanced a similar "readiness" theory, assuming that emotions are characterized by a balance between the ergotropic "action" system and the trophotropic "rest" system. This theory suggests that ergotropic emotions, such as anger or fear, are characterized by a predominance of the sympathetic over the parasympathetic nervous sytem, as shown in increased heart rate, asynchronous EEG, pupillary dilation, and increased muscle tone. The trophotropic system, responsible for rest and recovery, dominates in emotions, such as quiet happiness or sadness and depression.

## Instigation of Typical Adaptive Behavior Patterns

It is often difficult to differentiate between emotion per se and emotional behavior, since there seems to be little doubt that many emotional reactions smoothly blend into appropriate behavior patterns such as attack following anger or mourning following grief. Consequently, many emotion theorists have held that different emotions instigate concomitant or typical behavior patterns allowing an adaptive response of the organism to environmental events.

If one views emotion as an adaptive phenomenon which serves to motivate coping behavior, it seems highly reasonable to postulate a link between emotional states and adaptive behavior patterns occurring in response to the environmental contingencies that have given rise to these emotional states (Plutchik, 1962). The nature of the processes that determine whether or not a particular type of emotional behavior will follow a specific emotional state is quite unknown. Also, while an emotional state may instigate a particular type of behavior, it may not be actually shown by the organism due to conflicting behavior tendencies, external restrictions, or other factors. Thus, while one may legitimately assume that there is a motivational factor instigating specific behavior patterns, one has to distinguish carefully between the motivating emotional state on the one hand and the actual occurrence of a specific behavior pattern on the other.

## Emotional Expression and Communication

One aspect which is rarely disputed as a constitutive component of emotional processes is emotional expression. Endocrine and muscular activities leading to observable changes in the outward appearance of an organism, as well as definite patterns of facial, gestural, and postural movements and specific vocalizations, are direct signs that the organism is in an emotional state. While the existence of emotional expression is too obvious to be placed in doubt, the origin, nature, and function of emotional expression and its role in social communication is fiercely debated. Among the controversial issues, are those of whether emotional expression is innate or culturally learned; the role of expression in the subjective feeling accompanying emotional arousal; and the relationship between expression and impression, i.e., the attribution of an emotional state to an organism on the basis of expressive cues by an observer.

In the debate concerning innateness and universality versus learning and cultural specificity of emotional expression, ethologists and psychologists have generally followed the lead of Charles Darwin. He argued that patterns of emotional expression are remnants of adaptive behavioral responses ("serviceable associated habits"), as well as of general arousal (Darwin, 1872). Many sociologists and cultural anthropologists, however, maintain that the majority of emotional expressions are conventional signs shaped by custom and cultural norms. Both biological considerations (Leyhausen, 1967) and empirical data (Ekman, 1973, Izard, 1971) make it difficult to doubt that there is an innate, biological core to many emotional expressions and that many of these show evolutionary continuity; i.e., they can be found in species other than man. Neither ethologists nor psychologists, however, doubt that social norms and conventions in different cultures may exert considerable influence on whether particular emotional expressions will be shown and on the way in which they will be displayed (Ekman, 1973, Leyhausen, 1967).

Emotional expression plays a major role in the social communication between members of a species. As long as the behavior of an isolated organism is exclusively determined by physical stimuli in its environment, there is no need for expression or signals. However, if a species is socially organized and members of the species *interact*, rather than act in isolation, the action has to be coordinated. If there are only relatively few behavioral choices open, this coordination might be achieved through a number of simple cues. However, if behavior is highly flexible and if there are many options for different courses of action, as is the case in most higher organisms, more intricate signaling systems have to evolve to allow the organism to predict how other organisms are likely to behave in order to adjust its behavior accordingly. Emotional expression provides such a signaling system. Due to the important role of emotional expression in communication, it is possible that specific requirements of message transmission have modified the original expression pattern. Leyhausen (1967) provides a well-reasoned account of how the nature of "impression" processes (perception and inference) may have affected expression. This aspect will also be dealt with in more detail later in this chapter with special reference to the vocal communication of emotion.

## Subjective Awareness or Consciousness of Emotional States ("feeling")

In everyday usage we often equate feeling with emotion when we talk about "feeling angry" or "feeling sad." The feeling component of emotion has been the focus of attention of many phenomenologically oriented psychologists and philosophers (Klages, 1950; Lersch, 1962; Sartre, 1948) emphasizing the important role of emotional feeling in the conscious life of a human being. One particularly important aspect of the subjective feeling component of emotional states is, that feelings may persist for quite some time after the initial emotion-producing stimulus situation has passed. A persistence of emotional feelings over a fairly long period of time is generally referred to as "mood." Feelings and moods can affect the behavior of a person (including expressive phenomena), independent of the specific emotional arousal produced by specific stimulation. Emotional states are generally seen as adaptive responses, even though they may at times disorganize a plan for behavior in organisms. Moods may become dysfunctional if they fail to reflect the relationship of a person to his/her social or material environment realistically. The dysfunctional persistence of moods and feelings, such as dejection, can often lead to severe affect disturbances, such as depression and other psychopathological phenomena.

The subjective feeling of an emotional state plays an important role in research on emotion, since it is often via the verbal report of a person on his felt emotion that psychologists try to assess emotional processes. Due to the verbal nature of subjective reports, the language available to describe emotional experiences is of particular importance and may reflect fundamental dimensions of emotional experience (Davitz, 1969; Plutchik, 1962).

We are now in a position to turn to the question of the relationship between speech and emotional states. In order to facilitate understanding of the general effects of emotions on vocal behavior, we precede the investigation of the effects of emotional arousal on speech by a short survey on the effects of emotional arousal on nonlinguistic vocalizations.

## AFFECT VOCALIZATIONS IN ANIMALS AND MAN

Affect vocalizations in animals provide a starting base to explore the effect of emotional arousal on vocal behavior. Based upon Darwin's early speculations in his influential "The expression of the emotions in man and animals" (1872), Scherer (1979a) has argued for the existence of evolutionary continuities in the vocal expression of emotion. These continuities are not as evident (nor as well documented) as similarities in the facial expression of emotion, particularly within primates (Chevalier-Skolnikoff, 1973; van Hooff, 1973; Redican, 1975). Yet, the position that affect vocalizations in animals are both functionally and morphologically homologous with human affect vocalizations seems quite defensible. This is not very surprising if we assume emotion (as a mechanism of the organism to deal with environmental contingencies) to be evolutionary continuous. Both the definition of emotion-eliciting situations and the nature of physiological and motor response patterns may be highly similar across species. While the cognitive evaluation of situational cues and the ensuing emotion processes are much more differentiated in higher developed species, the nature of the basic components of emotion such as evaluation of situations, physiological arousal patterns energizing the organism, and typical modes of behavior are quite similar. Since the expression of affect is determined to a large extent by the arousal patterns and the nature of the adaptive behavioral response, evolutionary continuities in expressive behavior are to be expected. In different species different aspects of expressive signals may have selectively developed for special communicative purposes, however. Unfortunately, there have as yet been very few studies on similarities in the vocal expression of affect in different species including man. This is unfortunate since a comparative approach to the effects of affective arousal on nonlinguistic vocalizations may provide us with important insights into the nature of affective expression and signaling.

The literature on acoustic communication in nonhuman species is growing rapidly (Green, 1975; Marler and Tenaza, 1977; Tembrock, 1977). While animal call systems differ rather strongly in terms of the size of the "vocabulary" and the gradedness of the repertoire (i.e., the extent to which variations in acoustic patterns of a call communicate different aspects of meaning) there seem to be vocalization types for many states of the organism which we would call "emotional" in man, such as distress, anger, comfort, alarm, pleasure, etc. A review of the published accounts of call systems in different animal species suggests that there may be a systematic correspondence between motivational and emotional states and specific acoustic characteristics of vocalizations. Morton (1977) states that "birds and mammals use harsh, relatively low-frequency sounds when hostile and higher-frequency, more tonelike sounds when frightened, appeasing, or approaching in a friendly manner" (p. 855).

Similarly, Tembrock (1977) maintains, that states of comfort or playfulness are characterized by repeated short sounds within the middle range of the frequency spectrum (in the frequency range of the species). In states characterized by dominance, antagonistic behavior tendencies, and attempts to warn others of danger, calls are characterized mainly by lower frequencies. Defense calls are generally short, with strong attack or onset of sound, and usually have a broad frequency spectrum. Finally, calls of submission (implying fear or anxiety) generally have high frequencies, frequent shifts of fundamental frequency, and tendencies toward temporal prolongation. Tembrock bases these conclusions on regularities in observed acoustical patterns of animal calls observed under different states. While much of this is conjecture, relationships between emotional states and the acoustic nature of animal calls can be studied experimentally. Jürgens (1979), using systematic brain stimulation in addition to observation, carefully analyzed the vocal repertoire of the squirrel monkey (saimiri sciureus). He was able to group different vocalization types into several major classes, which are indicative of different emotional states of the animals. In addition, he found that an increase in the aversiveness of an emotional state seems to result in vocalizations characterized by an increase in total frequency range and intensity, a rise in fundamental frequency, a more irregular frequency contour and a level or descending contour.

It should be easily possible to subject human nonlinguistic affect vocalizations to similar analyses. Unfortunately, due to the almost exclusive preoccupation of most social and behavioral scientists with language, the enormous scope and variability of human soundmaking outside of language has been largely overlooked or disregarded. It would be most instructive to know what percentage of human vocalization time is filled with nonlinguistic vocalization such as sobbing, laughing, crying, whimpering, chuckling, moaning, etc. While this may certainly be greatly dependent on the situation, chances are that the occurrence of such nonlinguistic sounds are more frequent than we would normally assume and that these vocalizations may share many of the attributes of the respective animal vocalizations. In a study on the Japanese monkey (macaca fuscata), Green (1975) points out:

> Humans also employ roars, cries, shrieks, screams, screeches, and a variety of other sounds. These sounds are not only acoustically homologous with those described here for the Japanese monkey, but they are also used in analogous situations by primates with similar inferred internal states. Roars are used by enraged people, cries by babies abandoned or otherwise distressed, screeches in tantrums of youngsters, and whines as they reach the comfort of a mothers' embrace. . . . Shrieks and screeches are employed in stressful situations and screams are used by the victims of aggression. (p. 95)

The reliability with which such nonlinguistic affect vocalizations communicate the emotional state and frame of mind of the speaker has resulted in the integration of such sounds—often in a conventionalized and modified form—into the lexicon. The process whereby "reflex-like affect sounds" are "domesticated" and assimilated into linguistic form, has interested early linguists and psychologists in the evolution of language. Wundt (1900) has assumed that the linguistic assimilation of "primary affect sounds" into "secondary interjections" is a characteristic sign of cultural development in a society, reflecting the degree of normative constraints on affect expression. Both Wundt and, even earlier, Kleinpaul (1888) assumed that unarticulated affect vocalizations are similar in terms of production and acoustic features for both man and animal and across different cultures. Kainz (1962) has hypothesized that primary, nonlinguistic affect vocalizations are the result of very strong or extreme emotional states, whereas quasilinguistic secondary interjections are used in mild affect states in which the communicative behavior is more amenable to cortical control.

Scherer (1977), pointed out that quasilinguistic interjections, which he called "vocal emblems" (in accordance with Ekman's definition of gestural and facial emblems; Ekman, 1975), frequently substitute for verbal utterances. Unfortunately, we know little about the situations in which such substitution takes place. It seems highly likely that we use vocal affect emblems (in combination with facial and gestural affect emblems) in situations where we are not suddenly affected by an extreme emotion (in which case we would expect nonlinguistic affect vocalizations), but in which a reflective verbal utterance describing a state of emotion would also seem less than appropriate. This may be the case where our interlocutors expect messages concerning our emotional states and in which we try to appear spontaneous and genuine. For example, a drawn out "Oooh" might be considered a more spontaneous and sincere reflection of a person's admiration than the sentence: "This is nice." Consequently, the use of vocal affect emblems signals that the speaker experiences a relatively strong emotional state which does not lend itself easily to communication via cognitively planned verbalizations. While speakers may utter vocal affect emblems to convince interlocutors of the spontaneity and genuineness of their affective experience, it is possible that such vocal emblems are more easily elicited due to the neuronal prewiring of nonlinguistic affect vocalizations. The elicitation and production of affect vocalizations and vocal emblems makes a fascinating area of study with a high potential for insight into the relationship between emotion and vocalization.

The acoustic features of affective vocalizations are probably as reliably indicative of the underlying emotional states of the sender as animal calls seem indicative of specific motivational states of the animal. Situations in which a person encounters a harmful or unpleasant stimulus and has difficulties coping with it (as in fear-, anxiety-, or distress-evoking situations) call forth vocalizations that are described as screams, screeches, shrieks, cries, etc. These verbal descriptions point to the fact that most of these vocalizations have a fairly high fundamental frequency and a concentration of energy in the upper ranges of the spectrum. (It is interesting to note the onomatopoetic characteristics of the words which describe these sounds in many languages: often high front vowels such as [e] and [i] occupy the central voiced portion of the word.) Situations of comfort, satisfaction, or quiet happiness, on the other hand, are primarily characterized by energy concentration in the midfrequency range and lower fundamental frequency. Furthermore, attack (or onset) and decay (or termination) of these sounds are usually fairly rounded and soft, contrary to fear or anger vocalizations which are often characterized by a rather sharp onset with a quick rise in intensity. If a person feels powerful and in control of a situation, the fundamental frequency of a vocalization seems to be low and the energy concentrated in the lower parts of the spectrum, such as in roars, grunts, shouts, etc. It will be one of the major research tasks for the future to prepare an inventory of the repertoire of affect vocalizations and vocal emblems in different language and cultural groups in the world, to categorize these vocalizations according to the major dimensions of emotional states, and to provide a description of the acoustic characteristics of the respective classes of vocalizations. The results of such an undertaking could provide important leads for the study of the effect of emotional arousal on vocal behavior.

The same vocal apparatus that produces affect vocalizations is used for human speech. During the evolution of the human species the sound production apparatus has been modified for a communication system with special "design features", such as discreteness and arbitrariness of the sounds which constitute a message (Hockett, 1960; Thorpe, 1972). While there have been extensive changes in the neuronal and motor structures to allow the production of speech, this function has been superimposed on the earlier functions of affect vocalization, and we find a very intricate mixture of affect vocalization features, which are phylogenetically very old, and language features, which are phylogenetically very young in human speech (Lieberman, 1975). Many of the acoustic features of speech are not stringently constrained by the linguistic code but are free to vary with the underlying biological, psychological, and social characteristics of the sender (Scherer and Giles, 1979). Therefore, many of the prosodic or paralinguistic features, such as variation of fundamental frequency, intensity, energy, distribution in the spectrum, and some temporal and rhythmic patterns, play a major role in the "marking" of emotional states, even though they fulfill linguistic functions as well (Crystal, 1973).

It is difficult to assess whether these prosodic and paralinguistic features are the result of phonatory and articulatory processes similar to those involved in affect vocalizations, or whether they are the result of an interaction of the neuronal processes involved in speech production and the effect of the physiological state on the vocal organs. In addition to the effects of activation or arousal on phonatory and articulatory processes, emotional states may have an effect on speech planning and execution on a more central, cortical level. Apart from physiological arousal affecting the structures involved in speech production, the nature of emotional vocalization may be influenced by facial expressions affecting the shape of the vocal tract and by selective shaping of the acoustic characteristics according to a shared code within a speech community (Scherer, 1979 a,b). Before these mechanisms can be studied adequately we need empirical data on the objectively measurable effects of emotions on voice and speech. The major results of the relevant research to date are reviewed in the next section.

## REVIEW OF FINDINGS ON ACOUSTIC CORRELATES OF EMOTION IN SPEECH

It has been difficult for speech scientists and psychologists to study the effects of emotion on speech empirically (see reviews by Kramer, 1963; Scherer, 1979a; Starkweather, 1961). In spite of the pervasiveness of human emotions, they are very difficult to capture by means of objective scientific research. This is mostly due to the fact that emotions are considered in most cultures private experiences which, at least in their extreme manifestations, are to be hidden or suppressed in public. Even if their expression is allowed, such as grief at a burial, it is usually in highly ritualized and ceremonial situations in which recording or filming or systematic observation are deemed inappropriate. It is also difficult to produce emotions in the laboratory since they are emergency responses of the organism, and it would seem highly unethical to submit subjects to experimental situations with an extremely arousing character. While it may be legitimate and ethical to produce positive emotions, it is rather difficult to produce positive affect without a high investment of time and money. Perhaps this is the reason why negative emotions have been much more intensively studied. These difficulties account for the fact that the number of studies on the acoustical correlates of emotional speech is highly limited.

Generally, three major methods have been used to produce approximations to the natural vocal expression of emotion in the laboratory. Table 10-1 lists the most relevant studies in the field and their methodology. The production or induction method used most frequently is a straightforward encoding or simulation instruction. This consists of asking a number of speakers to produce a standard pattern of text (e.g., standard passages or sentences, letters of the alphabet, numbers) with a particular emotional expression. Somewhat related is the method of using excerpts from plays or having actors engage in

**Table 10-1**
Survey of Studies on Vocal Indicators of Discrete Emotions*

| Number | Study | Encoders | Induction | Voice sample | Instrument |
|---|---|---|---|---|---|
| 1. | Skinner (1935) | 9 male and 10 female drama students | Mood induction | "Ah" | Oscillograph |
| 2. | (a) Fairbanks & Pronovost (1939) (b) Fairbanks & Hoaglin (1941) | 6 male actors | Simulation | Standard sentences | Oscillograph |
| 3. | Eldred & Price (1958) | 1 female depressive | Interview topics | Interview responses poem | Ratings by 4 M.D.s |
| 4. | Zuberbier (1957) | 20 German students | Mood induction | | Amplitude level recorder |
| 5. | Sedláček & Sychra (1963) | 23 Czech actresses | Mood induction | Standard sentences | Pitch and amplitude level recorder |
| 6. | Davitz (1964, Ch. 5) | 3 male and 2 female speakers | Simulation | Standard sentences | Ratings by 5 judges |
| 7. | Davitz (1964, Ch. 8) | 3 male and 4 female speakers | Simulation | Standard sentences | Ratings by 20 judges |
| 8. | Bortz (1966) | 5 male German speakers | Simulation | Nonsense word | Filter bank analyzer |
| 9. | Huttar (1968) | 1 male speaker | Spontaneous | Selected utterances from natural speech | Spectrograph; Ratings by 12 judges |
| 10. | Costanzo, Markel, & Costanzo (1969) | 12 males and 11 female speakers | Simulation | Standard sentences | Ratings by 7 trained judges |

| Number Study | Encoders | Induction | Voice sample | Instrument |
|---|---|---|---|---|
| 11. Scherer, Koivu-maki, & Rosen-thal (1972) | 1 male and 1 female ac-tor | Playacting | Excerpts from play | Ratings by 61 judges |
| 12. Williams & Ste-vens (1972) | 3 male actors | Playacting | Standard sen-tences | Spectro-graph; Am-plitude level re-corder |
| 13. Markel, Bein, & Phillis (1973) | 50 male stu-dents | T A T cards | T A T re-sponses | Ratings by 15 trained judges |
| 14. Scherer, London, & Wolf (1973) | 1 male actor | Simulation | Standard text | Digital analy-sis; Ampli-tude level recorder |
| 15. Green & Cliff (1975) | 1 male drama student | Simulation | Letters of al-phabet | Ratings by 17 judges |
| 16. Levin & Lord (1975) | 1 male and 3 female dra-ma stu-dents | Simulation | Freely chosen words | Digital analy-sis |
| 17. Scherer & Wal-bott (in prep.) | 3 male and 3 female ac-tors | Playacting | Standard sen-tence | Digital analy-sis |

(Revised from Scherer, 1979a, pp. 510–511. Reprinted with permission of Plenum Press.)

short scenarios (with or without the insertion of standard text mate-rial in different emotion-related scripts or improvised interactions). The latter method has the advantage that there is a greater possibility for the speaker to create the emotion in a vicarious fashion by iden-tifying with a character or a role. Another attempt to provide a more naturalistic emotional experience for speakers is the mood induction technique in which music, poetry, or empathy techniques are used to produce a certain frame of mind in the speaker.

Only occasionally emotionally toned passages from natural speech samples have been selected and analyzed. Often the emotional expression contained in these samples is fairly mild and may not allow a direct comparison with more extreme forms of the expression of the respective emotion. Although it would be difficult to obtain speech samples of emotional expression, it is not impossible. Given the advances in sound recording technology, it would seem feasible to record samples of public displays of emotion unobtrusively, as long as it is ethically defensible. Possible sites for such efforts would be public situations in which the expression of emotion is licensed or at least not sanctioned. Examples are sports events where people are regularly allowed to show the whole gamut of emotions, games between a small number of players, or standardized interactions in public places with emotion producing potential.

In spite of the many methodological problems of simulation studies (Scherer, 1979 a, p. 509–512), it is probably impossible to avoid simulated emotional portrayals altogether. In part this is due to the fact that naturally recorded emotions are by definition singular cases, both in terms of speaker identity, situation context, and verbal content of the utterance. Therefore it is very difficult to separate the various factors that affect the speech pattern. Consequently, simulation studies have an important role in establishing the inter- and intraindividual variation of a vocal expression of emotion using highly controlled situational settings and verbal materials. Given the sensitivity of many of the acoustic and phonetic analysis parameters (e.g., formant structure) to such variations it seems desirable to render speech content and context comparable for different emotions and different speakers. Consequently, analysis of natural speech samples and of simulated portrayals should complement each other. The methodological problems previously described can be avoided by studying fairly standardized natural interactions. For example, one could use the situational context and the verbal material found in naturally occurring official–client interactions for simulation purposes, i.e., by having different speakers simulate a scenario with different emotions or attitudes (Scherer and Scherer, 1979, 1980).

One of the major problems with many of the studies listed in Table 10-1 is that they use only very few and unsystematically selected encoders. Obviously, if one of the advantages of the simulation method is to establish the intra- and interindividual constancy of emotional effects on speech, then this should be used to good advantage by selecting encoders and by using a fair number of them. In a recent study in our laboratory three male actors and three actresses were asked to impro-vise scenarios for different emotions in dyads (with a standard sen-tence which they had to introduce at the apex of the emotion display). In addition, scenarios were acted out in several different combinations of actor dyads allowing us to study not only the variability of the acoustic affects across persons but also to assess the variability of ex-pression within a person across several conditions, (Scherer and Wall-bott, in prep.).

Despite the large number of methodological flaws in many of the relevant studies, the pattern of results is surprisingly consistent, tes-tifying to the stability and strength of emotion effects on voice and speech. Detailed descriptions of analysis techniques and results of the more important studies are given in Chapter 11. Thus we can concen-trate here on the pattern of results for different discrete emotions and the evaluation, potency, and activity dimensions of emotions (Davitz, 1964). Table 10-2 shows the summary of the results on speech indica-tors of emotional states for some of the major vocal parameters. Ex-amination of this table shows that there are some systematic patterns. First, there seems to be a fairly high degree of covariation between the vocal indicators. One can distinguish the class of acoustic character-istics high in fundamental frequency with a wide range and variability of $F_0$, high amplitude or intensity, and fast tempo from an-other class of acoustic characteristics, with low fundamental frequen-cy, a narrow range and small variability, low intensity, and slow tempo. Looking at the discrete emotions which are characterized by each of these two patterns, the high frequency/amplitude/tempo pat-tern seems to correspond to a high degree of psychophysiological arou-sal (as one would expect from the activation dimension), whereas the latter pattern seems to be typical for low arousal, at least in terms of the ergotropic system.

One might well expect to find these patterns, given the nature of the effects of psychophysiological arousal on the various structures in-volved in voice and speech production (Scherer, 1979a; Chapter 11, this volume). However, such a simple dichotomy between high and low arousal correlates would imply that the different discrete emotions are not differentiated by specific combinations of acoustic patterns. In other words, the acoustic correlates would only reflect the location of this emotion on the activity or arousal dimension. The few research findings available to date do not provide a sufficient basis to answer the question whether only the activity dimension is reflected in vocal cues or whether there are specific patterns of acoustic cues for each emotion. This is partly due to the fact that the type of natural emo-tional expression studied or the simulation procedures used do not al-

**Table 10-2**
Summary of Results on Vocal Indicators of Emotional States

| Emotion | Pitch level | Pitch range | Pitch variability | Loudness | Tempo |
|---|---|---|---|---|---|
| Happiness/ joy | High 1,5,6,9 | ? | Large 5 | Loud 6,9 | Fast 6 |
| Confidence | High 9,14 | ? | ? | Loud 9,14 | Fast 9,14 |
| Anger | High 2a,3,6,9,12,16 | Wide 2a,12 | Large 2a | Loud 3,6,8,10,12 | Fast 2b,3,6,8,13 |
| Fear | High 2a,12 | Wide 2a | Large 2a | ? | Fast 2b |
| Indifference | Low 2a | Narrow 2a | Small 2a | ? | Fast 10 |
| Contempt | Low 2a | Wide 2a | ? | Loud 10 | Slow 2b |
| Boredom | Low 6,9 | Narrow 9 | ? | Soft 6,8,9 | Slow 6,8,9 |
| Grief/sad- ness | Low 2a,3,5,6,9 12,17 | Narrow 2a,12 | Small 2a | Soft 3,6,9 | Slow 2b,3,6,12,13 |
| Evaluation | ? | ? | ? | Loud 11 | ? |
| Activation | High 7,9,15 | Wide 9 | ? | Loud 4,7,9,11 | Fast 4,7,9,11 |
| Potency | ? | ? | ? | Loud 11 | ? |

(Revised from Scherer, 1979a, pp. 513. Reprinted with permission of Plenum Press.)

low us to be confident that specific discrete emotional expressions have really been produced. Furthermore, as the question marks in Table 10-2 show, we do not yet have a complete picture of the nature of vocal parameters for all emotions. In addition, Table 10-2 covers only some of the most central parameters, which are easily obtained and therefore have been analyzed often. It is possible, of course, that these parameters are representative of the central activation dimension, whereas other, more complex parameters, such as energy distribution in the spectrum, onset and termination of the signal, fine grained temporal and rhythmic patterns (Scherer, in press), are more specifically related to particular discrete emotions. It is to be expected that the recent advances in digital speech analysis techniques (Part I of this volume) will result in an increase of studies using a wider range of vocal parameters in their analyses.

## RECOGNITION OF EMOTION FROM SPEECH

While waiting for such studies to appear, there is one additional possibility to check on the specificity of the vocal patterning of emotional expression. It seems reasonable to assume that if different emotions are in fact characterized by specific combinations of vocal indicators, listeners ought to be able to differentiate discrete emotions on the basis of vocal displays only. If, on the other hand, only fairly general dimensions, such as activation, are reflected in acoustic characteristics, listeners should only be able to locate emotional displays on these emotional dimensions.

Unfortunately, the research evidence available does not provide us with a clear-cut answer to this question either. Most of the studies on the accuracy of emotion recognition from voice and speech have used the simulation or encoding method asking speakers, often actors or drama students, to read standard text material, such as standard sentences, letters of the alphabet, or numerals with specific emotional expressions. Apart from the artificiality of the verbal content underlying the emotional portrayal, one runs into more general problems with theatrical portrayals. First, renditions may be highly stereotypical and second, since the same actor encodes all emotions, differences between emotional portrayals may be exaggerated to permit easy discrimination. Furthermore, in most of the relevant studies, judges who are asked to listen to these emotional portrayals are requested to make decisions on discrete emotions only. Consequently, it is difficult to assess the accuracy with which vocal portrayals of emotions can be localized within the dimensional space of emotional expression.

Despite these shortcomings, it is instructive to examine the research results on emotion recognition from voice and speech cues. Table 10-3 shows a survey of most of these recognition studies, listing the material used for the vocal portrayals, the numbers of encoders and decoders, and the average percentage of accurate judgments. If one computes the average accuracy across all of those studies (excluding filtered speech, foreign language samples, and abnormal judge populations) one obtains a figure of about 60 percent accuracy. This is much higher than one would expect by chance, since judges in most of these studies had to make a choice between approximately four to

**Table 10-3**
Survey of Studies on Emotion Recognition from Speech

| Study | Speech Sample | Encoders | Decoders | Aver % Accur | Corr %Acc |
|---|---|---|---|---|---|
| Dusenbury & Knower, 1938 | letters of alphabet | 4 m, 4 f stud. | a) 135 m, 159 f b) 47 m, 17 f stud. | a) 83 b) 81 | a) 81 b) 79 |
| Fairbanks & Pronovost, 1933 | standard passage | 6 m amateur actors | 64 speech stud. | 79 | 74 |
| Knower, 1941 | letters of alphabet a) voiced forward b) whispered forward c) voiced reversed d) whispered reversed | 1 m, 1 f | 27 stud. | a) 89 b) 57 c) 43 d) 23 | a) 88 b) 53 c) 37 d) 15 |
| Pfaff, 1954 | numerals 1–8 | 1 m speech instructor | 304 stud. | 50 | 44 |
| Davitz & Davitz, 1959 | letters of alphabet | 4 m, 4 f stud. and faculty members, 1 actress | 30 grad. stud. | 37 | 30 |
| Pollack, Rubenstein, & Horowitz, 1960 | standard sentences a) 16 alternatives b) 8 alternatives | 4 | 18 | a) 42 b) 63 | a) 38 b) 58 |
| Soskin & Kauffman, 1961 | excerpts from real life recordings | 15 m | 22 | sign.* | |
| Lieberman & Michaels, 1962 | standard sentences | 3 m | 10 | 85 | * |
| Beldoch, 1964 | standard passage | 3 m, 2 f | 43 m, 46 f stud. | 54 | 49 |

| | | | | | |
|---|---|---|---|---|---|
| Dimitrovsky, 1964 | standard passage | 3m, 2 f | 224 children aged 5–12 yrs | 53 | 37 |
| Kramer, 1964 | standard passage a) American English b) filtered version (a) c) Japanese | a–b) 6 m speech stud. c) 3 Japanese stud. | a–c) 27 m stud. | a) 70 b) 61 c) 58 | a) 63 b) 51 c) 48 |
| Levitt, 1964 | standard passage | 25 m, 25 f stud. | 8 stud. | 47 | 36 |
| Levy, 1964 | standard passage | 3 m, 2 f | 32 m, 42 f stud. | 54 | 49 |
| Osser, 1964 | single word | 1 actress | 80 | 33 | 26 |
| Turner, 1964 | 36 nonsense sentences | 6 actors, 6 lay persons | a) 30 somatically ill patients b) 60 schizophrenic patients | a) 75 b) 59 | a) 70 b) 52 |
| Hornstein, 1967 | letters of alphabet | 124 f stud. | 124 f. stud. | 59 | 54 |
| Plaikner, 1970 | letters of alphabet | 1 German actor | 30 m, 19 f Germans | 53 | 49 |
| Wolf, Gorski, & Peters, 1972 | letters of alphabet | 25 m stud. | 25 m stud. (same as encoders) 45 | | 39 |
| Burns & Beier, 1973 | a) standard sentences b) filtered version (a) | a) 30 stud. b) 30 stud. | a) 21 stud. b) 21 stud. | a) 60 b) 39 | a) 52 b) 27 |
| Ross, Duffy, Cooker & Sargeant, 1973 | standard passage a) full range b) filtered 75–600 Hz c) filtered 75–450 Hz d) filtered 75–300 Hz e) filtered 75–150 Hz | 3 m, 3 f actors | 33 stud. | a) 70 b) 57 c) 55 d) 49 e) 26 | a) 66 b) 52 c) 49 d) 43 e) 17 |
| Schlanger, 1973 | standard sentences a) normals b) aphasics | * | * | a) 97 b) * | a) 96 b) * |

Table 10-3
Survey of Studies on Emotion Recognition from Speech

| Study | Speech Sample | Encoders | Decoders | Aver % Accur | Corr %Acc |
|---|---|---|---|---|---|
| Nash, 1974 | standard sentence | 1 m, 1 f | a) 45 m, 52 f hospital staff<br>b) 43 m, 91 f patients | a) 45<br>b) 32 | a) 40<br>b) 25 |
| McCluskey, Albas, Niemi, & Cuevas, 1975 | 2 improvised, emotion related sentences, content filtered | a) 3 f Canadian actresses<br>b) 3 f Mexican actresses | a) 10 f Canadian stud.<br>b) 10 f Mexican stud. | a) 73<br>b) 77 | a) 71<br>b) 69 |
| Sogon, 1975 | standard sentences | 12 Japanese | 30 Japanese | 57 | 46 |
| Zuckerman, Lipets, Koivumaki, & Rosenthal, 1975 | standard sentences | 27 m, 13 f stud. | a) 64 m stud.<br>b) 37 f stud. | a) 45<br>b) 46 | a) 38<br>b) 46 |
| Fenster, Blake, & Goldstein, 1977 | standard sentence | 30 m adults<br>30 m children 10–12 | a) 30 m adults<br>b) 30 boys 10–12<br>c) 30 boys 7–9 | a) 30<br>b) 28<br>c) 23 | a) 16<br>b) 14<br>c) 8 |
| Brown, 1980 | film description | 5 Spanish bilinguals | 18 stud. | 34 | 21 |
| Scherer & Walbott, in prep. | standard sentence | 3 m, 3 f German actors | 15 German stud. | 53 | 37 |

aver % accur = Average percentage of accurate judgments
corr % accur = accuracy percentage corrected for chance
* = relevant information not available
sign. = significant
m = male
f = female
stud. = students

ten emotions (i.e., accuracy to be expected by chance between 10 percent and 25 percent.) As the number of alternatives available in a judgment task strongly affects the probability of being correct (Pollack, Rubinstein, and Horowitz, 1960), the accuracy percentages should be corrected for guessing. The average for the corrected accuracy percentages listed in Table 10-3 is about 56 percent which should be compared to an average expected chance percentage of about 12 percent. This figure may be a somewhat conservative estimate, since in some studies rather esoteric affect states or emotional attitudes, such as pride, jealousy, love, nervousness, etc., had to be judged. These are probably much more difficult to recognize from very short standard sentence material than the fundamental discrete emotions such as anger, sadness, or happiness. Allowing for this possible attenuation in the average accuracy percentage, judges seem to be about equally capable to recognize emotion from the voice as from facial expression. A comparison of voice accuracy percentages for specific discrete emotions (for those studies in which a detailed breakdown by emotion is provided) with accuracy figures for recognition of facial expressions (Ekman, Friesen, and Ellsworth, 1972, p. 103) indicate that there is even a slight edge in favor of accurate recognition from speech in some cases. Due to the many methodological differences between these studies, such as type of simulation, number of alternatives, type of stimulus material, etc., an exact comparison of accuracy percentages is impossible.

Since most studies do not report accuracy percentages for specific emotions, it is difficult to tell which emotions are more easily recognizable from vocal expression. Judging from the data available, it looks as if negative emotions were generally more easily recognized than positive emotions (see also Fenster, Blake, and Goldstein, 1977). Anger often ranks first in terms of accurate recognition followed by sadness, indifference, and happiness. It would be most instructive for the question posed above, i.e., whether judges can really differentiate specific emotions, or whether they are merely able to locate emotional portrayals in a dimensional space, to have confusion matrices showing the patterns of errors in judgment (Brown, 1980). Unfortunately, the data are only very rarely presented in this form in the emotion recognition literature. Confusion matrices that have been published (e.g., Kramer, 1964) seem to allow the conclusion that errors are often made in incorrectly inferring emotions similar to the correct emotion in terms of their location on a particular emotional dimension. Thus, emotions which are fairly similar in terms of the arousal or activation involved, such as anger, elation, and fear may be more easily confused with each other than with emotions characterized by fairly low activation, such as grief, sadness, or indifference. Consequently, since the emotions that are generally studied occupy fairly discrete positions within the emotional space, an above chance discrimination may be possible even if judges only infer approximate positions on the important emotional dimensions.

In order to obtain a clear picture of the vocal communication of emotion we also need to know more about the vocal cues which serve as indicators of specific emotions for listeners. Since in all of these studies standard text or content-free material has been used, there is little doubt that emotional expression is communicated via nonlinguistic or paralinguistic cues. Even with standard content, however, it is possible that there is an interaction between verbal content and paralinguistic cues (e.g., selective emphasis on particular words). The studies in which filtered speech or foreign languages have been used show, however, that although the degree of accuracy is somewhat reduced, listeners can still recognize the emotion portrayed with better than chance accuracy. That the vocal cues which communicate emotion must be fairly basic and robust has been shown in a study by Scherer, Koivumaki, and Rosenthal (1972). Emotionally toned excerpts from a play were played back to listeners in a normal version, a content filtered version, a randomized spliced version (Scherer, 1971, randomly rearranging the sequence of subphonemic elements of speech), as well as a version which was *both* random spliced *and* content filtered. In the latter version, both sequence cues, (such as intonation contours, rhythm, pauses, etc.) *and* frequency cues (energy components above 650 Hz) were eliminated. In spite of this severe reduction of information, the ratings on adjectives reflecting the three major dimensions of active/passive, pleasant/unpleasant and strong/weak correlated highly ($r = .91$) with ratings of the original, unchanged speech sample. This result shows that some very basic acoustic cues, such as fundamental frequency and its variation, as well as intensity and its variation and other segmental cues, communicate the essential information concerning the location of a speech sample in the emotional space.

Exactly how different acoustic cues and their combinations are utilized by listeners to infer a particular emotional state is difficult to assess. One possible research approach is to attempt to manipulate these vocal cues systematically. Scherer has used a Moog synthesizer (Scherer, 1974; Scherer and Oshinsky, 1977) to vary configurations of acoustic cues systematically and asked judges to attribute emotional states. Table 10-4 shows the major results from these studies. Judges agreed remarkably well on the emotional meaning of particular cues

**Table 10-4**

Acoustic Parameters of Tone Sequences Significantly Contributing to the Variance in Attributions of Emotional States

| Rating scale | Single acoustic parameters (main effects) and configurations (interaction effects) listed in order of predictive strength |
|---|---|
| Pleasantness | Fast tempo, few harmonics, large pitch variation, sharp envelope, low pitch level, pitch contour down, small amplitude variation (salient configuration: large pitch variation plus pitch contour up) |
| Activity | Fast tempo, high pitch level, many harmonics, large pitch variation, sharp envelope, small amplitude variation |
| Potency | Many harmonics, fast tempo, high pitch level, round envelope, pitch contour up (salient configurations: large amplitude variation plus high pitch level, high pitch level plus many harmonics) |
| Anger | Many harmonics, fast tempo, high pitch level, small pitch variation, pitch contours up (salient configuration: small pitch variation plus pitch contour up) |
| Boredom | Slow tempo, low pitch level, few harmonics, pitch contour down, round envelope, small pitch variation |
| Disgust | Many harmonics, small pitch variation, round envelope, slow tempo (salient configuration: small pitch variation plus pitch contour up) |
| Fear | Pitch contour up, fast sequence, many harmonics, high pitch level, round envelope, small pitch variation (salient configurations: small pitch variation plus pitch contour up, fast tempo plus many harmonics) |
| Happiness | Fast tempo, large pitch variation, sharp envelope, few harmonics, moderate amplitude variation (salient configurations: large pitch variation plus pitch contour up, fast tempo plus few harmonics) |
| Sadness | Slow tempo, low pitch level, few harmonics, round envelope, pitch contour down (salient configuration: low pitch level plus slow tempo) |
| Surprise | Fast tempo, high pitch level, pitch contour up, sharp envelope, many harmonics, large pitch variation (salient configuration: high pitch level plus fast tempo) |

(Revised from Scherer & Oshinsky, 1977, p. 340. Reprinted with permission of Plenum Press.)

and cue combinations and, although only synthesized sound sequences rather than speech was used, the results provide a fairly clear picture of the inference processes involved in judging emotion from speech.

## CONCLUSION

The preceding review of the literature leaves little doubt that emotional states do affect voice and speech patterns and that listeners are generally able to correctly infer the affective state of the speaker. Yet, many questions remain. Among the important issues that could not be raised within the confines of this chapter are the existence of strong individual differences in both encoding and decoding emotions due to age, sex, or personality (see reviews in Rosenthal, 1979) and the role of different communication modalities (e.g., Cunningham, 1977; Ekman, Friesen, O'Sullivan, Scherer, 1980; Zaidel and Mehrabian, 1973). Clearly, further research is urgently needed, particularly with regard to the important practical implications of emotion communication in many kinds of social interactions.

In order to understand fully the communication of emotional meaning via voice and speech, however, we need to engage in more complex studies in which both expression and impression are jointly analyzed using standard procedures and parameters of measurement and in which individual differences are studied systematically. One particularly promising approach would be to design studies along the lines of the Brunswikian lens model which has been proposed for the study of speech and personality in Chapter 6. For each of the major dimensions of emotional meaning as well as for discrete emotions, we have to establish the nature of the externalization of the emotion in voice and speech in terms of the objective characteristics of emotional speech on the levels of the physiological substratum, the phonatory and articulatory processes, and the acoustic characteristics. Furthermore, we have to determine the perceptual representation of these acoustic characteristics as proximal cues in the listener. Finally, the nature of the inference processes resulting in predictable attributions on the basis of the proximal cues have to be established. Once we have this information it will be possible to obtain a more complete picture of the nature of emotional expression in voice and speech and to understand the factors underlying our ability to accurately recognize emotion from the voice and speech patterns of our interlocutors.

REFERENCES

Arnold, M. B. *Emotion and personality* (Vol. 1). *Psychological aspects.* New York: Columbia University Press, 1960.

Arnold, M. B. The *nature of emotion: Selected readings.* Baltimore: Penguin, 1968.

Beier, E. G., Zautra, A. J. Identification of vocal communication of emotions across cultures. *Journal of Consulting and Clinical Psychology*, 1972, *39*, 116.

Beldoch, M. Sensitivity to expression of emotional meaning in three modes of communication. In J. R. Davitz (Ed.), *The communication of emotional meaning,* New York: McGraw-Hill, 1964, pp. 31–42.

Bortz, J. Physikalisch-akustische Korrelate der vokalen Kommunikation. *Arbeiten aus dem Psychologischen Institut der Universität Hamburg*, 1966, 9.

Brown, B. L. The detection of emotion in vocal qualities. In H. Giles, P. W. Robinson, P. Smith (Eds.), *Language: Social psychological perspectives.* Oxford: Pergamon, 1980.

Burns, K. L., Beier, E. G. Significance of vocal and visual channels in the decoding of emotional meaning. *Journal of Communication*, 1973, *23*, 118–130.

Cannon, W. B. *Bodily changes in panic, hunger, fear, and rage.* New York: Appleton-Century-Crofts, 1915.

Chevalier-Skolnikoff, S. Facial expression of emotion in nonhuman primates. In P. Ekman (Ed.), *Darwin and facial expression.* New York: Academic Press, 1973, pp. 11–89.

Costanzo, F. S., Markel, N. N., Costanzo, P. R. Voice quality profile and perceived emotion. *Journal of Counseling Psychology*, 1969, *16*, 267–270.

Crystal, D. Nonsegmental phonology in language acquisition: A review of the issues. *Lingua*, 1973, *32*, 1–45.

Cunningham, M. R. Personality and the structure of the nonverbal communication of emotion. *Journal of Personality*, 1977, *45*, 564–584.

Darwin, C. *The expression of the emotions in man and animals.* London: John Murray, 1872 (Reprinted, Chicago: University of Chicago Press, 1965).

Davitz, J. R. Personality, perceptual, and cognitive correlates of emotional sensitivity. In J. R. Davitz (Ed.), *The communication of emotional meaning.* New York: McGraw-Hill, 1964, pp. 57–68.

Davitz, J. R. Auditory correlates of vocal expressions of emotional meanings. In J. R. Davitz (Ed.), *The communication of emotional meaning.* New York: McGraw-Hill, 1964, pp. 101–112.

Davitz, J. R. *The language of emotion.* New York: Academic Press, 1969.

Davitz, J. R., Davitz, L. J. The communication of feelings by content-free speech. *Journal of Communication*, 1959, *9*, 6–13.

Dimitrovsky, L. The ability to identify the emotional meaning of vocal expressions at successive levels. In J. R. Davitz (Ed.), *The communication of emotional meaning.* New York: McGraw-Hill, 1964, pp. 69–86.

Dusenbury, D., Knower, F. H. Experimental studies of the symbolism of action and voice (III): A study of the specificity of meaning in facial expression. *Quarterly Journal of Speech,* 1938, *24,* 424–435.

Ekman, P. Universal and cultural differences in facial expression of emotion. In J. R. Cole (Ed.), *Nebraska Symposium on Motivation,* 1971. Lincoln: University of Nebraska Press, 1972, pp. 207–283.

Ekman, P. Movements with precise meanings. *Journal of Communication,* 1976, *26,* 14–26.

Ekman, P. (Ed.) *Darwin and facial expression: A century of research in review.* New York: Academic Press, 1973.

Ekman, P., Friesen, W. V., O'Sullivan, M., Scherer, K. R. Relative importance of face, body, and speech in judgments of personality and affect. *Journal of Personality and Social Psychology,* 1980, *38,* 270–277.

Eldred, S. H., Price, D. B. A linguistic evaluation of feeling states in psychotherapy. *Psychiatry,* 1958, *21,* 115–121.

Fairbanks, G., Hoaglin, L. An experimental study of the durational characteristics of the voice during the expression of emotion. *Speech Monographs,* 1941, *8,* 85–90.

Fairbanks, G., Pronovost, W. An experimental study of the pitch characteristics of the voice during the expression of emotion. *Speech Monographs,* 1939, *6,* 87–104.

Fenster, C. A., Blake, L. K., Goldstein, A. M. Accuracy of vocal emotional communications among children and adults and the power of negative emotions. *Journal of Communication Disorders,* 1977, *10,* 301–314.

Gellhorn, E. *Biological foundations of emotion.* Glenview, Ill.: Scott, 1968.

Green, R. S., Cliff, N. Multidimensional comparisons of structures of vocally and facially expressed emotion. *Perception and Psychophysics,* 1975, *17,* 429–438.

Green, S. Variation of vocal pattern with social situation in the Japanese monkey (Macaca fuscata): A field study. In: L. A. Rosenblum (Ed.), *Primate behavior. Developments in field and laboratory research.* Vol. 4. New York: Academic Press, 1975, pp. 2–102.

Grossman, S. P. *Physiological psychology.* New York: John Wiley and Sons, 1967.

Hockett, C. F. Logical considerations in the study of animal communication. In W. E. Lanyon and W. N. Tavolga (Eds.) *Animal sounds and communication.* Washington, D.C.: American Institute of Biological Sciences, 1960, pp. 392–430.

Hooff, J. A. van, A comparative approach to the phylogeny of laughter and smiling. In R. Hinde (Ed.) *Nonverbal communication.* Cambridge: Cambridge University Press, 1972, pp. 209–241.

Hornstein, M. G., Accuracy of emotional communication and interpersonal compatibility. *Journal of Personality,* 1967, *35,* 20–28.

Huttar, G. L. Relations between prosodic variables and emotions in normal American English utterances. *Journal of Speech and Hearing Research,* 1968, *11,* 481–487.

Izard, C. E. *The face of emotion.* New York: Appleton-Century-Crofts, 1971.

Izard, C. E. On the ontogenesis of emotions and emotion–cognition relationships in infancy. In M. Lewis and L. A. Rosenblum (Eds.), *The develop-ment of affect*. New York: Plenum Press, 1978, pp. 389–413.

Izard, C. E., Buechler, S. Emotion expressions and personality integration in infancy. In C. E. Izard (Ed.), *Emotions in personality and psychopathology*. New York: Plenum Press, 1979, pp. 445–472.

Jürgens, U. Vocalization as an emotional indicator: A neuroethological study in the squirrel monkey. *Behaviour*, 1979, *69*, 88–117.

Klages, L. *Grundlagen der Wissenschaft vom Ausdruck*. (7th ed.) Bonn: Bouvier, 1950.

Kleinpaul, R. *Sprache ohne Worte - Idee einer allgemeinen Wissenschaft der Sprache*. Leipzig: Friedrich, 1888. (Reprinted, Den Haag: Mouton, 1972).

Knower, F. H. Analysis of some experimental variations of simulated vocal expressions of the emotions. *Journal of Social Psychology*, 1941, *14*, 369–372.

Kramer, E. Judgment of personal characteristics and emotions from nonverbal properties of speech. *Psychological Bulletin*, 1963, *60*, 408–420.

Kramer, E. Elimination of verbal cues in judgments of emotion from voice. *Journal of Abnormal and Social Psychology*, 1964, *68*, 390–396.

Lange, K. *The emotions*. Baltimore: Williams and Wilkins, 1922 (Originally published, 1885).

Lazarus, R. S. Emotions and adaptation: Conceptual and empirical relations. In: W. J. Arnold (Ed.), *Nebraska Symposium on Motivation (Vol. 16)*. Lincoln: University of Nebraska Press, 1968, pp. 175–270.

Lazarus, R. S., Averill, J. R., Opton, E. M. Towards a cognitive theory of emotion. In M. B. Arnold *(Ed.)*, *Feelings and emotions: The Loyola Symposium*. New York: Academic Press, 1970, pp. 207–232.

Leeper, R. W. The motivational and perceptual properties of emotions as indicating their fundamental character and role. In M. B. Arnold (Ed.), *Feelings and emotions: The Loyola Symposium*. New York: Academic Press, 1970, pp. 151–168.

Lersch, P. *Der Aufbau der Person*. (8th ed.) München: Barth, 1962.

Levin, H., Lord, W. Speech pitch frequency as an emotional state indicator. IEEE *Transactions on Systems, Man, and Cybernetics*, 1975, *5*, 259–273.

Levitt, E. A. The relationship between abilities to express emotional meanings vocally and facially. In J. R. Davitz (Ed.), *The communication of emotional meaning*. New York: McGraw-Hill, 1964, pp. 87–100.

Levy, P. K. The ability to express and perceive vocal communication of feeling. In J. R. Davitz (Ed.), *The communication of emotional meaning*. New York: McGraw-Hill, 1964, pp. 43–55.

Leyhausen, P. Biologie von Ausdruck und Eindruck (Teil 1). *Psychologische Forschung*, 1967, *31*, 113–176.

Lieberman, P. *On the origins of language: An introduction to the evolution of human speech*. New York: Macmillan, 1975.

Lieberman, P., Michaels, S. B. Some aspects of fundamental frequency and envelope amplitudes as related to the emotional content of speech. *Journal of the Acoustical Society of America*, 1962, *34*, 922–927.

Mandler, G. *Mind and emotions*. New York: John Wiley and Sons, 1975.

Markel, N. N., Bein, M. F., Phillis, J. A. The relationship between words and tone-of-voice. *Language and Speech*, 1973, *16*, 15–21.

Marler, P., Tenaza, R. Signaling behavior of apes with special reference to vocalization. In: T. A. Sebeok (Ed.), *How animals communicate.* Bloomington, Ind.: Indiana University Press, 1977, pp. 965–1033.

McCluskey, K. W., Albas, D. C., Niemi, R. R., et al. Cross-cultural differences in the perception of the emotional content of speech: A study of the development of sensitivity in Canadian and Mexican children. *Developmental Psychology,* 1975, *11,* 551–555.

Morton, E. S. On the occurrence and significance of motivation-structural rules in some bird and mammal sounds. *American Naturalist,* 1977, *111,* 855–869.

Mowrer, O. H. *Learning theory and behavior.* New York: John Wiley and Sons, 1960.

Nash, H. Perception of vocal expression of emotion by hospital staff and patients. *Genetic Psychology Monographs,* 1974, *89,* 25–87.

Osser, H. A. A distinctive feature analysis of the vocal communication of emotion. *Dissertation Abstracts,* 1964, *25,* 3708.

Pfaff, P. L. An experimental study of the communication of feeling without contextual material. *Speech Monographs,* 1954, *21,* 155–156.

Plaikner, D. Die Veränderung der menschlichen Stimme unter dem Einfluss psychischer Belastung. Unpublished doctoral dissertation, Philosophische Fakultät der Universität Innsbruck, 1970.

Plutchik, R. *The emotions: Facts, theories, and a new model.* New York: Random House, 1962.

Pollack, I., Rubenstein, H., Horowitz, A. Communication of verbal modes of expression. *Language and Speech,* 1960, *3,* 121–130.

Redican, W. K. Facial expressions in nonhuman primates. In L. A. Rosenblum (Ed.) *Primate behavior,* Vol. 4. New York: Academic Press, 1975, pp. 103–194.

Rosenthal, R. (Ed.) *Skill in nonverbal communication: Individual differences.* Cambridge, Mass.: Oelgeschlager, Gunn & Hain, 1979.

Ross, M., Duffy, R. J., Cooker, H. S. et al. Contribution of the lower audible frequencies to the recognition of emotions. *American Annals of the Deaf,* 1973, *118,* 37–42.

Sartre, J. P. *The emotions: Outline of a theory.* New York: Philosophical Library, 1948.

Schachter, S. The assumption of identity and peripheralist–centralist controversies in motivation and emotion. In M. B. Arnold (Ed.), *Feelings and emotions: The Loyola Symposium.* New York: Academic Press, 1970, pp. 111–121.

Scherer, K. R. Randomized splicing: A note on a simple technique for masking speech content. *Journal of Experimental Research in Personality,* 1971, *5,* 155–159.

Scherer, K. R. Acoustic concomitants of emotional dimensions: Judging affect from synthesized tone sequences. In S. Weitz (Ed.), *Nonverbal communication.* New York: Oxford University Press, 1974, pp. 105–111.

Scherer, K. R. Affektlaute und vokale Embleme. In R. Posner and H. P. Reinecke (Eds.), *Zeichenprozesse - Semiotische Forschung in den Einzelwissenschaften.* Wiesbaden: Athenaion, 1977, pp. 199–214.

Scherer, K. R. Nonlinguistic vocal indicators of emotion and psychopathology. In C. E. Izard (Ed.), *Emotions in personality and psychopathology*. New York: Plenum, 1979, pp. 493–529. (a)

Scherer, K. R. Personality markers in speech. In K. R. Scherer and H. Giles (Eds.), *Social markers in speech*. Cambridge: Cambridge University Press, 1979, pp. 147–209. (b)

Scherer, K. R. Methods of research on vocal communication: Paradigms and parameters. In K. R. Scherer and P. Ekman (Eds.), *Handbook of methods in nonverbal behavior research.* Cambridge: Cambridge University Press, in press.

Scherer, K. R., Giles, H. (Eds.) *Social markers in speech*. Cambridge: Cambridge University Press, 1979.

Scherer, K. R., Oshinsky, J. S. Cue utilization in emotion attribution from auditory stimuli. *Motivation and Emotion*, 1977, *1*, 331–346.

Scherer, K. R., Scherer, U. Nonverbales Verhalten von Beamten in der Interaktion mit dem Bürger: Erste Ergebnisse. In K. R. Scherer and H. G. Wallbott (Eds.), *Nonverbale Kommunikation: Ausgewählte Forschungsberichte zum Interaktionsverhalten*. Weinheim: Beltz, 1979, pp. 307–319.

Scherer, U., Scherer, K. R. Psychological factors in bureaucratic encounters: Determinants and effects of interactions between officials and clients. In W. T. Singleton, P. Spurgeon and R. B. Stammers (Eds.), *The analysis of social skill*. New York: Plenum, 1980, pp. 315–328.

Scherer, K. R., Koivumaki, J., Rosenthal, R. Minimal cues in the vocal communication of affect: Judging emotions from content-masked speech. *Journal of Psycholinguistic Research*, 1972, *1*, 269–285.

Scherer, K. R., London, H., Wolf, J. The voice of confidence: Paralinguistic cues and audience evaluation. *Journal of Research in Personality*, 1973, *7*, 31–44.

Scherer, K. R., Wallbott, H. G. Cues and channels in emotion recognition. Unpublished manuscript, University of Giessen, in preparation.

Schlanger, B. B. Identification by normal and aphasic subjects of semantically meaningful and meaningless emotional toned sentences. *Acta Symbolica*, 1973, *4*, 30–38.

Sedlacek, K., Sychra, A. Die Melodie als Faktor des emotionellen Ausdrucks. *Folia Phoniatrica*, 1963, *15*, 89–98.

Skinner, R. E. A calibrated recording and analysis of the pitch, force, and quality of vocal tones expressing happiness and sadness. And a determination of the pitch and force of the subjective concepts of ordinary, soft, and loud tones. *Speech Monographs*, 1935, *2*, 81–137.

Sogon, S. A study of the personality factor which affects the judgment of vocally expressed emotions. *Japanese Journal of Psychology*, 1975, *46*, 247–254.

Soskin, W. F., Kauffman, P. E. Judgment of emotions in word-free voice samples. *Journal of Communication*, 1961, *11*, 73–81.

St. Martin, G. M. Male/female differential encoding and intercultural differential decoding of nonverbal affective communication. *Dissertation Abstracts International*, 1976, *37*, 2499–2500.

Starkweather, J. A. Vocal communication of personality and human feelings. *Journal of Communication*, 1961, *11*, 63–72.

Strongman, K. T. *The psychology of emotion.* London: John Wiley and Sons, 1973.

Tembrock, G. *Tierstimmenforschung. Eine Einführung in die Bioakustik.* (2. Aufl.) Wittenberg Lutherstadt: A. Ziemsen, 1977.

Thorpe, W. H. The comparison of vocal communication in animals and man. In R. A. Hinde (Ed.), *Nonverbal communication.* Cambridge: Cambridge University Press, 1972, pp. 27–47.

Tomkins, S. S. *Affect, imagery, consciousness* (Vol. 1): *The positive affects.* New York: Springer, 1962.

Turner, J. le B. Schizophrenics as judges of vocal expressions of emotional meaning. In J. R. Davitz (Ed.), *The communication of emotional meaning.* New York: McGraw-Hill, 1964, pp. 129–142.

Williams, C. E., Stevens, K. N. Emotions and speech: Some acoustical correlates. *Journal of the Acoustical Society of America*, 1972, *52*, 1238–1250.

Wolf, G., Gorski, R., Peters, S. Acquaintance and accuracy of vocal communication of emotions. *Journal of Communication*, 1972, *22*, 300–305.

Wundt, W. *Völkerpsychologie.* (Vol. 1) Leipzig: Engelmann, 1900.

Zaidel, S. F., Mehrabian, A. The ability to communicate and infer positive and negative attitudes facially and vocally. *Journal of Experimental Research in Personality*, 1969, *3*, 233–241.

Zuberbier, E. Zur Schreib- und Sprechmotorik der Depression. *Zeitschrift für Psychotherapie und Medizinische Psychologie*, 1957, *7*, 239–249.

Zuckerman, M., Lipets, M. S., Koivumaki, J. H., et al. Encoding and decoding nonverbal cues of emotion. *Journal of Personality and Social Psychology*, 1975, *32*, 1068–1076.

Carl E. Williams
Kenneth N. Stevens

# 11

# Vocal Correlates of Emotional States

I ... uh ... can't even talk to people. It's a, it's a, it's a ... I, a, I can't talk, ladies and gentlemen ... I, I can hardly breathe. I, I'm going to step inside where I cannot see it. I, I can't a ... Listen folks, I, I'm going to have to stop for a minute because I've lost my voice. This is the worst thing I've ever witnessed.

(Radio announcer describing the crash of the *Hindenburg*)

When an individual is exposed to an emotion-producing situation, such as was the radio announcer who was describing the approach of the *Hindenburg* when the zeppelin suddenly burst into flames, various changes in bodily state occur. These changes, which are the result of changes in the activity of the sympathetic and parasympathetic branches of the autonomic nervous system, can affect speech behavior, even against the individual's will.

The purpose of this section is (1) to briefly discuss some of the acoustic characteristics of speech that can be influenced by an individual's physiological and emotional state, and (2) to bring together from a historical perspective the results of a few selected studies which have attempted to identify and measure those parameters in the speech signal that reflect an individual's emotional state. The latter purpose will focus primarily on a detailed description of some of the authors' own research (Williams and Stevens, 1972), and will also include the presentation of some data heretofore unpublished. [We will not attempt to provide a complete review of the acoustical correlates of emotional states, since there already exist a number of reviews of past research on this topic (Davitz, 1964; Kramer, 1963; Scherer, 1979 and Chapter 10 of this volume; Weitz, 1979).]

## SOME PHYSIOLOGICAL CONSIDERATIONS

Two general views regarding the relationship between bodily reactions and emotional experiences can be identified:*

> The first view maintains that bodily reactions play a controlling factor in emotions, that they to some degree control and determine what we feel. The second view posits that bodily reactions are secondary effects of emotion and, while they do not control emotions, they can be used as indicators of emotion. (Grings and Dawson, 1978, p. 3)

For various emotions, one can expect considerable individual differences in the degree of activation of the sympathetic nervous system (SNS) and parasympathetic nervous system (PNS) and in the specific structures affected, particularly when the PNS is involved. The two systems have opposing effects that serve the function of regulating visceral activities and maintaining stability in the physiological systems of the body.

Increased activation of the SNS occurs during the emotions anger and fear. A consequence of this activation is an increase in the heart rate and blood pressure, and in the distribution of blood in the exterior muscles. Further effects of this heightened activity are changes in the rate, depth, and pattern of respiratory movements and a decrease in secretion from the salivary glands, leading to an increase in viscosity of the saliva and a drying of the mouth. Sweating of the palms is frequently a concomitant of the emotional state associated with fear and anger. Tremor in muscle activity is also often observed for these emotional states, and occasionally for grief as well.

Increased activation of the PNS leads to a decreased heart rate, a reduction of blood pressure, a diversion of blood to the digestive tract and away from the external muscles, and an increase in salivation. The PNS is normally active when we are calm and relaxed, but is increased in activity when an individual feels dejection, defeat, and grief. This division of the autonomic system appears capable of selectively influencing individual structures in the body and can be subjected to some degree of voluntary control, whereas the sympathetic division tends to work as a unit and to be more general, or less specific, in its effects.

These various physiological effects of increased activity in the divisions of the autonomic system can have a direct influence on the

---

*For a review of the numerous contemporary theories of emotion, see Strongman, 1973.

control of the various articulatory and respiratory movements involved in speech production and can affect the manner in which the vocal cords vibrate to produce the acoustic sources for voiced speech sounds. Changes in activation of the muscles controlling the articulatory structures can lead to changes in the timing of movements and, presumably, to different amplitudes of motion of the structures. These changes would result in modification in the rate of articulation, the range of vowel qualities produced, and the range of frequencies of vocal cord vibration. Changes in the depth, rate, and pattern of respiration can have an influence on the magnitude and time pattern of the subglottal pressure and the position of the sternum (to which the larynx is attached through the strap muscles); these changes can modify the contour of fundamental frequency versus time and the acoustic characteristics of obstruent consonants, which are produced by buildup of pressure behind a constriction. For example, increased subglottal pressure would lead to a longer interval of turbulence noise generation at the release of a stop consonant. The condition of moistness or dryness of the vocal folds can modify the vibratory patterns and thus change the characteristics of the source of acoustic excitation of the vocal tract at the larynx. This modification of the source could lead to a different overall spectrum shape for vowels and possibly to deviations from regular periodic vocal cord vibration during voiced sounds. Thus there are potentially a number of acoustic characteristics of speech that are influenced by an individual's physiological and emotional state. It is not unreasonable to suppose, therefore, that certain acoustic characteristics of the speech produced by an individual may provide an indication of his or her physiological and emotional state.

## REVIEW OF SELECTED STUDIES

Historically, research studies directed toward the identification and measurement of those parameters in the speech signal that reflect an individual's emotional state have, for the most part, utilized speech samples obtained during simulated emotional situations. This approach provides investigators the best opportunity for obtaining good recordings that can be subjected to both quantitative and qualitative analyses. Recordings of vocal utterances in "real-life" situations, in which there is no question as to the emotion present, are difficult to acquire; moreover, they frequently reflect the simultaneous presence of several emotions, interfering background noises, and the lack of control of the speech material. Most of the data to be presented and discussed herein were obtained in studies utilizing simulated emotions.

## Studies Utilizing Simulated Emotions

Two classic investigations in the speech science area that utilized the simulated emotion approach were those of Fairbanks and Pronovost (1939),* who studied pitch characteristics of the voice during the expression of simulated emotions, and Fairbanks and Hoaglin (1941), who investigated the durational features of the same simulations.

THE FAIRBANKS AND PRONOVOST STUDY (1939)

In this study, voice recordings were obtained of six amateur male actors simulating five emotional states: anger, fear, grief, indifference, and contempt. The test passage employed by each of the actors during their simulations was: "There is no other answer. You've asked me that question a thousand times, and my reply has always been the same. It always will be the same." (p. 88)

A method of listener identification was used to validate the simulations. Sixty-four young adult speech students were provided with a list of 12 emotional states (the additional states being: astonishment, doubt, elation, embarrassment, jealousy, love, and amusement) and were asked to select from the list, as each recording was played, the term that most accurately described the simulated emotion. The listeners were not told that the emotions were simulated. Fairbanks and Pronovost considered the simulations to be highly satisfactory examples of the emotions studied, as indicated by the following percentages of correct listener identifications: indifference 88 percent; contempt 84 percent; anger 78 percent; grief 78 percent; and fear 66 percent. The most important results of measurements of fundamental frequency ($F_0$) obtained from the recorded voice samples are reproduced in Table 11-1 where all six voices are considered as a group. As can be seen, fear showed the highest median $F_0$ value, followed by anger, grief, contempt, and indifference. Fear, contempt, and anger gave rise to the greatest range of $F_0$, and anger showed the greatest mean rate of change in $F_0$. Fundamental frequency curves obtained of the simulated emotions (not shown) revealed generally wider, rapid inflections for anger, irregularity of $F_0$ changes for fear, a consistent vibrato for grief, and a lack of distinguishing features for indifference.

---

*See also Fairbanks, 1940.

**Table 11-1**
Measurements of Fundamental Frequency ($F_0$) for Five Simulated Emotions.

|                              | Contempt | Anger | Fear | Grief | Indifference |
|------------------------------|----------|-------|------|-------|--------------|
| Median $F_0$ (Hz)            | 124      | 229   | 254  | 136   | 108          |
| Mean total $F_0$ range (octaves) | 1.8  | 1.7   | 1.9  | 1.5   | 1.3          |
| Mean rate of $F_0$ change (octaves) | 2.8 | 4.3 | 3.2  | 2.6   | 2.8          |

(From Fairbanks & Pronovost, 1939; Fairbanks, 1940. Reproduced with permission.)

THE FAIRBANKS AND HOAGLIN STUDY (1941)

The major results of this study on the durational features of the five simulated emotions mentioned previously are reproduced in Table 11-2. A comparison of the emotions in the table shows that grief and contempt are characterized by a slow speaking rate and may be differentiated from each other and from the other emotions. Accounting for the slow rate for grief is the prolongation of pauses, particularly between phrases. The total pause time is nearly equal to the total phonation time. Anger, fear, and indifference are characterized by a relatively rapid speaking rate.

AUTHORS' STUDIES

Some of our own exploratory investigations into the acoustical correlates of emotions (Williams and Stevens, 1972) have also utilized simulated emotions. Whereas in other studies individuals were asked to simulate emotions on the basis of such instructions as, "read this as though you are angry" or "put yourself in this situation," it was our opinion that such limited instructions might be interpreted quite differently by individuals, and that they would tend to stereotype the emotions rather then attempt to experience true feelings. For this reason, in some of our studies we used professional "method" actors

**Table 11-2**
Measures of Total Speaking Time (in Seconds) and Speaking Rate (in Words per Minute). All Values Are Means for Six Speakers.

|                     | Contempt | Anger | Fear | Grief | Indifference |
|---------------------|----------|-------|------|-------|--------------|
| Total speaking time | 14.03    | 8.51  | 8.03 | 12.57 | 7.74         |
| Rate                | 116      | 190   | 202  | 129   | 209          |

(From Fairbanks & Hoaglin, 1941. Reproduced with permission.)

who presumably become deeply involved in the roles that they play. We felt that the emotions of interest might best be described in terms of specific situations involving emotional interaction among several people. Getting the actors involved in clearly defined situations would, hopefully, result in their experiencing and expressing the various emotions that were to be studied.

*Methodology.* A detailed outline of a short play involving three male characters was constructed and given to a playwright who wrote the dialogue for the three actors who would be speaking in various situations. The play served to provide smooth and logical transitions from one emotional situation to the next, and it gave each actor an opportunity to live through a number of related situations. The primary function of the play was to elicit the desired emotions from the actors and to serve as the carrier for selected phrases and sentences to be embedded in the different emotional situations. These phrases and sentences, so-called "control clusters," were then later subjected to detailed acoustical analyses. Because changes in the speech signal due to the presence of some emotions might be subtle, we considered it necessary to be able to compare utterances of identical material as it occurred in different emotional situations. In addition to having the control clusters as speech material to be examined, longer portions of the dialogue, usually several sentences surrounding a control cluster, were selected for study.

A professional director and three professional actors, (all former members of the Actor's Studio experienced in the "method" style of acting) were employed in recording the special scenario. Three rehearsals were held, and at each rehearsal the actors read and studied all three roles. To provide more emotional situations for each actor than could be included in a single role and to obtain the best casting of the roles, the actors were asked to portray each character. In rotating from role to role, the actors were cautioned against changing any vocal characteristics which might invalidate comparisons of utterances between roles. The recordings were made in a professional recording studio.

*Emotional exercises.* In addition to recording the scenario, recordings were also obtained of each of the three actors performing four emotional exercises: neutral, anger, fear, and sorrow. This particular type of exercise, part of the method actor's training, centers around the recall of past events to re-experience a particular feeling or emotion. The control clusters employed in the emotional exercises were a combination of two of the clusters employed in the scenario:

"Maybe that's true. I don't understand it." Control cluster tapes were prepared for each of the three voices, both for spectrogaphic analysis and for presentation to listeners.

Although a vast amount of data was made available from the various recordings of the scenario, only selected samples and results will be presented in order to demonstrate some of the ways in which the data were examined. Data included quantitative results that were obtained by making various measurements from wide- and narrow-band spectrograms, as well as graphic level recordings and qualitative observations that consisted simply of setting down impressions derived from visual examination of a number of spectrographic patterns.

*Listener identification of the emotions.* In order to determine the relative aural effectiveness of the actors' simulations of the emotions called for in the scenario, the recorded control clusters were played to twelve listeners. The listeners were provided with a list of five descriptors from which they were asked to select for a given vocal utterance the descriptor that described most accurately the speaker's emotional state. The results of the listening tests are shown in Table 11-3 in the form of a confusion matrix. The diagonal entries enclosed in boxes show for each of five types of situations in the scenario (neutral, happy, anger, fear, and sorrow) the percentage of correct identifications made by the listeners. The percentages are based on the total number of responses obtained from the twelve listeners for the three voices. Sorrow received the highest identification score (73 percent), and fear the lowest (27 percent). Identification scores of 51 percent and 47 percent were achieved for anger and neutral situations, respectively. Except for the 73 percent identification score for sorrow, these scores are somewhat lower than those reported in the Fairbanks and Pronovost study (1939), which employed considerably longer speech samples.

**Table 11-3**
Confusion Matrix of Listener Identifications of Selected Simulated Emotions as Defined by Situations in the Scenario.*

|         | Neutral | Happy | Anger | Fear | Sorrow |
|---------|---------|-------|-------|------|--------|
| Neutral | [47]    | 9     | 19    | 9    | 16     |
| Happy   | 30      | [28]  | 0     | 21   | 21     |
| Anger   | 22      | 2     | [51]  | 17   | 10     |
| Fear    | 25      | 10    | 32    | [27] | 6      |
| Sorrow  | 16      | 0     | 8     | 3    | [73]   |

*Entries are percentages based on the total number of responses obtained from 12 listeners for the three voices.

*Speech rate.* Mean speaking rates, in syllables per second, were determined from speech samples selected from points in the scenario where the emotional situation was clearly defined. Table 11-4 shows the mean speaking rate for each of the three voices. The ranking of the emotions according to speaking rate, from fastest to slowest, was, with one exception, the same for each of the three voices: neutral, anger, fear, and sorrow. The rate exhibited in sorrow situations was less than half that found for other situations. This finding is in agreement with the results of Fairbanks and Hoaglin (1941) who, as shown earlier, found marked decreases in rate for grief as compared with anger, sorrow, and indifference. The substantially slower rate for the emotion sorrow is presumably a consequence of decreased activation of the muscles used in speech production and possibly shallower respiration resulting in more frequent inspirations and hence more frequent pauses.

*Identification of emotions from visual examination of spectrograms.* In order to gain familiarity with the acoustic correlates of various emotions as manifested on spectrograms, an examination was made of some of the vocal utterances generated as part of the emotional exercises. We assumed that the emotions portrayed in these speech samples would be more clear-cut and extreme than those occuring in the scenario, and consequently we expected that the characteristics observed in these spectrograms would provide us with a point of departure for examining the more subtle and mixed emotions that might be found in the scenario itself.

A first informal examination of these spectrograms from the emotional exercises revealed fairly sharp differences among utterances obtained for the various emotions. These observations led us to explore whether it would be possible to assemble spectrograms of utterances taken from the scenario and to categorize them in terms of these emotions simply by informal examination of the wide- and nar-

**Table 11-4**

Mean Speaking Rate (Syllables per Second) for Each of the Three Voices Speaking in Different Situations.

|         | Neutral | Anger | Fear | Sorrow |
|---------|---------|-------|------|--------|
| Voice A | 4.03 | 4.26 | 3.92 | 1.84 |
| Voice B | 4.89 | 4.32 | 3.90 | 2.03 |
| Voice C | 4.02 | 3.88 | 3.57 | 1.86 |
| Mean | 4.31 | 4.15 | 3.80 | 1.91 |

(From Williams & Stevens, 1972. Reproduced with permission.)

row-band spectrographic patterns. For several different sets of spectrograms from the three actors, therefore, we attempted in a rather informal way to classify the individual items. The criteria used in this preliminary informal categorization experiment bore some relation to the characteristics that evolved as a result of more detailed study, but they were based more on overall pattern characteristics and impressions rather than on a detailed checklist of a number of well-defined attributes.

In our first attempt at such a classification of spectrograms, the two authors examined 57 spectrograms of utterances excerpted from the scenario, but not including the control clusters. The categorization was done without knowledge as to the content of the utterances. In situations where the emotion was not judged to be a clear example of neutral, anger, fear, or sorrow, a partial emotion or a combination of emotions was noted (e.g., "mild anger" or "fear and sorrow"). We were entirely unanimous (i.e., at least one component of a mixed response of either observer was unanimous) in 89 percent of the cases. Estimates of the emotion actually intended, based on the scenario text, were compared with our judgments on items that were unanimous. The agreement was 100 percent for items that were characterized by the emotions anger and sorrow, 57 percent for neutral items, and 67 percent for items identified by the emotion fear. Such a result suggests that sorrow and anger are portrayed most clearly on spectrograms.

Similar informal experiments with limited sets of control clusters from the scenario were conducted; categorization of spectrograms was carried out separately for each of the three voices. In general, the results were similar to those just cited, except that the identification scores tended to be somewhat lower. This poorer performance is not unexpected, since the amount of speech in the control clusters was less than that in the longer utterances examined in the first experiment. It was observed that the same general kinds of criteria were used for identifying emotions from a spectrographic pattern for each of the three actors, although it was clear that there were aspects of the patterns that were distinctive for each voice. There were some instances in which we correctly assigned utterances to a given category, whereas listeners in the identification tests judged the utterances as belonging to one or more different categories.

Examples of wide-band spectrograms of one of the control clusters produced under several emotional situations are given in Figure 11-1. These spectrograms illustrate some of the attributes that were used by the observers in making judgments of the emotional categories associated with the spectrograms. For this cluster, the total duration

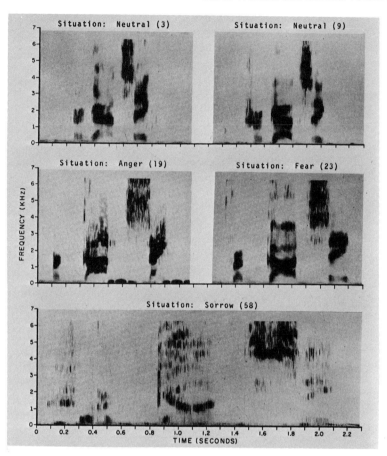

Fig. 11-1.  Wide-band spectrograms of the control cluster, "For God's sake," spoken by the same voice in five different emotional situations. (From Williams & Stevens, 1972. Reproduced with permission.)

was least for the neutral situation, and greatest for sorrow. The lengths of the utterances for fear and for anger were about the same. The increases in duration for the utterances made in anger, fear, and sorrow situations came in part from increases in vowel durations, but primarily from lengthened intervals of closure or vocal-tract constriction for the consonants. The vocal cord vibrations for the utterance exemplifying sorrow appeared to have considerable fluctuations in shape from one glottal pulse to the next. This voicing irregularity was manifested by a variation in darkness of individual voicing pulses, particularly in the high-frequency region above 2000 Hz. This effect is particularly evident in the word "God's" at the bottom of Figure 11-1 (0.8–1.3 sec on the time scale), in the entire frequency region above 2000 Hz. The spectrograms for the anger situation also demonstrate some anomalies that were presumably due to irregularities in the glottal output. For example, the pattern of glottal vibration is not uniform in the words "God's" and "sake," as evidenced by the irregular spectral pattern at high frequencies (above 3 kHz).

*Fundamental frequency ($F_o$) contours.* Figure 11-2 shows contours of the control cluster "maybe that's true" as uttered by Voice

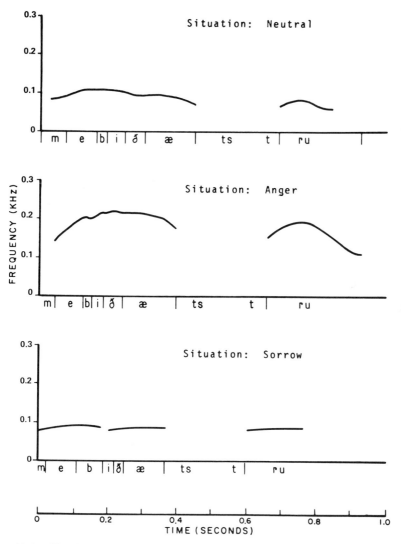

Fig. 11-2. Fundamental frequency contours of the control cluster, "Maybe that's true," as uttered by Voice B in neutral, anger, and sorrow situations in the scenario.

B in neutral, anger, and sorrow situations in the scenario. The contours were obtained by tracing harmonics on narrow-band spectrograms of the utterances. All the contours show the general form of a declination of the values of the $F_0$ peaks and valleys throughout the utterance, but the peak $F_0$ values and the amount of declination of the peaks differed from one emotion to another. For neutral utterances the shape of the contour was smooth and continuous and the changes in $F_0$ were relatively slow. Utterances produced in anger situations revealed an $F_0$ that was generally higher throughout the utterance and showed a greater range of $F_0$, suggesting that they were generated with greater activation of respiratory and laryngeal muscles. Although the excursions in $F_0$ were quite great, there appeared to be a relatively smooth overall contour with one or two major peaks, but with no large discontinuities. Relatively flat contours with few fluctuations were observed for utterances in sorrow situations and the $F_0$ peaks were usually lower than for neutral situations. Only rarely was emphasis placed on syllables in utterances in a sorrow situation. Contours for utterances made in fear situations (not shown) often departed from the smooth continuous prototype shape for utterances obtained in neutral situations. Occasionally there were rapid up-and-down fluctuations within a voiced interval and sometimes sharp discontinuities were noted from one syllable to the next. It should be noted, however, that not all contours for utterances in fear situations had these unusual or anomalous properties. One can only speculate on the nature of the physiological mechanism underlying these unusual contours. There would appear to be some lack of organization in the control of laryngeal muscles and of the respiratory system. Such disorganization of motor response is, apparently, often observed under an emotion of this kind. The speaker may fail to achieve coordination between the movements of the tongue, lips, and jaw on the one hand and the frequency-controlling laryngeal muscles on the other.

*Quantitative measures of $F_0$.* From narrow-band spectrograms of the longer speech samples, measurements of $F_0$ were obtained every 0.15 sec, and distribution curves were drawn to determine the median $F_0$ and a measure of the range of $F_0$ (10th–90th percentile). Measurements obtained from utterances of Voice A are shown in Table 11-5. For almost all samples (all three voices) there was a clear separation among data for the situations labeled neutral, anger, and sorrow. With one or two exceptions, the median $F_0$ was always lower for sorrow than for neutral and was higher for anger than for neutral. This finding is in accord with the observations noted earlier concerning the $F_0$ contours. The range in $F_0$ tended to be less for sorrow than for neutral and was greatest for anger. These differences in range were not consistent for all speech samples and all voices, however.

**Table 11-5**
Median Fundamental Frequency ($F_0$) for the Longer Speech Samples As Spoken by Voice A.*

| Speech Sample | Neutral Median $F_0$ | $F_0$ Range | Speech Sample | Anger Median $F_0$ | $F_0$ Range |
|---|---|---|---|---|---|
| a | 117 | 89–153 | j | 193 | 120–240 |
| b | 111 | 87–128 | k | 148 | 113-192 |
| d | 105 | 83–125 | l | 146 | 111-225 |
| q | 101 | 70–167 | p | 173 | 117–250 |
| r | 114 | 90–140 | $u_1$ | 150 | 125–226 |
| Mean | 110 | 84–143 | $u_2$ | 139 | 100–183 |
| | | | Mean | 158 | 114–219 |

| Speech Sample | Fear Median $F_0$ | $F_0$ Range | Speech Sample | Sorrow Median $F_0$ | $F_0$ Range |
|---|---|---|---|---|---|
| m | 150 | 113–260 | $e_2$ | 107 | 83–137 |
| o | 156 | 113–244 | $f_2$ | 128 | 89–233 |
| s | 125 | 94–210 | $g_2$ | 97 | 80–113 |
| w | 152 | 104–246 | $h_2$ | 88 | 67–107 |
| $b_2$ | 114 | 97–147 | $i_2$ | 84 | 67–120 |
| Mean | 139 | 104–221 | Mean | 101 | 77–142 |

*Categories of emotion refer to particular situations in the scenario.

The range of $F_0$ for fear was usually greater than for neutral and comparable to that for anger, but this finding also was by no means consistent. Speech samples generated in "happy" situations in the scenario usually had a higher median $F_0$ and a wider range of $F_0$ than samples uttered in neutral situations.

The data obtained for the three voices indicated certain consistent trends in $F_0$ distributions for different emotions, similar to those reported by Fairbanks and Pronovost (1939). The data suggest, however, that a single speech sample of a few seconds' duration may not be long enough to give a clear indication of the effective long-time median and range of $F_0$. Furthermore, whereas measurements of the median $F_0$ and range of $F_0$ for a given speech sample provide some evidence concerning the emotion of a speaker, they do not identify it unambiguously. Presumably an indication of contour shape (as noted earlier) in addition to median $F_0$ and range of $F_0$ can help to identify an emotion more reliably.

*Relative intensity.* Since the actors were not always at a constant distance from the microphone during the recording of the scenario, it was not possible to obtain accurate measures of changes in voice level for the various situations. Although graphic-level tracings were obtained for all utterances of the control clusters, only a selected few were examined in detail. Of the tracings examined, anger showed the highest level and sorrow the lowest. For sorrow situations, consonants generated with fricative noise, such as /s/, tended to be of higher intensity relative to vowels than in the other situations examined.

*Average spectrum.* Whereas utterances made in anger and fear situations showed less low-frequency energy in relation to high-frequency energy than did utterances in neutral situations, utterances from the latter did not differ in a consistent way from those for sorrow situations, at least as far as the low-frequency energy was concerned. The spectrum amplitude at high frequencies (above 1000 Hz) relative to low frequencies was always greatest for anger and least for sorrow. The implication is that anger is manifested in a high subglottal pressure and a narrower glottal pulse, leading to greater high-frequency spectral energy, while the reverse is true of sorrow.

*Limitations of our studies.* Because of the limited context in which the above studies were carried out, care should be exercised in generalizing the results to a variety of talkers and a variety of emotional situations. First, even though the actors were attempting to re-create real-life emotions, it must be recognized that they were involved in an acting situation. There is the possibility that while actors may portray an emotion in such a way that listeners will interpret it correctly, they may not fully achieve the physiological state which accompanies that emotion in real life. Thus there may be subtle acoustic effects in the voice that are a consequence of this physiological state but which would not appear in vocal utterances obtained when the emotion is being simulated.

Secondly, for the most part, the acoustic data that were examined in detail were taken from situations in the scenario where the emotion was clear-cut and definable in terms of a single unambiguous descriptor. In such situations it is possible that the actors may have tended to exaggerate the emotion, thus creating acoustic effects which would not have been present in vocal utterances obtained in a corresponding real-life situation.

A further limitation of the use of actors is that their voices tend to be characterized by "good" voice quality. In the situations described as neutral, the voices of the three actors used in the studies may not be representative of the acoustic characteristics of the "average" voice. It is probable that actors' voices tend to have more uniform glottal pulses (less voicing irregularity), a more well-defined formant structure during vowels, a more uniform level, and, perhaps, more clearly articulated consonants. Thus the acoustic manifestations of the various emotions by the actors may not be entirely similar to those of a normal sample of the population.

## Data from Real-life Emotional Situations

There have been a few studies which have described the acoustical analysis of voice recordings obtained in real-life situations in which the circumstances gave a clear indication of the emotions experienced by the speaker (Kuroda, Fujiwara, Okamura, et al., 1976; Popov, Simonov, Frolov, et al., 1971; Williams and Stevens, 1969). Brief mention will be made of findings from some of these studies, most of which were directed toward the assessment and/or control of the emotional state of aviation and space personnel during flight.

One recording we analyzed (1969) was that of a conversation between a civilian pilot and a control tower operator. During the course of the recording the pilot ran into serious difficulty with his aircraft, and the recording ended with the pilot losing control and crashing.

Figure 11-3 shows three narrow-band spectrograms sampled from various points throughout the recording. Portions of the speech in which the vocal cords are vibrating are indicated by a series of equally spaced horizontal lines on the spectrogram. Each of these lines represents a harmonic of the fundamental vocal-cord vibration frequency ($F_0$). The spacing between the lines indicates $F_0$, and the lines move up and down together as $F_0$ rises and falls. The more irregularly spotted regions on the spectrograms indicate the presence of noise, either in the speech itself or in the background. The top spectrogram portrays the pilot's voice when his difficulty was not serious. His problem had reached serious proportions in the middle spectrogram, and the bottom spectrogram represents one of the last utterances of the pilot when a crash appeared imminent. Evident from the contours is the increase in $F_0$ as the fear of the pilot increases. Furthermore, the contours become irregular and discontinuous. When the pilot is more or less terror stricken (bottom spectrogram), the $F_0$ becomes extremely high and undergoes large fluctuations.

Another recording we subjected to analysis (1969) was that of the radio announcer mentioned at the beginning of this section, who was describing the approach of the *Hindenburg* when it suddenly burst into flames. The announcer continued his description (with one or two short breaks) throughout the disaster. Figure 11-4 shows three narrow-band spectrograms that were made from excerpts of the announcer's voice before and after the crash occurred. As can be seen, the announcer's voice had a great deal of inflection before the crash, as indicated by the smooth up-and-down movements of $F_0$ in the upper spectrogram. Immediately after the crash (middle and lower spectro-

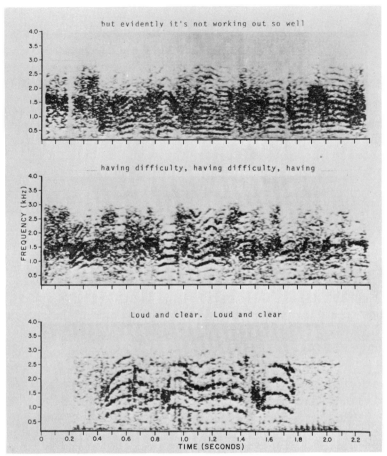

Fig.11-3.  Narrow-band spectrograms of civilian pilot requesting permission to land (*top*) and speaking during flight difficulty prior to fatal crash (*middle* and *bottom*). (From Williams & Stevens, 1969. Reproduced with permission.)

grams), there is an abrupt change in the shape of the $F_0$ contour. The average $F_0$ is considerably higher, and there is apparently much less fluctuation in frequency. There are some irregular bumps in the contour which might be interpreted as a kind of tremor. Examples of these irregularities can be seen in the bottom spectrogram, near 0.6 sec and again near 0.8 sec. The irregularities may reflect a loss of precise control of musculature and an irregular respiratory pattern. A combination of emotions is presumably involved in this situation—probably both grief (leading to a flatter $F_0$ contour) and fear (leading to a higher $F_0$).

The results of these and additional limited analyses of vocal utterances from real-life emotional situations led us (1969) to conclude

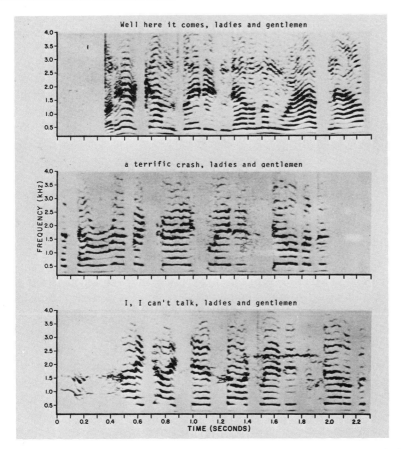

Fig. 11-4. Narrow-band spectrograms of radio announcer speaking before (*top*) and after (*middle* and *bottom*) the crash of the *Hindenburg*. (From Williams & Stevens, 1969. Reproduced with permission.)

that measurements of $F_0$ and range of $F_0$, together with observation of the $F_0$ contour, might serve to signify when a person is undergoing emotional stress.

Subsequently, Niwa (1970, 1971), Popov, Simonov, Frolov, et al. (1971), Simonov and Frolov (1973), and Kuroda, Fujiwara, Okamura, et al. (1976) reported additional data from real-life situations which confirmed the potential for utilizing the analysis of voice communications for determining the emotional status of aviation and space personnel. In the last study (Kuroda, et al., 1976) a methodology was developed for determining the emotional status of pilots involved in aircraft accidents. From spectrograms of the recorded voice communications of pilots involved in 14 aircraft accidents, the investigators calculated what they termed vibration space shift rate (VSSR). This quantity apparently represents the percentage change in average $F_0$ under the emotional situation relative to the normal situation. VSSR patterns (profiles) based on these calculations can reportedly be utilized to depict the relative variation of the emotional status of pilots in specific situations. In a retrospective analysis by those pilots who survived the emergency situations, the patterns were found to correlate with the degree of tension recalled.

## CONCLUSION

We have presented information and data from selected studies which have attempted to identify and measure those aspects of the speech signal that reflect an individual's emotional state. Although most studies in this area have utilized simulated rather than real-life emotions, limited data from the latter have not been inconsistent with data obtained utilizing method actors in scenario type situations.

As reported earlier by us (1972), vocal utterances obtained in anger, fear, and sorrow situations tend to produce characteristic differences in contour of fundamental frequency, temporal characteristics, average speech spectrum, precision of articulation, and waveform regularity of successive glottal pulses. Attributes for a given emotional situation are not always consistent from one speaker to another.

The aspect of the speech signal that appears to provide the clearest indication of the emotional state of a talker is the contour of $F_0$ versus time. This contour has a prototype shape for a breath group that is generated in a normal manner, without marked emotions of any kind. The normal contour is characterized by smooth, slow, and continuous changes in $F_0$ as a function of time, the changes occurring in syllables on which emphasis or linguistic stress is to be placed. Emotions appear to have several effects on this basic contour shape.

While at present it is certainly not possible to specify any quantitative automatic procedures that reliably indicate the emotional state of a talker, measurements of the median $F_0$ and range of $F_0$ for a sample of speech of several seconds' duration may at least serve to classify a talker's emotional state as one of sorrow (reduced $F_0$ and decreased range), or of anger or fear (increased $F_0$ and range), assuming that the normal $F_0$ and range of $F_0$ for the talker are known. Further identification of the emotions must be done by an experienced observer who must look for certain attributes of the $F_0$ contour, shifts in spectrum, changes in duration, and voicing irregularities.

(Williams and Stevens, 1972, p. 1249.)

One difficulty associated with most of the studies reviewed here is that the search for acoustic correlates of various emotions is *ad hoc* and is not based on any well-defined hypotheses. Such a search could be more systematic and soundly based if detailed information concerning the physiological correlates of various emotions were utilized. For example, if the respiration rate increases, or if there is excessive formation of mucus in the region of the larynx, there could be certain consequences in the acoustic properties of the speech signal. We would suggest, therefore, that future studies of the effects of emotion on speech should include an examination of the physiological effects as well as the acoustical ones.

REFERENCES

Davitz, J. R. Auditory correlates of vocal expressions of emotional meanings. In J. R. Davitz (Ed.), *The communication of emotional meaning*. New York: McGraw-Hill, 1964, pp. 101–112.

Fairbanks, G. Recent experimental investigations of vocal pitch in speech. *Journal of the Acoustical Society of America*, 1940, *11*, 457–466.

Fairbanks, G., Pronovost, W. An experimental study of the pitch characteristics of the voice during the expression of emotions. *Speech Monographs*, 1939, *6*, 87–104.

Fairbanks, G., Hoaglin, L. W. An experimental study of the duration characteristics of the voice during the expression of emotion. *Speech Monographs*, 1941, *8*, 85–90.

Grings, W. W., Dawson, M. E. *Emotions and bodily responses: A psychophysiological approach*. New York: Academic Press, 1978.

Kramer, E. The judgment of personal characteristics and emotions from nonverbal properties of speech. *Psychological Bulletin*, 1963, *60*, 408–420.

Kuroda, I., Fujiwara, O., Okamura, N., et al. Method for determining pilot stress through analysis of voice communication. *Aviation, Space, and Environmental Medicine*, 1976, *47*, 528–533.

Niwa, S. Changes of voice characteristics in urgent situation (1). Rept. Aeromedical Laboratory, Japan Air Self-Defense Force, 1970, *11*, 51–58.

Niwa, S. Changes of voice characteristics in urgent situation (2). Rept. Aeromedical Laboratory, Japan Air Self-Defense Force, 1971, *11*, 246–251.

Popov, V. A., Simonov, P. V., Frolov, M. V., et al. Frequency spectrum of speech as an indicator of the degree and nature of emotional stress. *Zh. Vysshey Nervnoy Deyatel 'nosti*, 1971, *1*, 104–109.

Scherer, K. R. Nonlinguistic vocal indicators of emotion and psychopathology. In C. E. Izard (Ed.), *Emotions in personality and psychopathology*. New York: Plenum, 1979, pp. 493–529.

Simonov, P. V., Frolov, M. V. Utilization of human voice for estimation of man's emotional stress and state of attention. *Aerospace Medicine*, 1973, *44*, 256–258.

Strongman, K. T. *The psychology of emotion*. London: John Wiley and Sons, 1973.

Weitz, S. Paralanguage. In S. Weitz (Ed.), *Nonverbal communication: Readings with commentary.* New York: Oxford University Press, 1979, pp. 221–231.

Williams, C. E., Stevens, K. N. On determining the emotional state of pilots during flight: An exploratory study. *Aerospace Medicine,* 1969, *40,* 1369–1372.

Williams, C. E., Stevens, K. N. Emotions and speech: Some acoustical correlates. *Journal of the Acoustical Society of America,* 1972, *52,* 4(2), 1238–1250.

# IV. Speech Behavior Associated with Character Disturbances and Neuroses

Bernard L. Diamond

# 12

# The Relevance of Voice in Forensic Psychiatric Evaluations

One of the most critical, yet most difficult, problems of diagnosis for the psychiatrist is the accurate differentiation of the three conditions: schizophrenia, borderline syndrome, and sociopathic personality disorder. Apart from the medical necessity for a clear differential diagnosis of these conditions, their differentiation from each other and from normal mental processes has special social and legal significance. The forensic psychiatrist or psychologist is frequently called upon to evaluate the psychological state of an accused criminal offender to determine competency to stand trial and sanity or insanity with respect to criminal responsibility, and often to give an expert opinion as to the offender's dangerousness, prognosis, the prognosis for the psychopathology, the need for institutional or other treatment or rehabilitation, and the anticipated response of the offender. Based upon such expert evaluation, important social and legal decisions are made concerning the disposition of the offender.

Despite the grave difficulties inherent in making such evaluations, the forensic specialist must base diagnosis upon the immediate cross-sectional examination of the subject, often with a minimum of longitudinal history and with no opportunity to validate one's professional judgment by long-term observation.

## DIFFERENTIAL DIAGNOSIS

Although the new *Diagnostic and Statistical Manual (DSM III)* of the American Psychiatric Association provides much improved criteria for the diagnosis of these mentally disturbed conditions, there is still apt to be much confusion over the precise categorization of a particular offender. Antisocial "acting-out" behavior is often an early sign of mental illness, and the more florid evidence of psychopathology may not yet be visible. Psychiatric examination of such persons must frequently be done under circumstances which are not conducive to trusting communication between examiner and subject. Dissimulation, suspiciousness, and reticence are commonly present, yet the examiner is expected to formulate an accurate evaluation, prognosis, and recommendation based upon much more superficial and ephemeral contact with the subject than would be tolerable in the usual therapeutic situation.

Under such circumstances experienced diagnosticians rely heavily upon their intuitive skills, skills acquired through many contacts with similar patients. Yet even the most skilled clinical teachers usually have difficulty in communicating to their students the precise basis upon which their intuition is based. They rely on statements such as, "I can just feel in my guts that this patient is schizophrenic" or "His affect was in a subtle way not congruent with his words" or "I could feel the barrier between him and me" or even "I just know, that's all, I just know."

Such statements are not likely to be helpful to the inexperienced clinician for they give no clues as to what skilled diagnosticians actually perceived about the patient, nor as to what they relied upon to make their intuitive diagnosis. Unless we believe in magical powers or mental telepathy, we must assume that the diagnostician is responding to some perceived clue: some aspect about the speech, body language, physical appearance, or perhaps even a distinctive odor of the patient. Whatever it might be it must be exceedingly subtle, for the diagnosticians can seldom describe what they have perceived that so firmly fixed their impression of the diagnosis.

Certainly, the speech content and the linguistic aspects of the patient's communications are most important in establishing the psychiatric diagnosis. Fundamentally, we rely upon what our patients tell us—on their history, their feelings and complaints, their present thoughts, and their hopes and their fears. These are the verbal communications that predominate among the diagnostic criteria. Nonverbal communications are also of importance. Body language, gestures, mannerisms, and unusual or odd behavior and activities, as well as facial expression and signs of emotion in expression or tone of voice, all communicate to experienced diagnosticians information about the patient's psyche and they have been trained to recognize such signs and to interpret their significance as evidence of psychopathology or of normal mental processes.

The traditional verbal and nonverbal communications from the patient, which permit diagnostic inferences, are reasonably well defined, however. They can be listed, described, defined, and recorded, and their nature and qualities can be transmitted from teacher to student with at least fair precision. The disturbances of language and thought in schizophrenia have received a great deal of attention ever since their emphasis by Bleuler (1911) in his monograph in which the name "schizophrenia" was coined and the famous four A's introduced. Kasanin (1944) edited an exceptionally fine collection of papers on schizophrenic thought disorders. Included are articles by pioneer researchers in this field, such as Kurt Goldstein (1944) whose original research was concerned with organic disorders of thought, such as the aphasias, and who was able to make clear distinctions between the language and thought disorders of schizophrenia and of organic brain disease. Of particular importance is the article by E. von Domarus (1944) who clarified the strange, paralogical grammar so often used by schizophrenic patients.

In clinical practice, however, it has not always been possible to accurately define or test for such thought disorder. Available tests, such as the Vigotsky Block Sorting test or the Proverb Interpretation test, are very helpful when they work. But many patients who show evidence of profound schizophrenic pathology may not reveal abnormality on such tests. Andreasen (1979) has carefully refined the definitions of the clinical terms used to describe thought and associational disorders and has raised many doubts about their incidence and specificity for the diagnosis of schizophrenia.

The growing discrepancy between the criteria used in America and England, and sometimes in other European countries, for the diagnosis of schizophrenia has led to the development of so-called "research diagnostic criteria." Schneider, as early as 1959, developed lists of "first rank" symptoms which, if present, made the diagnosis of schizophrenia certain. Such an approach is very useful for research purposes in which it is necessary to be certain that all of the subjects are actually suffering from the same mental illness, for false positive diagnoses are greatly reduced. It is less useful for clinical purposes for such rigid diagnostic criteria result in a heavy excess of false negative diagnoses. A number of other sets of research diagnostic criteria have been proposed. Overall and Hollister (1979) compared six different research diagnostic criteria systems as applied to a series of 166 patients who had received a clinical diagnosis of schizophrenia. These systems differed markedly in the proportion of clinical diagnoses that were confirmed. Moreover they disagreed with each other, therefore the authors concluded that alternative systems of research diagnostic criteria define different patient populations and that they represent varying arbitrary definitions of the underlying psychiatric disorder. This means that existing descriptions of the phenomena believed to be evidence of the existence of schizophrenia are insufficiently understood and recognized in ways which permit accurate, valid, and reliable diagnoses of that most important psychiatric disorder. Whether for research or purely clinical purposes, the important differential diagnosis between schizophrenia, borderline personality disorder, antisocial personality disorder, and the affective psychoses still cannot be accomplished with precision and validity. Systems of nosology such as the *DSM III* are valuable improvements in that they tend to increase the reliability of a psychiatric diagnosis.

Literally millions of such psychiatric patients have been closely observed and studied, and the manifestations of their psychopathology enumerated, described, defined, compared, and tested in a multitude of traditional, innovative, and sometimes exotic fashion (Bellak, 1979). In the absence of a nosology firmly based upon etiology, we must either look for new phenomena to study or concede defeat and reconcile ourselves to diagnostic failure.

## SPEECH BEHAVIOR AND PSYCHOPATHOLOGY

Is it possible that something has been overlooked about our patients—some product of the psyche that may reveal important clues as to the existence and type of psychopathology? Something which, perhaps, skilled and experienced clinicians intuitively utilize in their scheme of differential diagnosis but fails to consciously recognize. I suggest that the study of speech behavior might reveal such a clue. It is striking that in the many clinical and research descriptions of psychopathology so little attention has been made to the sound and enunciation of speech. Content of speech and nonverbal expression have been studied at great length and are familiar to every clinician and researcher (Ruesch & Bateson, 1951; Marcos, 1979). Yet other than imprecise, vague references to tempo, such as slowing or "pressure" of speech or to observations of the incongruity of tone of voice to speech content, little acknowledgment is made to the diagnostic importance of the nonlinguistic elements of communication. Even when we attempt to judge emotional expression by tone of voice, relating it to rage, depression, euphoria, or schizophrenic dissociation of affect, we rely on acoustic variations which are neither described nor defined in other than a conclusionary manner. What is actually the difference between a voice that expresses rage or excitement or affective flatness? (Williams & Stevens, 1972) Obviously we utilize speech behavior in every clinicial judgment we make each time we listen to our patients talk. But it is done intuitively, imprecisely, and without any attempt at scientific analysis.

Psychiatric and psychological clinicians seem to be generally unaware of the publications on speech behavior that have attempted to relate the sound, and not the meaning, of speech to psychopathology. As early as 1926, Sapir observed that there may be unconscious symbolic value to the sound of words apart from their meaning. Allport and Cantril (1934) performed careful experimental studies in which judgments of personality attributes were made from radio broadcast voices. A large majority of the subjects were successful in matching the voices to the personality attributes of the speakers.

Karl Menninger (1935) published a short paper giving a clinical demonstration of how a consistent mispronunciation of a word had specific unconscious significance. When interpreted to the patient the mispronunciation stopped. Brody (1943) entreated the psychoanalyst to attend to the voice as well as the meaning of verbal communications:

It has long been recognized that the voice is a sensitive reflector of emotional states. Speech . . . is not always used solely for the communication of meanings . . . but may also constitute the expression of feelings, in which case it may have less propositional value. This fact is so universally recognized that there is danger of it being taken for granted and overlooked. The analyst may tend to concentrate his attention solely on what the voice is saying (p. 371)

He continues:

. . . the voice is a sensitive reflector of emotional states and is used by the ego as a vector for neurotic symptoms and defense mechanisms. To hear the voice solely for what it has to say and to overlook the voice itself, deprives the analyst of an important avenue leading to emotional conflict. (p. 379)

It was Moses, a laryngologist, however, in 1954 who published the first extensive treatise on speech behavior as a diagnostic instrument of psychiatric disorder. Moses was convinced that both neuroses and psychoses manifested abnormalities of voice, which could be correlated with developmental fixations or regressions. Moses believed that characteristics of speech, other than content and meaning, were useful differentiators between neuroses, schizophrenia, and disorders of personality, and could sometimes reveal combinations of neurotic and psychotic conditions in the same patient.

The basic difference between the neurotic and the schizophrenic patient is audible in vocal expression: the neurotic voice reveals typical symptoms of fixation and regression through vocal patterns belonging to earlier phases in his development, whereas the schizophrenic voice has a marked archaic character, with primordial attributes. (p. 15)

The literature on the psychotherapeutic application of phonetics has been greatly expanded by Barbara (1958a, 1958b, 1960). Barbara's conviction of the importance of speech behavior is demonstrated by this statement:

Speech and personality are one . . . . The function of speech is not only that of verbal communication, but is also an expression of the individual's relationship to himself, to others and to groups. It is mainly through an understanding of their dynamic interaction, as observed in daily situations and under various stress circumstances, that we can find some of the answers to the riddle of the complexities of personality maladjustments and those of language. (1958a, p. xi)

Rousey and Moriarity (1965) have attempted the most specific correlation between particular phonetic qualities of speech and personality attributes, developmental psychological abnormalities, and specific emotional conflicts. Careful to label their conclusions as "working assumptions," they nevertheless propose a specificity that is not likely to be acceptable to most psychiatric clinicians. For example they assert that:

Persistent hoarseness in the sounds of speech (vowels) tends to occur in individuals manifesting socially distorted sexual identification and functioning." (p. 31)

and that:

Lateral lisping (a spilling of air over the sides of the tongue in articulating the s) appears in individuals whose narcissism has reached a pathological degree. (p. 41)

Although they give clinical illustrations to support these and many other working diagnostic assumptions, the authors provide no real justification for such specific inferences. Particularly, they do not evaluate the question of whether, and how often, persons without the ascribed clinical abnormalities also demonstrate the phonetic deviations. Although the evidence in support of their "working assumptions" is insufficient, and therefore, conclusions drawn from their hypotheses would have no validity in a legal context, further research might prove otherwise. One is reminded of the early research on the Rorschach test in which similar specific working assumptions were scoffed at as unscientific, even preposterous. Now it is not at all unusual for forensic psychiatrists to offer in part, as the basis, of their opinion of the mental state of a defendant, the findings on the Rorschach and similar projective tests.

## CONCLUSION

Even more than in clinical situations, the psychiatrist and psychologist in the legal arena require reliable, valid, and objective criteria for the differentiation of the major psychoses from borderline conditions, neuroses, and character disorders. Legal decisions that are of extreme importance to both society and the affected individual are frequently dependent upon evaluations of the forensic expert. False positives may result in the deprivation of liberty of persons who should not have been confined as homicidal or suicidal. False negatives may result in mentally ill persons being punished for crimes when they should have been treated for illness.

Existing systems of diagnosis, such as the *DSM III*, are improvements but are far from sufficient to make these difficult differentiations. Experienced clinicians rely heavily upon their intuitive skills, which make it impossible to persuade judges and juries that their opinions have credible scientific validity. It is likely that good clinicians already rely to some degree upon unconsciously perceived features of speech behavior in their patients. But these qualities have yet to be defined and scientifically correlated with varying psychopathological and normal conditions of the human mind. The existing literature is largely theoretical or based upon much too small clinical samples, relying heavily upon unsubstantiated inferences. As much, it falls far short of the standard set by the *Frye* court.

Nevertheless, if further research, utilizing better methodology with more controls, should validate even a small number of the diagnostic claims now existing in the literature on speech behavior, important benefits to the credibility of psychiatric and psychological expert testimony would inevitably follow. In the past several decades there has been a marked increase in the legal admissibility of such expert testimony, but the credibility of psychiatric and psychological expertise is lower than ever. Issues of admissibility are essentially legal matters to be resolved in legal ways. Issues of credibility are matters of science, research, and professional integrity, and cannot be solved by the law.

REFERENCES

Allport, G. W., Cantril, H. Judging personality from voice. *Journal of Social Psychology*, 1934, *5*, 37–55.

American Psychiatric Association, *Diagnostic and statistical manual of mental disorders* DSM III. (3d ed.) Washington, D.C.: American Psychiatric Association, 1980.

Andreasen, N. C. Thought, language, and communication disorders: I.Clinical assessment, definition of terms, and evaluation of their reliability. *Archives of General Psychiatry*, 1979, *36*, 1315–21. II. Diagnostic significance. *Archives of General Psychiatry*, 1979, *36*, 1325–1330.

Barbara, D. A. *Your speech reveals your personality.* Springfield, Ill.: Charles C. Thomas, 1958.

Barbara, D. A. *The art of listening.* Springfield, Ill.: Charles C. Thomas, 1958.

Barbara, D. A. (Ed.) *Psychological and psychiatric aspects of speech and hearing.* Springfield, Ill.: Charles C. Thomas, 1960.

Bellak, L. (Ed.) *Disorders of the schizophrenic syndrome.* N. Y.: Basic Books, 1979.

Bleuler, P. E. *Dementia praecox oder die Gruppe der Schizophrenien.* Leipzig: Wien, F. Deuticke, 1911.

Brody, M. W. Neurotic manifestations of the voice. *Psychoanalytic Quarterly*, 1943, *12*, 371–80.

*Frye v. United States,* 293 F. 1013, 1014 (D. C. Cir.1923).

Goldstein, K. Methodological approach to the study of schizophrenic thought disorder. In J. S. Kasanin (Ed.) *Language and thought in schizophrenia.* Berkeley: University of California Press, 1944, pp. 17–40.

Marcos, L. R. Nonverbal behavior and thought processing. *Archives of General Psychiatry*, 1979, *36*, 940–43.

Menninger, K. A. Unconscious values in certain consistent mispronunciations. *Psychoanalytic Quarterly*, 1935, *4*, 614–15.

Moses, P. *The voice of neurosis.* New York: Grune & Stratton, 1954.

Overall, J. E. Hollister, L. E. Comparative evaluation of research diagnostic criteria for schizophrenia. *Archives of General Psychiatry*, 1979, *36*, 1198–1205.

Rousey, C. L. Moriarity, A. E. *Diagnostic implications of speech sounds.* Springfield, Illinois: Charles C. Thomas, 1965.

Ruesch, J. Bateson, G. *Communication: The social matrix of society.* New York. W. W. Norton, 1951.

Sapir, E. Speech as a personality trait. *Mental Health Bulletin*, 1926, *5*, 1–7.

Schneider, K. *Clinical psychopathology* (M. Hamilton, trans.) New York. Grune & Stratton, 1959.

von Domarus, E. The specific laws of logic in schizophrenia. In J. S. Kasanin (Ed.), *Language and thought in schizophrenia.* Berkeley: University of California Press, 1944, pp. 104–114.

Williams. C. E. Stevens, K. N. Emotions and speech: Some acoustical correlates. *Journal of the Accoustical Society of America*, 1972, *52*, 1328–50.

# V. Speech Behavior Associated with Psychotic Disturbances

John K. Darby

# 13
# Speech and Voice Studies
# in Psychiatric Populations

## PSYCHIATRY AND SPEECH SCIENCE

### Purpose

Over the past 25 years, with the development of psychotropic drugs, major interdisciplinary efforts between psychiatry and the biological sciences have developed. Biochemistry, genetics, and psychopharmacology have all contributed enormously to our knowledge about psychoses.

This chapter explores the basis for an interactional framework between psychobiological research in psychoses and the study of nonlinguistic properties of speech. The chapter will present an overview of disease models and review the major psychoses and speech studies in these disorders.

### Disease Models and Psychoses

The best current conceptualization of psychoses is represented by a gene environment interactional hypothesis. A brief historical review of developments in disease causation theory is helpful in understanding the origins of this hypothesis.

#### UNIFACTORIAL CONCEPT

One of the most important developments in modern medicine was the unifactorial germ theory of disease. Pasteur (1833-1895 recognized the existence of germs, their reproductive capacities, and their specificity in causing disease. He demonstrated germ vulnerability to heating and also developed vaccines for anthrax and rabies. Antibiotic concepts developed by Erhlich (1854–1915) came to fruition with the development of penicillin by 1940.

The germ theory of disease represented a major achievement in medical treatment. While some brain diseases causing mental disturbance (Creutzfeldt-Jacob disease, kuru, syphillis, and cryptococcosis) fit this model, there is only weak evidence supporting the idea that a virus could be responsible for schizophrenic symptoms and mental illness.

MULTIFACTORIAL CONCEPTS

The development of a multifactorial concept of disease is well illustrated by the history of tuberculosis. This condition was proposed by Virchow (1821–1902) to be due to social and constitutional as well as bacteriologic factors. In the case of tuberculosis the presence in the lung of the bacillus represents "a necessary but not sufficient condition" (Wender, 1967) for the manifestation of the disease. Additional features, such as reduced resistance, susceptibility, and/or poor hygiene, need also be present.

Wender (1967) has compared mental illness and tuberculosis with regard to their multidetermined nature and pointed out that mental diseases, cancer, and arteriosclerosis may not yield to unifactorial explanations;l rather these may be syndromes which are the outcome of a constellation of factors, significantly more difficult to evaluate etiologically

PSYCHOSOMATIC CONCEPTS

Walter Cannon (1871–1945) observed that changes in emotional states, such as anxiety or rage, were accompanied by cessation of digestive movements in the stomach. He went on to describe the effects of adrenal secretions in the "fight or flight reaction," stimulated by environmental challenges. Franz Alexander in the 1940s suggested a relationship between psychodynamic features and peptic ulcer, hypertension, and several other "psychosomatic" illnesses. Jung (1908; trans. 1960) hypothesized that some cases of schizophrenia were precipitated by certain psychologically stressful events which in turn set off internal psychonoxious biochemical processes.

PSYCHOLOGIC CONCEPTS

In addition to biological models of disease, there is a long history of behavioral and psychological observations about mental illness.

Aristotle (384–322 B.C.) emphasized the purging of disturbing passions through catharsis. Over the past century a host of psychological formulations has been developed. These include psychosomatic theories (Jung), psychoanalytic (Freud, Sullivan), behavioral (Pavlov, Skinner), family (Lidz, Wynne), double-bind (Bateson et al.), and stress models.

GENETIC–METABOLIC CONCEPTS

Hippocratic writings (4th century B.C.) of neurohumeral theories and Paracelsus' (1493–1541) "tartaric" diseases anticipated later concepts of metabolic disease. In 1908, Garrod described alcaptonuria in his *Inborn Errors of Metabolism*. This was the first example of a recessive inheritance to be recognized in man. Beadle (1945) stated the one gene–one enzyme concept, which indicated that each biochemical reaction is under the control of a different single gene.

Over the past 20 years research has indicated that genetic and biochemical processes are significant factors in selected types of schizophrenia and certain affective disorders. Genetic influence has far-reaching consequences, and many of the mechanisms of its action are not clear. The onset of puberty, Huntington's Chorea, and dementia illustrate some of the age and time-related effects of genes. Some genetic diseases affecting the brain require specific dietary conditions or drugs to precipitate them.

In 1968, Pauling formulated a concept involving both genetic factors and vitamin deficiency effects upon the brain. Certain vitamin deficiency diseases are known to produce mental disturbances through their effects on the brain. Pauling suggested that schizophrenia resulted from a relative vitamin deficiency secondary to a genetically determined alteration in vitamin metabolism, thus producing an increased need for the substance. Strong evidence supporting this provocative postulate has not been developed.

HETEROGENEITY OF PSYCHOTIC SYNDROMES

The development of relevant models for schizophrenic and affective psychoses has been hampered by the heterogeneity of diagnostic classifications. It is likely that each of these gross classifications represents a variety of different disorders. A pluralistic approach, therefore, regards these classifications as representing a group of symptom complexes rather than as unitary disease processes. These syndromes may be analagous to fever or anemia as symptoms representing a class of disorders. Current subtyping classifications are based on historical information and behavior rather than along etiological or biochemical dimensions. The search for differentiation by biochemical, psychophysiologic, and psychological methodologies represents a key challenge in the coming decade.

GENETIC–ENVIRONMENTAL INTERACTION
CONCEPTS

There is as yet no definitive model for mental illness. From genetic–biochemical–pharmacologic studies and psychological conflict/ stress models come compelling evidence that both factors are involved. The multideterminant features of psychoses suggest a genetic–environmental interaction.

The hypothesis of genetic–environmental interaction in schizophrenia explores the specific nature of environmental stresses; how these stresses impact upon physiologic and biochemical processes; and how these processes trigger the illness in genotypically vulnerable individuals. In this model, stress is a bridge phenomenon involving an integration of biologic, psychodynamic, and social features (Pollin, 1972). This conceptual framework, although necessarily general, can encompass both genetic and environmental (psychological and constitutional) research to date.

Language acquisition and speech is one such example of behavior secondary to genetic–environmental interaction. Genetic influence dictates the development of the neural speech mechanism, while language form is determined by acculturation (Kety, 1979).

## Multidimensional Nature of Speech

GENETIC–ENVIRONMENTAL ADMIXTURE

Language and speech behaviors represent a composite of both genetic and environmental influences. In general, language content reflects cultural effects, while certain vocal and speech features tend to reflect biophysiologic information. Pittenger (1958) emphasized a link of paralinguistics to physiologic emotional responses and primitive drive states. The speech signal may reflect both fixed characteristics like age, sex, individual specific features (speaker identification research), personality (Scherer, Chapter 6), speech tract configuration (Laver, Chapter 3), or transient emotional states (Scherer, Chapter 10; Williams, Chapter 11) and neurological disorders (Aronson, in press).

SPEECH PRODUCTION AND NEUROLOGIC
INTEGRITY

Production of intelligible speech and language is a complex phenomenon involving major segments of brain function. Language function, abstraction, associative ideation, and planning are subserved by cortical function and are therefore very sensitive to conditions such as delirium tremens, drug toxicities (amphetamine psychoses, alcohol, LSD), and metabolic encephalopathies, which produce temporary but marked impairment of these higher cortical functions. Motor speech disorders are well described in diseases involving the cerebellum, extrapyramidal, and pyramidal systems (see Aronson, in press).

Activation, arousal, and attention mechanisms associated with environmental stimulation involve complex cortical and subcortical control mechanisms, which intertwine with speech and language function. Interestingly, a primary disturbance in attention and arousal has been considered by many researchers as a basic deficit in schizophrenia. Moses (1954) has proposed an internal constitutional rhythmic capacity that is utilized in speech and is sensitive to both psychologic and organic influence.

SPEECH IN GENETIC AND METABOLIC DISEASES

There are a few genetic diseases that mainly impact the language mechanisms. Audimutism, a rare disorder, results in a relatively permanent retardation of language function. Congenital aphasia and auditory agnosia appear to produce isolated defects in speech and language expression and reception.

On the other hand, metabolic diseases may affect the speech mechanism in a variety of ways. Myasthenia gravis, a defect in neurotransmission, may impair speech production by reducing power in the muscular apparatus. Diabetes millitus, a genetic metabolic disorder, may disturb speech function via a neuroendocrine mechanism (hyper or hypoglycemia) or anatomically by peripheral neuropathy or arteriovascular effect.

PSYCHOPHYSIOLOGIC DIMENSIONS

Affect and emotional coloring appear to be reflected through subtle tonal qualities involving pitch, stress, and intonation (see Williams, Chapter 11). Traditionally, psychophysiologic studies have rarely included speech as a parameter; however, Rice, Abroms, and Saxman (1969) reported a correlation between cardiovascular effect and fundamental frequency in a stress situation. Psychiatric patients with "flat affects" failed to respond as normal controls. At this time a good deal of research in progress is systematically evaluating vocal effects in stress and emotional conditions (see Scherer, Chapters 9 and 10; Williams, Chapter 11).

SPEECH AND PSYCHOSES

It is likely that some selected psychotic syndromes will be shown to reflect an underlying neuroregulatory or neurochemical disturbance. Alterations in speech behavior may be expected, along with disturbances in psychomotor activity, mood, thinking, and planning. The relationship between selected speech parameters and their biophysical correlates should provide a fruitful area for investigation.

## SPEECH AND NONVERBAL COMMUNICATION

Some researchers have divided communication into verbal (content) and nonverbal channels. Nonverbal behaviors include paralinguistics, facial expressions, posture, and movement. Concepts behind this research include: (1) hidden or unconscious messages are unwittingly expressed in nonverbal channels of behavior; (2) ethological and sociologic phenomena are revealed in these nonverbal channels (see Scherer, Chapter 10); (3) incongruency in messages between verbal and nonverbal channels may reveal areas of conflict.

Incongruency between verbal and nonverbal channels has been particularly noted in clinical descriptions of schizophrenia. Flat or inappropriate affectual tone as compared to content message or situational context is one of the salient features of the syndrome. This alteration of affect in chronic schizophrenia may exhibit a fixed or frozen character which is quite apparent in the speech behavior of these patients. While the cause of this curious symptom is unclear, there is evidence which justifies searching for a physiological basis of this effect.

## CHILDHOOD PSYCHOSIS

### Discussion of the Syndrome

"Childhood schizophrenia" and "childhood psychoses" are broad terms used to describe a number of schizophrenialike syndromes, which have their onset from birth to age 12. In general, affected children manifest marked deviations in their relationships to people, maturational development, and perceptual, motor and/or intellectual skills (Lauffer and Gair, 1969). Goldfarb (1972) has pointed out the heterogeneity of this diagnostic grouping on the basis of their individual differences in genetic background, congenital disposition, psychosocial experience, defensive characteristics, and response to treatment.

There are a number of different syndromes and models for childhood psychoses in the literature. Particular areas of concern are (1) age of onset, (2) signs of organic involvement, (3) the role of biological/ hereditary aspects, (4) the importance of family dynamics, (5) I.Q., (6) developmental history, (7) current level of functioning.

Rutter (1967, 1968) suggested a simplified classification system based upon age of onset: (1) a schizophrenic syndrome developing around the time of adolescence (ages 8–18) that appears similar to adult schizophrenia; (2) a psychotic syndrome appearing at age 3–5 with a normal earlier development (in this group regression, deterioration, and loss of speech may suggest degenerative brain disease); (3) infantile autism with its onset from birth through 30 months. This latter syndrome is a severe disorder, usually beginning in infancy, which shows profound speech and language impairment (100 percent), social "aloofness" (100 percent), ritualistic behavior (90 percent), abnormal motor phenomena (75 percent), and mental retardation (75 percent).

### Etiological Considerations

While early investigators emphasized psychodynamic features in childhood psychoses, more recent neurophysiological studies (Schopler and Reichler, 1971; Walter, et al., 1971), and neuropathological reviews (Creak, 1963; Darby, 1976) implicate organic impairments. The interactional aspects of organic and psychological effects produce a syndrome which is difficult to untangle. Menolascino (1970) suggests that poor impulse control, temper tantrums, disorganization under minimal stress, and aloofness may be secondary consequences of cerebral dysfunction. Clark (personal communication), using an operant conditioning paradigm, has demonstrated that repetitive, ritualistic movements, hand flapping, twirling and stereotypy increase proportionately with frustration, lack of rewards, and defeat. Clark has also shown specific memory and learning disabilities and uneven learning performance curves in autistic children as compared with aphasics and mongols. Walter et al. (1971), describing a dissociation between cerebral and autonomic responses in autistic children, has shown an absence of nonspecific EEG responses to visual and auditory stimuli in selected autistics. Schopler and Reichler (1971) suggest that functionally autism seems to be associated with disruption in organizing sensory perception and cortical association and control. A defect in perceptual constancy, therefore, may be one frequent concomitant of autism.

While autistic children share many pathologic signs, there is, nevertheless, a wide diversity of outcomes, behavioral capabilities, neurophysiologic, and neuropathologic findings. These facts suggest that autism may represent several separate disease processes, since autism includes defects in memory, learning, speech, and language function (including planning, organization, and associative function), autonomic disturbance, visual integrative phenomena, and tactile and kinesthetic senses.

## Review of Studies

SPEECH AND VOICE CHARACTERISTICS

The speaking and communicative capabilities of psychotic children show a wide variability ranging from simple grunts through fluency. Hirsch (1967) suggests that the schizophrenic child produces idiosyncratic language exhibiting a lack of functional relationships between words. Pitch, intonation, and stress show marked deviation from normal.

Goldfarb, Braunstein, and Lorge (1956) and Goldfarb et al. (1972) noted a "flat, unfinished quality," which has been referred to as a "monotone." This quality was attributed to insufficient and peculiar intonation, linked with reduced pitch variation. The "chanting" quality of speech, frequently observed in these children, was caused by prolongation of sounds, syllables, or words, combined with inappropriate rate changes from phrase to phrase. Finally, inadequate and unrelated language reinforcement through facial expression and gesture produced an impression of "wooden features" with staring but apparently "unseeing eyes." While insufficient and inappropriate volume and pitch changes were noted, total pitch range was narrowed, with a tendency to excessively high pitch. Rhythm distortions resulted particularly from insufficient or inappropriate stress and from hesitation and repetition of sounds.

A CENTRAL REGULATORY DEFECT

These children showed significant deviations from normals in 50 of 82 speech and language parameters appraised. Overall they seemed to show either too much or too little of various speech qualities. Antipodal effects were prominent in volume, force, rate, stress, pitch, and inflection. Many divergencies were noted in individual patterns, so that no specific cluster of speech faults seemed uniquely characteristic. Goldfarb et al. (1972) concluded that a primary disturbance was shown in the control and regulation of voice and speech communication, and that this defect in self-regulatory control of speech provided a key to impairment in other adaptive functions.

### SCHIZOPHRENIA

#### Clinical Symptoms

The term schizophrenia describes a group of diseases with a symptom complex that produces massive disruptions of thinking, mood, and behavior. The acute stage of decompensation may include: (1) perceptual disturbances with auditory, visual, olfactory, gustatory, or somatic hallucinations; (2) cognitive disturbances with delusions, loose associations, impairment of reasoning and logic; (3) affect disturbance with flat, "blunted" or inappropriate emotional display, anhedonia, apprehension or frenzy; (4) mood disorder with exaltation, oceanic feelings, and excitement or depressions; (5) deficits of attention with easy distractibility or an inability to filter or screen out irrelevant stimuli; (6) sensorimotor aberrations with stereotypy, psychomotor agitation or retardation, grimaces, robotlike movement, gait and posture peculiarities, and speech and voice abnormalities.

Kraepelin (1919) required a deteriorated outcome to confirm the diagnosis of *dementia praecox*. He also suggested that more than two-thirds of the cases developed between the fifteenth and thirtieth years. Jung (1908, trans. 1960) suggested a psychosomatic model for schizophrenia. He believed that certain psychological conflicts triggered a psychonoxious biochemical process which then manifested as schizophrenia. Langfeldt (1939) proposed a distinction between process schizophrenia (*dementia praecox*) and reactive schizophrenia (schizophreniform psychoses). Process schizophrenia (Kraepelinian concept) was considered to arise without significant trauma, to eventually lead to deterioration, and to have a biological basis. Acute reactive schizophrenia appeared in individuals (who were not schizoid) with good premorbid adjustment and work patterns as a response to traumatic, environmentally produced stress and conflict. The prognosis was considered good without evidence of subsequent deterioration of residua.

Recent genetic and biochemical research in schizophrenia lends support to the Langfeldt hypothesis and theories of Meehl (1962), which suggest that chronic process schizophrenia is more dependent upon biological factors (Kallman, 1950; Kety, 1965; Rosenthal, 1961, 1963). Acute reactive schizophrenia, on the other hand, may be more significantly influenced by environmental stress factors.

The controversy of nature versus nuture may be partially resolved by a stress hypothesis of schizophrenia. Here the schizophrenia may be conceptualized as representing a continuum of illnesses of multifactoral causation, with biological loading at one end of the spectrum and environmental stress at the other. An individual who is genetically vulnerable would exhibit schizophrenic symptoms upon exposure to proper stress factors. While many psychodynamic models have been documented, the integration of both biological and psychological factors has received less attention.

**Biochemical Models**

Hollister (1977) indicates that while genetic predisposition to schizophrenia exists, phenotypic expression may be contingent upon the degree of genetic loading, intelligence, developmental influence, and stress.

Two principal hypotheses have emerged relating to the biological substrate of schizophrenia. These are well described in *Psychopharmacology* (Barchas, et al., 1977).

The transmethylation hypothesis implicates endogenous production of psychotogenic compounds. Osmond and Smythies (1952) indicated that mescaline could result from the O-methylation of dopamine. They postulated that an accumulation of hallucinogenic methylated metabolites might produce a schizophrenic condition. N-methylation of tryptamine or methylation of dopamine are two of numerous possible methods of producing endogenous psychotogens. Although no psychotogens have been shown to occur exclusively in schizophrenia, this hypothesis opens up a number of possibilities for further research due to the biochemical potential for a wide variety of endogenous psychotogens.

The dopamine hypothesis postulated that schizophrenia correlates with a functional hyperactivity of one or more cerebral dopaminergic pathways. The most important evidence for this hypothesis is based on information that suggests that antipsychotic drugs act by decreasing dopaminergic transmission. In addition to a psychic effect, these drugs produce significant motoric effects, such as the Parkinson-like reaction. The mechanism of action of the motoric effect is thought to be similar to that of the psychic effect, i.e., postsynaptic dopamine blockade, although separate receptor sites could be involved.

While dopamine would appear to play a central role in schizophrenia, other neurotransmitter systems also seem to be involved. Neuroregulators work in parallel or in opposition to one another. Examples of this "balancing" may be seen in Parkinson's disease and in tardive dyskinesia. In these two disorders the balance between dopaminergic and cholinergic systems appears to have been disturbed. In Parksonism, the scale of dopaminergic activity appears reduced when compared with the cholinergic system. An opposite "balance hypothesis" has been suggested for schizophrenia. Other "balance hypotheses" can be postulated involving serotonergic and dopaminergic systems. Due to the genetic involvement in these systems, future biological research is likely to pay close attention to DNA structure and to the enzymes that regulate neurochemical reactions.

In summary, the studies of chronic schizophrenia through clinical observation, genetic background, and neurochemical studies point towards a biological substrate. As the schizophrenic symptoms manifest so should a derangement reflect itself in the fine parameters of speech. A great deal of neural control is necessary to produce controlled frequency, intensity, and rate modulations. These modulations involve very finely tuned and complex neurological feedback systems. If schizophrenia is conceived as a disease where neuroregulatory and modulatory mechanisms suffer dysfunction, then one would expect concomitant disturbances in language, speech, and voice control mechanisms.

## Review of Studies

### VOICE CHARACTER AND QUALITY

Moses (1954) made several clinical observations of schizophrenic voice changes and suggested similarity to a child's voice due to the marked regression. He noted an androgynous character with male patients frequently using "head register" typical of females. Melody was found never to glide but rather to jump intervals without correlation to speech content. He noted inappropriate accents and emphasis and rhythmic repetition of vocal patterns. Moses emphasized rhythmic repetition of vocal and language patterns as a basic feature of schizophrenic expression.

Moskowitz (1951) studied a group of 40 schizophrenics matched with 40 controls and concluded that (1) certain voice qualities appeared in the schizophrenic populations, such as "monotony, weakness, unsustained auditory gloominess, and flat, colorless tone quality"; and that (2) male subjects seemed to show a great degree of "unsustained voice quality." Spoerri (1966) also noticed certain voice qualities in schizophrenics. He characterized the schizophrenic voice timbre as gloomy, dull, or metallic, and melody as monotonous and idiosyncratic.

### DISCRIMINATION STUDIES

Hollien and Darby (1979) utilized a perceptual identification schema involving 58 subjects (23 schizophrenics, 15 involutional depressives, 20 controls). Ten (naive) listeners were provided 8–10 second speech samples of a standard prose passage. Controls were correctly classified as normal 88 percent of the time, while schizophrenics were classified as abnormal 70 percent of the time.

Bannister (1972) compared 8 adolescent schizophrenics to 17 hospitalized nonpsychotic patients and to a control population. The schizophrenic subjects (7 males and 1 female) showed significantly reduced fundamental frequency deviation (FFD) when compared to their nonpsychotic cohorts and the normal controls. Bannister noted that this decrease in fundamental frequency deviation was compatible with Moskowitz's (1951) perceptual study of schizophrenics in which a monotony in pitch was reported.

Chevrie-Muller et al. (1971) studied 53 hospitalized adolescent schizophrenics (ages 12–23). The most striking finding reported was that the female schizophrenics showed reduction in fundamental frequency deviation (pitch range) relative to normal females. The males showed a similar trend but not of statistical significance. The authors suggested that from the symptomatic aspect the female schizophrenics were more homogenous than the male population, and this could be one explanation for the sex difference. Pause times and reading times were longer in the schizophrenic group but not at a statistically significant level. Some patients showed prolonged duration of words. The authors point out a lack of consistency and indicate some variability of findings. They also suggest that phenothiazine medications may be a significant factor in their results.

Denber (1978) reported that jitter (based on pitch differences at 10 millisecond intervals) is significantly lower in schizophrenics as compared to normals. Denber suggests that the lower jitter value could be one acoustic correlate of "flatness" or monotone effect sometimes reported in schizophrenia.

VOICE DEVIATION

Spoerri (1966) in a study of 350 schizophrenics found the following speech deviations: (1) dysarticulation (90 percent), (2) consonant formation deficiency (56 percent), (3) beginning speech (25 percent), (4) melody (23 percent), (5) volume (20 percent), (6) rhythm (18 percent). Spoerri reported that deteriorated forms of schizophrenia show a higher preponderance of deviation.

Harlan (1974) using speech pathologists' ratings found a mixed psychotic population (schizophrenia, paranoia, and affective) to have a 48 percent incidence of voice disturbance. He reported abnormalities of intonation (100 percent), breathiness and tension (93 percent), low pitch (43 percent), intensity irregularity (36 percent), and glottal fry (35 percent) in his sample of 14 schizophrenic patients.

VOCAL REGULATORY PHENOMENA

Ostwald (1961, 1963, 1974, 1966) was one of the pioneers in the study of speech disturbances in psychiatric patients. In 1964 he published a study detailing eight different acoustic patterns of soundmaking found in psychiatric patients. One adolescent schizophrenic male showed patterns of ultrarapid frequency shifts and rapid intermittent sound production.

In 1966 Ostwald and Skolnikoff published a study detailing a number of speech disturbances in a 15-year-old adolescent schizophrenic male. His speech was described as strikingly abnormal. Voice quality was nasal and indistinct. Articulation was impaired due to insufficient mouth closure, and consonants sounded mushy and unclear. Breath control was poor, and rate, rhythm, and intonation were disturbed. Physical action of the mouth and pharynx were studied radiographically. At times the soft palate did not close off the nasopharynx, resulting in a fuzzy nasal sound.

In the same year that Ostwald and Skolnikoff published their study, Spoerri (1966) reported antipodal effects in pitch, volume, speed, and idiosyncratic melodic movement of syllables in schizophrenia. Similarities in Ostwald's findings when compared to the Goldfarb (1956, 1972) and Spoerri (1966) studies include: (1) the difficulties noted in distinct articulation; (2) excessive variability of rate and rhythm; and (3) an apparent lack of finely tuned, integrated, and modulated control over the speech apparatus.

TREATMENT EFFECTS

Ostwald (1961, 1963) reported the case of a 16-year-old girl who entered the hospital in an acute schizophrenic state characterized by withdrawal and apathy. A monotonous sound quality pervaded her speech and an acoustic analysis at the time of admission showed a pattern characteristic of "sharp" voices. (See Ostwald, 1963, for definition of four acoustic stereotypes.) Following 5 weeks of hospitalization, psychotropic medication, and therapy, several changes were noted: (1) the spectral power curve showed a rise in intensity and a reduction of "sharpness"; (2) motant 3 (at 1430 Hz) showed appreciable change; (3) reading had speeded up an average of 0.06 seconds per syllable.

Scherer (1979), in a study of 11 schizophrenic females, found that 7 patients showed a relative decrease of low band energy (whole group mean–7.5 percent) following hospital treatment.

Spoerri (1966) reports that when intensive social therapy is utilized, the number of speech irregularities are lower. Deteriorated conditions show the greatest distortion of speech, simplest of rhythms, largest irregularity of dynamics, and greatest defects in articulation.

SEVERITY AND PROGNOSIS

Saxman (1968) studied 37 hospitalized schizophrenic females and compared this group to 22 mentally healthy females. He analyzed the two groups cross-sectionally by instrumental analysis of fundamental frequency level (FFL), fundamental frequency deviation (FFD), and mean overall and mean sentence reading rate. The schizophrenic group showed statistically significant differences in having a slower oral reading rate and a larger FFD. The schizophrenic group was subdivided into diagnostic types and levels of severity, and variations were noted between these groups. The subgroup classification of severity proved useful. Where significant differences were observed between schizophrenics and control groups, the mild/moderate/severe subgroup means were ordered in the direction of difference such that the severe subgroup represented one extreme and the control group the other. The authors suggest that these speech measures may have diagnostic and prognostic implications.

MEDICATION EFFECT

As is noted above, Saxman's and Burk's findings of increased fundamental frequency deviation are in contrast to studies of adolescent schizophrenia by Chevrie-Muller and Bannister. Saxman and Burk tested their patients 48 hours after discontinuation of psychotropic medications. In severely ill chronic schizophrenic patients this must be seen as a powerful variable. Did this effect unleash an acute schizophrenic process covered up in other studies by medication effect? There is a pressing need for clarification as to how these drugs interact with voice and speech analysis in schizophrenia.

SUMMARY

While these studies on schizophrenia fail to show any consistent abnormality, some considerations emerge.

1. Perceptual impressions of monotony may be correlated with findings of narrowed fundamental frequency deviation, with differences more marked for females than males.
2. The effect of medication upon this parameter requires careful exploration.
3. In the one study (Saxman and Burk) where medications were discontinued, fundamental frequency deviation was increased significantly in the direction of severity.
4. Antipodal effects were noted for rate, pitch, volume in several studies involving childhood psychosis, adolescent, and adult schizophrenia. These defects may suggest a regulatory or modulatory defect in speech production and control.
5. Intonational abnormalities seem frequently associated with all types of schizophrenia. The relationship (if any) between intonational defect and antipodal effect is unclear.
6. Prolonged reading times and pause rates (causing reduced phonation ratios) might be attributed to medication effect. The Saxman and Burk (1968) study, however, does not confirm this notion.
7. Power spectral analysis emerges in several studies as a potentially significant feature in before and after treatment studies.

## AFFECTIVE DISORDERS

### Discussion

The term affective disorder is used to refer to a broad category of psychiatric syndromes which have at their core a disturbance of mood or affect. Affective disorders are separated from the schizophrenias when a disturbance of thinking is the most prominent feature. In most syndromes depression is the major symptom; however, other alterations of mood include elation, mania, hypomania, euphoria, and rapidly fluctuating moods (cyclothymic).

Sadness and disappointment are normal emotions, although the term depression has been used to describe both normal and abnormal states. The distinction between a normally depressed state and an abnormal depression is not always clear, because affective disorders involve accentuation in duration and intensity of otherwise normal emotions. For example, severe depressive symptoms in a 60-year-old man could represent an endogenous depression. This disorder is thought to have an endogenous biological substrate and usually presents a distinct symptom complex. On the other hand, depressive symptoms in a young adult could reflect some recent traumatic loss and, as such, might represent a normal grief reaction.

A depressive or pessimistic attitude may describe an individual's life-long outlook or adaption pattern, in which case the problem is seen as part of the individual's character structure. Depression is also used to refer to syndromes overshadowed by symptoms such as headaches, phobias, or obsessive ideas ("atypical depressions") (Detre, 1971). This confusing multiple usage is partly an outgrowth of the difficulties in distinguishing the person who is disturbed by some current life event from one who is mentally ill (Hudgens, 1967). The situation is further confounded by the fact that many psychiatric patients with schizophrenia, borderline personality disorders, organic brain syndromes, paranoid disorders, and various physical illnesses suffer varying degrees of depression as a part of these mental processes.

### Clinical Symptoms

In general, severe psychopathological depressive illnesses are marked by: (1) depression of mood, (2) the presence of neurovegetative signs, (3) suicidal thoughts, (4) disturbances in reality testing with hallucinations or delusions and impaired performance.

1. Depression of mood manifested by sadness, tearfulness, hopelessness, and gloominess (90 percent). Changes in speech, facial expression, posture, and dress may be observed.

2. Neurovegetative signs manifested by:
   * Loss of appetite with weight loss (70–80 percent).
   * Sleep disturbance (80–90 percent), which may involve early morning awakening, difficulty in falling asleep, midsleep awakenings, or a feeling of exhaustion upon arising.
   * Reduced sexual interest and a lack of enjoyment of life.
   * Disturbance of gastrointestinal function. Many patients complain of constipation and focus attention on their bowel habits.
   * Psychomotor disturbance, with either agitation or retardation of movement present. Anxiety and tension discharge movements (such as pacing, wringing of hands, or reciprocal repetitions) frequently occur together. Speech, gestures, and movement in these patients may be rapid, explosive, or clipped.
   * Psychomotor retardation appears to be the opposite of agitation with generally slowed movements, fixed gaze, slow, dull, monotonous, listless speech, and lethargy.
   * Psychomotor alterations with impaired concentration, slowed thinking, "mind thick like a fog." Mental speed and performance are decreased, although accuracy is retained.
3. Suicidal thoughts occur in the majority of depressions. Death by suicide will occur in 1 percent of acute depressions, and in 15 percent of severe chronic recurrent depressions (Klerman, 1978). Suicidal behavior is probably related to cognitive, perceptive, and mood distortions suffered during the depressive episode, even though most suicides occur after symptomatic improvement.
4. Impaired reality testing, with disturbances of perception, may involve derogatory hallucinations, somatic delusions, delusions of poverty, a sense of helplessness or impotence, a sense of being unworthy, and a profound loss of self-esteem.

Traditional divisions have been made between character, neurotic, and psychotic depressive states. Factors involved in differentiation include: (1) age of onset, (2) duration of illness, (3) severity and extent of symptom complex, (4) nature of precipitating event, (5) recurrent history, (6) personality style, and (7) family history.

With the development of psychotropic drugs, it has become useful to characterize the level of psychomotor agitation, retardation, or anxiety present. To some extent these features may provide "target symptoms" for selection of medications. As a general rule, benzodiazepines are effective for treating anxiety, sedating tricyclics or phenothiazines for treating agitation, and activating tricyclics for treating retarded depressions.

## Diagnostic Classification

Parallel with the schizophrenias, manic and depressive reactions represent a number of different disease processes. The causes for these disturbances include environmental stress and biological factors, individually and in combination with one another. A spectrum thesis of etiology represents a reasonable conceptual framework for this group of disorders. Robins and Guze (1972) proposed a distinction between primary and secondary affective disorders based on chronology of onset and the presence of associated illness. Primary disorders occur in patients who have been previously well or who have manic depressive illness, and secondary disorders occur in mentally ill persons or as a secondary symptom to medical diseases or drug reactions. Further differentiation between unipolar (depression only) and bipolar (mania and depression) is included as an elaboration of Kraepelin's (1921) early concept of manic-depressive illness. Genetic studies have shown that families with bipolar illness have a higher frequency of psychiatric disorders than unipolar families. While psychodynamic theories of depression are well understood, biochemical correlates of depressed behavior and their relationship to genetics and psychological events are current areas of research interest.

## A Biochemical Model of Depression and Mania

Mania and depression may be viewed as representing opposite poles in a continuum of psychomotor activity. These states are thought to be related to excesses or deficiencies of certain brain neurotransmitters: norepinephrine and serotonin. The "catecholamine hypothesis" suggested that an excess of noradrenergic activity would produce mania, while a deficiency would lead to lassitude and depression. The "indoleamine hypothesis" suggested that serotonin played a large role in depression.

Early research on these ideas was based on clinical effects of reserpine and iproniazid. Reserpine, when used to treat hypertension, produced a depressive syndrome in a subgroup of patients. Iproniazid, used for tuberculosis, was noted to produce euphoria and increased activity in some patients. Subsequent pharmacological research revealed that reserpine had the effect of depleting serotonin, epinephrine, and dopamine, while iproniazid inhibited monomine oxidase, thereby increasing the concentrations of catecholamines and serotonin. These two hypotheses taken together have been termed the "biogenic amine hypothesis" of affective disorders.

Further research has suggested that there may be subgroups of depressed patients who show selective deficiencies and/or imbalances of either serotonin or norepinephrine systems. Initial results suggested that serotonin deficient patients were agitated, while norepinephrine deficient patients had retarded psychomotor activity. Although these results have not been consistently confirmed, and therefore cannot be considered established, they do provide a conceptual framework for understanding the biological substrates of affective disorders. These biochemical hypotheses are fully described in *Psychopharmacology* (Barchas, et al., 1977).

## Review of Studies

DEPRESSIVE SYMPTOMS

*Voice character and quality.*   Newman and Mather (1938) perceptually studied the speech of 40 depressed patients whom they classified into four separate subgroups: "classical depressions," "dissatisfaction/gloom states," "mixed," and maniac states. The "classical depressions" comprised several diagnostic groupings, but for the most part consisted of patients who exhibited sadness, retardation, constipation, anorexia, and insomnia. These patients showed "dead, listless" voice qualities. Pitch range was narrow with infrequent stepwise pitch changes. Speech tempo was slow with frequent pauses and hesitations. Emphatic accents were lacking. Resonance was described as pharyngeal and nasal. Syntax was limited, and length of response was short.

The second grouping of depressions included patients experiencing chronic states of gloom, self-pity, and dissatisfaction. These patients showed a different speech pattern from those of the classical depressions. Articulation was fairly crisp, and pitch revealed long gliding intonations extended over a wide tonal range. The voice was described as relatively lively and, although tempo was average, pauses were frequent. Glottal rasping was particularly noted in this group.

Moses (1954) has characterized the depressed voice as exhibiting a uniformity with a regular repetition of the same gliding down interval. When the tone goes down intensity decreases proportionately, and he felt that this regular repetition was responsible for the monotonous voice quality attributed to depressive states.

*Severity effect.*   Whitman and Flicker (1966) studied three patients in an attempt to correlate the degree of improvement or deterioration of depression in psychiatric disease by means of sound spectrograph. Each of their patients had different disorders: simple schizophrenia, manic depressive–depressed type, and ambulatory schizophrenia. They clinically differentiated agitated depression (found in the manic depressive and ambulatory schizophrenics) from a more retarded form (found in the simple schizophrenic). In each case they found average pitch and second formant rate change increased with depression and the level of severity of the patient's symptom complex. They also found that a reduction in intensity correlated with greater depression. Syllable rate increased in the two patients with agitated depression, whereas it fell in the patient who became more depressed without concurrent agitation.

Moses (1954) had previously suggested that anxiety may be associated with higher pitch, and depression with lower pitch; yet Whitman's and Flicker's findings would appear to contradict this idea. It is important to note that "agitated" forms of depressive symptomatology are generally considered to contain significant levels of anxiety. Therefore, agitated depression would represent at the least a combination of two emotional states: anxiety and depression.

*Treatment effect.* Eldred and Price (1958) perceptually studied one patient's speech and voice patterns extensively through a 13-month period of psychoanalysis. Although the diagnosis of the patient was not given, the study investigated the overt and suppressed emotions of depression and anger. They reported decreases in pitch, rate, and volume with depressed states and increases with anger. Suppressed emotional states were associated with break-up, whereas overt expression showed little or none.

Hargreaves and Starkweather (1964) studied eight psychiatrically hospitalized patients (with different diagnoses) in which depression was a prominent feature of their illness. The study attempted to track changes in mood concomitant with various treatment procedures utilizing power spectrum analyses. Several of the patients, with improvement, showed an anticipated pattern of increase in overall power, with greater relative increases in the higher formants. The authors suggested it might be possible to identify subgroup voice patterns in a larger study, but that no uniform pattern should be expected within the broad category of depression of mood.

Hargreaves, Starkweather, and Blacker (1965) correlated mood ratings and power spectra before, during, and after treatment of 32 depressed patients (ages 20–72). Predictions of mood ratings from voice spectra correlated significantly for 25 of the 32 patients. Correlations were largest for those patients who showed considerable change in their mood. Some of the patients also showed organic impairment or confusion secondary to treatment (electroconvulsant therapy and/or antidepressant medications), which the authors felt was reflected in their voices. The ten patients who showed the largest changes were selected from the population to see if there was a uniform voice quality of depression. Five of these patients showed a depressed voice reduced in loudness and lacking in high overtones, giving the effect of a dull, lifeless quality with diminished inflection. There were two or three patients who showed a reversal, since their voices were actually louder and sometimes higher in pitch during depression. Thus, this study demonstrates the importance of examining a population from two standpoints: from that of the group as a whole and from that of the individuals within the group.

## INVOLUTIONAL DEPRESSION
## (ENDOGENOUS DEPRESSION)

*Clinical discussion.* Kraepelin (1896) first separated involutional melancholia from other periodic forms of depression. The illness is a psychotic depression occurring in the involutional period, usually in individuals of compulsive personality type but without prior history of manic depression. It is characterized by a long course manifested by worry, intractable insomnia, guilt, anxiety, agitation, delusional ideas, somatic concern, and a high suicide rate when untreated.

Its cardinal featuress include: (1) personality predisposition; (2) no prior mental disorder; (3) occurrence within the involutional phase; (4) a very severe depressive syndrome of psychotic proportion that may include paranoid delusions. Many researchers feel this disorder has strong biological determinants (Ford, 1967).

*Review of studies: Voice character.* Moses (1954) described the voice of individuals in the climacteric. Males were reported to lose strength and volume with the range becoming both narrowed and higher. Females sometimes showed lowering of range. These changes were presumably due to the accompanying physiologic changes of old age.

*Review of studies: Treatment effect.* Darby and Hollien (1977) studied six patients with primary depressions (ages 50–72) before and after electroconvulsive treatment. Prior to treatment the voices were characterized as "dull" and lacking in vitality. Following treatment and moderate clinical improvement, the voices were judged to have regained some of their normal vitality in distinction to the pretreatment "dull" quality. Perceptual analysis by a speech pathologist showed improvement in articulation and pitch inflection (five patients) and stress (four patients). While listener judgment showed change, it was not striking. Instrumental analysis was also carried out, yet no significant trends were detected. The paucity of significant instrumental findings in this study would appear to contradict Ostwald's (1963) findings of increased intensity centered around 500 Hz. following electroconvulsant therapy. The explanation for this may be due to either a different type of study approach, a different method of statistical analysis, or a marked sex ratio difference of patients between the two studies.

In an unpublished pilot study, Darby and Simmons (1979) found primary depressions (8 cases) to show significant changes in stress, monopitch, loudness decay, loudness level, and trends for reduction in monoloudness and imprecise consonants after antidepressant drug treatment. Hamilton depression ratings were reduced by a highly significant level signifying improvement of depression.

Scherer (1979) reports a mean decrease of fundamental frequency of 9.6 Hz for 9 depressed patients following hospital treatment. Six of these 9 patients showed a relative increase of low band energy (260–440 Hz) as compared to high bands (440–9040 Hz). Mean change for all 9 patients was 10.2 percent following therapy.

## MANIC DEPRESSIVE ILLNESS

*Clinical discussion.* This disorder has received attention in the past ten years due to research indicating a genetic basis and the advent of lithium treatment. Current research investigations have focused on the oscillatory nature of the syndrome with reference to unipolar and bipolar manifestations. Patients may cycle through periods of manic elation and depression in a sinusoidal manner (bipolar form). Other states may be observed where the individual is subject only to periodic recurrent depressions (unipolar form). Kahlbaum (1882) described mania and melancholia as stages of the same disease. Kraepelin (1896) proposed the term manic-depressive insanity for this group of disorders.

The manic patient exhibits elation, irritability, pressure of speech, flight of ideas, increased motor activity, and a markedly reduced sleep pattern, whereas the depressive patient shows quite the converse. Manic-depressive reactions in contradistinction to many of the schizophrenias do not progress to a state of mental deterioration (Cohen, 1967). Manic depressives provide a particularly useful model for experimental study, as the disorder shows oscillation of mood from depression to normal to manic with certain regularity or periodicity.

Because patterns of change are repetitive and characteristically quite similar for an individual patient, the opportunity to study the speech changes associated with each phase could produce important clues to the voice and speech correlates of depressive psychoses.

*Review of studies: Manic depressive-manic phase and voice character.* Newman and Mather (1938) described manic patients as "good speakers" with vigorous articulation. The voice was clear, lively, and vital. The pitch range was wide with frequent, gliding changes. Emphasis and accent were frequent; pauses were rhythmical, but exaggerated in length. Resonance was oral and pharyngeal. Syntax was described as rich but loose, and response initiation was rapid. With improvement of their condition, the patients showed relaxation of articulation, a narrowing of pitch range, and reduction of emphatic accent. Pauses and hesitation began to appear. Syntax tightened up and became more coherent. These findings were partially supported by Moses (1954) who described manic voices as exhibiting wide pitch range, uncontrolled intensities, fast tempo, and highly dynamic action.

*Review of studies: Manic depressive-depressed phase.* Ostwald (1961, 1963) acoustically analyzed a depressed manic depressive 64-year-old man before and after treatment with electrocovulsant therapy. The initial acoustic pattern on the power spectral curve was predominantly "flat." Motants 3 and 4 were not clearly defined for reading voice. After treatment, reading voice and high voice showed strikingly different curves characterized as "robust" and evidencing more intensity and acoustical energy. The voice showed a loudness rise of 4.3 sones with the band of maximum increase (2.2 sones) centered at 500 Hz. Read speech had slowed down 0.06 seconds per syllable.

SUMMARY

The review of the available studies on affective disorders suggests that: (1) subgroups sets of speech and vocal patterns will emerge; (2) a classical pattern of depression indicates presence of reduced intensity, reduced pitch range, slower speech, lack of intonation and lack of stress; (3) there may exist another subgroup that (due to anxiety and agitation) exhibit opposite findings from the classical pattern, and (4) manic patients may present a pattern of rate, loudness, pitch, and rhythm abnomalities. Certain of these patients may have voice effects which mirror their mood states in periods of fluctuation.

## MIXED POPULATION STUDIES

### Discussion

Studies of mixed psychiatric populations may attempt: to find some basic variable that separates emotionally disturbed individuals from normals; to monitor some basic symptom that is found in several psychopathological disorders (e.g., depression or flat affect); to monitor some general treatment variable; or to monitor some independent variable (such as institutionalization).

The clinical manifestations of psychiatric disorders are the outcome of complex interacting forces—biological, sociocultural, and psychological (Linn, 1967). Many researchers feel that the multifactorial point of view is not embodied in traditional clinical psychiatric nosology. One may be concerned more with a specific symptom or characteristic that is deviant from normal behavior but which occurs in a variety of behavioral patterns. For example, symptoms of depression, anxiety, suggestibility, disturbances of judgment, altered levels of consciousness, and multiple other states (including illusions and delusions) may be seen at various times in the majority of people. Speech analysis may provide valuable insights into some of these states, which may have specific psychophysiologic correlates.

### Review of Studies

AIR LOSS AND RESTRICTION OF FUNDAMENTAL
FREQUENCY: DEVIATION IN HOSPITALIZED
ADOLESCENTS

Bannister (1972) studied a mixed population of 45 hospitalized adolescents (ages 14–18) in a cross-sectional manner compared to 45 matched normals. The psychiatric population contained 12 diagnostic entities ranging from schizophrenia to adjustment reaction. The common denominator was emotional disturbance. The analytic method consisted of evaluating voice recordings of impromptu and read speech by selected instrumental (FFL, FFD) and perceptual parameters (vocal fry, air loss, and effort). Bannister found that psychiatrically hospitalized females demonstrated significantly lower FFL from controls on reading. Both hospitalized males and females showed more restricted FFD than their control counterparts. The difference for males was statistically significant. Air loss was perceived as greater among the hospitalized group. Listeners were able to differentiate hospitalized from nonhospitalized by judging recordings of read speech.

## TREATMENT AND POWER SPECTRUM ANALYSIS

Ostwald (1963) studied 30 hospitalized patients (ages 13–74) with mixed psychiatric disorders. The patients were recorded before and after various forms of treatment including chemotherapy and electroconvulsant therapy. Ostwald directed his attention to motants 1–4 on the power spectra. The 9 patients who received ECT showed significant trends towards intensity increases at 500 Hz; but the 21 patients who did not tended to show either no change or a decrease of sound pressure level at 500 Hz. Changes in time duration of soundmaking were also noted; younger patients sped up their reading after treatment, and older patients slowed down.

## FLAT AFFECT, STRESS, AND FUNDAMENTAL FREQUENCY

Rice, Abroms, and Saxman (1969) studied a mixed group of 9 psychiatric patients in an experiment designed to measure psychophysiologic responses under emotional and neutral circumstances when compared to normals. The patient group included 5 schizophrenics, 2 borderline disorders, and 2 personality disorders. The common factor was flat affect. The aim of the research was to determine whether constriction of affect correlated with constricted automonic, skeletal system, or voice qualities. Heart rate, body movement, galvanic skin response, finger blood volume, frontalis EMG, and vocal analysis (FFL, FFD, vocal inflection) were measured. Heart rate, body movement, and fundamental frequency level revealed parallel results. Emotionally flat patients showed a decrease in response level to emotional conditions compared with that of a neutral condition. Controls showed an increased response. The experimental group showed lower FFL under the emotional conditions, while the controls showed increased FFL.

## SUMMARY

Mixed population studies show: (1) the importance of power spectral curves in studies of psychiatric patients with special reference to formant structure; (2) a relationship between "flat affect," emotionality, stress, and FFL; and (3) the importance of rate phenomena in psychiatric patients, especially in before and after treatment studies.

## COMPARATIVE STUDIES

### Review of Studies

Several studies have compared and contrasted speech/voice parameters between different psychiatric populations. Harlan (1974) studied the comparative incidence of vocal disturbances among schizophrenic, paranoid, and manic depressive populations with subjective ratings by three speech pathologists. Spontaneous and read samples from 14 subjects in each population were evaluated for 14 voice parameters. Harlan found a 48 percent incidence of voice disorders in the combined psychotic groups (estimate of 1 percent in general population). Intonation, however, was rated to be abnormal in 100 percent of all subjects studied, and breathiness (air loss) abnormalities were noted in 83 percent of all subjects. The only significant intergroup difference was for pitch breaks between schizophrenics (0 percent) and manic depressives (29 percent). Harlan studied each factor individually and did not attempt a cluster analysis. It should be noted also that virtually all of his subjects were medicated.

Scherer (1979) compared 9 depressive and 11 schizophrenic female patients (ages 20–59) before and after hospital treatment. He analyzed FFL, FFD, and relative amplitude levels in third octave bands. Scherer found a mean decrease in fundamental frequency level (FFL) of 9.5 Hz for depressive patients and 5.4 Hz (not significant) for schizophrenic patients following treatment. He reported that 6 of the 9 depressive patients showed a relative *increase* of energy in low bands (260–440 Hz) as compared to high bands (440–9040 Hz). Seven of the 11 schizophrenic patients showed a relative *decrease* of energy in the low bands. The difference between the two groups was significant. Scherer suggests that after therapy the depressive patients' voices sounded more resonant, suggesting a more flexible control of laryngeal musculature and possibly a relaxation of muscular tone.

Hollien and Darby (1979) compared 15 involutional depressives, 23 schizophrenics, and 20 controls with respect to a perceptual identification schema, FFL, FFD, reading time, and phonation–time (P/T) ratios. All subjects read a standard prose passage. There was suggestion of a bimodal distribution of FFD among some of the schizophrenics. The involutional depressives took substantially longer to read the 132-word passage than did the schizophrenics or controls. Schizophrenic females also took longer to read the passage than did the controls. Mean phonation–time ratios for involutional depressives

(.64), schizophrenics (.73), and normals (.81) suggest an order effect. However, these differences, while discriminating psychotic from nonpsychotic, would not appear to discriminate schizophrenics from involutional depressives. Further evaluation of rate phenomena should be undertaken.

Denber (1978) developed a computerized spectral analysis approach and compared 61 depressed males with 20 schizophrenic males and 31 control males. Speech samples of read prose material (12 sec.) were analyzed for 21 parameters including maximum, average, and minimum pitch and power, jitter, and pitch reversals. Denber found significant differences between the control and experimental groups in power variation and jitter. The depressed group when compared to controls appeared quite similar to the schizophrenic group with the exception of the jitter measurement, which differentiated it from the schizophrenic group. The similarity in the results for the two experimental groups suggested that voice changes were similar for these groups, but the effects of medication could not be overlooked as one powerful (and uncontrolled) variable. Denber suggests that more research is warranted and points to the importance of further jitter measurements, voice onset times, speech to silence ratios, formant transitions, and vowel duration.

SUMMARY

The more recent comparative studies appear to substantiate some of the relationships suggested in earlier studies.

1.  Psychotic populations appear to exhibit voice disturbances and different speech features from nonpsychotic populations.
2.  Differences between normals and psychotics are more readily identified than are those between and among subgroups of psychotic populations.
3.  Psychotropic medications continue to be an important uncontrolled variable.
4.  Longitudinal studies of patients are seriously needed.
5.  Certain measures may provide etiological clues for some of the major psychotic disturbances. Newer measurement techniques involving power spectral curves, rate phenomena, jitter, formant structure, and intonation features may prove useful in the differential diagnosis of psychoses and in the assessment of treatment effects.
6.  The potential of a cluster analysis technique is suggested in order

to factor multiple parameters into coherent patterns, as psychiatric populations probably involve several subgroups.

7. The development of automated, computer-based systems to analyze the speech and voice characteristics of subjects is now a possibility.

8. Finally, it would appear possible to establish a tentative model of the speech and voice relationships with some of the clinical entities discussed above; current technology would appear robust enough to permit the testing of certain relationships specified by such a model.

### Table of Studies Reviewed

Table 13–1 recapitulates the reviewed studies according to psychopathological diagnoses. The basic method of sound analysis employed is labeled as perceptual (P) or instrumental (I). Only five studies used both approaches in a combined or correlative fashion (C). A multitude (over 82) of speech parameters were measured in these studies, making comparison or correlation nearly impossible. While most of these studies were cross-sectional (CS) in nature, 10 of them attempted before and after treatment (BA) comparisons.

### CONCLUSION

The overview of literature demonstrates a potentially vast field for study. While there are as of yet few studies that yield systematic data, a structural foundation for further work is provided by those studies reviewed.

An initial difficulty in reviewing these studies had to do with the interdisciplinary nature of the research. Because psychiatry, psychology, speech pathology, and speech science originate from very different roots and lend diverse perspectives, there are often problems in terminology, classification, and even research objectives. It appears that the most successful approach to resolving these interdisciplinary communication problems will involve active participation by each discipline involved in a given study.

When there is good interdisciplinary collaboration in a study, the potential yield of knowledge is impressive. For example, the finding of antipodal effects and excessive variability in speech patterns has broad ramifications with respect to schizophrenia, since: the disturbance of modulatory control and regulation in speech is also manifest-

**Table 13-1**

Studies According to Psychopathological Populations

| Diagnosis or Group | Author | Year | N | Ages | Method | Study |
|---|---|---|---|---|---|---|
| *CHILDHOOD PSYCHOSES* | | | | | | |
| | Goldfarb et al. | 1956 | 12 | med.=8 | P | CS |
| | Goldfarb et al. | 1972 | 25 | med.=8 | P | CS |
| *SCHIZOPHRENIAS* | | | | | | |
| Adolescent | Ostwald | 1961,1963 | 2 | 14,16 | I | BA |
| Schizophrenia | | 1964 | | | I | BA |
| | Ostwald & Skolnikoff | 1966 | 1 | 15 | I | CS |
| | Chevrie-Muller et al. | 1971 | 53 | 12–23 | I | CS |
| | Bannister | 1972 | 8 | 14–17 | C | CS |
| Adult | Moskowitz | 1951 | 40 | — | P | CS |
| Schizophrenia | Spoerri | 1966 | 350 | — | C | CS |
| | Saxman and Burk | 1968 | 37 | med.=42 | I | CS |
| *AFFECTIVE DISORDERS* | | | | | | |
| Depressive | Eldred & Price | 1958 | 1 | — | P | BA |
| Symptoms | Whitman & Flicker | 1966 | 3 | 40–53 | I | CS |
| Depression | Newman & Mather | 1938 | 40 | — | P | CS |
| | Hargreaves & Starkweather | 1964 | 8 | — | I | BA |
| | Hargreaves et al. | 1965 | 32 | 20–72 | I | BA |
| Involutional Depression | Darby & Hollien | 1977 | 6 | 50–72 | C | BA |
| Manic Depression | | | | | | |
| Depressed phase | Ostwald | 1961,1963 | 1 | 64 | I | BA |
| Manic phase | Newman & Mather | 1938 | — | — | I | CS |
| *MIXED POPULATIONS* | | | | | | |
| | Ostwald | 1963 | 30 | 13–74 | I | BA |
| | Rice et al | 1969 | 9 | med.=23 | I | BA |
| | Bannister | 1972 | 45 | 14–17 | C | CS |
| *COMPARATIVE STUDIES* | | | | | | |
| | Scherer | 1979 | 20 | 20–59 | I | BA |
| | Harlan | 1974 | 42 | — | P | CS |
| | Denber | 1978 | 81 | — | I | CS |
| | Hollien & Darby | 1979 | 39 | 24–72 | C | CS |

ed in other areas of adaptive behavior; speech disturbances accurately mirror some more basic deficit present in these subjects; and there may be a reasonable clinical cross-correlation between behavioral and cognitive deficits and speech disturbances in patients. Observations of this type can provide a powerful base both for the development of measurement parameters and for hypotheses concerning basic defects and etiological considerations in these disorders.

Review of these studies demonstrates the complexity of speech research in psychiatric populations. There is neither a comprehensive model for the psychotic disorders, nor one for speech and language production. Knowledge of the impact of diseases upon speech has been obtained largely through clinical observation and deduction. It has been assumed that speech and language mirror internal events, yet some researchers believe that language may serve a central planning and organizational function. This latter thesis would implicate speech and language in a broad spectrum of central nervous system activity.

Another feature of complexity is the large number of factors which can be subjected to analysis. The Goldfarb study (1972) looked at 82 parameters of speech and language faults. When one considers the other significant variables, such as number of subjects, diagnosis, severity, medications, etc., the need for systematized mathematical analyses becomes apparent. Studies with a smaller number of factors appeared tighter in construction and were perhaps more reliable, but produced fewer comprehensive results.

The overview demonstrates areas of interest in which little or no research has been done. They are (1) longitudinal studies on schizophrenics, manic depressives, and various other syndromes; (2) the effect of psychotropic medications on speech; (3) cross-correlation work between instrumental and perceptual methodology; and (4) cross-correlation work with speech and other phenomena (e.g., behavioral, psychophysiologic, and neurochemical parameters).

As a final note, this review demonstrates that, while there are as yet no specific clusters of speech disturbances for any given syndrome, there is an indication that specific clusters or subgroup factors will emerge as products of further research. This potential is one of the exciting possibilities in the field, since, when developed, it may yield significant new information in areas such as the identification of neurobiological and environmental correlates for various speech parameters.

REFERENCES

Aronson, A. E. Motor speech signs in neurologic disease. In J. Darby (Ed.), *Speech evaluation in psychiatry.* New York: Grune & Stratton, in press.
Bannister, M. L. An instrumental and judgmental analysis of voice samples from psychiatrically hospitalized and nonhospitalized adolescents. Doctoral thesis, University of Kansas, 1972.
Barchas, J. D., Berger, P. A., Ciaranello, R. D., et al. (Eds.), *Psychopharmacology from theory to practice.* New York: Oxford University Press, 1977.
Beadle, G. W. Biochemical Genetics. *Chem Rec,* 1945, *37,* 15.

Chevrie-Muller, C., Dodart, F., Sequier-Dermer, N., et al. Étude des parametres acoustiques de la parole au cours de la schizophrenia de l'adolescent. *Folia Phoniatrica*, 1971, *23*, 401–428.

Cohen, R. A. Manic depressive reactions. In A. M. Freedman and H. I. Kaplan (Eds.), *Comprehensive textbook of psychiatry*. Baltimore: Williams and Wilkins, 1967, Chap 17.1, 676–687.

Creak, E. M. Childhood psychosis: A review of 100 cases. *British Journal of Psychiatry*, 1963, *109*, 84–89.

Darby, J. K. Neuropathologic aspects of psychosis in children. *Journal of Autism and Childhood Schizophrenia*, 1976, *6*, 229–252.

Darby, J. K., Hollien, H. Vocal and speech patterns of depressive patients. *Folia Phoniatrica*, 1977, *29*, 279–291.

Darby J. K., Sherk, A. Speech studies in psychiatric populations. In H. and P. Hollien (Eds.), *Current issues in the phonetic sciences*, Vol. 9. Amsterdam: John Benjamins B. V., 1979, pp. 599–609.

Denber, M. A. Sound spectrum analysis of the mentally ill. Unpublished Master's thesis, University of Rochester, 1978.

Detre, T. P., Jarecki, M. G. Affective disorders. In *Modern psychiatric treatment*. Philadelphia: J. B. Lippincott Company, 1971.

Eldred, S. H., Price, D. B. A linguistic evaluation of feeling states in psychotherapy. *Psychiatry*, 1958, *21*, 115–121.

Ford, H. Involuntional psychotic reaction. In A. M. Freedman and H. I. Kaplan (Eds.), *Comprehensive textbook of psychiatry*. Baltimore: Williams and Wilkins, 1967, Chap 17.3, 697–703.

Garrod, A. E. Inborn errors of metabolism, Croonian Lectures. *Lancet*, 1908, *2*, 1, 73, 142.

Goldfarb, W., Braunstein, P., Lorge, I. A study of speech patterns in a group of schizophrenic children. *American Journal of Orthopsychiatry*, 1956, *26*, 544–555.

Goldfarb, W., Goldfarb, N., Braunstein, P., et al. Speech and language faults of schizophrenic children. *Journal of Autism and Childhood Schizophrenia*, 1972, *2*, 219–233.

Hargreaves, W. A., Starkweather, J. A. Voice quality changes in depression. *Language and Speech*, 1964, *7*, 84–88.

Hargreaves, W. A., Starkweather, J. A., Blacker, K. H. Voice quality in depression. *Journal of Abnormal Psychology*, 1965, *70*, 218–220.

Harlan, C. D. Incidence and relationship of voice disorders within divergent psychotic populations. Unpublished Ph.D. dissertation, University of Utah, 1976.

Hirsch, K. Differential diagnosis between aphasic and schizophrenic language in children. *Journal of Speech and Hearing Disorders*, 1967, *32*, 3–10.

Hollien, H., Darby, J. K. Acoustic comparisons of psychotic and non-psychotic voices. In H. and P. Hollien (Eds.), *Current issues in the phonetic sciences*, Vol. 9. Amsterdam: John Benjamins B. V., 1979, pp. 609–615.

Hollister, L. E. Antipsychotic medications and the treatment of schizophrenia. In J. D. Barchas, P. A. Berger, R. D. Ciaranello, et al. (Eds.), *Psychopharmacology from theory to practice*. New York: Oxford University Press, 1977.

Hudgens, R. W., Morrison, J. R., Barcha, R. G. Life events and onset of primary affective disorders: Study of 40 hospitalized patients and 40 controls. *Archives of General Psychiatry*, 1967, *16*, 134–145.

Jung, C. G. *The psychogenesis of mental disease. In H. Read, M. Fordham, G. Adler, et al. (Eds.), The collected works of C. G. Jung*, Vol. 3. Princeton: Princeton University Press, 1960.

Kallman, F. J. The genetics of psychosis. *American Journal of Human Genetics*, 1950, *2*, 385.

Kety, S. S. Biochemical theories of schizophrenia. *International Journal of Psychiatry*, 1965, *1*, 409.

Kety, S. S. Disorders of the human brain. *Scientific American*, 1979, 241, *3*, 202–219.

Klerman, G. L. Affective disorders. In A. M. Nicholi (Ed.), *Harvard guide to modern psychiatry*. Cambridge, Mass: Belknap Press of Harvard University Press, 1978, 253–283.

Kraepelin, E. *Psychiatrie, ein Lehrbuch für studierende und Artzte* (Ed.5). Leipzig: Barth, 1986.

Kraepelin, E. *Lectures in clinical psychiatry*. London: Bailliere, Tindall and Cox, 1913.

Kraepelin, E. *Dementia praecox and paraphrenia*. Edinburgh: Livingston, 1919.

Kraepelin, E. *Manic-depressive insanity and paranoia*. In G.M. Robertson (Ed.), Edinburgh: Livingston, 1921.

Langfeldt, G. *The schizophreniform states*. Copenhagen: Murkgaard, 1939.

Lauffer, M. W., Gair, D. S. Childhood schizophrenia. In L. Bellak and L. Loeb (Eds.), *The schizophrenic syndrome*. New York: Grune & Stratton, 1969, Chap 11, 378–461.

Linn, L. Clinical manifestations of psychiatric disorders. In A. M. Freedman and H. I. Kaplan (Eds.), *Comprehensive textbook of psychiatry*. Baltimore: Williams and Wilkins, 1967, Chap 13.1, 546–577.

Meehl, P. E. Schizotaxia, schizotypy, schizophrenia. *American Psychology*, 1962, *17*, 827–838.

Menolascino, F. J. Infantile autism: Descriptive and diagnostic relationships to mental retardation. In F. J. Menolascino (Ed.), *Psychiatric approaches to mental retardation*. New York: Basic Books, 1970, Chap 5, 115–140.

Moses, P. J. *The voice of neurosis*. New York: Grune & Stratton, 1954.

Moskowitz, E. Voice quality in the schizophrenic reaction type. Doctoral thesis, New York University, 1951. Abstracted by D. Mulgrave in *Speech Monographs*, 1952, *19*, 118–119.

Newman, S. S., Mather, V. G. Analysis of spoken language of patients with affective disorders. *American Journal of Psychiatry*, 1938, *94*, 912–942.

Osmond, H., Smythies, J. Schizophrenia: A new approach. *J Ment Sci* 1952, *98*, 309–315.

Ostwald, P. F. Acoustic manifestations of emotional disturbance. In *Disorders of Communication*, 1964, *42*. Research Publications, A.R.M.N.D.

Ostwald, P. F. *Soundmaking: The acoustic communication of emotion*. Springfield, Illinois: Charles C. Thomas, 1963.

Ostwald, P. F. The sounds of emotional disturbance. *Archives of General Psychiatry,* 1961, *5,* 587–592.

Ostwald, P. F., Skolnikoff, A. Speech disturbances in a schizophrenic adolescent. *Postgraduate Medicine,* 1966, 40–49.

Pauling, L. Orthomolecular psychiatry. *Science.* 1968, *160,* 265–271.

Pittinger, R. E. Linguistic analysis of tone of voice in communication of affect. *Psychiat. Res. Rep.,* 1958, *8,* 41–54.

Pollin, W. The pathogenesis of schizophrenia. *Archives of General Psychiatry,* 1972, *27,* 29–37.

Rice, D. G., Abroms, G. M., Saxman, J. H. Speech and physiological correlates of "flat" affect. *Archives of General Psychiatry,* 1969, *20,* 566–572.

Robins, E., Guze, S. 1972 classification of affective disorders. In T. A. Williams, M. M. Katz, and J. A. Shield (Eds.), *Recent advances in the psychobiology of the depressive illnesses.* Washington, D.C.: Government Printing Office, 1972.

Rosenthal, D. Sex distribution and the severity of illness among samples of schizophrenic twins. *Journal of Psychiatric Research,* 1961, *1,* 26.

Rosenthal, D. (Ed.). *The Genain quadruplets.* New York: Basic Books, 1963.

Rutter, M. Concepts of autism: A review of research. *Journal Child Psychology and Psychiatry,* 1968, *9,* 1–25.

Rutter, M. Psychotic disorders in early childhood. In A. J. Coppen and A. Walk (Eds.), *Recent developments in schizophrenia: A symposium.* London: R. M. P. A., 1967.

Saxman, J. M., Burk, K. W. Speaking fundamental frequency and rate characteristics of adult female schizophrenics. *Journal of Speech and Hearing Research,* 1968, *11,* 194–203.

Scherer, K. R. Nonlinguistic vocal indicators of emotion and psychopathology. In C.E. Izard (Ed.), *Emotions in personality and psychopathology.* New York: Plenum Press, 1979. pp 493–529.

Schopler, E., Reichler, R. J. Psychobiological referents for the treatment of autism. In D. W. Churchill, G. A. Alpern, and M. K. DeMyer (Eds.), *Infantile autism.* Springfield, Ill: Charles C. Thomas, 1971, Chap 15, 243–264.

Spoerri, T. H. Speaking voice of the schizophrenic patient. *Archives of General Psychiatry,* 1966, *14,* 581–585.

Walter, W. H., Aldridge, V. J., Cooper, R. et al. Neurophysiological correlates of apparent defects of sensorimotor integration in autistic children. In D. W. Churchill, G. A. Alpern, and M. K. DeMyer, (Eds.), *Infantile autism.* Springfield, Ill: Charles C. Thomas, 1971, Chap 16, 265–276.

Wender, P. H. On necessary and sufficient conditions in psychiatric explanation. *Archives of General Psychiatry,* 1967, *16,* 41–47.

Whitman, E. N., Flicker, D. J. A potential new measurement of emotional state: A preliminary report. *Newark Beth-Israel Hospital,* 1966, *17,* 167–172.

Christiane A. M. Baltaxe
James Q. Simmons, III

# 14

# Disorders of Language in Childhood Psychosis: Current Concepts and Approaches

Childhood psychosis is a broad diagnostic label for a group of profound behavioral disorders of early childhood. This group of disorders was first systematically examined from a general perspective (Bender 1942) and then from the more narrow perspective of one subgroup (Kanner 1943). Although relatively low in prevalence, childhood psychosis has been the subject of an unusually large number of scientific and clinical studies (Tilton, DeMeyer, and Loew, 1966). The unique estrangement of these children from their parents and other human beings has probably been the driving force behind this extraordinary curiosity. It may also be significant, however, that various subcategories within this group were thought to be reflective of psychopathology occurring at various stages along the continuum of social development. Unfortunately, one serious flaw that has reduced the usefulness of the literature has been the lack of clearly defined criteria for inclusion and exclusion that would permit comparison among studies (Lockyer and Rutter, 1967). Despite this limitation there is considerable information to be gleaned from the literature.

Early in the study of childhood psychosis most of the emphasis was focused on trying to understand the impairment of interpersonal parent/child relationships from a psychodynamic perspective (Des-Lauriers, 1962; Call, 1963; Bettelheim, 1967). The subcategories of ear-

This research was supported in part by Maternal and Child Health Grant MCT-927-09, Developmental Disabilities Grant 59-P-45192-9-07, USPHS MH 30897-2, and IROINS 16479-01

ly infantile autism (Kanner, 1944), symbiotic psychosis (Mahler, 1952), atypical ego development (Rank, 1949), borderline psychosis (Geleerd, 1958), and childhood schizophrenia (Bender, 1947) were thought to represent differing degrees of disturbance along a continuum of social, psychological, and biological development. A number of these studies were heavily influenced by psychoanalytic thinking, and thus certain behavioral and family characteristics were emphasized without, at times, focusing on the cardinal characteristics that were common to all. In addition, many of these characteristics were seen in the context of disturbed interpersonal relationships. That deficits of language and cognition may have precluded normal interpersonal relationships was not seriously investigated.

    More recently, many authors have begun to delineate a group of characteristics which, with minor variations, cut across all of the diagnostic categories described above and define the disorder (Creak, 1961; Ornitz and Ritvo, 1968; Simmons and Tymchuk, 1973; Freeman and Ritvo, 1977). Six cardinal characteristics of the disorder, described by Simmons and Tymchuk (1973) contain the fundamental elements of all of them. These include:

1.  Impairment of interpersonal relationships characterized by aloofness, decreased physical contact, and lack of eye contact
2.  Deficits in social behavior seen in severe limitations in cooperative play, toy play, and self-care skills
3.  Stereotyped activities including self-stimulatory behavior, various kinds of repetitions, and preoccupations with sameness
4.  Impairment of intellect manifested by concreteness of thought, school performance deficits, and difficulties with judgment and abstract thinking
5.  Disturbances of speech and language seen in various forms, such as mutism, echolalic speech, delayed development, and a variety of other idiosyncrasies in word usage, speech modulation and content
6.  Onset prior to the age of 30 months

    Despite the similarity in observable characteristics across subgroups, it must be remembered that these disorders are behaviorally defined but may be etiologically different. It has already been shown that conditions originally diagnosed as variants of childhood psychosis have been sequestered, once a clear cut etiology has been demonstrated. This has been especially true in the case of phenylketonuria (Knobloch and Pasamanick, 1975), but has also been reported where postmortem examination of children who had been diagnosed as having the behavioral picture of childhood psychosis were revealed to have been suffering from known neurological disorders, such as tuberose sclerosis, cerebral lipidosis, and other neuropathologies (Rutter and Lockyer, 1967; Darby, 1976).

Within recent years studies of childhood psychosis have tended to support an organic etiology for this group of disorders (Tanguay, 1972; Damasio and Maurer, 1978). As this trend has prevailed, there has been a parallel tendency to examine various characteristics of the disorder in terms of the neurophysiological subsystems thought to underlie these characteristics. Examples include studies of the vestibular system (Ornitz, 1970), the neurotransmitter systems (Yuwiler, Geller, and Ritvo, 1976), perception and cognitive functions (Hermelin and O'Connor, 1970; Tymchuk, Simmons, and Neafsey, 1977), and speech and language (Dawson, 1979; Baltaxe, 1979b).

The purpose of this paper is to examine the contributions from the area of speech and language in order to understand this group of disorders and to relate them to other characteristics of the disorder.

## APPROACHES TO THE STUDY OF SPEECH AND LANGUAGE DISTURBANCES IN CHILDHOOD PSYCHOSIS

Since the initial description of the disorder, language related studies have constituted a major area of investigation. This may be due to a particular interest in the specific peculiarities of the linguistic constellation of deficits as well as the importance of such deficits in diagnosis and prognosis.

Speech and language characteristics in childhood psychosis have been studied by a number of disciplines from several directions. Based on differences in underlying interest and focus, these studies can be grouped into the following broad categories with some overlap between groups:

1. Studies of the general characteristics of speech and language and their significance in differential diagnosis and prognosis
2. Studies of more specific aspects of speech and language, such as those which have focused on phonology, syntax, semantics, prosody, pragmatics, echolalia, pronoun use, and other aspects of language
3. Studies of language intervention techniques
4. Studies of language in autism in relation to other linguistic, cognitive, or social functions and abilities or disabilities.

In all of the above types of studies, depending on the discipline involved, a wide variety of approaches has been used. These have included longitudinal, cross-sectional, single subject and multisubject, descriptive and experimental studies, and observational reports. Contrast groups have included normal, mentally retarded, brain damaged, and language disordered subjects. In the language disordered group the most commonly used subjects have been those with developmental aphasia. Because of the heterogeneous origins of the autistic disorder and the previously mentioned problems with diagnostic labels, however, problems in controls have been numerous. The most serious may be that many of the autistic subjects may not have been adequately differentiated from the control group and may have common underlying characteristics.

The following discussion will cover each of these general types of studies with a slightly different focus.

### Studies Concerning the General Description of Speech and Language and their Significance to the Autistic Disorder

Early approaches to the study of language in childhood psychosis were dominated by clinicians viewing the problem from a general syndrome point of view. Thus, the language deficit was seen as one of the many abnormalities thought to be a function of the basic disorder. The current general trend in language research, however, is characterized by a search for explanations of language in a broader context. Thus, recent studies of linguistic deficits in autism appear to investigate language not as an isolated phenomenon, but in relation to other aspects of behavior, cognitive function, and brain function. Also the more recent directions in clinical studies concern themselves with the interrelationship between different types of language disturbances in the autistic person; a greater effort to establish differences between the autistic language deficits and those of other disorders; the reinterpretation of specific linguistic deficits in terms of alternate strategies in language acquisition and in the communicative process; the extension of language intervention to include nonvocal systems of communication; and, finally, the relationship of language deficits to recent findings in neurophysiological studies involving autistic children.

GENERAL CHARACTERISTICS OF SPEECH
AND LANGUAGE

Kanner's (1943) original description of speech and language in the autistic disorder was clear, concise, and remains today a valid description of most of the abnormalities seen. Thus, we will restate Kanner's original description and then examine the various characteristics on the basis of subsequent studies. These characteristics included echolalia, literalness, bizarre content and structure, and abnormalities in rhythm, volume, and pitch.

Echolalia, or the tendency to repeat rather than construct original remarks, was the characteristic that drew most attention. This repetition generally occurred in close association with a verbal stimulus, but often was removed from it in time. Kanner designated these immediate and delayed echolalia. Mitigated echolalia was a term used when the autistic child made modifications in the utterance repeated. Pronoun reversal in echolalic verbal productions was another unique feature that led to considerable speculation concerning ego development and the ability of the autistic individual to separate the self from others (Griffith and Ritvo, 1967).

The second characteristic was the extreme literalness with which verbal autistic children interpreted language. They seemed unable to use language to fit new situations and had difficulty in understanding utterances except in their originally acquired situational sense. Extreme literalness has been found to be a persistent deficit extending into adolescence and young adulthood (Rutter, Greenfeld, and Lockyer, 1967; Ornitz and Ritvo, 1976), and has subsequently been verified in experimental approaches using standard intellectual testing (Tymchuk et al., 1977). Scheerer, Rothman, and Goldstein (1945) interpreted this extreme literalness or concreteness on the part of the autistic as an impairment in abstract thinking. Extreme literalness was studied from a somewhat different perspective in the context of language use by Baltaxe (1977).

Bizarre, irrelevant, metaphorical language was another of the original characteristics that has subsequently been explored and somewhat clarified in terms of the possible linguistic processes and structures involved.

A final characteristic related to disturbances of speech output is the quality of speech of autistic children, which was described as wooden and monotonous, with distortions of volume, stress, rhythm, and pitch. Such disturbances in prosody or the melody of speech first received detailed attention by Goldfarb, Braunstein, and Lorge (1956). Prosodic disturbances and their possible significance to other linguistic deficits will be discussed in detail later.

The studies that concern themselves with language as a general phenomenon are mostly psychiatric or medical. Such studies generally focus on the diagnostic and prognostic significance of linguistic disturbances in childhood psychosis. In these studies, language is frequently described as showing the most severe and noticeable deficit in the autistic child. The specific constellation of language deficits is of value in terms of differential diagnosis. In addition, age of onset of speech, type, and persistence of language impairment are of considerable significance in terms of prognosis. Studies that consider the language deficit central to the psychotic disorder, and possibly as its primary defect, also belong to this group of studies (Rutter, 1968; Rutter, Bartak, and Newman, 1971; Ricks and Wing, 1975). In this context, Ricks and Wing (1975) note that impairments in speech and language also have major importance in practice, since they are primary determining factors in the education and management planning in the autistic child.

Support for the claim that language defects may be more central to the disorder is provided by follow-up studies. Such studies have shown that despite improvement in other areas of dysfunction, peculiarities of speech and language persist into adolescence and adulthood (Kanner and Eisenberg, 1955; Eisenberg, 1956; Creak, 1963; Brown and Reiser, 1964; Rutter, Greenfeld, and Lockyer, 1967; Rutter, 1966; Kanner, 1971). Simmons and Baltaxe (1975) and Baltaxe (1977) have shown that major deficits tend to persist in the area of semantics, prosody, and the use of language.

Among the studies dealing with the more general characteristics of speech and language are those with a focus on the heterogeneity of the disorder. Attempts to find linguistic subcategorizations have included those based on the organic versus nonorganic etiology (Goldfarb et al., 1956) and the distinction between autistics with and without mental retardation (Bartak and Rutter, 1976). The heterogeneity of the autistic condition in terms of specific underlying neurological or neurophysiological deficits was considered by Simon (1975), Darby (1976), and Damasio and Maurer (1978).

## LANGUAGE IN THE CONTEXT OF DIAGNOSIS
## AND PROGNOSIS

As noted, speech and language deficits are quite significant in both diagnosis and prognosis. Only about 50 percent of all children with the disorder acquire functional speech (Rutter, 1966). Language development in autism has been associated with several distinct early developmental patterns which are of diagnostic and prognostic importance. These are (1) mutism or a lack of acquisition of speech, which is observed in approximately 50 percent of all autistic children; (2) early normal onset of language followed by a subsequent loss and a possible gradual reacquisition, sometimes after years of silence (Wing, 1966; Rutter and Lockyer, 1967); and (3) delayed development with a wide range of linguistic disturbances, all of which appear to be reducible to a common core of the above stated peculiarities. Language histories are thus of considerable diagnostic significance. Kanner and

Eisenberg (1956) have described the vicissitudes of language development as the most striking and challenging of the presenting phenomena.

The most interesting, and at the same time most perplexing, language histories are those in which an early normal onset and subsequent loss is reported. This group of children present an interesting parallel, but at an earlier age, to the syndrome of acquired aphasia of childhood that is associated with a convulsive disorder and a bilaterally abnormal EEG (Landau and Kleffner, 1957; Gascon, Lambroso, and Goodglass, 1973; Shoumaker et al., 1971; Baltaxe, 1976; Cooper and Ferry, 1978). An early onset with subsequent loss of both language comprehension and production, as well as a history of slow reacquisition, is reported in these cases (van Harskamp, van Donger, and Loonen, 1978); however, in none of these cases is language loss reported prior to three years of age. In contrast, loss of speech after an early normal onset and after the first steps of language acquisition is reported between the ages of 18 months and approximately 30 months in the autistic group. Thus, the autistic group appears to complement the aphasic group in terms of age of loss after an early normal onset.*

Interestingly, EEG abnormalities, frequently bilateral, have also been reported to accompany a diagnosis of autism. Rutter (1966) also reported that in approximately 25 percent of the cases, seizures developed in adolescence. These previously mentioned instances of the acquired aphasia syndrome have also included cases with subclinical seizure symptomatology, a possible plausible explanation for brain dysfunction in autistics who develop overt seizures later in life. Thus research relating to the variables of language development, EEG abnormalities, and seizure development, would appear fruitful.

To date, there has only been one study that has investigated age and type of onset as possible variables in early infantile autism. Harper (1975) completed a retrospective study of 131 autistic children in which he divided the children into 2 groups, defined on the basis of age and type of onset: those whose autism was natal and those whose autism was acquired. Prenatal and perinatal variables were found to be significantly related to age of onset at birth in the natal group, while the significant variables in the acquired group were those events occurring in early childhood between the years of one and three. Based on follow-up data in intellectual functioning and language development, a better prognosis was found for the acquired group with early normal onset of speech and subsequent loss.

---

*It should be noted here that loss of language prior to the age of three years has been reported for other *types* of acquired aphasia (Basser, 1962; Lenneberg, 1967; and others).

Development of some communicative language has been considered of good prognosis value by many investigators (Eisenberg, 1956; Creak, 1961; Ornitz and Ritvo, 1968; Rutter, 1974). In addition to age of onset of language development, level and type of communicative function have received attention and validation in terms of prognosis. For example, Rutter, Greenfeld, and Lockyer (1967) found that the symptoms of isolation and withdrawal had no significant association with outcome, but that the presence or absence of language development was significant. Rutter (1974) considered the ability to use speech communicatively as the best predictor of outcome in autistic children. Creak (1961) considered the prognosis as guarded for children with a prolonged failure to develop speech. Worst (1977), who found a high correlation between development of speech, improved intelligence, and social interest, also considered at least minimal speech development necessary for a better prognosis. An improvement in the overall autistic condition was noted by Ward and Hoddinott (1968) in an 18 month follow-up study, which correlated highly with improvement in verbal abilities, especially spontaneity.

Prognostically, the failure to develop speech by the age of five has been associated with poor outcome (Kanner and Eisenberg, 1955; Eisenberg, 1956; Creak, 1961). Rutter, Bartak, and Newman (1971) noted that prognosis was particularly poor when poor language development was coupled with low IQ. Interestingly, recent neurolinguistic studies have posited a critical age for language acquisition. Such studies have pointed to the age of five as the outer limit for language lateralization in the dominant hemisphere (Krashen, 1973), although earlier estimations extended the period to the age of puberty (Lenneberg, 1967). Language acquisition presumably becomes more difficult after the age of five, may not be as easily lateralized, and the effects of brain lesions on linguistic performance take on more specific characteristics (Basser, 1962; Lenneberg, 1967; Krashen, 1973). It would therefore also be reasonable to consider prognostic factors relating to lack or time of onset of speech in the light of the critical age hypothesis for language acquisition in the autistic condition.

SPEECH AND LANGUAGE CHARACTERISTICS
IN AUTISM IN RELATION TO OTHER DIAGNOSTIC
CATEGORIES

The relationship of speech and language abnormalities in autism to those of other diagnostic categories is complex, controversial, and remains without resolution. As noted earlier, autism is a behavioral syndrome probably with multiple etiologies. Studies whose objective it is to identify the 'distinctive features' of autistic language may suffer from several major difficulties. For example, the autistic disorder is not always clearly delineated, which may make comparison of results across studies difficult. Also, the autistic group may unwittingly include those with underlying etiologies, which are the same as those of the control group. Results may thus be confounded for several reasons.

Diagnostic categories that serve as control groups in experimental studies and that also appear in the differential diagnosis include mentally retarded, brain-damaged, and language-impaired subjects. The choice of mentally retarded subjects as a control group is fraught with difficulties, because of the presence of mental retardation in many autistic children. An estimated 75 percent of all autistic children are also mentally retarded (Rutter, 1974; Freeman and Ritvo, 1977). In this context, Bartak and Rutter (1976) make a distinction between language and other cognitive abilities for autistics with an IQ above or below 70. Presence or absence of mental retardation thus needs to be considered when planning experimental studies. In many instances, underlying brain damage can also be demonstrated and can therefore confound the results in the case of a control group with brain damage (Goldfarb, Braunstein, and Lorge, 1956; Darby, 1976; Damasio and Maurer, 1978). A diagnosis of autism or developmental aphasia in some cases may also depend on the specific discipline of the experimenter or practitioner or on the facility to which referral was made.

Another area of difficulty in terms of other diagnostic categories relates to the individual parameters of language under investigation. Results may be different or the same as those of control groups, depending on the parameter of language measured. Even though recent studies seem to indicate that autistic children have their own specific constellation of linguistic deficits, this is not a universally accepted position.

Rutter (1968; Rutter et al., 1971) has likened the language abnormalities in autism to those found in disorders of language, such as developmental receptive aphasia. Despite the noted similarities, however, the autistic deficits were distinguished from those of the developmental disorders of language by several features. These included echolalia, pronoun reversal, a good short term memory, and the lack of gestures for communicative purposes. All of these were found to be less characteristic of developmental receptive aphasia. More recently, however, Bartak, Rutter, and Cox (1977) in a psychometric, observational, and interview study of infantile autism and developmental receptive disorders of language, appeared to find little overlap between clinically defined autistic and dysphasic children. They noted that the discrimination between these diagnostic entities could be made as clearly on language and cognitive characteristics as on social and behavioral ones. Interestingly, language characteristics and behavioral characteristics interrelated within the autistic subgroup. Their final conclusion was that autism and dysphasia differed in important ways and that a cognitive deficit was an additional important aspect of the syndrome of autism.

Churchill (1972) compared nonpsychotic brain damaged and psychotic children and offered a "degree of impairment" hypothesis. He maintained that the language impairment in autism was closely related to, but more severe than, that found in various aphasic or central language disturbances.

In contrast, Simon (1975) considered the linguistic impairment in childhood autism the reverse of that in the aphasic disorder, based on intactness of discrimination of phonemic features and impairment of intonational features. She maintained that aphasic children show impairment in phonemic discrimination but intactness of intonational features, while the reverse was true for the autistics.

In a comparison of the psycholinguistic profile of matched normals, subnormals, and psychotics, Tubbs (1966) used the Illinois Test of Psycholinguistic Abilities to show differences in the linguistic profiles of these groups. She showed that, except for digit span, psychotics scored lower than either subnormals or normals. The overall profile of linguistic abilities was also different and included poor understanding, difficulties in transfer from one sensory modality to the other, and poor digit span. In contrast, poor auditory memory but good gestural ability is commonly noted for the developmental disorders of language. Using standard intelligence tests, DeMeyer (1975) compared high functioning autistics and subnormal subjects and found that autistics were similar to subnormal children on verbal subtests, but that subnormal children were superior to autistics in some performance areas.

Hesse and Wallstein (1976) compared psychotic, language handicapped, and linguistically normal children for natural preferences of intelligible and distorted speech and found the psychotic group to be qualitatively different from the two nonpsychotic control groups. The psychotic group showed an overall preference for unnatural distorted speech, while the two nonpsychotic groups did not. The authors concluded that the acoustic novelty of the stimuli, rather than linguistic intelligibility, may have motivated the psychotic group. They further hypothesized that speech and language may have a distinctly different functional significance for the psychotics than for the comparison group. More recently, Morton-Evans and Hensley (1978) compared autistic, (receptive) developmental aphasic, mentally retarded, and normal subjects on a paired associate learning task. They found that autistics and aphasics were similar in that they were unable to associate sounds with their visual counterparts at the same rate as normal children. The aphasics overcame their difficulty at a faster rate than did the autistics, however.

Experimental studies, such as the above, demonstrate that the issues involved in differential diagnosis from a language perspective are complex and include such variables as the parameters of language compared and the choice of acceptable control groups. Although, generally speaking, most of the above studies find differences between individual groups supporting the distinctive linguistic behavior of autistic children, the presence of such deficits is not sufficient to make a differential diagnosis.

## Studies That Focus on Specific Aspects of Language and Its Use

By far the largest group of studies concern themselves with specific aspects of language and its use. A general observation is that such studies have developed from an earlier, more general focus, such as the number or variety of words in an utterance (McCarthy, 1954), to more specifically linguistic studies, in which individual aspects of the grammatical development in the autistic child are examined. They include studies related to the development of the phonological, syntactic, and semantic systems. More recent studies have also viewed specific speech and language deficits, such as prosodic deficits and echolalia, in the light of new theories, including possible alternate strategies of the autistic for the acquisition of better communicative skills.

SOUND OR PHONOLOGICAL DEVELOPMENT

In those children who develop speech, the development of the sound system appears to be the least disturbed, although some difficulties have been reported and some controversy exists. In a study of babbling, a precursor of phonological and grammatical development, Ricks (1972) found diminished babbling in autistics when compared to normals. Ostwald (1963) claimed that autistics lacked the capacity to adhere to linguistic constraints of sound making. Shervanian (1959) found normal, but greatly delayed development in the sound system, with considerable individual differences in the acquisition of specific sounds. Deficiencies were reported for stops, fricatives, and semi-vowels, while vowels and nasals appeared to follow normal development.

Nasals are among the first sounds acquired in normal children. In contrast, vowels appear to be aspects of later stages of development in terms of differential features of vocalic length and quality (Jakobson, 1968; Ervin-Tripp, 1966; Stampe, 1969; Ingram, 1976).

Of the sounds mentioned by Shervanian to be deficient, fricatives, such as f, v, θ, d, and the sibilants s, š, z, and ž, require complicated fine motor control and coordination of the various aspects of the vocal mechanism.

Hermelin (1971) also supported Shervanian's earlier findings, but made a further important observation. She noted an apparent discrepancy between phonological development and the development of other grammatical systems, with phonological development advanced over other levels of grammar. In normal acquisition, the outer limit for the development of the sound system is approximately 7 years, a time when other levels of language, such as syntax and morphology, are deemed to have reached adultlike levels (Brown, 1973). An inverse relation may thus be true for the autistics.

In contrast to the above study, Bartolucci, Pierce, Steiner, et al. (1976) examined the phonological development in verbal autistics and compared it to that of mentally retarded controls. Despite a general finding of delay in phonological development in both subject groups, these authors noted atypical development in their autistic subjects. Autistics as well as retardates were found to be delayed in phoneme acquisition. The autistics, however, differed significantly from the retarded group by the type of phoneme substitutions. These investigators corroborated the findings of their phonological study in a series of experiments, which demonstrated that the autistics were deficient in extracting the components of structured auditory input when compared to their controls. A high correlation between frequency of phonological errors and overall level of language development was also established.

In apparent contrast, Boucher (1976), using standardized articulation tests, found that the autistics' articulation was significantly superior to that of a subnormal and developmentally aphasic, language matched, control group.

Our own clinical observations support good phonological development, when compared to other levels of linguistic function. These observations are general and do not necessarily hold for individual cases, however. Better development on the phonological level can be tentatively linked to the good auditory memory skills seen in autistics (Tubbs, 1966; Frith, 1969; Hermelin and O'Connor, 1967; O'Connor and Frith, 1973).

## SYNTACTIC AND SEMANTIC STUDIES

Syntax and semantics appear to have received even less systematic attention than studies of phonology. One plausible explanation for such a lack may be the inherent difficulty in differentiating between more spontaneous, propositional speech and echolalia.

Autistics appear to have less difficulty in acquiring individual nouns than they do in acquiring more complex syntactic structures (Baltaxe and Simmons, 1975), probably because nouns only require an ability to label and relate sound to symbol. On the other hand, the production of syntactic structures consisting of more than one word requires the recognition of linguistic functional relations within an utterance, which is a more difficult task. Baltaxe and Simmons (1975) suggest that autistics may be deficient in this latter capacity because of corresponding underlying cognitive deficits in recognizing functional relationships in the real world (Piaget and Inhelder, 1969).

Bartolucci and Albers (1974) investigated aspects of morphology in autistic children and found significant differences in the use of past tense markers by autistic children when they were compared to mentally retarded and normal children. Such a finding is also supported by Baltaxe (1979d). In examining the application of various measures of psycholinguistic age to normal, aphasic, and autistic children, a lack of expected correlation was found between the measures of mean length of utterance and the grammatical morpheme index in the case of the autistic subjects. Both are recognized measures of psycholinguistic age in normals and are highly correlative with each other (Brown, 1973; deVilliers and deVilliers, 1973). The past tense morpheme studied by the above investigators is one of the fourteen morphemes in the grammatical morpheme index.

Pierce and Bartolucci (1977) subsequently systematically investigated the syntax of verbal autistics who were matched for linguistic age with a group of mentally retarded and normal subjects. They used a developmental sentence scoring technique (Lee, 1974) and a Chomsky-based transformational analysis. Based on the developmental scoring technique, the autistic group ranked significantly lower than either of the two control groups. The autistics also showed a higher error rate and a lower level of complexity in a transformational analysis of their utterances. Of particular significance in this study, however, was their finding that the grammatical system of the autistics was not only rule governed, but that the syntactic abnormalities in autism were due to extreme language delay as well as to an impairment in using linguistic rules. Inconsistent rule application was also found in an earlier study of the language patterns of adolescent autistics by Simmons and Baltaxe (1975). Following a transformational model of linguistic analysis, Dalgleish (1975) had noted earlier that autistics failed to analyze their sentences for deep structures. In an attempt to explain such deficits, this author noted that the autistics may be impaired in coordinating visual and aural stimulation, which would inhibit the necessary underlying lexical development.

Deficits in the development of semantics and in associated concept formation and concept usage appear closely related to the autistics' cognitive level. Linguistically, they are inherent in the autistics' reported "extreme literalness," "metaphoric language," and deficits in language use in context. Concept formation and semantic aspects of language are the most difficult to study, even in normal development. Again, this may explain a relative absence of such studies for autistic populations. Apart from such general observations that the autistics' language is concrete and lacks in abstraction (Scheerer, Rothman, and Goldstein, 1945), there have been few studies that address semantic development in more specific terms.

One such study, Ricks and Wing (1975), compares the extent to which autistics and normals could use spoken and unspoken language and develop an inner language. This was previously suggested by the literature on normal development (Luria, 1959; Vygotsky, 1962). Their conclusion was that the central problem in autism was an impairment in complex symbolic function, affecting all forms of communication including the development of inner language.

Walker and Bortner (1975) examined concept usage in young autistic children with normal and brain damaged comparison groups. They used an object matching task based on class, function, and stimulus similarity. These authors found significant improvement in task performance with increased age in utilizing class or function concepts for all groups. But unlike the control groups, their autistic group did not consistently benefit from a reduction in stimulus competition. Furthermore, a dichotomy in concept usage was found based on IQ. In the autistic population, surprisingly, the high IQ group produced more bizarre and irrelevant responses than the lower IQ group.

A more specific semantic investigation was carried out by Shapiro and Kapit (1978) who examined the semantic concept of negation in a group of young autistics, based on a production/imitation/comprehension paradigm. They used the categories of nonexistence, denial, and rejection. Their study indicated poor production, superior imitation, and some skills in comprehension of the concepts associated with these categories in their experimental group. Their conclusion was that the autistics appeared to make greater use of imitation as a major strategy in linguistic coding of the semantic concept of negation.

The results of these numerous studies in phonology and grammar appear to indicate that autistics are not only delayed, but also deviant in specific ways.

## PROSODIC DEFICITS IN AUTISM

Among the linguistic deficits in autism, prosody has remained the least studied. Those studies available are generally observational with few involving systematic investigation. Prosody consists of the acoustic parameters of pitch, intensity, and duration, and their covariations. Phonologically these features assist the listener in the segmentation of the speech stream by contouring words. Lexically they differentiate between syntactic categories, such as noun and verb, by differences in stress. Syntactically these parameters make up sentence intonation and differentiate various sentence types. In addition, connotative and denotative meaning and the emotional aspects of a linguistic interchange are often solely expressed by differences in prosody (Lieberman and Michaels, 1962; Abercrombie, 1968). In normal language acquisition, prosodic features are presumed to fulfill an organizational function. They appear to be acquired as a first step in the acquisition process and prior to other units for which they provide guiding principles (Crystal, 1969; Pike, 1972; Lieberman, 1968; Kaplan, 1970; Lenneberg, 1967; Macken, 1978).

Autistic speech has often been described as dull, wooden, improperly modulated, and having a singsong quality. Distortions in rhythm, loudness, and pitch, as well as overprecision in articulation, have been noted (Goldfarb, Braunstein, and Lorge, 1956; Pronovost, Wakstein, and Wakstein, 1966; Goldfarb, et al. 1972). Even those autistic children with high language function often have demonstrable difficulties in the use and interpretation of the fine nuances of language. Such difficulties have contributed to their language being characterized as "extremely literal" and "concrete." The autistics' failure to use and interpret prosodic features appropriately may be responsible, at least in part, for this "literalness," since fine nuances of meaning are most often signaled by prosodic features. A flat affect, which relates to mood and other emotional aspects of communication, has also been described in the speech of autistic individuals as sounding "atonal, arhythmic, and hollow" (Ornitz and Ritvo, 1976). Goldfarb, Braunstein, and Lorge (1972) observed that the description of the schizophrenic child's speech patterns, in terms of flatness, is based upon the listener's response to the schizophrenic's broad range of errors in stress, pitch, phrasing, intonation, inflection, meaning, and mood expression.* Deficits in prosody have also been reported in the speech of non-English speaking autistic children. For example, Sedlackova and Neshidalova (1975) found that Czech autistic children had abnormal prosody. Likewise, Baltaxe and Simmons (1977a), in a comparison of English and German speaking autistic adolescents, found that abnormal prosody was also characteristic of their German subjects.

Follow-up studies reporting the speech and language deficits of autistics in adolescence still refer to residual difficulties in prosody in the presence of much improved speech (Rutter, 1966; deMeyer, 1973; Rutter, Greenfield, and Lockyer, 1967; Kanner and Eisenberg, 1956; Kanner, 1971). The prosodic deficits described in these follow-up studies refer to a lack of lability or cadence and difficulties with inflection and intonation. Simmons and Baltaxe (1975) and Baltaxe and Simmons (1977a) also noted the persistent nature of such problems into adolescence, and Ornitz and Ritvo (1976) commented on their presence in adulthood.

The earliest studies which addressed prosodic abnormalities were those of Goldfarb and his coworkers (1956; 1972). The first study showed that schizophrenic children had a wide range of deviations in rhythm and intonation in terms of voice volume changes, excessively high pitch with narrow pitch range, and a lack of pitch fall in the final position of an utterance. They also showed atypical durational characteristics. In the 1972 study of a larger group of schizophrenic children, Goldfarb and his team, using a more refined technique of observations, showed that there was no specific clustering of linguistic deficits characteristic to this specific group. They did note, however, that schizophrenic children showed either too much or too little of a given prosodic feature with the "presence of antipodal phenomena fluctuating from one extreme to the other in many of the voice and speech elements" (Goldfarb et al., p. 219). More recently sound spectrography has been used to physically demonstrate the dissimilarity of the prosodic characteristics of autistic and normal children (Fletcher, 1976; Bagshaw, 1978).

In a study of seven autistic adolescents, Baltaxe (1975) found that autistics fell into two groups, which could be characterized by the presence or absence of deficits in the production of prosody, syntax, and semantics, and by differences in the perception of tone and rhythm on the Seashore Test of Musical Abilities. These authors

---

*Goldfarb and the Ittleson group of investigators use the term childhood schizophrenia roughly synonymous with autism. For a more detailed review of differences in terminology, see Baltaxe and Simmons (1975).

hypothesized that prosodic deficits and other linguistic abnormalities were interrelated. They also felt that deficits in prosody might play a fundamental role in the deficient acquisition of syntactic and semantic structures. A more recent study by Baltaxe (1979a) seems to support this general contention. Her findings also support those of Goldfarb, Braunstein, and Lorge (1956) in showing that autistics operated with a narrower frequency range than normals. The autistic subjects had a greater intensity range and showed a lack of the expected covariation of intensity and frequency in certain intonational contours, however. Here again, some subjects used intensity appropriately to signal rising intonation, although they lacked of covariation in frequency. Other subjects, however, used intensity inappropriately and showed increased intensity for each individual syllable, obliterating the sentence-specific prosodic effect and creating the impression of overprecision and deliberateness in articulation. The autistic group in that study also showed difficulties with durational characteristics. The author felt that autistics might "overselect" intensity to express prosodic information and, with respect to duration, may follow a different model of speech production than normals (Baltaxe, 1979a; 1979b).

Extrapolating from production deficits to perceptual deficits, it may also be plausible to explain some of the autistics' difficulties in language acquisition, based on difficulties in prosody. Echolalia, for example, may be the result of a difficulty in breaking down the flow of speech the way normals do aided by prosodic abilities. Unable to do so, the autistics may require differential strategies for better communicative language, using echolalic patterns as an intermediary stage.

Because of the considerable attention to autistic echolalia and its possible significance in terms of language acquisition, relevant studies in echolalia will be described in greater detail.

ECHOLALIA AND LANGUAGE ACQUISITION

The phenomenon of echolalia remains one of the most cited linguistic characteristics in autism and has been studied from a variety of perspectives. Echolalia may also hold the most promise for examining language acquisition strategies in autistic children.

An estimated 75 percent of all autistic children who develop communicative speech have been reported to go through an echolalic phase (Rutter, 1974; Ricks and Wing, 1975). The question may well be whether echolalic is not a necessary stage of language development in autism. Prizant (1978) noted that echolalic autistic children represent approximately 40 percent of the entire autistic population. The phenomenon of pronoun reversal has also been considered, at least by some investigators, to be an artifact of echolalia (Fay, 1971; Baltaxe and Simmons, 1977b). The pronoun system is one aspect of deixis, the linguistic expression of placing objects and events in place and time. The autistics' reported difficulties with deixis (Silberg, 1978; Bartolucci and Albers, 1976; Bartak and Rutter, 1974) could similarly be interpreted as such artifacts.

Echolalia is not unique to autism. It is also reported in mental retardation (Ausman and Gaddy, 1974) developmental aphasia (de-Hirsch, 1967; Cohen, Caparulo, and Shaywitz, 1977), transcortical aphasia, epilepsy, senile dementia, and catatonic schizophrenia (Stengel, 1947), blindness (Fay, 1973), carbon monoxide poisoning (Geschwind, Quadfasal, and Segarra, 1968), and clouded levels of consciousness (Stengel, 1974). A recent comprehensive review of echolalia was provided by Schuler (1979). Several characteristics appear to set autistic echolalia apart from that appearing in other abnormal states, however. These include age of onset, rigidity of repetition, and peculiarities of both suprasegmental patterns and paralinguistic features (Fay, 1969; Simon, 1975; Prizant, 1978). Heightened rigidity of the autistics' imitations of a model has been observed by several investigators, giving the impression of mimicry (Shapiro, Roberts, and Fish, 1970; Ricks and Wing, 1975). Echolalia in autism has also been discussed in relation to imitation in normal children (Baltaxe and Simmons, 1975).

It has been demonstrated that in normal language acquisition some children use imitation as a developmental strategy (Brown, 1973). Normal imitation differs from that in the autistic child, however, in that the normal child's productive language system and level of linguistic competence appears to be reflected in the modifications in the child's imitations (Fraser, Bellugi, and Brown, 1963; Menyuk, 1969; Smith, 1970). This may only be the case in a special sense in the autistic child. Also, in the normal child, imitation is rarely reported past the age of three. In contrast, autistic echolalia has been observed in both preschool and school years (Rutter, 1974; Prizant, 1978). Shapiro and Lucy (1979) attempted to differentiate experimentally between normal and autistic imitation by the use of latency measures. Differences between the two groups related to shorter response latencies for autistic echolalia. These investigators concluded that autistic echolalia involved a process which was different from that used by normals, but also different from that used by the autistics' spontaneous verbalizations. Shapiro and Lucy proposed that the autistics might bypass the usual (black box) processing reflective of actual development in normals.

Recently, the communicative potential of echolalia has come

more sharply into focus. A review of the echolalia literature indicates two basic positions. The first is that echolalia is an abnormal behavior to be eradicated and replaced by more appropriate linguistic target behaviors. Thus, in terms of language intervention, the aim is to eliminate echolalia prior to language therapy (Risley and Wolf, 1967; Coleman and Stedman, 1974; Freeman, Ritvo, and Miller, 1975; Lovaas, 1977; Schreibman and Carr, 1978).

The second, more recently developed position is based on a closer study of the nature of autistic echolalia. Investigators sharing the second perspective postulate that echolalia may represent an important intermediary step in the acquisition of better communicative skills and as such should be incorporated into therapy programs.

While the earlier literature had defined echolalia as a meaningless repetition of words or utterances spoken by another, recent investigators have suggested that it may represent the child's attempt to maintain social interaction in the face of a severe communicative disorder (Fay, 1971). Schuler (1979) also maintained that most echolalia was not random, but needed to be interpreted as a response to communicative pressures in a dyadic interaction. She interpreted this as the child's ability to perceive that he was expected to respond. Kanner (1943) in his initial description of the disorder had focused on the affirmative function of autistic echolalia as "affirmation by repetition." Similarly, Shapiro (1977) also attributed the function of social facilitation to immediate echolalia. It is of interest to note that echolalia has been shown to decrease with an increase in more communicative, spontaneous speech (Prizant, 1978). Based on such observations, Philips and Dyer (1977) have gone as far as to propose that echolalia is a necessary stage in the development of language in the autistic child.

Based on a hypothesis of alternate language strategies in the autistic child, Baltaxe and Simmons (1977b) investigated the potential importance of mitigated echolalia in the autistics' acquisition process. In analyzing the bedtime monologues of an autistic child, they reached the conclusion that the autistic may use verbal play with echolalic patterns as a language learning strategy, similar to that reported for normal subjects (Weir, 1962). In addition, the mitigations which occurred in the echolalia in the course of such verbal play evidenced some linguistic abilities. The echolalic patterns, used by the autistic child tended to be partially broken down and then resynthesized with similar chunklike units originating from other echolalic patterns. Breaks in the echolalia were shown to occur at particular syntactic junctions, such as the junction between noun and verb phrase. Accordingly, there appeared evidence of some knowledge of basic linguistic structures. Baltaxe and Simmons thus have suggested that the autistics' major acquisition strategies may be the reverse of that of normal children and may be one of gradual breakdown of larger echolalic patterns into smaller, more useable chunks. For the normals, the strategy is one of a gradual building up of linguistic patterns from smaller to larger units. Although normals and autistics may use both of these strategies, the order of their importance may be reversed. Mitigated echolalia may thus also play a particular intermediary role and in that sense may be considered as reflective of the autistics' level of linguistic development.

The first systematic study of echolalia from a functional perspective was done by Prizant (1978), who used response latency measurements. He found autistic echolalia to serve several distinct functions which included nonfocused, turntaking, declarative, rehearsal, self-regulatory, yes-answer, and report functions. Prizant's findings were based on a multilevel structural analysis, which included attention to and analysis of such variables as natural contexts and nonverbal behaviors. Prizant's findings suggest that echolalia is used both communicatively and noncommunicatively, with comprehension as well as without comprehension. Interestingly, greater production of echolalia was also seen in dyadic in contrast to group situations. Moreover, an inverse relationship emerged between the various functions performed by echolalia and the development of spontaneous language skills. Prizant also found differences in the use of echolalia in the individual subject, suggesting possible individualized strategies of use consonant with the particular child's level of cognitive and social abilities.

DEFICITS OF LANGUAGE USE OR PRAGMATICS
IN AUTISTIC LANGUAGE

Prizant (1978) considered echolalia from a functional or pragmatic perspective. Pragmatics can be defined as the use of linguistic skills in face-to-face interaction. The acquisition of pragmatic competence can be understood as the interface between social, cognitive, and linguistic development. It is therefore reasonable to assume that impairment in any one of these areas could also be reflected in language use in context. Although linguistic disturbances in autism have been studied from many perspectives, few have addressed the area of actual language use and considered the possible interplay of other skills, abilities, and variables in that context. Linguistic deficits in autism in the area of pragmatics include the absence of spontaneity in the initiation of a conversation and an overall lack of skills in the interpersonal use of language. The extreme literalness and metaphoric use of language and the use of some linguistic routines also can be interpreted in many instances as an inability to translate or modify language use from one communicative context to the other. Other pragmatic components already discussed are evident in the use of echolalia; difficulties with deixis; the inability to interpret the fine nuances of language; difficulties in the linguistic expression of emotions; and difficulties in the use of prosody.

There have been very few studies of language use in relation to overall interactional skills in normal and clinical populations. Earlier studies, seeking psychogenic explanations for the disorder, have implied such potential deficits, however. Among such studies are those suggesting a frigid parent–child relationship as the underlying cause of the disorder (Bateson, Jackson, and Haley, 1956; Goldfarb, 1961; Bettelheim, 1967). Inadequate or absent linguistic interaction between mother and child would be a natural concomitant. The interactions between mothers and schizophrenic children were examined linguistically by Goldfarb, Braunstein, and Lorge (1956) who reached the conclusion that they generally provided poorer communicative models than mothers of normals; but correlations between the communicative patterns used by the mothers and children were not analyzed. Cantwell, Baker, and Rutter (1978) analyzed interactional language of autistic and aphasic children and their mothers. Although they found no essential differences, their analysis stopped at a listing of utterance types. Baltaxe and Simmons (1975) reported on the interactional patterns of five psychotic and five normal controls and their mothers, as contrasted with their caretakers. They found that the verbal interaction between psychotic children and their mothers was less than with their caretakers and the reverse was true for the normals. A possible explanation for the greater interaction with the caretakers was the latter's professional training, which allowed them to be more at ease with the psychotic condition.

An analysis of linguistic structures beyond the sentence through a discourse analysis of bedtime soliloquies of a seven-year-old girl by Baltaxe and Simmons (1977b) showed that the autistic subject used discourse devices, including substitution, expansion, and deletions, and alternations of major discourse themes in similar ways to normal children (Weir, 1962). Interesting differences were also noted, however. Weir (1962) had described the discourse of her subject in terms of the child's dialogue with an imaginary interlocutor, in which the child alternated between the roles of speaker and listener. The soliloquies of the autistic subject showed no evidence of such a dialogue and may have been reflective of the autistics' inability to alternate between hearer's and speaker's roles. Such a role-taking capacity has been noted as one of the basic principles in the acquisition of interactional linguistic skills (Bates, 1976; DeVries, 1970; Maratsos, 1973) and to be in evidence as early as three years of age. In normal cognitive, social, and linguistic development, a progression is seen from an earlier "egocentric stage" to a subsequent socializing and role-taking stage (Flavell, Botkin, Fry, et al., 1968). The capacity to take the perspective of the hearer seems to solidify the speaker's point of view and role taking has consistently been implicated in improved communicative competence (Kraus and Glucksberg, 1969).

Baltaxe (1977) analyzed the dialogue of five adolescent autistics and found a pattern of impairment in speaker–hearer role relationship as one of the major deficits. The autistic subjects appeared to remain in the hearer's role and appeared to have difficulties in switching to a speaker's role and assuming concomitant presuppositions of what the listener knew about the discourse situation. Difficulties relating to speaker–hearer role taking were seen in the use of direct quotes, the continuing confusion of "I" and "you," and confusion of linguistic styles in which linguistic patterns were not adapted to fit a particular hearer or situational context. In addition an impairment in the rules of conduct governing a conversation were also noted. Keenan (1974) found that in order to interact effectively, speaker and hearer must adhere to a code of conduct superimposed on a common linguistic code. This code also includes the principle of acceptability and politeness (Lakoff, 1973; Bates, 1976). Autistics in the above study had not acquired such rules, whereas normal children have been shown to acquire this concept around the age of three (Bates, 1976). Awareness of the contextual variables of an interchange clearly play a decisive role. An explanation for the autistics' deficiencies in the acquisition of such rules may lie in their withdrawal and general aloofness in a social situation and their inattention to the total dialogue situation in which such variables appear to be learned.

Another pragmatic deficit noted in the adolescent study was the difficulty in differentiating between old and new information. To introduce or foreground new information or to mark comment in a topic–comment context, different linguistic devices can be used. These include fully specified noun phrases, word order, cleft constructions, the use of pronominal reference, and contrastive stress. The general use of such devices depends on speaker–hearer presuppositions and may depend on the subject's age as well. Differentiating between old and new information is often accomplished by putting what is known into reference and what is recently acquired into fully specified noun phrases. The pedantic literalness and redundancy in the autistics' discourse were explicable in terms of the autistics' difficulties in such differentiation, which also extended to the dichotomy of relevant versus irrelevant information.

Pragmatic deficits also became apparent in the autistics' lack of adequate use of prosodic features. As noted above, these have been consistently identified as deviant in autism. Contrastive stress, a prosodic feature, is an early primitive device used to differentiate between old and new information. New information is stressed and old information remains unstressed (Miller and Ervin, 1964; Slobin and Welsh, 1967; Atkinson-King, 1973; Wieman, 1976). Baltaxe (1979c) examined contrastive stress in a group of normals, aphasics, and autistics and found that autistics have difficulties with distinguishing old and new information as well as with topic–comment differentiation at an early age. This is probably based in part on an inability to make adequate use of prosodic devices to express and perceive such distinctions. The lack of this skill, coupled with an additional lack in social and cognitive skills, may handicap the autistic in more than one way in developing interactional competence.

These examples have been presented to show that a functional pragmatic analysis of individual features in the autistics' speech and language can provide additional insights over and above those gained when language analysis stops at the level of the sentence. It might be useful in language intervention programs to take such additional findings seriously. All of these studies suggest that language behavior must be viewed more closely in the context of its use and of other social behaviors.

## APPROACHES TO LANGUAGE THERAPY

As has been noted, language intervention techniques are taking on new directions. Most therapy programs to date consider a structured situation essential, and most programs are still based on an operant model of language function (Lovaas, 1966; Freeman, Ritvo, and Miller, 1975; Lovaas, 1977; Schreibman and Carr, 1978). Intervention programs have utilized a variety of different reinforcers. These have included food (Lovaas, Freitag, and Kinder, 1966), food and social contact (Hingtgen and Trost, 1966), food and tokens (Martin, England, Kaprowy, et al., 1968), games (Shaw, 1969), visual color displays (Fineman, 1968), tape recordings and voices (Marr, Miller, and Straub, 1966), kaleidoscopic patterns (Jellis and Grainger, 1974), music (Schmidt, Frankling, and Edwards, 1976), and self-stimulation (Hung, 1978). Varying degrees of success have been reported using these reinforcers in operant conditioning paradigms. More recently, psycholinguistic research and an examination of the fundamentals of normal acquisition have found some application in language intervention strategies (Rubin, Bar, and Dwyer, 1967; Hirsch, 1975; Baltaxe and Simmons, 1975).

Currently the major thrust of research in language intervention is toward alternative approaches in therapy. Colby and Kraemer (1975) used a computer program for stimulation of language behavior in mute autistic children. Hargrave and Swisher (1975) used the Bell and Howell Language Master with audiorecordings to modify the verbal expression of a nine-year-old-boy with autistic behaviors. They reported equal or better success than with live-voice presentations for their language lessons. Programs with limitations on gross motor behavior were also found to be effective in increasing vocalizations (Bram and Meir, 1977). There is also one study that reports success with a group interactive format utilizing an interactive language developmental teaching procedure (Ratusnik and Ratusnik, 1976).

Because 50 percent of all autistic children are also mute, and because of major limitations in teaching speech to mute autistic children, recent attention has focused on nonvocal systems of communication (Schull, Stark, and Giddan, 1967; Lovaas, Freitag, and Kinder, 1968). Teaching the autistic child to communicate through sign language is one of the major current efforts in experimental language training methods in autism, although other symbol systems have also been used. For example, Lavigna (1977) considered writing a viable alternative in the communication training with mute autistic adolescents. Similarly, Widman and Simon (1978) used handwriting and observed a dramatic improvement in a nine-year-old autistic child's ability to reproduce the alphabet. More important, however, was an increase noted in the rate of social interaction between the child studied and the members of his family. Based on theoretical implications of earlier work with chimpanzees, Premack and Premack (1974), using plastic chips as symbolic for language, replicated the procedure with an eight-year-old autistic boy and reported success for subsequent generalization to language proper. Similarly, McLean and McLean (1974) used a nonvocal system developed by Carrier (1974) and found that two of their three subjects were able to generalize within a linguistic category. Language intervention through signing has been reported for autistic children by numerous investigators: Miller and Miller (1973); Bonvillian and Nelson (1976); Fulwiler and Fouts (1976); Konstantareas, Oxman, and Webster (1977); Benaroya, Wesley, Ogilvie, et al. (1977); Salvin, Routh, Foster, et al. (1977); and Brady and Smouse (1978).

Most of the programs described above have used a system of total communication, including both auditory and visual stimuli. In addition to improvement in speech, several of these studies have also noted improvement in social behavior. In all of the studies, however, nonverbal systems appear to act as a catalyst to language acquisition in the more usual language modalities. These studies would support the hypothesis that access to the autistics' linguistic potential may be facilitated through nonvocal modalities. It should be noted in passing that the results of the above studies are somewhat surprising, since autistics have been found to have poor natural gesture ability (Tubbs, 1966), and recent research relating to hemispheric specialization tends to indicate that gestural behavior is associated with left hemisphere function (Dawson, 1978), which has been shown to be deficient in autistics (Blackstock, 1978; Dawson, 1978; Hier, LeMay, and Rosenberger, 1979).

## ABILITIES AND ABNORMALITIES OF INTEREST IN THE CONTEXT OF LANGUAGE

The previous sections have dealt primarily with linguistic deficits. In addition to such deficits, however, autistics have also been noted to have special abilities, sometimes described as "idiot savant" abilities (Rimland, 1964; Cain, 1969; Viscott, 1970). Two of these are of interest from a language perspective: hyperlexia (a special ability to read) and musical abilities. Hyperlexia is also of interest in terms of developmental language histories. In many autistic children with hyperlexia, a high incidence of early normal development of language with subsequent loss has been reported (Ross, 1979). Hyperlexia thus may be a compensatory mechanism after loss of language.

Musical abilities are related to language somewhat differently. The acoustic parameters of music, pitch, intensity, and duration are the same as those for prosody, an area where consistent deficits have been reported. Furthermore, musical abilities and prosodic abilities seem interrelated with respect to hemispheric specialization. This unusual combination of deficits and outstanding abilities may therefore provide some insight into the difficult question of hemispheric specialization. A discussion of hyperlexia, musical abilities, and neurophysiological studies in autism will constitute the final section of this review.

### Hyperlexia

Several studies have reported on the autistics' special ability to read (Silberberg and Silberberg, 1967; Cobrinick, 1974; Ross, 1979). Such an ability has also been reported for brain damaged children (Elliott and Needleman, 1976) and aphasic children (personal communication, Hirsch, 1978). Hyperlexia is defined as an advanced ability to recognize the written word in the presence of delayed and deviant language development (Silberberg and Silberberg, 1967; Mehegan and Dreifuss, 1972). It frequently occurs with a lack of comprehension, although some hyperlexics have been reported to read with comprehension (Huttenlocher and Huttenlocher, 1973; Ross, 1979). Children who show evidence of the phenomenon of hyperlexia are not directly taught to read, but teach themselves at a very early age. Hyperlexia has been reported for autistics as young as two years of age, usually it is quite pronounced by the age of five, and quite often it is reported to occur in a particular ritualistic fashion. Mehegan and Driefuss (1972) described it as a compulsive preoccupation with the written word. As already noted, the history of many hyperlexics reveals an early normal onset of speech, with a subsequent abrupt stop (Cobrinick, 1974; Huttenlocher and Huttenlocher, 1973; Mehegan and Dreifuss, 1972). Ross (1979) postulated that the sound system in the hyperlexic continues to be acquired during a time at which other linguistic skills appear at a standstill. This would allow the child to connect the written to the spoken mode without necessarily comprehending it. The autistics' unusual reading skill, when it occurs, has been attributed to unusual underlying cognitive abilities involving visual imagery and auditory and visual memory (Cobrinick, 1974; Symmes, 1971; Huttenlocher and Huttenlocher, 1973; and others). The possibility of specific brain damage, such as in the case of some types of dyslexia, may also be considered (Benton, 1975). Certain psychological factors have also been suggested as the underlying basis for hyperlexia in the autistic subject (Huttenlocher and Huttenlocher, 1973).

To date, the 1979 study by Ross is the only one that systematically examined the linguistic features and cognitive abilities associated with hyperlexia in a search for underlying explanations and connections. She measured the performance of eight hyperlexic autistics in terms of pattern perception, sequential ordering, and visual memory. She also analyzed spontaneous language samples and experimentally tested other linguistic functions, such as comprehension, sentence completion, and the ability to produce specific types of utterances. The findings indicated that the subjects were heterogeneous in terms of cognitive and/or linguistic abilities. The individual subjects' reading behavior was predictive of their performance on other linguistic and cognitive tests, however. Ross concluded that hyperlexia may contain separate subgroups based on communicative function. Poor or nonexistent comprehension of written material and poor performance on other linguistic and cognitive tasks were seen as characteristic of one group, while better comprehension and higher linguistic and cognitive abilities characterized the other.

## Musical Abilities

There is an apparent interrelationship between prosody and music. Both use the same acoustic parameters and, in the context of language, the literature on the two is often confused (Miller and Toca, 1979). Furthermore, some interesting observations on the interrelationship of musical and verbal abilities can be surmised from the literature. In addition, as will become evident in the discussion of hemispheric specialization, there may be an important interrelationship between the prosody of language and music, since the same mechanism may underlie both functions (Gates and Bradshaw, 1977). Interestingly, music has also been shown to provide a seemingly successful strategy for language intervention in the autistic child (Miller and Toca, 1979), modeled on music intonation therapy in aphasia (Sparks, Albert, and Helm, 1973; Sparks and Holland, 1976; Berlin, 1976).

There have been numerous descriptive reports indicating good musical ability and unusual interest in music among autistic children. Rimland (1964; 1978) described special abilities in 10 percent of his sample of 5400 autistic individuals, and musical talent was the ability most identified. Some of these reports note an attempt at communication through singing on the part of the autistic subjects. Hollander and Juhrs (1974) cited several case studies in which the autistic subjects were especially attracted to music. Musical abilities have been described in a variety of ways, including humming and singing, a compelling interest in listening to music, identification and recognition of tunes, preoccupations with music, and unique abilities with instruments, pitch recognition, and in reproducing tunes with extraordinary accuracy. For example, Wing (1966) found that many autistic children reproduced tunes and TV commercials with considerable accuracy, even when very limited in language usage. Similar reports were presented by Kanner (1951) on 100 children, many of whom had an extraordinary memory for songs. Another finding of significance relates to the very early age at which these abilities are noted. Viscott (1970) reported on a seven-month-old child who was able to hum a complicated melody. This musical ability was noted on follow-up in the child's ability to play the piano. Even at that age, however, the child only knew a few words, and apparently communicated through music. Sherwin (1975) described three autistic children ages fourteen to eighteen months with similar abilities which, although notable, were varied in degree. Sherwin also noted a relationship between echolalia in music, rocking in rhythm, and being most attracted to "strong rhythms." With improvement in communication, Sherwin found a decline in musical ability and interest. A recent study by Applebaum, Egel, Koegel, et al. (1979) appears to be the only experimental study available. In a behavioral paradigm, these investigators studied the perception of musical stimuli in three autistic subjects with reported good musical abilities and in three normal controls who had musical experience. The results of the study showed that autistics performed as well as or better than their normal counterparts.

Explanations for this musical ability have varied, ranging from psychodynamic to biological. Viscott (1970) reported in his follow-up that "the production of music seemed . . . a way of recreating a motherly presence and dealing with feelings of loneliness." Sherwin (1975) speculated on the musical interest in terms of fixation in early psychosexual development. Rimland (1978) pointed out the possible relationship between these abilities and left temporal lobe impairment suggested by EEG, dichotic listening, and anatomical studies. The question of hemispheric specialization and musical ability is not entirely clear. Music can be processed differentially depending on individual subcomponents, such as rhythm, pitch, intensity, duration, tonal variation, and simultaneity (Gates and Bradshawy, 1977). Other variables that might affect hemispheric specialization include the experience of the listener, whether or not music is viewed as a notational system (writing or reading of music), and whether the expressive or receptive aspect of music is involved.

### Neurophysiological Studies

One of the most promising research approaches offering insight into these peculiarities of prosody and musical abilities and into the broader study of language and cognition in autism has been the rapidly expanding field of clinical neurophysiology and, in particular, the area of hemispheric specialization. The functional properties of the right and left hemispheres have been investigated in a variety of ways. These have included dichotic listening studies (Kimura, 1961; 1964; Milner, 1962; Sparks and Geschwind, 1968), sodium amytal (Wada, Clarke, and Ham, 1975), electrical stimulation (Penfield and Roberts, 1959), clinical studies with split brain patients (Sperry, Gazzaniga, and Bogen, 1969), and more recently laboratory studies, using EEG, auditory evoked response, and bloodflow studies (Molfese, 1976; Gardiner and Walter, 1976; Lassen, Ingvar, and Shinoff, 1978). These studies have demonstrated differential processing of information by the right and left hemispheres. An excellent general characterization of these differences was provided by Bogen (1969a; 1969b), who described left hemisphere function as involved in language, time-related events, and propositional thought. The right hemisphere is involved in spatial relations, Gestalt perceptions, part–whole judgments, and music and appositional thought. The studies which have helped establish these differential functions also support the notion of the relative independence of prosodic abilities and musical abilities. Although this characterization of right/left differential functioning is not as clear cut as it appears, particularly in the light of more recent studies (Gates and Bradshaw, 1977; Bever and Chiarelli, 1974), it does serve as sufficient introduction to the studies which have been carried out on autistic children and adolescents.

Attention was first drawn to the possibility of subtle cortical dysfunction underlying the autistic disturbance from clinical studies on the peculiarities of perception and performance on various levels of psychological tests. Lockyer and Rutter (1970), using the WISC and WAIS to analyze intellectual functioning in autistic children showed that their lowest scores were in the left hemisphere related functions of vocabulary, information, arithmetic, and the similarities subtests, while higher scores were obtained on right hemisphere related block design and object assembly. Similar findings were reported by Tymchuk, Simmons, and Neafsey (1977) who showed that these kinds of impairments in autistic children extended into adolescence. Also, a number of experimental studies was carried out that showed a deficiency in autistic children in encoding and spontaneously generating patterns (Frith, 1970a; 1970b; 1971). In addition, there were a number of general clinical observations involving musical abilities (Rimland, 1978), problems in comprehension (Simmons and Tymchuk, 1973), and prosody and language (Simmons and Baltaxe, 1975), as well as speculations from clinicians (Damasio and Maurer, 1978) and clinical investigators (Tanguay, 1976) who helped to focus attention on the cortical mechanisms underlying autism.

Recently these clinical and experimental observations have given rise to a significant number of studies designed to test the hypothesis that there is a differential defect in hemispheric function in autistic children. These studies have generally involved (dichotic) listening, evoked response, and anatomical studies. Blackstock (1978) conducted two listening studies utilizing a behavioral paradigm on autistic and normal controls. The first study showed that when asked to choose between verbal stimuli and musical stimuli, autistics preferred the music and normals showed no preference. In a somewhat more rigorous second study, Blackstock showed that when forced to use one ear or the other, the autistics listened to both verbal and musical stimuli with the left ear. Although there was considerable variation, normals tended to listen to verbal stimuli with the right ear and musical stimuli with the left. Prior and Bradshaw (1979) in a dichotic listening study using single syllable word pairs, found that autistic children showed a definite left ear advantage, while normals showed a right ear advantage.

Dawson (1979) in her doctoral dissertation, examined alpha rhythm asymmetries from homologous parietal areas during verbal, spatial, and gestural imitation tasks. The results indicated greater left hemisphere dominance in normals during verbal testing when compared with spatial tasks. During spatial tasks, both autistic and normal subjects had similar right hemisphere activation, whereas during language processing there was less hemisphere involvement for the autistics. In this same study on hemispheric specialization in autism, Dawson utilized neuropsychological testing to demonstrate a greater degree of left hemisphere dysfunction in autistics when compared to mentally retarded subjects and patients with bilateral or diffuse brain damage. These tests involved performance on cognitive tasks known to be mediated by one or the other hemisphere, right–left differences in perceptual motor and sensorimotor abilities, and tests of aphasia and apraxia. While autistic children had a significantly greater degree of left hemisphere dysfunction than the two control groups, no significant degree of difference in right hemisphere function was seen. In other studies, Tanguay (1976) showed that during REM sleep, normal children showed larger evoked responses over the right hemisphere, but no consistent differences were found with autistics.

Despite the large number of studies of autism dating back to Kanner's original description, there are few anatomical studies which have proven of significance in understanding the etiology of this condition. Darby's (1976) study, mentioned earlier, basically concerned itself with the gross neuropathology of the brains of autistic individuals who had come to postmortem examination. Although a variety of CNS disorders were described, no mention of specific abnormalities as they might relate to function was made. Hauser, DeLong, and Rosman (1975) reported that in 15 of 17 language retarded autistic children air pneumonencephalography showed left temporal horn enlargement with a deficiency in brain substance in the left cerebral hemisphere. On the basis of some similarities in behavior noted between animals with left temporal lobe defects and autistics, they postulated a left cerebral abnormality in autism. Although this study has not been replicated, another study by Hier, LeMay, and Rosenberger (1979) also reported right–left cerebral differences in autism. In a study of 16 autistic children utilizing computerized axial tomography, they found that in 50 percent of those children the right parieto-occipital region was wider than the left. This finding was noted in 23 percent of retarded and 25 percent of neurologically damaged controls. They postulated that those morphological asymmetries of the brain in the posterior language zone may contribute to the difficulties autistic children have with language. Finally, Blackstock and Mavestutio (1978), postulating that right–left cerebral hemisphere asymmetries would be reflected in right–left body asymmetries, examined right–left size and function in autistic and normal controls. They found that severely autistic children were larger and more functional on their left sides, whereas normals were larger on the right. The relationship between handedness and these right–left asymmetries is unclear. In the Hauser, Delong, and Rosman (1975) study, 8 of 17 subjects were left–handed and in the Prior and Bradshaw (1979) study, a significant number had not established handedness. However, Kinsbourne and Hicks (1978), Colby and Parkinson (1977), Levy, Mack, and Staikoff (1978), and Galaburda, LeMay, Kemper, et al. (1978) concluded that the issue of handedness has not been satisfactorily resolved.

It is obvious that the data available from these studies support the notion that autistic individuals are defective in left hemisphere functioning and are predominantly right hemisphere processors. In viewing these studies in isolation and without corroboration, however, one runs the risk of oversimplification, since there are other areas of information processing and central nervous system function that have been shown to be abnormal in autism, and the deficits are quite complex (Damasio and Maurer, 1978; Darby, 1976; Simon, 1975).

CONCLUSION

Speech and language have been considered as significant aspects of childhood psychosis since the first clinical descriptions were made, some of which remain valid today. Initially the deficits in these areas were considered as evidence of disturbances in the interpersonal domain and reflected pathology in psychosocial development. As the trends in research and treatment moved in the direction of organic etiology, however, the disorder began to be viewed in terms of mechanisms that may underlie specific deficits. Further studies in speech and language demonstrated clearly that not only was language delayed but it was deviant, and these deficits persisted into adolescence and adulthood. It is particularly the deviances, such as echolalia, disturbances in prosody, and disturbances of language use in context, that have stimulated the interest of researchers in the various phys-

iological, anatomical, and linguistic areas. Also, some of the idiosyncrasies of autistic language, such as echolalia, have begun to appear
as the autistic's initial steps in language acquisition.

In recent years some of the fundamental neurophysiological
mechanisms of language acquisition and production have been partially clarified and have led to speculations that the deficits in autism
may well be explained in part by impairment in left hemisphere function. In addition, careful analysis of language in the context of social
and cognitive functioning has demonstrated deficits which point to a
complex interrelationship between these three areas of impairment in
the autistic individual. These findings also tend to support some of the
speculations made on the basis of neurophysiological and anatomical
studies.

Treatment of the language problem in autism has focused heavily
on the use of reinforcement learning paradigms which continue to be
useful in the delivery of intervention programs. However, the studies
in neurophysiology and developmental psycholinguistics have led to a
more synthesized view, not only of the mechanics of language reme-
diation through reinforcement learning, but, more importantly, of the
content and sequencing of the therapeutic effort. Despite considerable
work in the speech and language area, the specific mechanisms underlying this deficit have not been totally delineated, and further work
in pragmatics and prosody in autism and the physiology of normal
language needs to be carried out. One of the problems of past
studies is the comparability of the techniques and patient populations. Thus, various methodologies utilized with one or another population must be used across populations in order to obtain comparable
findings. Also, control groups for autistic populations need to be more
accurately defined and differentiated before applying various research strategies.

REFERENCES

Abercrombie, D. Paralanguage. *British Journal of Disorders of Communica-
tion,* 1968, *3,* 55–59.
Applebaum, E., Egel, A., Koegel, R., et al. Measuring musical abilities of au-
tistic children. *Journal of Autism and Developmental Disorders,* 1979,
*9*(3), 279–285.
Atkinson-King, K. Children's acquisition of phonological stress contrasts.
*Working Papers in Phonetics,* 1973, No. 21, Los Angeles: University of
California.
Ausman, J., Gaddy, M. Reinforcement training for echolalia. *Mental Retarda-
tion,* 1974, *12,* 20–21.

Bagshaw, N. An acoustic analysis of fundamental frequency and temporal parameters of autistic children's speech. Unpublished Master's thesis, University of California, 1978.

Baltaxe, C. Recovery patterns in a case of acquired aphasia of childhood. *Proceedings of a conference on human brain function.* Los Angeles: Brain Information Service: University of California, 1976, 131–137.

Baltaxe, C. Pragmatic deficits in the language of autistic adolescents. *Journal of Pediatric Psychology,* 1977, *2*(4), 176–180.

Baltaxe, C. Prosodic abnormalities in autism. *Journal of Speech and Hearing Disorders,* 1979a, (in press).

Baltaxe, C. Acoustic characteristics of prosody in autism. In P. Mittler (Ed.), *Proceedings of the Fifth International Congress for the Scientific Study of Mental Deficiency: New Frontiers of Knowledge.* Baltimore: University Park Press, 1979b, (in press).

Baltaxe, C. Contrastive stress and topic–comment in autistic, aphasic, and normal children. Paper presented at the Annual National Convention American Speech and Hearing Association, Atlanta, Ga., November, 1979c.

Baltaxe, C. Measures of psycholinguistic abilities for normal, aphasic, and autistic subjects. 1979d. Paper presented at the Annual National Convention of American Speech and Hearing Association, Detroit, Mich., November 1980.

Baltaxe, C., Simmons, J. Q. Language in childhood psychosis: A review. *Journal of Speech and Hearing Disorders,* 1975, *40,* 439–458.

Baltaxe, C., Simmons, J. Q. Language patterns of German and English autistic adolescents. In P. Mittler (Ed.), *Proceedings of the International Association for the Study of Mental Deficiency.* Baltimore: University Park Press, 1977a, 267–278.

Baltaxe, C., Simmons, J. Q. Bedtime soliloquies and linguistic competence in autism. *Journal of Speech and Hearing Disorders,* 1977b, *42*(3), 367–393.

Bartak, L., Rutter, M. Differences between mentally retarded and normally intelligent autistic children. *Journal of Autism and Childhood Schizophrenia,* 1976, *6*(2), 109–120.

Bartak, L., Rutter, M., Cox, A. A comparative study of infantile autism and specific developmental receptive language disorders III: Discrimination function analysis. *Journal of Autism and Childhood Schizophrenia,* 1977, *7,* 383–396.

Bartolucci, G., Albers, R. Deictic categories in the language of autistic children. *Journal of Autism and Childhood Schizophrenia,* 1974, *14*(2), 131–141.

Bartolucci, G., Pierce, S., Steiner, D., et al. Phonological investigations of verbal, autistic, and mentally retarded subjects. *Journal of Autism and Childhood Schizophrenia,* 1976, *6*(4), 303–316.

Basser, L. Hemiplegia of early onset and the faculty of speech with special reference to the effects of hemispherectomy. *Brain,* 1962, *88,* 427–460.

Bates, E. *Language and context: The acquisition of pragmatics.* New York: Academic Press, 1976.

Bateson, G., Jackson, D., Haley, J., et al. Toward a theory of schizophrenia. *Behavioral Science*, 1956, *1*, 251–264.

Benaroya, S., Wesley, S., Ogilvie, H., et al. Sign language and multisensory input training of children with communication and related developmental disorders. *Journal of Autism and Childhood Schizophrenia*, 1977, *7*(1), 23–31.

Bender, L. Childhood schizophrenia. *Nervous Child*, 1942, *1*, 138–140.

Bender, L. Schizophrenia in childhood: A clinical study of one hundred schizophrenic children. *American Journal of Orthopsychiatry*, 1947, *17*, 40–56.

Benton, A. Developmental dyslexia: Neurological aspects. In W. Friedlander (Ed.), *Advances in neurosciences*. New York: Raven Press, 1975.

Berlin, C. On melodic intonation therapy for aphasia by W. R. Sparks and A. L. Holland. *Journal of Speech and Hearing Disorders*, 1976, *41*, 298–300.

Bettelheim, B. *The empty fortress: Infantile autism and the birth of the self.* New York: Free Press, 1967.

Bever, T., Chiarelli, R. Cerebral dominance in musicians and nonmusicians. *Science*, 1974, *185*, 537–539.

Blackstock, E. Cerebral asymmetry and the development of infantile autism. *Journal of Autism and Childhood Schizophrenia*, 1978, *8*, 339–353.

Blackstock, E., Malvestuto, G. Anatomical and neuroanatomical asymmetries in autistic children. Paper presented at the National Conference of the Canadian Society for Autistic Children, 1978.

Bogen, J. The other side of the brain I. Dysgraphia and dyscopia following cerebral commissuratomy. *Bulletin of the Los Angeles Neurological Society*, 1969a, *34*, 73–105.

Bogen, J. The other side of the brain II. An appositional mind. *Bulletin of the Los Angeles Neurological Society*, 1969b, 34, 135–162.

Bonvillian, J., Nelson, K. Sign language acquisition in a mute autistic boy. *Journal of Speech and Hearing Disorders*, 1976, *41*(3), 339–347.

Boucher, J. Is autism primarily a language disorder? *Journal of Disorders of Communication*, 1976, *11*(2), 135–143.

Brady, D., Smouse, A. A simultaneous comparison of three methods for language training with an autistic child, an experimental single case analysis. *Journal of Autism and Childhood Schizophrenia*, 1978, *8*(3), 271–279.

Bram, S., Meir, M. A relationship between motor control and language development in an autistic child. *Journal of Autism and Childhood Schizophrenia*, 1977, *7*(1), 57–67.

Brown, J., Reiser, D. Follow-up study of preschool children of atypical development (infantile psychosis)—later personality patterns in adaptation to maturational stress. *American Journal of Orthopsychiatry*, 1963, *33*, 336–338.

Brown, R. *A first language, the early stages.* Cambridge, Mass.: Harvard University Press, 1973.

Cain, A. Special isolated abilities in severely psychotic young children. *Psychiatry*, 1969, *32*, 137–149.

Call, J. Interlocking affective freeze between an autistic child and his "as if" mother. *American Academy of Child Psychiatry*, 1963, *2*, 2–15.

Cantwell, D. P., Baker, L., Rutter, M. Families of autistic and dysphasic children. II. Mothers' speech to the children. *Journal of Autism and Childhood Schizophrenia,* 1977, *7*(4), 313–327.

Cantwell, D., Baker, L., Rutter, M. A comparative study of infantile autism and specific developmental receptive language disorder. IV. Analysis of syntax and language function. *Journal of Child Psychology and Psychiatry,* 1978, *19,* 351–362.

Carrier, J. Nonspeech noun usage training with severely and profoundly retarded children. *Journal of Speech and Hearing Research,* 1974, *14,* 510–517.

Churchill, D. The relation of infantile autism and early childhood schizophrenia to developmental language disorders of childhood. *Journal of Autism and Childhood Schizophrenia,* 1972, *2*(2), 182–197.

Cobrinick, L. Unusual reading ability in severely disturbed children. *Journal of Autism and Childhood Schizophrenia,* 1974, *4*(2), 163–175.

Cohen, D., Caparulo, B., Shaywitz, B. Primary childhood aphasia and childhood autism. *Journal of the American Academy of Child Psychiatry,* 1977, *15,* 604–645.

Colby, K., Kraemer, H. An objective measurement of nonspeaking children's performance with a computer-controlled program for stimulation of language behavior. *Journal of Autism and Childhood Schizophrenia,* 1975, *5*(2), 139–146.

Colby, K., Parkinson, C. Handedness in autistic children. *Journal of Autism and Childhood Schizophrenia,* 1977, *7*(1), 3–9.

Coleman, S., Stedman, J. Use of a peer model in language training in an echolalic child. *Journal of Behavioral Therapy and Experimental Psychiatry,* 1974, *5,* 275–279.

Cooper, J., Ferry, C. Acquired auditory verbal agnosia and seizures in childhood. *Journal of Speech and Hearing Disorders,* 1978, *43*(2), 176–184.

Creak, E. Schizophrenic syndrome in childhood: Progress report of a working party. *Cerebral Palsy Bulletin,* 1961, *3,* 501–504.

Creak, E. Childhood psychosis: A review of 100 cases. *British Journal of Psychiatry,* 1963, *109,* 84–89.

Crystal, D. Prosodic systems and language acquisition. In P. Leon (Ed.), *Prosodic Feature Analysis.* Montreal: Didier, 1969, 77–90.

Dalgleish, V. Cognitive processing and linguistic reference in autistic children. *Journal of Autism and Childhood Schizophrenia,* 1975, *5*(4), 353–361.

Damasio, A., Maurer, R. A neurological model for childhood autism. *Archives of Neurology,* 1978, *35,* 777–786.

Darby, J. Neuropathologic aspects of psychosis in children. *Journal of Autism and Childhood Schizophrenia,* 1976, *6,* 339–352.

Dawson, G. Early infantile autism and cerebral hemispheric specialization. Unpublished Doctoral dissertation, University of Washington, 1979.

DeHirsch, K. Differential diagnosis between aphasic and schizophrenic language in children. *Journal of Speech and Hearing Disorders,* 1967, *32,* 3–10.

DeMeyer, M. The nature of the neuropsychological disability in autistic children. *Journal of Autism and Childhood Schizophrenia,* 1975, *5*(2), 109–128.

DesLauriers, A. *The experience of reality in childhood schizophrenia.* New York: International University, 1962.

deVilliers, J., deVilliers, P. A cross-sectional study of the development of grammatical morphemes in child speech. *Journal of Psycholinguistic Research,* 1973, *2,* 267–278.

Devries, R. The development of role taking as reflected by behavior of bright, average, and retarded children in a social guessing game. *Child Development,* 1970, *41,* 759–770.

Eisenberg, L. The autistic child in adolescence. *American Journal of Psychiatry,* 1956, *112,* 607–613.

Elliott, D., Needleman, R. The syndrome of hyperlexia. *Brain and Language,* 1976, *3,* 339–349.

Ervin-Tripp, S. Imitation and structural change in children's language. In E. Lenneberg (Ed.), *New directions in the study of language.* Cambridge, Mass.: M.I.T. Press, 1966, 163–189.

Fay, W. On the basis of autistic echolalia. *Journal of Communication Disorders,* 1969, *2,* 38–47.

Fay, W. On normal and autistic pronouns. *Journal of Speech and Hearing Disorders,* 1971, *36,* 242–249.

Fay, W. On the echolalia of the blind and of the autistic child. *Journal of Speech and Hearing Disorders,* 1973, *38,* 478–479.

Fineman, K. Shaping and increasing verbalization in an autistic child in response to visual color stimulation. *Perceptual Motor Skills,* 1968, *27,* 1071–1074.

Flavell, J., Botkin, P., Fry, C., et al. *The development of role taking and communication skills in children,* New York: John Wiley & Sons, 1968.

Fletcher, C. A comparison of pitch patterns of normal and autistic children. Unpublished Master's thesis, University of California, Santa Barbara, 1976.

Fraser, C., Bellugi, U., Brown, R. Control of grammar in imitation, comprehension, and production. *Journal of Verbal Learning and Verbal Behavior,* 1963, *2,* 121–135.

Freeman, B., Ritvo, E. Diagnostic and evaluation systems: Helping the advocate cope with the "state of the art." In J. Budde (Ed.), *Advocacy and autism.* Lawrence, Kansas: University of Kansas Press, 1977.

Freeman, B., Ritvo, E., Miller, R. An operant procedure to teach an echolalic autistic child to answer questions appropriately. *Journal of Autism and Childhood Schizophrenia,* 1975, *5,* 169–176.

Frith, U. Emphasis and meaning in recall in normal and autistic children. *Language and Speech,* 1969, *12,* 29–38.

Frith, U. Studies in pattern detection I. Immediate recall of auditory sequences. *Journal of Abnormal Psychology,* 1970a, *76,* 413–420.

Frith, U. Studies in pattern detection II. Reproduction and production of color sequences. *Journal of Experimental Child Psychology,* 1970b, *10,* 120–135.

Frith, U. Spontaneous pattern production produced by autistic, normal, and subnormal children. In M. Rutter (Ed.), *Infantile autism: Concepts, characteristics, and treatment,* Edinburgh: Churchill Livingstone, 1971, 113–132.

Fulwiler, R., Fouts, R. Acquisition of American sign language by a noncommunicating autistic child. *Journal of Autism and Childhood Schizophrenia,* 1976, *6*(1), 43–51.

Galaburda, A. M., LeMay, M., Kemper, T., et al. Right–left asymmetries in the brain. *Science,* 1978, *199,* 852–856.

Gardiner, M., Walter, D. Evidence of hemispheric specialization from infant EEG. In S. Hormad, R. Doty, L. Goldstein, et al. (Eds.), *Lateralization in the nervous system.* New York: Academic Press, 1976, 481–502.

Gascon, V., Lambroso, C., Goodglass, H. Language disorder, convulsive disorder and electroencephalographic abnormalities acquired syndrome in children. *Archives of Neurology,* 1973, *28,* 156–162.

Gates, A., Bradshaw, J. The role of cerebral hemispheres in music. *Brain and Language,* 1977, *4,* 403–431.

Geleerd, E. Borderline states in childhood and adolescence. *Psychoanalytic Study of the Child,* 1958, *13,* 279–295.

Geschwind, N., Quadfasal, F., Segarra, J. Isolation of the speech area. *Neuropsychologia,* 1968, *6,* 327–340.

Goldfarb, W. *Childhood schizophrenia.* Cambridge, Mass.: Harvard University Press, 1961.

Goldfarb, W., Braunstein, P., Lorge, I. A study of speech patterns in a group of schizophrenic children. *American Journal of Orthopsychiatry,* 1956, *26,* 544–555.

Goldfarb, W., Goldfarb, N., Braunstein, P., et al. Speech and language faults of schizophrenic children. *Journal of Autism and Childhood Schizophrenia,* 1972, *2,* 219–233.

Griffith, R., Ritvo, E. Echolalia: Concerning the dynamics of the syndrome. *Journal, American Academy of Child Psychiatry,* 1967, *6,* 184–193.

Hargrave, E., Swisher, L. Modifying the verbal expression of a child with autistic behaviors. *Journal of Autism and Childhood Schizophrenia,* 1975, *5*(2), 147–154.

Harper, J. Age and type of onset as critical variables in early infantile autism. *Journal of Autism and Childhood Schizophrenia,* 1975, *5*(1), 25–36.

Hauser, S., Delong, G., Rosman, N. Pneumoencephalographic findings in the infantile autism syndrome. *Brain,* 1975, *98,* 667–688.

Hermelin, B. Rules and language. In M. Rutter (Ed.), *Infantile autism: Concepts, characteristics, and treatment.* Edinburgh: Churchill Livingstone, 1971, 98–113.

Hermelin, B., O'Connor, N. Remembering of words by psychotic and normal children. *British Journal of Psychology,* 1967, *58,* 213–218.

Hermelin, B., O'Connor, N. *Psychological experiments with autistic children.* London: Pergamon Press, 1970.

Hesse, G., Wallstein, R. Psychotic children's free-choice selection of natural and distorted speech. *Journal of Communication Disorders,* 1976, *9*(1), 19–25.

Hier, D., LeMay, M., Rosenberger, P. Autism and unfavorable left–right asymmetries of the brain. *Journal of Autism and Developmental Disorders,* 1979, *9*(2), 153–159.

Hingtgen, J., Trost, F. Shaping cooperative responses in early childhood schizophrenics: Reinforcement of mutual physical contact and vocal responses. In R. Ulrich, T. Stacknick, and J. Malry (Eds.), *Control of human behavior.* Glenview, Illinois: Scott Foresman, 1966, 110–113.

Hirsch, R. Personal communication on hyperlexia in aphasia, 1978.

Hollander, F., Juhrs, P. Orff: Schulwork: An effective treatment tool with autistic children. *Journal of Music Therapy,* 1974, *11,* 1–12.

Huttenlocher, P., Huttenlocher, J. A study of children with hyperlexia. *Neurology,* 1973, *23,* 1107–1116.

Hung, D. Using self-stimulation as reinforcement for autistic children. *Journal of Autism and Childhood Schizophrenia,* 1978, *8*(3), 355–366.

Ingram, D. Issues in child phonology. In Morehead and Morehead (Eds.), *Normal and deficient child language.* Baltimore: University Park Press, 1976, 3–27.

Jakobson, R. *Child language, aphasia, and phonological universals.* Mouton: The Hague, 1968.

Jellis, T., Grainger, S. The back projection of kaleidoscopic patterns as a technique for eliciting verbalizations in an autistic child. A final note. *British Journal of Disorders of Communication,* 1974, *9*(1), 65–68.

Kanner, L. Autistic disturbances of affective contact. *Nervous Child,* 1943, *2,* 217–250.

Kanner, L. Early infantile autism. *Journal of Pediatrics,* 1944, *25,* 211–217.

Kanner, L. The conception of wholes and parts in early infantile autism. *American Journal of Psychiatry,* 1951, *108,* 23.

Kanner, L. Follow-up study of eleven autistic children originally reported in 1943. *Journal of Autism and Childhood Schizophrenia,* 1971, *1*(2), 119–145.

Kanner, L., Eisenberg, L. Notes on the follow-up studies of autistic children. In H. Hoch and J. Zubin (Eds.), *Psychopathology of childhood.* New York: Grune & Stratton, 1955.

Kanner, L., Eisenberg, L. Early infantile autism, 1943–1955. *American Journal of Orthopsychiatry,* 1956, *26,* 55–65.

Kaplan, E. Intonation and child acquisition. *Papers in Research in Child Language Development,* 1970, 1, 1–21.

Keenan, E. Conversational competence in children. *Journal of Child Language,* 1974, *1,* 163–183.

Kimura, D. Cerebral dominance and the perception of verbal stimuli. *Canadian Journal of Psychology,* 1961, *15,* 166–171.

Kimura, D. Left–right differences in the perception of melodies. *Quarterly Journal of Experiment Psychology,* 1964, *16,* 355–358.

Kinsbourne, M., Hicks, R. On the genesis of human handedness: A review. Division of Neurology, Department of Pediatrics, Hospital for Sick Children, Toronto, Ontario, Canada, 1978.

Knobloch, H., Pasamanick, B. Some etiologic and prognostic factors in early infantile autism and psychosis. *Pediatrics,* 1975, *55,* 182–191.

Konstantareas, M., Oxman, J., Webster, C. Simultaneous communication with autistic and other severely dysfunctional nonverbal children. *Journal of Communication Disorders,* 1977, *10*(3), 267–282.

Krashen, S. Lateralization, language learning, and the critical period: Some new evidence. *Language Learning,* 1973, *23,* 39–55.

Kraus, R., Glucksberg, S. The development of communication competence as a function of age. *Child Development,* 1969, *40,* 255–266.

Lakoff, R. The logic of politeness: Minding your p's and q's. *Papers from the Ninth Regional Meeting of the Chicago Linguistic Society.* Chicago, Ill.: 1973.

Landau, W., Kleffner, F. The syndrome of acquired aphasia with a convulsive disorder in children. *Neurology,* 1957, *7*(8), 523–530.

Lassen, N., Ingvar, D., Shinoff, E. Brain function and blood flow. *Scientific American,* 1978, *289*(4), 62.

Lavigna, G. Communication training in mute autistic adolescents using the written word. *Journal of Childhood Schizophrenia,* 1977, *7*(2), 135–149.

Lee, L. *Developmental sentence analysis.* Evanston, Illinois: Northwestern University Press, 1974.

Lenneberg, E. *Biological foundations of language.* New York: John Wiley and Sons, 1967.

Levy, J., Meck, B., Staikoff, J. Dysfunction of the left cerebral hemisphere in autistic children. *Brain,* 1978.

Lieberman, P. *Intonation, perception, and language.* Cambridge, Mass.: M.I.T. Press, 1968.

Lieberman, P., Michaels, S. Some aspects of fundamental frequency, envelope, amplitude, and the emotional content of speech. *Journal of the Acoustical Society of America,* 1962, *34,* 922–927.

Lockyer, L., Rutter, M. A five to fifteen year follow-up study of infantile psychosis IV: Patterns of cognitive ability. *British Journal of Social and Clinical Psychology,* 1970, *9,* 151–163.

Lotter, V. Factors related to outcome in autistic children. *Journal of Autism and Childhood Schizophrenia,* 1974, *4,* 263–277.

Lovaas, I. A program for the establishment of speech in psychotic children. In J. Wing (Ed.), *Early childhood autism.* London: Pergamon, 1966, 115–144.

Lovaas, I. A program for the establishment of speech in psychotic children. In H.N. Sloan and B.D. MacAulay (Eds.), *Operant procedures in remedial speech and language training.* Boston: Houghton Mifflin, 1968.

Lovaas, I. *The autistic child: Language development through behavior modification.* New York: Halstead Press, 1977.

Lovaas, I., Freitag, G., Kinder, M. Establishment of social reinforcers in two schizophrenic children on the basis of food. *Journal of Experimental Child Psychology,* 1966, *4,* 109–125.

Luria, A. The directive function of speech in development and dissolution. Part I. Development of the directive function of speech in early childhood. *Word,* 1959, *15,* 341–352.

Macken, M. Permitted complexity in phonological development: One child's acquisition of Spanish consonants. *Lingua,* 1978, *44,* 219–253.

Mahler, M. On child psychosis and schizophrenia: Autistic and symbiotic infantile psychosis. *Psychoanalytic Study of the Child*, 1952, *7*, 286–305.

Maratsos, M. The effects of stress on the understanding of pronominal coreference in children. *Journal of Psycholinguistic Research*, 1973, *2*(1), 1–8.

Marr, J., Miller, E., Straub, R. Operant conditioning of attention with a psychotic girl. *Behavioral Research Therapy*, 1966, *4*, 85–87.

Martin, G., England, G., Kaprowy, E., et al. Operant conditioning of kindergarten class behavior in autistic children. *Behavioral Research Therapy*, 1968, *6*, 281–294.

McCarthy, M. Language development in children. In L. Carmichael (Ed.), *Manual of child psychology*. New York: John Wiley and Sons, 1954.

McLean, L., McLean, J. Language training program for nonverbal autistic children. *Journal of Speech and Hearing Disorders*, 1974, *39*, 186–193.

Mehegan, C., Dreifuss, F. Hyperlexia. Exceptional reading ability in brain-damaged children. *Neurology*, 1972, *22*(11), 1105–1111.

Menyuk, P. *Sentences children use*. Cambridge, Mass.: M.I.T. Press, 1969.

Miller, W., Ervin, S. The Development of Grammar in Child Language. In Bellugi, U. and Brown, R. (eds) *The Acquisition of language*. Monographs of the Society for Research in Child Development (1964), 29. 9–34.

Miller, A., Miller, E. Cognitive developmental training with elevated boards and sign language. *Journal of Autism and Childhood Schizophrenia*, 1973, *3*, 65–85.

Miller, S., Toca, M. Adapted melodic intonation therapy: A case study of an experimental language program for an autistic child. *Journal of Clinical Psychiatry*, 1979, *80*, 201–203.

Milner, B. Laterality effects in audition. In V. Mountcastle (Ed.), *Interhemispheric relations and cerebral dominance*. Baltimore: Johns Hopkins University Press, 1962, 177–195.

Molfesse, D. The ontogeny of cerebral asymmetry in man: Auditory evoked potentials to linguistic and nonlinguistic stimuli. In J. Desmedt (Ed.), *Recent developments in the psychology of language: The cerebral evoked potential approach*. London: Oxford University Press, 1976.

Morton-Evans, A., Hensley, R. Paired associate learning in early infantile autism and receptive developmental aphasia, *Journal of Autism and Childhood Schizophrenia*, 1978, *8*(1), 61–69.

O'Connor, N., Frith, U. Cognitive development and the concept of set. In A. Pragishvil (Ed.). *Psychological investigations: A commemorative volume dedicated to the 85th anniversary of the birth of D. Uzandze*, Metsnierba, Tbilisi, USSR: 1973, 296–300.

Ornitz, E. Vestibular dysfunction in schizophrenia and childhood autism. *Comprehensive Psychiatry*, 1970, *11*, 159–173.

Ornitz, E., Ritvo, E. Perceptual inconstancy in the syndrome of early infantile autism and its variants. *Archives of General Psychiatry*, 1968, *18*, 76–98.

Ornitz, E., Ritvo, E. Medical assessment. In E. Ritvo (Ed.), *Autism, diagnosis, current research and management*. New York: Spectrum Publications, 1976, 7–26.

Ostwald, P. *Soundmaking*. Springfield, Illinois: Charles C. Thomas, 1963.

Penfield, W., Roberts, C. *Speech and brain mechanisms.* Princeton, New Jersey: Princeton University Press, 1959.

Piaget, J., Inhelder, B. *The Psychology of the child* (H. Weaver, trans). New York: Basic Books, 1969.

Pierce, S., Bartolucci, G. A syntactic investigation of verbal autistic, mentally retarded, and normal children. *Journal of Autism and Childhood Schizophrenia,* 1977, *7*(2), 121–134.

Philips, G., Dyer, C. Late onset echolalia in autism and allied disorders. *British Journal of Disorders of Communication,* 1977, *12*, 47–59.

Pike, K. Several characteristics of intonation. In D. Bolinger (Ed.), *Intonation.* Baltimore: Penguin Books, Ltd., 1972.

Premack, D., Premack, A. Teaching visual langauge to apes and language deficient persons. In R. Schiefelbusch and L. Lloyd (Eds.), *Language perspectives: Acquisition, retardation, and intervention.* Baltimore: University Park Press, 1974.

Prior, M., Bradshaw, J. Hemisphere functioning in autistic children. *Cortex,* 1979, *15*, 73–81.

Prizant, B. An analysis of the functions of immediate echolalia in autistic children. Unpublished Doctoral Dissertation, State University of New York, 1978.

Pronovost, W., Wakstein, M., Wakstein, P. A longitudinal study of the speech behavior and language comprehension of fourteen children diagnosed atypical or autistic. *Exceptional Children,* 1966, *33*, 19–26.

Rank, B. Adaptation of the psychoanalytic technique for the treatment of young children with atypical development. *American Journal of Orthopsychiatry,* 1949, *19*, 130–139.

Ricks, D. Vocal communication in preverbal normal and autistic children. In N. O'Connor (Ed.), *Language, cognitive deficits, and retardation.* London: Butterworth, 1972.

Ricks, D., Wing, L. Language, communication, and the use of symbols in normal and autistic children. *Journal of Autism and Childhood Schizophrenia,* 1975, *5*, 191–221.

Ratusnik, C., Ratusnik, D. A therapeutic milieu for establishing and expanding communicative behaviors in psychotic children. *Journal of Speech and Hearing Disorders,* 1976, *41*(1), 7–72.

Rimland, B. *Infantile autism.* New York: Appleton-Century-Crofts, 1964.

Rimland, B. Inside the mind of the autistic savant. *Psychology Today,* 1978, *12*, 68–80.

Risley, T., Wolf, M. Establishing functional speech in echolalic children. *Behavior Research and Therapy,* 1967, *5*, 73–88.

Ross, N. Manifestation of hyperlexia in eight autistic boys. Unpublished Master's thesis, University of California, 1979.

Rubin, H., Barr, A., Dwyer, J. An experimental speech and language program for psychotic children. *Journal of Speech and Hearing Disorders,* 1967, *32*, 242–248.

Rutter, M. Prognosis: Psychotic children in adolescence and early adult life. In J. Wing (Ed.), *Early childhood autism: Clinical, educational, and social aspects.* London: Pergamon Press, 1966, 83–100.

Rutter, M., Lockyer, L. A five to fifteen year follow-up study of infantile psychosis. I. Description of sample. *British Journal of Psychiatry*, 1967, *113*, 1169–1182.

Rutter, M., Greenfeld, D., Lockyer, L. A five to fifteen year follow-up study of infantile psychosis. II. Social and behavioral outcome. *British Journal of Psychiatry*, 1967, *113*, 1183–1199.

Rutter, M. Concepts of autism: A review of research. *Journal of Child Psychology and Psychiatry*, 1968, *9*, 1–25.

Rutter, M., Bartak, L. Causes of infantile autism: Some considerations from recent research. *Journal of Autism and Childhood Schizophrenia*, 1971, *1*, 20–32.

Rutter, M., Bartak, L., Newman, S. Autism: A central disorder of cognition and language. In M. Rutter (Ed.), *Infantile autism: Concepts, characteristics, and treatment*. Edinburgh: Churchill Livingstone, 1971, 148–172.

Rutter, M. The development of infantile autism. *Psychological Medicine*, 1974, *4*, 147–163.

Salvin, A., Routh, D., Foster, R., et al. Acquisition of modified American sign language by a mute autistic child. *Journal of Autism and Childhood Schizophrenia*, 1977, *7*(4), 359–371.

Scheerer, M., Rothman, E., Goldstein, K. A case of "idiot savant": An experimental study of personality organization. *Psychological Monographs*, 1945, *58*(4), 63.

Schmidt, D., Frankling, R., Edwards, J. Reinforcement of autistic children's responses to music. *Psychological Reports*, 1976, *39*(2), 571–577.

Schreibman, L., Carr, E. Elimination of echolalic responding to questions through the training of a generalized verbal response. *Journal of Applied Behavior Analysis*, 1978, *11*, 453–463.

Schuler, A. Echolalia: Issues and clinical implications. *Journal of Speech and Hearing Disorders*, 1979, *44*(4), 411–435.

Schull, R., Stark, J., Giddan, J. Development of language behavior in an autistic child. *Journal of Speech and Hearing Disorders*, 1967, *32*, 51–64.

Sedlackova, E., Neshidalova, R. Development of autistic children with special regard to their means of verbal expression. *Folia Phoniatrica*, 1975, *27*, 157–165.

Shapiro, T. The quest for a linguistic model to study the speech of autistic children. *Journal of the American Academy of Psychiatry*, 1977, *16*, 608–619.

Shapiro, T., Kapit, R. Linguistic negation in autistic and normal children. *Journal of Psycholinguistic Research*, 1978, *7*(5), 337–351.

Shapiro, T., Lucy, P. Echoing in autistic children: A chronometric study of semantic processing. *Journal of Child Psychology and Psychiatry*, 1978, *19*, 373–378.

Shapiro, T., Roberts, A., Fish, B. Imitation and echoing in young schizophrenic children. *Journal of the American Academy of Child Psychiatry*, 1970, *9*, 548–565.

Shaw, W. Treatment of a schizophrenic speech disorder by operant conditioning to play therapy. *Canadian Psychiatric Association Journal*, 1969, *14*, 631–634.

Shervanian, C. The speech development of precommunicative psychotic children. Unpublished doctoral dissertation, University of Pittsburgh, 1959.

Sherwin, A. Reactions to music of autistic (schizophrenic) children. *American Journal of Psychiatry*, 1953, *109*, 823–831.

Shoumaker, R., Bennet, D., Bray, P., et al. Clinical and EEG manifestations of an unusual aphasic syndrome in children. *Neurology*, 1971, *24*, 10–16.

Silberberg, N., Silberberg, M. Hyperlexia: Specific word recognition skills in young children. *Exceptional Children*, 1967, *34*, 41–42.

Silberg, J. The development of pronoun usage in the psychotic child. *Journal of Autism and Childhood Schizophrenia*, 1978, *8*(4), 413–425.

Simmons, J., Baltaxe, C. Language patterns of autistics who have reached adolescence. *Journal of Autism and Childhood Schizophrenia*, 1975, *5*, 333–351.

Simmons, J., Tymchuk, A. The learning deficits in childhood psychosis. *Pediatric Clinics of North America*, 1973, *20*, 665–679.

Simon, N. Echolalic speech in childhood autism. *Archives of General Psychiatry*, 1975, *32*, 1439–1446.

Slobin, D., Welsh, C. Elicited imitation as a research tool in developmental psycholinguistics. In C. Ferguson and D. Slobin (Eds.), *Studies of child language development*. New York: Holt, Reinhardt, and Winston, 1967.

Smith, C. An experimental approach to children's linguistic competence. In J.R. Hayes (Ed.) *Cognition and the development of language*. New York: John Wiley and Sons, 1970, 109–136.

Sparks, R., Albert, M., Helm, N. Melodic intonation therapy for aphasics. *Archives of Neurology*, 1973, *29*, 13–131.

Sparks, R., Geschwind, N. Dichotic listening in man after section of neocortical commisures. *Cortex*, 1968, *4*, 3–16.

Sparks, R., Holland, A. Method: Melodic intonation therapy for aphasia. *Journal of Speech and Hearing Disorders*, 1976, *41*, 287–297.

Sperry, M., Gazzaniga, M., Bogen J. Interhemispheric relationships: The neocortical commisures. Syndromes of hemispheric disconnection. In P.J. Vilden and G.W. Bruyn (Eds.), *Handbook of clinical neurology*, Vol. 4: *Disorders of speech, perception, and symbolic behavior*, Amsterdam: Northolland Publishing, 1969.

Stampe, D. The acquisition of phonetic representation. *Papers from the Fifth Regional Meeting of the Chicago Linguistic Society*. Chicago, Ill.: 1969, 443–454.

Stengel, E. A clinical and psychological study of echo reactions. *Journal of Mental Science*, 1947, *93*, 598–612.

Symmes, J. S. Visual imagery in brain-damaged children. *Proceedings from the Seventy-ninth Annual Convention of the American Psychological Association*, Washington, D.C.: American Psychological Association, 1971, 179–180.

Tanguay, P. Neurophysiological models of early infantile autism. *University of Ottawa Medical Journal*, 1972, *17*, 3–6.

Tanguay, P. Clinical and electrophysiological research. In E. Ritvo (Ed.), *Autism, diagnosis, current research, and management*. New York: Spectrum Publications, 1976.

Tilton, J., DeMeyer, M., Loew, L. *Annotated bibliography on childhood schizophrenia, 1955–1964.* New York: Grune & Stratton, 1966.

Tubbs, V. Types of linguistic disability in psychotic children. *Journal of Mental Deficiency Research*, 1966, *10*, 23–24.

Tymchuk, A., Simmons, J., Neafsey, S. Intellectual characteristics of adolescent childhood psychotics with high verbal ability. *Journal of Mental Deficiency Research*, 1977, *21*, 133–138.

van Harskamp, F., van Dongen, J., Loonen, M. Acquired aphasia with convulsive disorders in children: A case study with a seven year follow-up. *Brain and Language*, 1978, *6*(2), 141–148.

Viscott, D. A musical idiot savant. *Psychiatry*, 1970, *33*, 494–515.

Vygotsky, L. *Thought and language* (E. Hanfmann and G. Vakar, trans). Cambridge, Mass.: M.I.T. Press, 1962.

Wada, J., Clarke, R., Hamm, A. Cerebral hemispheric asymmetry in humans. *Archives of Neurology*, 1975, *32*, 239–246.

Walker, H., Bortner, M. Concept usage in schizophrenic children. *Journal of Autism and Childhood Schizophrenia*, 1975, *5*(2), 155–167.

Ward, T., Hoddinott, B. The development of speech in an autistic child. *Acta Paedopsychiatrica*, 1968, *35*, 199–215.

Weir, R. *Language in the crib.* The Hague: Mouton and Company, 1962.

Wieman, L. Stress patterns in early child language. *Journal of Child Language*, 1976, *3*, 283–286.

Wildman, R., Simon, S. An indirect method for increasing the rate of social interaction in an autistic child. *Journal of Clinical Psychology*, 1978, *34*(1), 133–139.

Wing, J. *Early childhood autism: Clinical, educational and social aspects.* Oxford, England: Pergamon Press, 1966.

Worst, E. Intelligence prognosis for autistic children. *Paediatric Paedology*, 1977, *12*(2), 112–117 (translation).

Yuwiler, A., Geller, E., Ritvo, E. Neurobiochemical research. In E. Ritvo (Ed.), *Autism: Diagnosis, current research and management.* New York: Spectrum Publications, Inc., 1976.

Peter F. Ostwald

# 15
# Speech and Schizophrenia

This chapter deals with the problems of schizophrenia: a group of psychiatric illnesses that are frequently but not inevitably associated with disturbances of speech and communication. Our focus is on the history of the schizophrenia concept, the major symptoms of these diseases, and aspects of their phenomenology that are pertinent to the science of speech. Spectrographic examples and other objective data from the clinical analysis of schizophrenic speech are included.

## HISTORY AND DEFINITIONS OF SCHIZOPHRENIA

Schizophrenia is a disease concept that originiated in psychiatric practice at the beginning of the 20th century when Emil Kraepelin (1855–1926) successfully described and classified the major mental illnesses prevalent at this time. Specific remedies for certain brain conditions, especially those caused by syphilitic infection, were then being discovered. Under the label "dementia praecox," Kraepelin lumped a number of different psychoses that were apparently not of infectious or traumatic origin but made their appearance during relatively early phases of life, especially in the second and third decade. Although numerous physical manifestations characterized these illnesses, including marked disturbances of speech, no brain pathology was demonstrable at autopsy. (It should be mentioned that today's methods of studying the living brain, by means of sophisticated scanning procedures, suggest that there may indeed be organic deficits.) Eugen

Bleuler (1857–1939), a Swiss psychiatrist, suggested that dementia praecox might be caused by a chemical toxin. He gave the term "schizophrenia" to this group of diseases, and his protegé Carl Jung (1875–1961) reasoned that psychological factors—he called them "mental complexes"—were responsible for the release of these chemical substances. The assumption that neurochemical imbalances may play an essential role in the onset and duration of schizophrenic illnesses has gained increasing support over the years.

Bleuler and Jung both were influenced by the theories of Sigmund Freud (1856–1939) who believed that "unconscious" mental processes have the power to provoke psychiatric illness. Adolf Meyer (1866–1950), a Swiss-born psychiatrist who, by virtue of his professorships in New York and Maryland, had great influence on American psychiatry, promoted a viewpoint that emphasized social stresses as causative factors in mental disease. American psychiatry has in general leaned toward this position, and one man in particular, Harry Stack Sullivan (1892–1949), championed the idea that schizophrenia results from disturbances in interpersonal relationships.

Thus we see a variety of viewpoints in the field of schizophrenia research today (Fann, Karacan, Pokorny, et al., 1978). Neurobiologists explore chemical and anatomical factors; social psychiatrists look at the family and its cultural roots; psychotherapists emphasize the patients' thoughts and feelings; while other scientists investigate hereditary determinants. The schizophrenia concept has been much criticized, but in spite of several efforts to eliminate it altogether from psychiatric diagnosis, it seems to survive and certainly continues to be quite useful in medical practice (Wing, 1978). The incidence of schizophrenia ranges between one and six percent of the world's population, depending on the criteria used to define these illnesses. A very broad definition considers schizophrenia to be "trouble in maintaining self-esteem, security, and intimacy in human relationships (Will, 1975)." A much narrower definition is proposed by psychiatrists in the *Diagnostic and Statistical Manual* for the American Psychiatric Association. According to the *Manual,* schizophrenia must "always involve at least one of the following: delusions, hallucinations, or certain characteristic types of thought disorder" (*DSM*-III, 1980).

No matter what definition applies, the analysis of speech is of primary importance in diagnosing schizophrenic illnesses, since neither "trouble in human relationships" nor "delusions, hallucinations and thought disorder" can be ascertained without engaging the patient in verbal discourse.

Above all, it must be remembered that schizophrenia is not a unitary clinical entity but pertains to processes that can be phasic or continuous, quiescent or alarming, overt and covert. Speech may be totally absent during states of "catatonic" stupor or may be over productive when patients are excited. Vastly disorganized speech, accompanied by a great deal of silly or inappropriate behavior, is called "hebephrenic" schizophrenia, while "paranoid" and "pseudoneurotic" forms of the illness may present with only minimal speech pathology.

## PRIMARY AND SECONDARY DISTURBANCES IN SCHIZOPHRENIA

In his highly original monograph (Bleuler, 1950), the psychiatrist who coined the term "schizophrenia," attempted a clinical description on two levels. First he proposed an *internal* disorganization of the sequential process of thought, which produces a chaotic muddling of memories, feelings, perceptions, and motivational impulses. This Bleuler called the primary manifestations of schizophrenia. He then went on to describe how patients also show secondary or accessory disturbances, reflecting an attempt to compensate for, or to hide, control, or transform their primary difficulties. When only "mildly sick," writes Bleuler, schizophrenic patients may show little if any change in the *form* of their speech. But the *content* is altered, specifically in regard to the wish to "convey anything to, or communicate with their environment. Their thoughts are transformed into speech without relation to the environment. Many patients are constantly uttering chains of words; they talk but do not say anything." (p.147)

Bleuler further observed that more severely sick patients "may show *every imaginable* speech abnormality," citing for example peculiarities of intonation.

There is often an absence, exaggeration or misplacement of modulation. Speech may be abnormally loud, abnormally soft, too rapid, or too slow. Thus, one patient speaks in a falsetto voice, another mumbles, a third grunts. A catatonic speaks in precisely the same fashion during inspiration as during expiration, another has no intonation at all. (pp. 148–149)

Speech at times sounds inappropriate in relation to its content according to Bleuler, a person may say cheerful things in a sorrowful tone, or may giggle while talking about something sad. Above all, "the connection between concept and linguistic expression has loosened" (p. 149). New words ("neologisms") are coined without regard to the usual rules of language. Schizophrenics may distort the grammatical structure of sentences ("paragrammatisms"). In far advanced cases of schizophrenia the result is that the patient's speech becomes unintelligible, resembling a "word salad" or an "artificial language."

The idea that a breakdown of association patterns is the primary mechanism in schizophrenia has been challenged. Bleuler probably overemphasized it because of his own synesthetic way of associating sounds with visual sensations (Ostwald, 1964). Association psychology was of much greater interest to psychiatrists of the early twentieth century than it is today, and we now know that many people, when they are sleepy, exhausted, intoxicated, inattentive, or emotionally excited, can produce speech errors and disturbed behavior that resembles schizophrenia. In some countries, such as the U. S. S. R., psychiatrists adhere to the idea of a "spectrum" or schizophrenic illnesses which blend into the affective, the psychoneurotic, and the sociopathic forms of psychopathology (Ostwald and Zavarin, 1980); a similar notion, of "borderline syndromes," is currently popular in the U. S. A. Harrow and Prosen (1979) recently demonstrated that much of the bizarreness in schizophrenic speech is a product of the way these patients, while talking, are able to intermingle information from their past and their current life experiences. Thus, there does not seem to be one central "complex" of mental or emotional concern, but rather a multitude of problem areas with which schizophrenic patients cannot cope efficiently.

**SCHIZOPHRENIA AND COMMUNICATION**

It is important to emphasize that advances in speech science generally and studies of schizophrenic speech in particular have been influenced by the newer models of "communication" (Ostwald, 1977). An early proponent of these theories, Jurgen Ruesch (1957) urged investigators to focus on specific elements of the communication process involving schizophrenic patients and to recognize that nonverbal as well as verbal behavior is involved. Verbal behavior—words and sentences—is processed according to grammatical rules that drastically restrict meaningful discourse to logical categories. To reduce ambiguity, one strikes an acceptable balance between conventional and unconventional meanings. Nonverbal behavior, by contrast, is less rigidly tied to the dictionary. But using it effectively nevertheless requires a knowledge of conventions and the willingness to conform to certain standards.

Ruesch pointed out that many adult schizophrenics display uncoordinated movements, conducted with uneven acceleration or deceleration, at a tempo that seems too slow or too fast. This may influence speech, for example if a patient "jumps" two or three intermediary steps of a dialogue, or gives "tangential" responses that are insufficient or misleading for sensible conversation (Ruesch, 1972).

Forrest and his colleagues (1969) have described the "wandering quality" of schizophrenic speech. They attribute this to abnormal learning experiences within the family. Unfortunately, parents, especially mothers, are often blamed for producing psychiatric problems in their children. But social transmission may not be the basic mechanism involved. There seems to be a hereditary factor in schizophrenia, since genetic transmission may be involved (Cancro, 1978). Disorders in focusing on the surface structure of language (Pavy, 1968), an inability to disambiguate redundant speech signals (Maher, 1972), distractibility (Grant et al., 1975), and disattention (Cromwell and Dokecki, 1968) have all been postulated in schizophrenia. Roger Brown (1973), a noted psycholinguist, has criticized much of this research, stating that "the formal cues of grammar and prosody seem of little or no importance" in giving the impression that a person is schizophrenic. According to Brown it is "the meaning or content that guides the judgment." He points out that rules of grammar may be easier to specify than rules of meaning, and suggests that mental illness is a judgment made about people who depart from the rules governing how "we really use" rather than how we "ought to use" rational mental operations.

Wynne and colleagues (1970) have worked with clinical observations, conjoint family therapy, Rorschach protocols, and other psychological test methods to demonstrate differences between the *expressive* and the *instrumental* use of communicative behavior. Expressive relatedness has to do with the more affectionate and spontaneous aspects of being together, the human contact and intimacy people generally seek in their relationships with each other. Instrumental relatedness requires shared and focused attention to specific tasks that are external to the human participants, a kind of being together which is forced on them in the course of having to get a particular job done. Both the speech and the paralanguage of schizophrenics seems to indicate a quest for "instant relatedness" at the expense of conventional task orientations. This results in the breakdown of language as an instrumentality for mutual problem solving and may be part of the patients' "dismissal and neglect of the more grubby aspects of task orientation and attention to specific content in communication."

### Studies of Schizophrenic Speech

The possibility of recording on magnetic tape all of the sounds that people make when they engage in speech, or when they are trying to inhibit their speech, has radically changed our understanding of communication (Ostwald, 1963). Whereas in the past, transcripts of psychiatric interviews drew attention mainly to the spoken words of the patient—those that could be understood and transcribed—today we have virtually all acoustical events of such interviews available.

Tapes usually include what the psychiatrist has said to the patient, in addition to the patient's own speech. An objective analysis of these tapes reveal a wealth of data. Teams of investigators, usually interdisciplinary groups composed of psychiatrists and linguists, have consumed months if not years transcribing mere bits and pieces of dialogue (Pittenger, Hockett, and Danehy, 1960; Labov and Fanshel, 1977).

When tape-recorded speech is analyzed, serious questions may arise as to the interpretation of what the patient has actually said. For example, after it was subjected to a fine-grained linquistic analysis including articulatory and vocal features (Ostwald, 1964), a single sentence spoken by an acutely excited adolescent diagnosed to be schizophrenic, suggested seventy-two different meanings. The sentence in question was

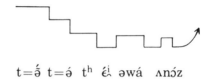

t=ə́ t=ə́ tʰ ɛ́ⁱ əwá ʌnɔ́z

and the possibilities of interpretation included the following:

$$\text{(Don't) don't tell} \begin{Bmatrix} \text{her} \\ \text{him} \end{Bmatrix} \begin{Bmatrix} \text{what} \\ \text{why} \\ \text{by} \end{Bmatrix} \begin{Bmatrix} \text{you} \\ \text{yours} \\ \text{her} \end{Bmatrix} \begin{Bmatrix} \text{knows} \\ \text{nose} \end{Bmatrix}$$

Even when embedded in dialogue, this patient's sentences were extremely difficult to disambiguate. For example, at one point in the interview the psychiatrist asked whether the patient had any brothers or sisters. The patient answered:

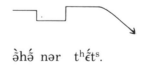

ə̀hə̰́ nər tʰɛ́tˢ.

The doctor assumed this meant "a hundred ten," clearly a crazy answer. By repeating "a hundred ten?" the psychiatrist indicated his disbelief, and the patient then responded as follows:

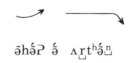

ə̀hə̰́ʔ ə́ ʌr̰tʰə̰́n̰

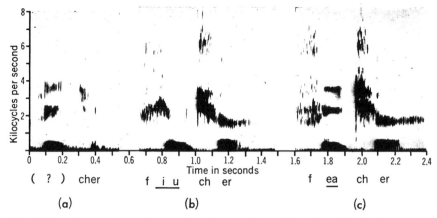

Fig. 15-1.  Comparison of a word spoken by the patient (a) with similar words spoken by normal persons (b) and (c). The spectrogram reveals a lack of proper acoustic cues for identifying the patient's vowel sounds, particularly in the first syllable. (From Ostwald and Skolnikoff, 1966. Reproduced with permission of the publishers of *Postgraduate Medicine*.

This response sounded like both agreement ("ahah") and denial (rise in pitch), followed by an "uh" and then a statement that the psychiatrist took to mean "under ten," a somewhat more rational yet still quite puzzling answer to his question.

Acoustic spectrography enables investigators to analyze samples of defective speech without having to rely solely on phonetic notation, which, at best, is only an approximation and cannot do justice to the complexity of an actual speech signal.

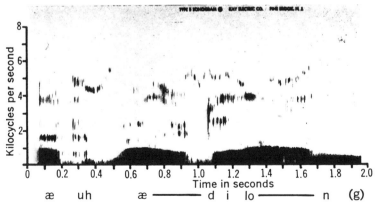

Fig. 15-2.  Spectrogram illustrating the patient's speech. (From Ostwald and Skolnikoff, 1966. Reproduced with permission of the publishers of *Postgraduate Medicine*.)

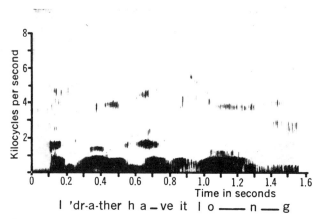

I 'dr-a-ther h a _ ve it I o ——— n __ g

Fig. 15-3.   Spectrogram illustrating the patient's speech. (From Ostwald and Skolnikoff, 1966. Reproduced with permission of the publishers of *Postgraduate Medicine.)*

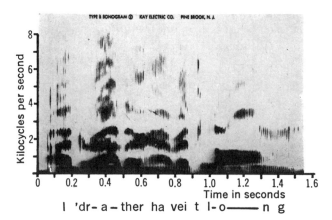

I 'dr- a – ther ha vei t I-o——— n g

Fig. 15-4.   Spectrogram of a normal person saying the same sentence as that shown in Figures 15-2 and 15-3. Note the absence of distinctive acoustic features in the patient's speech, particularly the poor quality of his vowel formants (resonance-energy bands) and lack of clearly articulated stop consonants. (From Ostwald and Skolnikoff, 1966. Reproduced with permission of the publishers of *Postgraduate Medicine.)*

In one such study with a fifteen-year-old schizophrenic, Ostwald and Skolnikoff (1966) selected by ear those segments that sounded most strikingly abnormal. Words containing unidentifiable vowels often could not be understood. For example, a word uttered by the patient sounded like "teacher," or possibly "preacher," but the patient was trying to say "future." Spectographic analysis showed an absence of discriminative phonations. Friction noises for the perception of the consonants *f* and *ch* were missing. Also, there was such paucity of acoustical energy above 4,000 Hz that the formant structure of the vowels remained obscure. Compare the patient's speech (a) with a normal speaker saying "future" (b) versus "feature" (c) (see Figure 15-1). With persistent effort, this patient was still unable to enunciate clearly. Spectrographic analysis of an obscure sentence, "I'd rather have it long," showed an absence of upper formants (see Figure 15-2). Even after practicing how to say the sentence more distinctly, the patient produced an abnormal pattern (see Figure 15-3), as shown if one compares it to normal speech (see Figure 15-4).

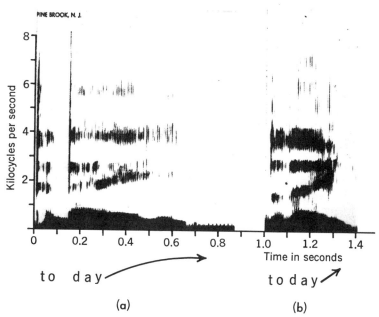

Fig. 15-5. Spectrograms comparing certain vocal and paralinguistic patterns of a schizophrenic and normal person's speech: (a) elongation of patient's terminal vowel sounds producing a baby-like pleading sound at the end of questions; (b) the same question as spoken by a normal person. (From Ostwald and Skolnikoff, 1966. Reproduced with permission of the publishers of *Postgraduate Medicine.)*

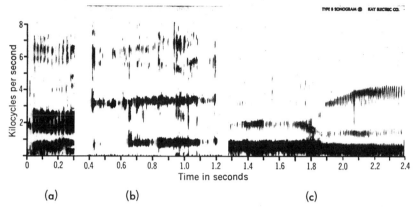

(a)                    (b)                                    (c)

Fig. 15-6. Spectrograms of noises produced by the patient at times of great emotional tension or excitement: (a) a rasp; (b) a froglike "squeak squawk", (c) a growl that sounded like "aw-er." (From Ostwald and Skolnihoff, 1966. Reproduced with permission of the publishers of *Postgraduate Medicine*.)

Spectrographic methods have also been used to study certain vocal and paralinguistic anomalies associated with schizophrenia. For example, the patient mentioned in the previous case study manifested an exaggerated intonation pattern. Where a brief rise of pitch at the end of questions would be sufficient to produce the required effect, the patient emitted inappropriately prolonged elevation of pitch. Compare the .45 second terminal pitch-rise at the end of the patient's utterance "today" (a) with the same word spoken in the same context by a normal subject (b) (see Figure 15-5). This patient occasionally made noises resembling animal calls that defy phonetic transcription. Here are spectrograms of a sort of rasp (a), squeak (b), and growl (c) (see Figure 15-6).

### The "Speaking Voice" of the Schizophrenic Patient

Disturbances in vocal behavior associated with mental disease have long been of interest to psychiatrists. Eight anomalous patterns were described in a spectrographic study of several different illnesses (including schizophrenia) by Ostwald (1964):

1. Rapidly intermittent sounds
2. Predominance of noises
3. Prolonged emission of continuous sound

4. Ultra rapid frequency shifts
5. Sustained and unvarying frequency levels
6. Abrupt lapses of acoustic output
7. Sudden increased sound levels
8. Hyperresonant tonal sounds

Such findings may be used clinically in the analysis of schizophrenic speech. For example, when separated into "chant," "screech," and "normal" vocalization and analyzed in terms of three levels of verbal meaning—utter nonsense, stereotyped slogans, meaningful messages—a patient's voice was shown to be "screechy" almost exclusively while uttering meaningful verbal material (Ostwald, 1965). By contrast, this patient's "normal" voice accompanied slogans, nonsense, and messages almost equally (see Figure 15-7). These findings led the treating physician to assume that the patient reserved his verbally most meaningful speech for those times when, by screeching, he indicated an urgency to be heard. One is reminded of the parable of the boy who cried "wolf" so often that his calls finally were ignored. The phenomenon has been called a double-bind—the patient wants to be heard but doesn't want to speak.

Spoerri (1964) has given the label "paraphonia" to vocal phenomena of this sort. His treatise has not yet been translated, but an article published in the United States (Spoerri, 1966) showed spectrograms of the breathy, squeaky voice of a chronically ill woman, together with the monotonous and noisy voices of two male schizophrenics. The following incidence figures referable to schizophrenic speech pathology were included:

| | |
|---|---|
| Dysarticulation | 90% |
| Unusual consonant forms | 56% |
| Difficulties with beginning of speech | 24% |
| Intonation disturbances | 23% |
| Abnormal volume | 20% |
| Rhythm disturbed | 18% |
| Abnormal timbre (tone-quality) | 18% |
| Unusual register | 10% |
| Unusual tone | 6% |

Without information about the precise age, educational level, language background, and neurological status of psychiatric patients, it would be hazardous to draw any conclusions about the diagnostic significance of their "paraphonias," and Spoerri (1964) has clearly cautioned that *it is not possible to make a diagnosis of schizophrenia from the voice changes alone.*

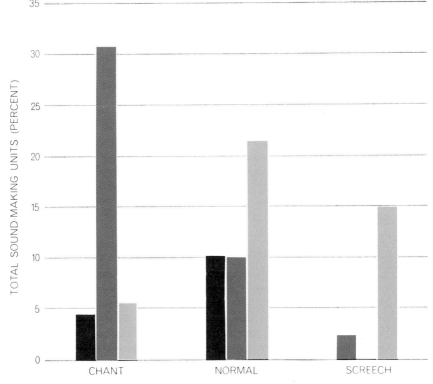

Fig. 15-7. CONTENT AND STYLE of a patient's speech are correlated in this
chart. The entire verbal output of a schizophrenic boy was divided
into three categories with meaningful statements called "message,"
advertisements and other set expressions classed as "slogan," and
meaningful statements called "nonsense." The child's vocal styles
were then divided into three predominant types: a screech, a chant
and a normal voice characteristic of healthy boys his age. By this
technique it was shown that the boy spoke his most meaningful statements in the voice of high frequency that expressed the greatest de-
sire to be heard. (From Ostwald, P.F. Acoustic methods in psychiatry,
© by Scientific American, Inc. All rights reserved.)

Since voice changes that involve disturbances of respiration, intonation, and tone quality are more continuous than the articulatory
defects described by acoustic spectrography, it has been useful to apply other methods of analysis. Octave, half-octave, and third-octave
band filtration readily demonstrates certain audible features of
schizophrenic speech (e.g., the inhibited voice of a terribly frightened
patient and the improved vocalization resulting from effective treatment [Ostwald, 1965]). Voice is of course a prime instrument for display of emotion, and part of the so-called "inappropriate affect" shown

by schizophrenics may well reflect their inability to verbalize feelings of panic, hostility, and despair (Gottheil, Thornton, and Exline, 1976). Darby and Sherk (1979) have reviewed several other studies of schizophrenic vocal behavior, including the effects of sex differences (Chevrie-Muller *et al.*, 1971) and of antipsychotic medication (Bannister, 1972) on a variety of auditory—acoustic parameters. In terms of the differential diagnosis of mental illness, a recent study of 52 patients whose speech was subjected to computerized analysis of its spectral characteristics showed that acoustical parameters were definitely useful in classifying patients as being manic, schizophrenic, or depressed (Andreason, Alpert, and Martz, 1979).

## ACQUISITION OF PATHOLOGICAL SPEECH

Fundamental to the problem of speech pathology in schizophrenia is the question of its acquisition. One assumption stemming from newer models of language acquisition (McNeill, 1970) is that schizophrenic speech may be acquired as a result of faulty learning experiences. While there continues to be a debate about how much of the capacity for language acquisition is built into the brain as an "innate" or prenatal propensity versus how much of this depends on interpersonal and social experience following birth, considerable evidence points toward the fact that the first 10 to 15 years of life are crucial for learning how to speak. Children deprived of linguistic input because of hearing problems and/or social neglect appear to show striking language deficits as they grow older, and after puberty the acquisition of communicative skills proceeds quite differently from those acquired during earlier formative years, presumably because of irreversible sensory-neuromuscular maturations that preclude the plasticity and spontaneity so characteristic of first-language learning (Lenneberg and Lenneberg, 1975).

A correlate of this statement would be that the earlier the onset of a schizophrenic illness, the more profound and debilitating are the patient's defects in communication and language. With early onset (childhood) autism, for example, there may be a total delay of speech development and muteness, or fixations along the course of development, echolalia, misuse or reversal of pronouns, and speech lacking appropriate intonation and rhythm (Ornitz and Ritvo, 1976). Most follow-up studies show a major language handicap, with about 50 percent of the patients remaining mute. That a peculiarity in the realm of audition is involved has been suggested by several studies, including the observation of unusual musicality among autistic children

(Ostwald, 1973), and the findings that autistic adolescents who demonstrate the most linguistic difficulty also do the most poorly on the Seashore Musical Tests (Simmons and Baltaxe, 1975).

Schizophrenic children show far more speech faults than do normal children, and the defects range broadly through many elements of vowel production, consonant articulation, rhythmic fluency, intonation, symbolization, and paralanguage. There appears to be no specific clustering of defects, but rather a marked tendency for schizophrenic children to "fluctuate from one extreme to the other in a number of voice and speech elements" (Goldfarb, Levy, and Meyers, 1972).

It is impossible to separate problems of speech acquisition from social interaction, particularly the mother–child relationship, wherein linguistic skills are acquired. As Bruner (1974) has so elegantly stated, "language acquisition occurs in the context of an 'action dialogue' in which joint action is being undertaken by infant and adult. The joint enterprise sets the deictic limits that govern joint reference, determines the need for a referential taxonomy, establishes the need for signaling intent, and provides a context for the development of explicit predication." Thus, it comes as no surprise that where there are schizophrenic children one also finds disturbed adults. One of the first studies of the speech of mothers of schizophrenic children (Goldfarb, Goldfarb, and Scholl, 1966) suggested a remarkable mutual impoverishment, and attributed this primarily to "the fact that these mothers of schizophrenic children are poor models for their children to emulate (and) are impaired in ability to communicate meaning and mood." (The fact that more of the mothers of patients were from upper-class families than the nonpatient control group did not seem to impress these investigators.) Their later study (Goldfarb, Yudkovitz, and Goldfarb, 1973) indicated that the mothers of schizophrenic children were more inclined to respond to the children's feedback responses in a fashion that "weakened the child's discriminations." During a "surprise visit" to the hospital, Goldfarb and colleagues (1972) found these mothers to demonstrate quite remarkable "failures" in stimulating, correcting, and responding to their children's speech.

The question arises whether parents of schizophrenic children may be trying to accommodate their own speech to that of the children. Frank et al. (1976) have described a tendency generally for mothers to speak with preschoolers at a level "much less complex than the one used in speaking with other adults, but slightly more complex than the language level of the child." When a child is autistic, the mother has more difficulty than the mother of a normal child to "simplify her language below a certain natural lower limit if she is to say anything substantial." That difficulty, in turn, may further upset a sick child.

Colby (1968) has experimented with the use of a digital computer, programmed to give verbal responses, as one way to circumvent the potentially disruptive effects of a human caretaker on the schizophrenic child. While results seem encouraging, at its present stage of development this method still requires an adult to help the child focus attention on and play with the machine.

An important problem is the diagnostic distinction between early-onset schizophrenia, infantile autism, and childhood aphasia—three conditions that may be associated with similar patterns of speech pathology. Developmental vicissitudes have to be considered as well. In a pioneering effort to correlate articulation errors with psychosexual immaturity, Rousey and Moriarty (1965) described a variety of defects that seem to indicate faulty emotional development. But the connection, if any, between these speech defects and schizophrenia remains obscure.

## THE INNER SPEECH OF SCHIZOPHRENIA

No discussion of speech and schizophrenia would be complete without mentioning the problems schizophrenic patients have with their nonvocalized or "inner" speech. It is part of everyone's experience that verbalizations—words, phrases, sentences, etc.—can appear in conscious awareness. This "inner" speech may be especially noticeable when one reminisces, or during the planning process in preparing to speak or to write. States of aloneness, or of meditation, can also draw attention to the inner speech. There may even be the perception of the sound of the speaker's voice as one thinks of what he or she is saying (Ostwald, 1967).

There is considerable clinical and experimental evidence to suggest that with schizophrenia the inner speech is altered in some substantial way. Especially when their emotions run high and their thinking becomes loosened, patients report intrusive "voices." Without recognizing these voices to be products of their own imagination, they report "broadcasts" or "messages" from outer space or even from within their own bodies. There may be entire "conversations" in which frightening, threatening, or mocking content is revealed. Patients are "criticized," or told to carry out unacceptably erotic, hostile, violent, or suicidal acts. No longer recognized as obsessional ideas, these demands or commands may then be put into action, sometimes with disastrous results.

Lauretta Bender (1967) observed that schizophrenic children, unlike schizophrenic adults, do not experience hallucinations of the projected type. Theirs is more of the introjected type—"they hear voices inside their head or other parts of the body, feel that they [the voices] originate inside themselves and do not feel persecuted by them." Among adults, in a study comparing schizophrenics with patients who had toxic psychoses and medical illnesses, Mott (1965) found that only the schizophrenics localize their hallucinations internally to any degree. Alpert and Silvers (1970) found that compared with hallucinating alcoholics, the schizophrenics' hallucinations are less localized in space and have more of a cognitive "taint" of audible thoughts. The voices not only speak to the patients, but also about them. Modell (1960) observed that schizophrenic hallucinations tend to be voices of people who have been significant in the patient's life—parents, siblings, acquaintances, friends, and lovers, but with whom the patient has lost contact.

It has been suggested that schizophrenics, while hallucinating, may be speaking to themselves. As pointed out earlier, their overt speech is not clear; they seem almost to mumble at times. The listener gets a sense of noncommunication. The patient's attention seems to turn inward, and there is more involvement with the inner flow of perceptions than with the outer world of persons and things. Gould (1949) in an interesting study of laryngeal movements, suggested that hallucinatory experiences occur while the patient is subvocalizing, a process that normally occurs without conscious awareness or with the realization that the inaudible speech is self-produced. In an unpublished study we attempted to record movements of the middle-ear muscles, using a Zwyslocki bridge. Our assumption was that a detectable disturbance of auditory physiology might accompany the hallucinatory experience. Unfortunately it was impossible to obtain the necessary consent and cooperation for such an investigation.

Patients who are gifted poets or writers have often shed light on the inner speech of schizophrenia (Freedman, 1974). For example:

Suddenly my thoughts went slower and slower, like a gramophone running down. Or else they dashed ahead faster and faster and to my horror I was thinking gibberish.

The process of thought is like a chain that has become clogged with muddy oil.

Sounds came to my ears. They meant little to me besides just noise—my immediate environment was blurred.

My conscious mind is like an information center whose staff are sick: as more of them become incapacitated, so the rest become more severely overworked. To send them a mass of new material to be worked out at this moment makes disorganization complete. Reason clocks off and leaves the door open to the inner mind. Unconscious impulses, like a band of irresponsible children, take over the telephone exchange and play around with the controls. (pp.335–337)

Other less talented schizophrenics may coin bizarre words or try to invent new languages. Forrest (1969) collected ninety new words ("neologisms") from a single patient, including such jaw-breakers as:

Pyrolegislation: laws pertaining to fire
Disproportionability: act of getting out of proportion
Superstylophototutorization: higher education

One of our patients seemed intent on creating her own alphabetical system. She was a poorly educated Black woman from a small southern town who in a northern metropolis felt handicapped by her regional dialect. During states of panic she would withdraw socially and begin to work out a complex scheme for transforming english letters into more accurate representations of her own idiolect. The result was an encyclopedia of phonetic transformations, of greater interest to psychopathologists than to phycholinguists.

Begaining of xspessing. By affurbetercul. Arranging from Z thee ending two thee a weich waars. Thee begaining.


## CONCLUSION

Schizophrenia is a clinical concept that has been used for the past three-quarters of a century to recognize, diagnose, and treat a group of mental illnesses. This chapter has focused on the following problems of schizophrenic speech disturbances: (1) disorganization of thinking and cognition; (2) fragmentation and projection of covert (inner) speech; (3) reduction and overabundance of overt (outer) speech; and (4) the transmission and acquisition of pathological patterns of communication. Clinical, phonetic, and spectrographic examples of schizophrenic speech have been given.

Application of acoustic—phonetic methodology to the analysis of schizophrenic behavior is presently at an early stage, but it appears promising and has already contributed to improvements in diagnosis and treatment. Discovery of more precise and pathognomonic speech patterns may be expected in due time, as progress is made in understanding the more manageable schizophrenic syndromes and relating them to biochemical, neurophysiological, and psychosocial determinants of disease.

REFERENCES

Alpert, M., Silvers, K. N. Perceptual characteristics distinguishing auditory hallucinations in schizophrenia and acute alcoholic psychosis. *American Journal of Psychiatry,* 1970, *127,* 298–302.

American Psychiatric Association, *Diagnostic and statistical manual of mental disorders.* (3rd ed.) Washington, D. C: American Psychiatric Association 1980.

Andreasen, N. C., Alpert, M., Martz, J. Acoustic analysis: A diagnostic aid in psychosis. In *Research Report No. NRI, American Psychiatric Association,* 1979.

Bannister, M. L. Unpublished Doctoral Dissertation, University of Kansas, 1972.

Bender, L., quoted in *Psychotomimetic Drugs,* D. Efron (Ed.). New York: Raven, 1969. p. 267.

Bleuler, E. *Dementia praecox or the group of schizophrenias.* J. Zinkin (trans.) New York: International Universities Press, 1950.

Brown, R. Schizophrenia, language, and reality. *American Psychologist,* 1973, *28,* 395–403.

Bruner, J. S. From communication to language: A Psychological perspective. *Cognition,* 1974, *3,* 255–287.

Cancro, R. Genetic factors in the group of the schizophrenias. In W. E. Fann, I. Karacan, A. D. Pokorny, et al. (Eds.), *Phenomenology and treatment of schizophrenia.* New York: Spectrum Publications, Inc., 1978, pp. 73–82.

Chevrie-Muller, D., Dodart, F., Sequier-Dermrer, N. et al. *Folia Phoniatrica,* 1971, *23,* 401–428.

Colby, K. M. Computer-aided language development in nonspeaking children. *Archives of General Psychiatry,* 1968, *19,* 641–651.

Cromwell, R. L., Dokecki, P. R. Schizophrenic language: A disattention interpretation. In S. Rosenberg and J. H. Kaplan (Eds.), *Developments in applied psycholinguistic research.* New York: MacMillan, 1968.

Darby, J. K., Sherk, A. Speech studies in psychiatric populations. In H. and P. Hollien (Eds.), *Current issues in the phonetic Sciences (Vol. 9, Part II).* Amsterdam: John Benjamins B. V., 1979, pp. 599–609.

Fann, W. E., Karacan, I., Pokorny, A. D., et al. (Eds.) *Phenomenology and treatment of schizophrenia.* New York: Spectrum Publications, Inc., 1978.

Forrest, D. V. New words and neologisms. *Psychiatry,* 1969, *32,* 44–73.

Forrest, A. D., Hay, A. J., Kushner, A. E. Studies in speech disorder in schizophrenia. *British Journal of Psychiatry,* 1969, *115,* 833–841.

Frank, S. M., Allen, D. A., Stein, L., et al. Linguistic performance in vulnerable and autistic children and their mothers. *American Journal of Psychiatry,* 1976, *133,* 909–915.

Freedman, B. J. The subjective experience of perceptual and cognitive disturbance in schizophrenia: A review of autobiographical accounts. *Archives of General Psychiatry,* 1965, *28,* 1–18.

Goldfarb, W., Goldfarb, N., Scholl, H. The speech of mothers of schizophrenic children. *American Journal of Psychiatry,* 1966, *122,* 1220–1227.

Goldfarb, W., Levy, D. M., Meyers, D. I. The mother speaks to her schizophrenic child: Language in childhood schizophrenia. *Psychiatry*, 1972, *35*, 217–226.

Goldfarb, W., Yudkovitz, E., Goldfarb, N. Verbal symbols to designate objects: An experimental study of communication in mothers of schizophrenic children. *Journal of Autism and Childhood Schizophrenia*, 1973, *3*, 281–298.

Gottheil, E., Thornton, C. C., Exline, R. V. Appropriate and background affects in facial displays of emotion: Comparison of normal and schizophrenic males. *Archives of General Psychiatry*, 1976, *33*, 565–568.

Gould, L. N. Auditory hallucinations and subvocal speech: Objective study in a case of schizophrenia. *Journal of Nervous and Mental Disease*, 1949, *109*, 418–427.

Grant, S., Steingart, I., Freedman, N., et al. Organization of language behavior and cognitive performance in chronic schizophrenia. 1975, *84*, 621–628.

Harrow, M., Prosen, M. Schizophrenic thought disorders: Bizarre associations and intermingling. *American Journal of Psychiatry*, 1979, *136:3*, 293–296.

Labov, W., Fanshel, D. *Therapeutic discourse.* New York: Academic Press, 1977.

Lenneberg, E. H., Lenneberg, E. (Eds.). *Foundations of language development.* (Vol. I and II) New York: Academic Press, 1975.

Maher, B. The language of schizophrenia: A review and interpretation. *British Journal of Psychiatry*, 1972, *120*, 3–17.

McNeill, D. *The acquisition of language: the study of developmental linguistics.* New York: Harper and Row, 1970.

Modell, A. H. An approach to the nature of auditory hallucinations in schizophrenia. *Archives of General Psychiatry*, 1960, *3*, 259–266.

Mott, R. H. Comparative study of hallucinations. *Archives of General Psychiatry*, 1965, *12*, 595–601.

Ornitz, E. M., Ritvo, E. R. The syndrome of autism: A critical review *American Journal of Psychiatry*, 1976, *133*, 609–621.

Ostwald, P. F. *Soundmaking: The acoustic communication of emotion.* Springfield, Illinois: Charles C. Thomas, 1963.

Ostwald, P. Color hearing: A missing link between normal perception and the hallucination. *Archives of General Psychiatry*, 1964, *11*, 40–47.

Ostwald, P. F. How the patient communicates about disease with the doctor. In T. A. Sebeok, A. S. Hayes, M. C. Bateson (Eds.), *Approaches to semiotics.* The Hague: Mouton, 1964.

Ostwald, P. F. Acoustic manifestations of emotional disturbance. *Disorders of communication.* (Vol. XLII) Research Publications, A. R. N. M. D., 1964.

Ostwald, P. F. Acoustic methods in psychiatry. *Scientific American*, *1965, 212*, 82–91.

Ostwald, P. F., Skolnikoff, A. Z. Speech disturbances in a schizophrenic adolescent. *Postgraduate Medicine*, 1966, *40*, 40–49.

Ostwald, P. F. The inner speech psychotherapy. *American Journal of Psychotherapy*, 1967, *21*, 757–766.

Ostwald, P. F. Musical behavior in early childhood. *Developmental Medicine Child Neurology*, 1973, *15*, 367–375.

Ostwald, P. F. (Ed.) *Communication and social interaction.* New York: Grune & Stratton, 1977.

Ostwald, P. F. Language and communication problems with schizophrenic patients: A review, commentary and synthesis. In W. E. Fann, I. Karacan, A. D. Pokorny, et al. (Eds.), *Phenomenology and treatment of schizophrenia.* New York: Spectrum Publications, Inc., 1978, pp. 163–191.

Ostwald, P. F., & Zavarin, V. Studies of language and schizophrenia in the U.S.S.R. In R. Rieber (Ed.), *Applied psycholinguistics and mental health.* New York: Plenum Press, 1980, pp. 69-92.

Pavy, D. Verbal behavior in schizophrenia: A review of recent studies. *Psychological Bulletin*, 1968, *70*, 164–178.

Pittenger, R. E., Hockett, C. F., Danehy, J. J. *The first five minutes: a sample of microspcopic interview analysis.* Ithaca: Paul Martineau, 1960.

Rousey, C. L., Moriarty, A. E. *Diagnostic implications of speech sounds.* Springfield, Illinois: Charles C. Thomas, 1965.

Ruesch, J. The schizophrenic patient's ways of communication. In J. Ruesch (Ed.), *Semiotic approaches to human relations.* The Hague: Mouton, 1972, pp. 635–647.

Ruesch, J. The tangential response, In J. Ruesch (Ed.), *Semiotic approaches to human relations.* The Hague: Mouton, 1972, pp. 354–364.

Simmons, J. Q., Baltaxe, C. Language patterns of adolescent autistics. *Journal of Autism and Childhood Schizophrenia*, 1975, *5*, 333–351.

Spoerri, T. H. *Sprachphänomene und psychose.* Basel: Karger, 1964.

Spoerri, T. H. Speaking voice of the schizophrenic patient. *Archives of General Psychiatry*, 1966, *14*, 581–585.

Will, O. A. Schizophrenia: Psychological treatment. In A. M. Freedman, H. I. Kaplan, B. J. Sadock (Eds.), *Comprehensive textbook of psychiatry/II* (Vol. 1) Baltimore, Md.: WIlliams and Wilkins, 1975, pp. 939–954.

Wing, J. K. *Reasoning about madness.* London and New York: Oxford University Press, 1979.

Wynne, L. C. Communication disorders and the quest for relatedness in families of schizophrenics. *American Journal of Psychoanalysis*, 1970, *30*, 100–114.

Hemmo Müller-Suur

# 16
# Spoerri's Descriptions
# of Psychotic Speech

## EDITOR'S PREFACE

Theodor Spoerri published the results of his extensive study of speech and language phenomena in psychoses as *Sprachphänomene und Psychose* in 1964. Unfortunately, Spoerri died in 1973, and his studies have never been translated from the original German. His book emphasized the expressive, emotive, and communicative aspects of both speech and language disturbances in psychotic patients. This was the first such study in Europe and represented an original approach.

Spoerri's primary interest was in the unique nature of each individual as a creative human being. Consequently, his research placed a secondary emphasis on diagnosis and the nature of disease process. Much of Spoerri's work was of a descriptive nature, and his case portraits reveal sensitive and keen observational powers. Herein lies one of the great values of his research. It appears that Spoerri provided detailed descriptions of speech and language alterations in certain psychoses which bear close resemblance to findings in America. Sufficient information is available which suggests that certain patterns of disturbance can be discerned within and among selected psychotic conditions.

Due to the descriptive nature of Spoerri's work and the lack of measurement systems, cross case comparisons are not possible.

---

This chapter was translated by Karl Kaussen and edited by John K. Darby

Spoerri's original work has been summarized by Professor Hemmo Müller-Suur, translated into English by Karl Kaussen, and revised, edited, and organized into diagnostic groupings by the editor of this volume. Occasional editorial remarks are noted in brackets.

## SPOERRI'S METHODS AND CONCEPTS

Spoerri's research was carried out in a standardized situation with a protocol. A microphone was placed 50–60 centimeters in front of the patient in a soundproof room. A remote controlled recorder was placed in an adjacent room. After proper patient preparation, conversations of 10–40 minutes were recorded. In each case nonverbal behaviors were noted, and in several cases the interviews were filmed.

Spoerri intensively evaluated 400 cases who were selected from a population of 14,500 patients. Ninety-two percent of the subjects were schizophrenic. Diagnosis, however, was of secondary importance to Spoerri. His primary intent was to capture the peculiarity of the psychotic patient's speech and language behaviors.

Spoerri observed three dimensions of speech and language behavior: (1) expressive, emotive value, (2) communicative value, and (3) informational value. He believed that the order of importance of these elements in the "speaking voice" (expressive, communicative, informative) was reversed for that of language. He noted that these paralinguistic features could serve to influence the expressive emotive value, as well as to cause semantic shifts of meaning. Spoerri also paid close attention to the congruity between *what* the patient said and *how* the patient said it.

For purposes of this chapter, selected case examples have been excerpted from four patterns of speech and language alterations.

1. *Language destruction* with disorganized speech patterns in acute psychoses
2. *Language reduction* with depletion and restriction of linguistic facility in chronic psychoses
3. *Neoformation of language* in late stages of schizophrenia
4. *Unique linguistic phenomena* in which language is reduced to mere voice patterns without expressive, communicative, or informational value.

Each case is typically described with reference to language function, speech behavior, and interpretation of the phenomena.

## CASE STUDIES: LANGUAGE DESTRUCTION

### Alcohol Delirium

One case of subacute alcohol delirium served to demonstrate how interrupted continuity of speech flow with a rapid succession of fragments ("language segments") resulted in a "telegram style." Here the voice was loud, well articulated, and harsh at the onset, but would become slow or hurried in accordance with outside experiences. The "speech segments" consisting of one- or two-word groups were self-contained melodious units. Quite often one or two short sentences were bunched together, which terminated with falling pitch.

In a second case of severe alcohol delirium, not only the flow of language was destroyed, but also the unity of the sentence and of the vocal acoustic figure. The phenomenon of such a radical disturbance in which the semantic units of speech disintegrate was defined as a "language whirl."

In this case the voice was described as being chopped up, bleating, hurried, and bursting out in spurts, while at the same time rapid panting and strongly aspirated sounds were heard. Often there were repeated attempts to begin a sentence. Articulation was described as slurred and indistinct. Often the first syllable of a word and single sounds were repeated in the middle of a word. There was a rapid variation of sound intensity even within the words, resulting in a "phonatory tremor." Abrupt interruptions with screams and stammering produced haphazardly assembled sound combinations. Declarative sentences with adequate dynamic intonation were reported as being sporadic and occurred only as answers to questions.

### Depression

In a case of agitated depression there was repetition of short sentences or sentence fragments that tended to turn into amorphous wailing coupled with monotonous language that centered on the theme of sin. The pattern was defined as "speech circling" as an indication of the patient's obsession with himself and his limited ability to communicate.

The speaking voice showed a strikingly fast speech pattern. The patient burst out in whimpering lamentation, ending up with anxious breathing or convulsive sobbing. The sobbing seemed to remain even as a subliminal part of slow moving speech. With each new sentence, a new intonation or melodic pattern began. The repetitions were observed to be interrupted by sobbing, often uttered in the same vocal pattern. The appearance of monotony was produced by the fact that certain utterances of like configuration were constantly repeated. The vocal monotony combined with halting speech and monotonous whimpering produced a serious dissolution of form.

[Editor's note: The combination of convulsive sobbing interspersed with melodically repetitious speech patterns produces a striking effect, which the editor has observed in other cases.]

### Excitation States

A case of hypomanic excitation exhibited accentuated speech, which was melodically flowing in its repeated patterns. The conversational pattern was disorganized ("fleeting ideas"), and reference to the addressed person was lacking, which gave an overall impression of superficial linguistic "gliding." The speaking voice was described as full, vocalic, strongly accentuated, and flowing in a swaying, melodious pattern. The tempo was fast, but there were slowdowns accompanied by syllable stress, and seemingly casual pauses. Strong accents were distinct, but since the intonation was uniformly monotonous, the emphasizing effect was reduced. The prominent factor was the melodic pattern with many dynamic rises of the pitch level.

[Editor's note: This hypomanic speech pattern has been similarly reported by Newman and Mather, 1938.]

In a case of acute catatonic excitation strongly articulated speech was delivered in a tense, thrusting, and staccato voice. Sentences and word groups were incoherent. Spoerri referred to this combination of speech and language alterations as "speech waves" and interpreted the psychological state as one of severe personal angst.

[Editor's note: The distinct differences in speech patterns suggest a possible link to the diagnostic differences.]

### Paranoid Schizophrenia

A patient with acute hallucinations of a paranoic type exhibited a speech and language pattern described as "disproportionate." The sentences contained heterogenous elements, without communicative value, and the vocal qualities and nonverbal behaviors were similarly not in connection or congruity with one another. The more the patient spoke for himself, the more disconcerting was the effect upon both the patient and the interviewer.

The sentences were often unconnected, incompletely articulated, and delivered in a "telegram-style." The flow of speech was frequently interrupted by hallucinatory voices. These interruptions were followed by a repetition of sentences which had occurred prior to the interruption.

The speaking voice was rather rapid with medium sound volume. Articulations were frequently unclear. The nonrelated word groups at times melted together into a melodic dynamic unit without concern for customary emphasis.

[**Editor's note:** In the editor's experience the speech and language features observed in certain individuals with paranoid schizophrenia give an impression of "peculiarity," which is particularly difficult to portray or describe.]

## CASE STUDIES: LANGUAGE REDUCTION

### Depression

One patient, who was a depressed chronic schizophrenic with a guilt complex, produced an impression of "speech stagnation," due to slow speech, sound lengthening, and long pauses.

Sounds were clearly articulated but exceptionally lengthened, and voice onset was hesitating. First syllables or words were frequently repeated. Melodic movement was minimal, and timbre was low and hollow. Seemingly tense pauses of up to 3 seconds duration occurred in the middle of sentences. Language was intact except for a propensity toward short sentences.

Another patient, with an endogenous depression, exhibited a "language dwindling," in which utterances were only half finished, the speech was meager, and the language seemed to "dry up." Spoerri felt this speech pattern reflected the patient's shrinking withdrawal from the outside world. Language content was related to somatic concerns.

The "speaking voice" was monotonous and exhibited psychomotor retardation. The voice was described as shaky, with a slow tempo, and low volume, which diminished further at the end of a word. The timbre was dull, vowels were shortened, and the volume dynamics markedly restricted.

Special mention was made of *sighs* occurring in the pauses. The sighs had no connection to speech content or surroundings, but were an expression of despair. The sighs were caused by slow inhalation where the rib case expands as under heavy pressure. The air was sucked in at a slowly increasing rate and was exhaled with strong pressure after a short pause. During inhalation and exhalation the mouth remained nearly closed and tense, accounting for the fricative character of the sighs.

[Editor's note: Although the above two cases have been translated and severely edited, the richness of their clinical description is still apparent. While the "language dwindling" excerpt is clinically familiar, the "speech stagnation" presents a new perspective on a pattern that clinicians today may associate with blocking.]

### Organic Psychoses

A patient with Korsakoff syndrome, due to chronic alcoholism, engaged in empty chatter of formulalike, rhythmic, repetition produced "meaningless phrases." This stereotyped conversation was considered to be a perseverative phenomenon. The speech revealed repetitious patterns of melody and rhythm, which gave the impression of droning recitations. Spoerri pointed out that the perseverative qualities of this speech should be differentiated from the automatic, reflexlike qualities of verbigeration seen in schizophrenia.

### Schizophrenia

Spoerri described a "driven-restricted" quality of speech as one of the common patterns seen in schizophrenia. Here, a mechanically driven speech tempo becomes increasingly faster until it is suddenly interrupted (restricted) by a pause due to inhalation. The case example illustrated a monotonous and mechanically speeded up "speaking, voice" with minimal melody, pitch contours resembling a straight line, and shortened vowels.

In another case Spoerri described a "syndrome of the submerged-distressed" schizophrenic speech pattern where the patient whispered monologues to himself. The "speaking voice" would vary from a pattern of slow tempo, low and hollow timbre, pauses, and monotonous pitch (submersion) to a faster, high timbre, and rising intonation pattern (distress).

In a third case, a "syndrome of a tense-relaxed" speech pattern occurred. Here the tense voice was whispered and interrupted by a choking voice ("Würgstimme") produced in strong, short bursts. Alternatively, the patient would speak in a lively, resonant, and relaxed manner.

[**Editor's note:** The above three cases testify to the fact that schizophrenic symptomatology has always been diverse and difficult to describe or decipher. One of the central features of the syndrome is an oscillation between polar opposite positions. This phenomenon may be interpreted either psychoanalytically (ego defense mechanisms) or biologically (failure of regulatory and modulatory damping mechanisms). In any case, Spoerri has elucidated this principle in speech patterns.]

## CASE STUDIES: NEOFORMATION OF LANGUAGE

Phenomena of new language formations were only observed in schizophrenia. Both the language structure and the "speaking voice" were altered so that language was changed in its expressive and referential aspects. Spoerri emphasized the finding of grammatical peculiarities and a propensity toward an accumulation of nouns and modifying adjectives. Hyperbole, paralogism, and contamination were prominent.

In two cases an artificial language was constructed from incomprehensible sound conglomerations which were produced in a stiff and automatic manner. The artificial language (which was also incomprehensible to the patient) was spoken in a loud and rhythmic but pathetic voice. The language through its sound qualities was actually a medium for the expression of emotion. Spoerri referred to this phenomenon as an automatically occurring "language ecstasy."

[**Editor's note:** These two cases may be seen as regressions to a primitive level where only sound and rhythm conveyed emotional meaning. In fact, their language was no longer useful.]

In a third patient, with poetic inclination, neologisms were used to develop a primeval language. The combination of German, Italian, French, English, and Spanish created the impression of a "world of words," but without consideration as to whether or not the listener understood anything. Here the patient's "language serves as an adornment." The patient had also set some of his poetic creations to music and sang them monotonously in a folksonglike manner.

## CASE STUDIES: UNIQUE LINGUISTIC PHENOMENA

These unique phenomena occur in combination with other speech and language abnormalities. They are automatically occurring speech, language, and voice patterns that proceed motorically as sound productions without expressive, communicative, or informational value.

## Schizophrenia

*Verbigeration* is described in one patient where he kept repeating the same word groups softly and without accentuation or intonation.

In another patient a "pseudodialogue" gave the false impression of a conversation with a partner.

In one patient a "linear arrangement" was observed with enumeration of alphabet letters and numbers carried in a primitive rhythm.

## Dementia

A patient with dementia showed "iteration phenomena" (repetition of words) and "logoklonia" with strenuous repetition of final syllables and "pseudodialogic monologue."

[Editor's note: It is possible that a study of the late and final stages of language deterioration may improve our knowledge of language development and its relationship to the neurological hierarchy of language.]

## CHARACTERISTIC FEATURES OF SPOERRI'S RESEARCH

A characteristic feature of Spoerri's study is a description of speech and language phenomena that is detailed (but never loses itself in details) and that consequently evokes in the reader a picture of another human being. Through the medium of Spoerri's "speaking voice" and Spoerri's language analysis of psychotic patients, the reader begins to see the patients as real people. This was due to a combination of his observational and descriptive power, blended with his interest in the patient as an individual.

An investigation of Spoerri's texts can lead to further interpretations of speech and language phenomena, both of which are of psychopathological interest and general human importance. His research deals with issues of import to both psychiatry and language philosophy.

REFERENCES

Spoerri, Theodor. Der Ausdruck der gepressten Sprechstimme ("Wurg-stimme") bei chronischen Schizophrenen. *Confin. Psychiat,* 1961, *4,* 123–132.

Spoerri, Theodor. *Sprachstörungen bei Psychosen, 2 Schallplatten mit 27 akustischen Beispielen.* Munchen: J.F. Lehmanns Verl. o.J.

Spoerri, Theodor. *Sprachphänomene und Psychose.* Basel/New York: S. Karger, 1964.

Spoerri, Theodor. Speaking voice of the schizophrenic patient. *Arch. of General Psychiat.,* 1966, *14,* 581–585.

Murray Alpert

# 17
# Speech and Disturbances of Affect

As we listen to a person produce connected discourse, we can make valid assessments as to certain fixed or inherent characteristics of the speaker, such as sex, age, education, and a number of other factors. These features are carried in the speech signal in fairly specific ways, although some variation may be produced through cultural effect. Extrasemantic information on transient characteristics of the speaker is also communicated in speech. This chapter will focus on the vocal encoding of information concerning disturbed moods, affects, and emotions. The affect and mood disturbances seen in psychotic disorders may be separate processes representing alterations of distinct mechanisms. These separate processes may be distinguishable through acoustical analysis of voice. This chapter will discuss psychiatrically significant alterations of affects and will attempt to differentiate among affects, moods, and emotions. An important relationship between affect and cognition will be discussed. It is hoped that one outcome of this research will be to provide a functioning and operational separation of the terms, affect and mood, since there has been little systematic work on this issue.

## DEFINITION OF CLINICAL TERMS

The terms: affective disorder, affect, mood, emotion, and feeling have not always been used clearly and consistently in the clinical literature.

*Affective disorder* is used to refer to psychiatric disorders of mood which include depressions and manic states. The term *affective disorder* should be clearly differentiated from the term *affect*. In current usage, *affect* refers to an individual's monetary emotion or "feeling state." Two features distinguish affect from other feelings: (1) affects are brief in duration, and (2) affects are associated with external manifestations that can be objectified. Affects are reflected in a variety of behavioral modes which include eye contact, facial expression, expressive gestures, posture, speech, etc. It should be noted that affects need not be disturbed in affective disorders; and where they are described as being disturbed (such as euphoric or depressed affect), frequently the word "mood" can be substituted for affect without altering the description.

Affects may also be described as disturbed in schizophrenic states, but here the reference is not to a quality of feeling but, rather, to a lack, constriction, *blunting*, or *flatness* of expressed feelings. In this situation the word "mood" cannot be substituted for the word "affect." *Inappropriate affects* are also described for schizophrenia where there is a discrepancy between the content of speech and the feelings expressed. This is frequently noted when the content is sad and the feelings or affects are mirthful. *Inappropriate affect* appears to be less common than *flat affect*.

*Mood* refers to the sustained feeling tone found in manic and depressive illnesses. Mood disturbances tend to persist for weeks or months, although, rarely, rapidly cycling manic depressives may show abrupt bipolar swings within periods of days or even hours. Depressions frequently present with both *subjective* dysphoric reports as well as *objective* manifestations (such as psychomotor retardation or agitation). Manic patients, on the other hand, frequently report a *subjective* sense of well being despite objective evidence of disturbance (such as loud and rapid speech, agitation, etc.).

The term *emotion* is usually restricted to several well defined psychophysiological reaction patterns such as anger, fear, and rage. Here, a stimulus response pattern is generally understood to operate, for example, fight or flight reactions. Less often are positive feelings such as love or friendliness included. *Feelings* are generally not referred to as *emotions* unless a well defined stimulus physiological response pattern has been established. Emotions also tend to be of a transient nature, referred to as states rather than traits.

The terms *feeling* or *feeling tone* are more general terms, usually referring to the subjective aspects of affects, moods, and emotions.

The inconsistent and overlapping uses and definitions of feeling terms point out the need to develop operational definitions for these concepts.

## ACOUSTICAL FEATURES OF VOICE

Our research approach to the study of vocal encoding of moods and affects has been through measurement of the physical characteristics of speech sounds. Although we aim toward study of speech samples like those presented to clinicians during interviews, we have sometimes used reading, monologues, and other less naturalistic samples.

The issues involved in decoding the talker's feelings from his vocal acoustics are complex, and many difficult questions arise. In what way are feelings encoded in voice? How specific are the acoustic patterns of a specific feeling? How do cultures and dialects affect the encoding process? To what extent must we limit generalizations by consideration of the talker's age, sex, education, dentition, drug status, hospital role, and so forth?

From the acoustic standpoint, talking consists of a stream of sound pulses and pauses. These pulses can be characterized by their intensity (loudness), fundamental frequency (pitch), and a higher frequency structure (quality). The pulses and pauses, distributed in time, yield a sense of rate and rhythm. Usually a series of pulses is bounded by a longer pause. If one examines the grammar of what is being said, the longer pause tends to coincide with a stop, usually transcribed as a period or comma. Between stops the distribution of intensities across the string of sound pulses provides our impression of stress, and the distribution of fundamental frequencies provides our impression of inflection. Stress, inflection, and rhythm work together in complex ways to provide a pattern of emphasis. The components of emphasis must interface with the requirements of the phonics so that the message will be intelligible. Relatively little of the energy in the vocal message is required for the verbal channel, however. It has been estimated that 90 percent of the intelligibility of a speech signal may be preserved if only the crucial 10 percent of the energy is retained. Ninety percent of the acoustic energy is available for encoding infra content information.

### Description of the Acoustical Analysis

Our acoustical analysis is done by dividing high quality voice recordings into two channels. In one channel we analyze for the durations of articulations and pauses and the levels (loudness) of each sound pulse. In the second channel we measure the fundamental frequency of each sound pulse at the point of its peak amplitude.

The signal in the first channel is led into a rectifier-demodulator network that provides an output corresponding to the amplitude waveform of the voice. The second channel is led through a low pass filter (adjusted for the sex of the talker) to include the fundamental frequency but not its harmonics. The filtered signal is led into an analogue circuit that counts zero axis crossings providing an output voltage proportional to input frequency.

These two signals, amplitude and frequency, are led into a small lab computer which samples the amplitude channel one hundred times per second and decides whether there is "speech" (above the "noise" threshold) or "silence" at that moment. Durations of successive samples above and below threshold are measured and referred to as run length and pause length.

During periods of "speech" the computer notes the heights of peaks and valleys in the amplitude signal. Periods from valley to valley are defined as "syllables," and their durations are noted. The highest point between two valleys is also noted, and the log of its height is taken as the signal amplitude. When the computer determines that there is a peak in the amplitude channel, it looks at the frequency channel, and the log of the fundamental frequency is noted. The computer sorts the runs by length, so that it will provide means and standard deviations of syllable durations, log amplitudes, and log fundamental frequencies (Martz and Alpert, 1980).

## ENCODING OF EMOTIONAL AROUSAL

It appears that emotional arousal may alter some of the physiologic systems required for the speech act. These physiologic alterations may be detectable by either a skilled listener or by acoustical analysis. They appear as nonlexical disruptions in the course of speech. Consider, for example, a typical interview in which the clinician is enquiring about the patient's functioning in a broad range of situations. The patient's responses are uniformly noncommital and superficial, but on some topics the patient's voice rate, level, or pitch changes. Respiration may also intrude into the middle of an utterance. Here, it is not the content but the infra content that reveals the significance to the patient of the topic under discussion. We have studied this "vocal broadcasting of emotional arousal" in several artificial experimental situations (Friedhoff, Alpert, and Kurtzberg, 1962, 1964a, 1964b; Alpert, Kurtzberg, and Friedhoff, 1963) that were modeled on this commonplace observation.

In several studies we instructed subjects to always answer a series of questions with the single word "no." About once every ten questions, there was a question to which the correct answer was "yes." Examination of the loudness of each response showed that over a series of truthful "no's" the subject departed very little from his average response level. With the emotional stimulus of lying, however, the level of the response changed. Most subjects became louder, though a few tended to become quieter when lying. We further examined the spectrum of the subject's voice and found that most of the change in energy was in the amplitude of the fundamental frequency (Alpert, Frosch, and Fisher, 1967).

One possible explanation for this finding was that the subjects were experiencing changes in the muscle tone of the vocal folds and respiratory muscles, and consequently voice dynamics were affected. In other studies we used other emotionally arousing stimuli, such as mild electric skin shock, and found similar effects on the voice (Friedhoff, Alpert, and Kurtzberg, 1964a). We assume that the physiological (muscle) changes would have occurred whether the subject was talking or not. Vocal broadcasting of emotional arousal appears as nonlexical disruptions in talking, reflecting the transient emotional state of the·subject. These effects are, most likely, distinguishable from the more enduring voice changes associated with disorders of mood.

## ENCODING OF FLAT AFFECT

In an unpublished study, we examined schizophrenics rated as showing flattening of affect in the lie situation described above. In those studies our ability to detect the change in voice level in the emotional (lie) situation was dependent on having stable responses to the neutral stimuli. We were less successful in establishing a stable baseline of responses to the neutral stimuli for schizophrenics. With these limitations in mind, it was our impression that flat schizophrenics showed as much of a vocalized response to the emotional stimuli as the nonflat schizophrenics. Flattening of affect in schizophrenia did not appear to be reflective of a failure of emotional responsivity.

These observations, taken together with results from studies in which we had judges rate affect from recordings, led us to revise our approach to the study of the acoustic encoding of flat affect. We found that flat affect could be rated from recordings of interviews about as well as it could in face-to-face interviews (Alpert, Kurtzberg, and Friedhoff, 1963). We found, also, that the topic being discussed didn't seem to affect the clinician's ability to rate a vocal sample. Patients did not appear to be flatter when discussing neutral topics, nor did flat patients appear less flat when personally important issues were discussed.

The difference between the groups appeared to reside in the relative lack of *emphasis* in patients who appear flat. The nonflat talker emphasizes the more significant words, helping the listener to focus his attention appropriately. Talkers appear to emphasize significant words by using stress, inflection, and pausing. Amplitudes were easiest for us to measure, and we were able to demonstrate that patients rated as showing flattening of affect showed constricted dynamic vocal range, even while reading (Alpert, Kurtzberg, and Friedhoff, 1963; Alpert and Anderson, 1977). Generalization about affect from reading has to be guarded. However, it was helpful to eliminate the influence of phonetic and semantic differences that occur in free speech samples.

## MECHANISMS OF "NORMAL" EMPHASIS

Somehow, readers without flat affect, even while reading unfamiliar material, can decide where to distribute emphasis. Independently, different individuals can agree with each other as to which words to say louder and which softer. It is not clear how this complex feat is accomplished, and we thought that examination of underlying mechanisms might give some insight into the behavioral mechanisms that are defective in flat schizophrenics. We noted that word class syntax appeared to contribute to differential loudness, with nouns tending to be said louder than other grammatical classes.

We found little useful information in psycholinguistic theory to explain the mechanisms underlying this ability to utilize consensual emphasis patterns. However, the work of Allan Paivio and his colleagues (1971) had shown that word *imagery* is a potent attribute of nouns which affects word-learning rates and word memory. In converging experiments we found that word imagery predicted word emphasis for nonflat schizophrenics, but not for flat schizophrenics in a reading task. We also found that word imagery was a less potent predictor of learning rate in a paired associate learning paradigm for flat schizophrenics (Alpert and Anderson, 1977).

Thus, we were able to replicate our finding that emphasis patterns were deficient in schizophrenics with flat affect and that at least part of this deficiency was associated with a reduction in the potency of word imagery. In another study we examined the role of word emphasis in clinical ratings of flat affect. Through electronic compression of a recorded passage it is possible to constrict the dynamic range of stress without altering the intelligibility of the passage or its inflection or timing. When passages of nonflat sounding patients were compressed the patients were rated as flatter. The opposite phenomena could not be demonstrated, however. It did not appear that patients rated as flat were made to seem less flat when their vocal dynamics were expanded. These results are preliminary and more work has to be done, both with the electronic transforms and the ratings.

## FLAT AFFECT AND DEPRESSION

To improve clinical rating of flat affect Andreasen (1979) has recently developed a behavioral rating scale in which a patient can be rated separately for items such as eye contact, facial expressivity, associated hand gestures, etc. Utilizing this scale it is possible to develop a parameter of "flatness" that correlates with clinical impressions. However, when the scale is used systematically, some patients who are classified as depressed by Research Diagnostic Criteria (Spitzer, *et al.,* 1978) will show significant amounts of the "flat" behaviors when rated on the behavioral scale.

We examined the vocal acoustics of "flat" and "nonflat" schizophrenic and depressed patients as they produced five minute monologues (Alpert, Martz, and Andreasen, 1980). In depression "flatness" was associated with an increase in pause duration, but this was not so in schizophrenia. In depression "flat" behaviors appeared to be associated with retardation. In schizophrenia we were again able to show that "flat" behaviors were associated with reduction in emphasis. Reduction in emphasis was not associated with "flat" behaviors in depression (Alpert, Martz, and Andreasen, 1980).

Thus we see, in the acoustics of voice, evidence that flat affect is associated with unique behavioral patterns distinguishable from emotions and moods. In contrast with the latter two, the encoding mechanism for affects appears to involve the appropriate adjustment of voice value to word value. Affects may be thought of as feelings invested in symbols. This view departs from traditional definitions of affects based on a subjective–objective dimension, and may also be different from definitions articulating the duration of the feeling state. Our definition may have several advantages in that it may: (1) provide a quantifiable measure through acoustic study of the distribution of emphasis in a patient's speech; (2) be more directly related to semiotic theory than traditional views; and (3) be easier to teach and a more reliable clinical sign.

## ENCODING OF MOODS

Acoustic study of voice may also contribute to the differentiation of emotions and moods. We have initiated some study attempting to characterize voice in mood disorders. Depressions appear to be behaviorally heterogenous with agitation or retardation affecting voice in different and not necessarily polar ways. Affective disorders appear to affect rates and rhythms of speech more than stress or inflective patterns (Alpert, Frosch, and Fisher 1967; Alpert, Martz, and Swanson 1979). Some increase in verbal productivity is required for the diagnosis of mania, but increase in speech output also may appear in agitated depressions and schizophrenia. Even flat affect is frequently associated with increases in speech rates. We are currently studying a number of psychopathological conditions with high talking rates to see if they can be distinguished on the basis of their acoustics.

Normally an utterance consists of a string of sound pulses terminated by a longer pause. We use the longer pause in our acoustic analysis to mark grammatical stops. Even for normal speakers there is a tendency for voice level to decrease as the talker gets further into the utterance. In depression, this tendency to lose power over the course of long sentences is more marked, especially for retarded depressions (Alpert, Martz, and Swanson, 1979). Talking down the breath stream may be associated with the sighing communications of the depressed, reflecting a failure to inhibit the expiration of air. However, the most striking characteristic of the retarded depressed talker, when producing enough speech to permit acoustic analysis, is the increase in pause duration. These longer pauses may reflect slowing of thought processes. Finally, in addition to prolonged pauses and articulations, depressed patients may also show alterations in brief pausing and articulatory time.

## CONCLUSION

In this chapter we have suggested that affects, moods, and emotions may influence separate and distinct acoustic dimensions of the speech signal. It would appear that, from an acoustic standpoint, moods and emotions are only remotely related to the symbolic aspects of language. For affect, however, the relationship between symbols and prosody appears to be much closer. Flat affect, as seen in schizophrenia, appears to manifest acoustically as an alteration or absence of the normal emphasis patterns, and part of this deficiency is associated with word imagery. Further study of the relationship between the symbolic level of communication and the acoustic correlates is indicated.

Much more work also needs to be done to characterize the vocal acoustics of various psychopathological states. There is an especially great need for normative data. With adequate normative data, the study of vocal acoustics may provide objective and quantitative measurement systems for psychiatry.

In order to develop a meaningful clinical picture, it will always remain necessary for the clinician to integrate quantitative measures. Further interaction between the analytic and synthetic processes, however, may help to clarify the current confounding information about moods, affects, and emotions.

REFERENCES

Alpert, M., Anderson, L. T. Imagery mediation of vocal emphasis in flat affect. *Archives of General Psychiatry,* 1977, *34,* 208–212.

Alpert, M., Frosch, W. A., Fisher, S. Teaching the perception of expressive aspects of vocal communication. *American Journal of Psychiatry,* 1967, *124,* 202–211.

Alpert, M., Kurtzberg, R. L., Friedhoff, A. J. Transient voice changes associated with emotional stimuli. *Archives of General Psychiatry,* 1963, *8,* 362–365.

Alpert, M., Martz, M. J., Swanson, D. Vocal acoustic correlates of depression. Presented at the NCDEU Annual Meeting in Key Biscayne, Florida, May 21–24, 1979.

Andreasen, N., Alpert, M., Martz, M. J. An objective measure of affective flattening. Acoustic analysis *Archives of General Psychiatry,* 1980, (in press).

Friedhoff, A. J., Alpert, M., Kurtzberg, R. L. An effect of emotion on voice. *Nature,* 1962, *193,* 357–460.

Friedhoff, A. J., Alpert, M., Kurtzberg, R. L. An electroacoustic analysis of the effects of stress on voice. *Journal of Neuropsychiatry,* 1964a, *5,* 266–272.

Friedhoff, A. J., Alpert, M., Kurtzberg, R. L. Infracontent channels of vocal communication. *Disorders of Communication,* Vol XLII. Research Publications, A.R.N.M.D., 1964b, 414–423.

Martz, M. J., Alpert, M. In preparation, 1980.

Paivio, A. *Imagery and verbal processes.* New York: Holt, Rinehard and Winston, Inc., 1971.

Spitzer, R. L., Endicott, J., Robins, E. The research diagnostic criteria: Rationale and reliability. *Archives of General Psychiatry,* 1978, *35,* 773–782.

Stanley Feldstein
Herbert Weingartner

# 18
# Speech and Psychopharmacology

In spite of the prominent role of speech and language in human behavior, the psychopharmacological literature includes relatively few
studies about the effects of drugs on verbal and coverbal behavior. Indeed, in one of the most recent handbooks of psychopharmacology
(Lipton, DiMascio, and Killam, 1978), there is no mention made of any
studies in which drug effects on speech were the focus of attention. On
the other hand, few of those investigators who are primarily concerned with speech behavior have examined the influence of drugs on
speech. Both areas of study undoubtedly suffer from the lack of such
inquiry since a powerful behavioral referent system is required for
precise biological specification to be meaningful. There are, moreover,
some indications that psychopharmacology may be able to provide a
new kind of framework that can be useful in describing the psychobiology of speech and language.

There is no question that speech is a powerful behavioral system;
it is certainly the primary way in which people transmit information
(Rommetveit, 1968), including the information used by physicians and
psychopharmacologists to evaluate the results of their drug treatment
and/or research: "... spoken language is the most important tool in
medicine. ... At least in our sophisticated society, no operation, treatment, medication or even diagnostic test is carried out without pertinent speech" (Cassell and Skopek, in press).

The general purpose of this chapter is to explore how the analysis
of changes in speech may provide a particularly useful system for
evaluating the effects of psychoactive drugs. In her excellent 1967 re-

view of the literature, Waskow pointed out that psychoactive drugs are presumed to affect "psychomotor, cognitive, affective, and complex interpersonal and psychodynamic processes" (p. 355), and noted that it is logical to expect that speech reflects these processes. A steadily increasing number of studies provides the basis for such an expectation (e.g., Davitz, 1964; Feldstein, 1964, 1978; Scherer, 1974; Scherer, Rosenthal, and Hall, 1977; Siegman, 1979; Starkweather, 1967). Waskow also noted that speech is used by practitioners to assess their patients' clinical states and/or responses to drugs. Whether or not clinicians are aware of it, their assessments are often based upon the paralinguistic aspects of the patients' speech as well as the content. Such informal usage appears to be sufficiently helpful to raise the hope that systematic relationships can be established among the various facets of speech and certain types of drug activity.

Luria (1961, 1966) provides further support for the expectation that speech may be useful for monitoring drug activity. He demonstrated that, given the appropriate neurophysiological development, children learn to utilize speech—first the speech of others and then their own speech—to regulate their behavior. He has also shown that the impairment of this directive function of speech reflects frontal lobe pathology. It is conceivable that this information can help to identify the sites of the activity of psychoactive agents that modify or eliminate the regulatory function of speech.

Another reason for using speech to evaluate drug effects is psychometric. Speech involves a set of stable but nonetheless responsive behaviors. Changes in speech can be reliable measures of alterations in the environment and factors that distinguish individuals from one another. For instance, individuals develop idiosyncratic styles of word use, in terms of the frequencies with which they use particular words and/or word classes and the ways in which they combine words. (It is for this reason that word concordances often help to determine the authorship of anonymous writings.) Timbre is another stable quality of the voice and, in combination with fundamental frequency, allows for quite accurate auditory identification of individual voices. The temporal aspects of speech, such as the durations of its vocalizations and silences, are stable enough to be considered individual characteristics (Jaffe & Feldstein, 1970). The consistency of these speech behaviors means that, at the least, if they are shown to vary with drug activity, the variations are not likely to be random. But these are some of the formal, vocal, and structural components of speech. There are also content measures of speech, and the best among them (e.g., Gottschalk, 1967) have quite acceptable levels of reliability and validity.

Finally, there are traditional psychometric instruments that can be used to assess certain influences of certain drugs; but the instruments must be explicitly administered before, after, and/or during the course of the drug treatment or testing and are subject to the effects of attention, motivation, social desirability, etc. By contrast, speech measures are essentially unobtrusive in that they can be derived from verbal interactions that occur primarily, or also, to serve other purposes.

The issue of the behavioral specificity of psychoactive drugs is beginning to be addressed. For its successful pursuit it requires not only the specification of how particular neurons are altered by the drugs, but also a behavioral system capable of sufficiently sensitive and potentially discriminative responses to reflect the different neurobiological and neurochemical actions of different psychoactive drugs. No behavioral system is likely to be as flexible, sensitive, and tied to so many other aspects of human behavior as speech and language.

It should be noted, however, that no attempt will be made to review those investigations of how drugs affect such cognitive processes as learning and memory even though the studies that are relevant usually use language to examine such processes. However, learning and memory can be studied without the use of language. The concern of this chapter is speech, and its specific intent is: (1) to provide a brief description of the site and action of psychoactive drugs; (2) to review a selection of studies concerned with the influences of psychoactive drugs on speech; and (3) to explore some interesting and possibly useful directions for further research.

## SITE AND ACTION OF PSYCHOACTIVE DRUGS

The behavioral effects of psychoactive drugs derive from their action on the central nervous system (CNS). Such effects can be described in terms of topographical (neuroanatomical) responses, neuroelectrical activity, and neurochemical events. Drugs that have psychoactive properties ultimately effect CNS function by altering the excitability of CNS neurons. The neuron is the functional unit of the CNS, and it is the activity of neurons in relation to one another that becomes the primary physiological focus of drug effects that ultimately determine changes in behavior. Neurons either fire or do not fire in response to some chemical change in their environment; psychoactive drugs alter the probability of such activation.

Inasmuch as a good part of the effects of the drugs must, directly or indirectly, involve events at the synapse, it is worth summarizing those events. First, some stimulus activates an action potential in an axon. This activation involves a depolarization of the membrane potential above threshold level. The action potential is transmitted along the neuron to its terminal where the depolarization activates a process that allows chemical substances (neurotransmitters) specific to that neuron to be released from the vesicles contained within the neuron near the synapse. Other substances (e.g., enzymes) are also released that can modulate (neuromodulators) the amount and/or effectiveness of the neurotransmitter available for stimulating the postsynaptic neuron. When the transmitter substance is released from the storage site in the presynaptic neuron, its effect on the postsynaptic cells is to initiate either excitatory or inhibitory postsynaptic potentials, depending upon the nature of the postsynaptic receptor for that particular neurotransmitter. Thus, the two types of chemical substances that are thought to be crucial to neural functioning are *neurotransmitters* (which act to transmit information between adjacent nerve cells) and *neuromodulators* (which act to increase or decrease neuronal activity). Together, the two classes of substances are called *neuroregulators,* and it is one of the basic assumptions of neurochemistry that they are responsible for communication among nerve cells (Barchas, Huda, Elliott, et al., 1978). Some of the more extensively studied substances thought to be CNS neuroregulators include acetylcholine, serotonin, beta-endorphin, and the catecholamines (dopamine, norepinephrine, etc.).

There are various ways of categorizing and discriminating among psychoactive drugs. Some of these ways are based upon the behavioral properties and the clinical applications of the drugs. They also can be classified on the basis of their chemical structure, their similarity to neurotransmitter substances, their interactive effects with chemical processes at presynaptic and postsynaptic sites, and the localization of their effects to a specific class of neurons or particular region of the brain. One scheme that combines some of the properties of these different classificatory systems has grouped drugs as sedatives, anesthetics, hypnotics, narcotics, anticonvulsants, analeptics, neuroleptics, and psychotomimetics.

It is difficult to specify the neurochemical and neuroanatomical responses of a drug and systematically relate these effects to specific behavioral changes. Despite the enormous increase in the activity and scientific yield of neuropharmacological research, few of the details of the biological action of most psychoactive drugs are known. For example, it is known that a primary site of the action of barbiturates is the reticular activating system, but little is known about the specific mode of the neurobiological action of this system in modulating behaviors in man or how the barbiturate molecule interacts with the synapses in that system. It is clear that the neuroanatomical system is complex and sensitive, and at least one reflection of that sensitivity is seen in the qualitatively different kinds of responses that are induced by small changes in the structure of psychoactive drugs. Indeed the drugs can be made either very active or totally inactive by minimal alterations of their chemical structure (Snyder, Weingartner, Richelson, et al., 1970).

Physiological and behavioral studies suggest that some of the specificity of drug action is determined by whether a drug activates or blocks neurochemical activity at the presynaptic or postsynaptic neuron. Presynaptic activation can take place by stimulating the production or release of neurotransmitter substances, by inhibiting their reuptake at the presynaptic neurons, or by blocking the production or release of enzymes that degrade neurotransmitter substances. Postsynaptic activation can be altered by changing the amounts of neurotransmitter substances that reach the postsynaptic receptors. One way to change the amount of a neurotransmitter that reaches a postsynaptic neuron is to substitute a psychoactive drug that mimics the structure of the neurotransmitter so that the postsynaptic receptor can interact with the molecules of that drug as if they were those of the neurotransmitter. Note that different neurons react to different neurotransmitter substances (e.g., cholinergic neurons versus catecholaminergic neurons) and that the consequences of the resulting activation are different for different sets of neurons. Illustrative of several of these strategies, by means of which psychoactive drugs achieve their effects, are the actions of the neuroleptics and scopolamine.

The neuroleptic, or antipsychotic, drugs appear to act by blocking the postsynaptic receptor sites for the neurotransmitter dopamine, i.e., they inhibit the electrical response of the neurons to the neurotransmitter action of dopamine (Snyder, 1976). They may also act by stimulating the release of the hormone prolactin (Berger, Elliott, and Barchas, 1978), and apparently the prolactin response is closely related to the drug's antipsychotic potency (Sacher, Gruen, Altman, et. al., 1977). However, many of the neuroleptics, both reduce psychotic symptomatology and produce Parkinsonian symptoms by virtue, apparently, of the weakness of their anticholinergic activity (i.e., by comparison with the effectiveness of their dopamine blockade). In other words, there appears to be an inverse relation between the degree to which neuroleptics block the action of the neurotransmitter acetylcholine and the extent to which they produce Parkinsonian symptoms.

Scopolamine, a powerful drug that mimics behaviorally many aspects of a dementia (Caine and Weingartner, in press), produces its effects by blocking the release of a cholinergic neurotransmitter at the presynaptic site. Treated with arecoline, the scopolamine effect is reversed (Sitaram, Weingartner, and Gillin, 1978). Arecoline, by itself, produces its effects by directly activating the postsynaptic cholinergic receptor.

It might be noted that effects similar to those of scopolamine and its treatment with arecoline can be obtained by altering the amount of material available for the synthesis of a cholinergic neurotransmitter substance at the presynaptic site.

Apart from their particular neurochemical actions, some of the psychoactive drugs also appear to have lateralized effects on the brain. That is, drugs such as marijuana, alcohol, and amphetamine may affect the functions of the left and right hemispheres differently (Stillman, Welkowitz, Weingartner, et al, 1977). Inasmuch as the dominant and nondominant areas of the CNS are not entirely redundant, the lateralized effects of the drugs could be quite important in defining specific drug-induced changes in behavior (especially speech behavior).

### EFFECTS OF PSYCHOACTIVE DRUGS ON SPEECH

Waskow (1967) characterized the studies she reviewed in terms of the type of functioning (e.g., affective, cognitive, psychomotor) presumably affected by psychoactive drugs and the speech measures that seemed to index the effects. Of the studies, she said, "they are too few, and the differences among them and their methodological weaknesses are too great to allow for any valid conclusions to be drawn" (p. 356). Her conclusions, however, remain valid. The methodological weaknesses she described are still characteristic of many of the more recent studies that have appeared in the literature. In spite of these problems, however, enough of the studies are sufficiently interesting and potentially important to be worth reviewing with the hope that not only will more work be done in the area, but that it will be methodologically more adequate.

What follows is the review of a selection of the studies that have appeared in the literature at the same time as or after the publication of the Waskow report. Also included is a study that has come to the authors' attention that is still in progress. The studies are classified not in terms of the type of psychological functioning affected by the drugs but in terms of whether content or noncontent speech measures were used as dependent variables. There are two reasons for this division. One reason is that there are not enough studies to render their formal classification into areas of psychological functioning worthwhile. The other is that many of the preceding chapters are specifically concerned with the actual and potential roles of various types of content and noncontent speech measures in the evaluation of medical and psychiatric problems.

## Effects on Speech Content

Most of the recent studies that have investigated the effects of psychoactive drugs on the content of speech have used either antipsychotic (neuroleptic) or psychotomimetic agents. Natale and his associates have examined the effects of LSD-25 and dextroamphetamine (psychotomimetics) on several aspects of spoken language. One study (Natale, Dahlberg, and Jaffe, 1978) was concerned with the influence of the two drugs on primary- and secondary-process language during psychoanalytic sessions, while another (Natale, Kowitt, Dahlberg, et al., 1978) with their influence on the use of figurative language. A third study (Natale, Dahlberg, and Jaffe, 1979a) explored the effects of the drugs on the use of defensive language. The first study cited above found that for one patient LSD was associated with a decreased use of secondary-process language but not, apparently, an increased use of primary-process language; there were no dextroamphetamine or placebo effects. For another patient, LSD was associated with an increased use of primary-process language, dextroamphetamine with an increased use of secondary-process language, and placebo with no significant changes. The two remaining patients in the study showed no drug or placebo effects. In the second study, two of the three patients examined exhibited LSD-induced increases in the use of figurative language. In the third study, the authors reported that LSD was associated with a decreased use of three of the seven categories of defensive language (Weintraub and Aronson, 1962) when the LSD condition was compared with the placebo condition, and dextroamphetamine was associated with a decreased use of one category. In this study, as in the first two, the speech samples were five-minute monologues. In this study, however, the data of 7 patients were analyzed together, i.e., a separate analysis was not done for each patient.

The data used in the three studies were obtained from a research project described in some detail by Mechaneck, Feldstein, Dahlberg, et al. (1968). Briefly, 7 patients (3 males and 4 females) engaged in long-term psychoanalytic therapy, participated in 7 LSD-25, 7 dextroamphetamine, and 7 placebo sessions at fairly regular intervals over the course of about a year to a year and a half. It is not clear why the data for all 7 patients were not used in each of the first 2 studies by Natale and his associates. The results of the studies, as they stand, are suggestive but inconclusive. Results obtained from 7 patients and the use of a technique for combining the 7 separate statistical analyses may have allowed for some definitive conclusions. In the third study, one-tailed tests were incorrectly used to compare the drug and placebo conditions. The use of two-tailed tests would have yielded only one significant finding: patients used more personal references in the LSD condition than in the placebo condition. Given, however, that the data of the patients were combined for the statistical analysis and that there were only 7 patients, there may not have been sufficient statistical power to yield the expected differences.

A possibly more productive approach Natale and his associates could have taken would have involved combining the dependent variables of the 3 studies into one multivariate analysis performed for each patient or for all 7 patients together. It may well be that only in combination can the aspects of speech that they investigated reflect the effects of drugs on central nervous system functioning. Such a finding would not diminish the importance of the drugs' influence; it would suggest that the drug effect is more subtle than had been expected.

Another study of the effects of LSD-25 on speech also used 5-minute monologues (Cheek and Amarel, 1967). The subjects were 10 alcoholics who were participating in group therapy. The monologues were elicited under four conditions: predrug, 100 mg of LSD, 200 mg of LSD, and postdrug. The investigators used the Cloze technique (Taylor, 1956) to determine the "predictability" of the transcribed monologues, i.e., the ease with which readers of the monologues could guess words that had been deleted from them. Such predictability, quantified as the number or proportion of correct guesses, is considered to be an estimate of the redundancy, or comprehensibility, of spoken or written passages. Cheek and Amarel found that the monologues were significantly less predictable in the LSD conditions than in the pre- or postdrug conditions, although their analysis also indicated that the drug conditions did not affect the predictability of all the subjects in the same way.

Weil and Zinberg (1969) studied the effects of low and high doses of marijuana on five-minute monologues obtained before and after drug administration. They also investigated the comprehensibility of the transcribed monologues by means of the Cloze procedure. In addition, the monologues were rated in terms of the Gottschalk-Gleser (1969) scales for the analysis of content and in terms of nine seven-point scales concerned with such qualities as "narrative quality," "coherence," "awareness of listener," etc. The subjects were chronic users, who received only high doses, and a group of naive users who received high and low doses and a placebo. Interestingly, the naive subjects never became "high" despite the dose level.

Apparently, the monologues obtained after the use of either high or low doses were rated differently on the nine seven-point scales from the predrug monologues, although the differences were greater between the pre- and postdrug monologues in the high dose condition. There seemed, however, to be no differences between the two sets of monologues with regard to social alienation, presumably measured by the Gottschalk-Gleser scales. Unfortunately, the report does not indicate whether any statistical analyses of the data were conducted and the lack thereof makes it difficult to know how to evaluate the results. The investigators simply present some samples of the data and a pre- and postdrug monologue. Nor did Weil and Zinberg describe the ways in which the monologues were transcribed for the purpose of rating them on the seven-point scales; in the two published examples, dots were used to indicate pauses and the postdrug monologue had many more pauses than the predrug one. The investigators themselves, however, listened very carefully to the monologues and speculated, on the basis of their listening, that "... a high individual appears to have to expend more effort than when not intoxicated to remember from moment to moment the logical thread of what he is saying" (p. 436). It may be that the speculation is an inference based upon frequent pausing. (It does seem, however, that short term memory is adversely affected by high doses of marijuana [Volavka, Dornbush, Feldstein, et al., 1971].)

A somewhat more sophisticated assessment of the effects of marijuana on speech content was conducted by Crockett, Klonoff, and Clark (1976). They divided 81 normal volunteers into 7 experimental conditions in which they responded twice to a selection of 10 pictures from the Thematic Apperception Test (TAT). The conditions represented different pairings of placebo, low-dose marijuana, and high-dose marijuana (controlling for order) and the two trials were separated by a week. The recorded verbal productions were transcribed and analyzed in terms of a set of 13 rating scales designed to measure changes in thought processes, emotional tone, aggression, sexual content, and control.

A multivariate analysis and subsequent comparisons revealed that the TAT responses produced under the effects of low and high doses of marijuana were rated as less organized and integrated than those produced in the placebo conditions. In addition, those produced in the high-dose conditions exhibited less sensitivity to the anxious content of the TAT pictures and were more concrete and descriptive than those from the low-dose conditions. The marijuana had no effect on the variables associated with the categories of control, aggression, and sexual content.

A somewhat more indirect way of measuring the content of

speech is by examining aspects of its syntactic structure. While such an approach may not reveal anything about the semantic meaning of the speech, it may detect drug-induced changes in how the meaning is expressed. For example, Levy (1968) used a measure called the subordination index to investigate the effects of the neuroleptic drug, chlorpromazine, on the sentence structure of 4 schizophrenic patients. The index is the ratio of subordinate propositions to the total number of propositions in a speech sample. (A subordinate proposition appears to be very similar to a subordinate clause.) Four speech samples were elicited on each of three different occasions. The four samples were (1) interview speech, (2) descriptions of pictures, (3) proverb interpretations, and (4) "abstract" speech. The occasions were (1) soon after admission but prior to drug administration, (2) 48 hours after the ingestion of chlorpromazine, and (3) just prior to discharge.

The subordination index tended to be lower 48 hours after chlorpromazine administration than in the speech samples obtained either before the drug was taken or at discharge, except in the case of descriptive speech. Unfortunately, Levy compared the first and second and the first and third occasions (not all of which yielded significant differences) for each type of speech rather than perform trend analyses over the three occasions. Given the size of the subject sample, the results ought not to be generalized beyond the particular subjects used, but they do suggest that it may be worth looking at the effects of drugs on grammatical structure more closely.

The Gottschalk-Gleser scales were used in another study (Gottschalk, Bates, Waskow, et al., 1971) of the effects of amphetamine and chlorpromazine on achievement strivings. The data of the study were drawn from those of a much larger, double-blind study; the data were from those 41 subjects in the earlier study who had been able to provide adequate speech samples. Of the 41—all of whom were prisoners at a special corrections institution in Maryland—18 had been given amphetamine, 8 chlorpromazine, and 15 a placebo. Speech samples had been obtained prior to the drug administration and at about 2 hours and 4 hours after the administration. The analysis of the ratings made about the speech samples compared the amphetamine, chlorpromazine, and placebo samples obtained 2 to 4 hours after the drug administration while taking into account the predrug ratings.

The results indicate that the samples obtained 2 hours after the ingestion of amphetamine revealed a significant increase in achievement strivings over the predrug samples but the effect was reduced considerably by the fourth hour after drug ingestion. (Again, a trend analysis would have been more appropriate than the one employed.) The investigators had also expected a depressing effect on achievement strivings from the chlorpromazine but the results did not indicate that one had occurred.

Gottschalk and another group of associates (Gottschalk, Elliott, Bates, et al., 1972) used the content-analytic scales to explore the effects of a benzodiazepine called *lorazepam*. Lorazepam is neither a psychotomimetic nor a neuroleptic; it is an anxiolytic, or antianxiety, agent. The study compared 4 dose levels of lorazepam with a no-drug condition and various doses of pentobarbital and sodium phenobarbital. The comparisons do not, however, seem to have been intended seriously; each of the 4 individuals who received barbiturates was given a different dosage; the no-drug condition involved 6 prisoners who assisted in the study and "therefore were in the same environment;" and no dose of lorazepam was received by more than four subjects either intravenously or intramuscularly. Again, the speech samples obtained were 5-minute monologues. The statistical analysis of the data adjusted for the predrug levels of verbally reflected anxiety but was only done for some of the groups. In any case, 0.5 mg of lorazepam appeared to decrease the anxiety reflected by the content analysis whereas 8.0 to 9.0 mg seemed to increase the anxiety both several hours after administration and 23 hours afterwards. In short, the results are clearly inconclusive.

The studies reviewed thus far indicate that evidence of the effects of LSD, marijuana, and dextroamphetamine on the *content* of speech remains only suggestive. Some alterations do seem to occur, but they are not marked and are not easily identified. Part of the difficulty may be that the rationale for expecting speech content to be affected by the drugs has been made neither clear nor specific. At the time that LSD began to attract public attention, for example, it was thought that, within a therapeutic context, LSD would aid in the recall of early memories, loosen and enrich associations, increase emotional responsiveness, and decrease defensiveness (e.g., Abramson, 1959; Chandler and Hartman, 1960; Dahlberg, 1963). For the most part, these expectations were derived originally not from the bio- or neurochemical actions of the drugs but from "street use" reports of the drugs' effects. Perhaps amphetamine is the exception, inasmuch as controlled clinical observations have been reported about the effects of chronic amphetamine use (e.g., Bell, 1973). The continued use of amphetamine results in motor and cognitive patterns that become increasingly "constricted and repetitive" (Groves and Rebec, 1976). Such repetitiveness may make for increased verbal repetition which could be reflected by a higher "predictability" score as measured by the Cloze procedure. It is not at all certain, however, that such constriction and repetition follows the occasional use of amphetamine.

(Indeed, there is some evidence [Reuss, Silberman, Post, et al., 1979] that acute amphetamine treatment enhances some cognitive processes.)

Another part of the difficulty is that there are few content-analytic measures that are both reliable and valid, measures that get at the "meaning" of the verbal content. The Gottschalk-Gleser scales (Gottschalk and Gleser, 1969) are probably the best, but their intent is not so much to get at the meaning of a language sample as to reveal the psychological states of the individual who produced it.

The Cloze procedure is an intriguingly simple technique to use but its meaning is open to a variety of interpretations. It is not clear, in other words, what aspects of the message are being used by those asked to guess the deleted words. Salzinger (1967) noted that it is ". . . sensitive to chains of responses or syntax, rather than single-word variables" (p. 353) and Honigfield (1967) asserted that it ". . . is sensitive to states of the human organism . . ." (p. 352). It is called a measure of comprehensibility but, interestingly, no one has attempted experimentally to validate that interpretation.

Part of the problem of formulating content-analytic measures is definitional. The term, *content,* used as a characteristic of spoken (or written) language, usually refers to the meaning of the language. But the notion of "meaning" is rather complex. The study of meaning tends to be subsumed under the general construct of "semantic meaning," although the construct is not easily defined in an unambiguous and operational fashion. Moreover, the relevant literature refers to "lexical meaning," "associative meaning," "sentence meaning" (the meaning of combinations of words), and others. Even the term, *content,* is open to various interpretations. Haas (1979), for example, distinguishes between "content" and "topic." She uses the term, *topic,* to refer ". . . to the subject matter of the spoken utterance, to what the conversation is about" (p. 619). *Content,* on the other hand, ". . . refers to the more general concept of how topic is referenced" (p. 620). Thus, the content of an utterance may be more or less emotional, more or less value-laden, more or less action-oriented, etc. It is not clear that this distinction makes it easier to formulate more useful content-analytic measures. It does tend, however, to emphasize an important point that Berelson (1952) made in his definition of content analysis: ". . . content analysis is ordinarily limited to the manifest content of the communication and is not normally done directly in terms of the latent intentions which the content may express nor the latent responses which it may elicit. Strictly speaking, content analysis proceeds in terms of what-is-said, and not in terms of why-the-content-is-like-that (e.g., 'motives') . . ." (p. 16). Many of the content-analytic procedures devised by psychologists and psychiatrists have failed to observe this constraint. At least one consequence of this failure is the difficulty or impossibility of demonstrating acceptable reliability and validity.

More to the point, however, is the question implied earlier of whether psychoactive drugs can be expected to affect the meanings of spoken messages. Speakers usually have greater control over the content of their speech than they do over its form or structure. Most speakers tend to monitor much of *what* they say to others but only occasionally do they attempt to control *how* they say it. Depending upon the situation, for instance, speakers may try to use the more "correct" grammatical forms, or to use words they do not commonly use (or to not use words they do commonly use). In certain circumstances, such as the presence of persons who do not (or are thought not) to know the language well, speakers may even deliberately alter the intensity and rate of their speech (by speaking more loudly and slowly than they usually do). In general, however, speakers do not attempt to change—indeed, they are not even aware of—the characteristic coverbal patterns of their speech. These may be the patterns, therefore, that are best able to reflect the effects of psychoactive drugs.

The term *coverbal* is meant to include such vocal and structural characteristics of speech as its pitch, its loudness, its timbre, its disturbances, its rate, and the frequencies and durations of its sounds and silences. (This use of the term presumes that the term *verbal* refers to the words, syntax, and semantics of the speech.) Among the advantages of these coverbal characteristics is that they can be defined with some precision and, in many cases, can be derived automatically from ongoing speech. More interestingly, perhaps, is that there is increasing evidence (e.g., Feldstein, 1964; Scherer, 1974; Siegman and Feldstein, 1979) that they are capable of indexing important psychological and affective states. Their use as variables in psychopharmacological studies, however, is relatively new.

### Effects on Coverbal Aspects of Speech

An exciting study now in progress (Jaffe, unpublished manuscript) involves the prediction of blood plasma levels of imipramine by the use of such a predrug interview measure as the average duration of vocalizations. A preliminary analysis of the data obtained thus far suggests that there is a nonlinear relationship between the measure and the plasma levels. If borne out by further data, the finding can produce an important application of the relation between coverbal measures and drugs.

Helfrich and Scherer (1977) studied the effects of two tricyclic antidepressants on a number of spectral measures of the voice. Their subjects were 23 healthy male students who were divided into high and low depression groups on the basis of their scores on a personality questionnaire. The drugs imipramine and lofepramine and a placebo were administered in a double-blind, counterbalanced procedure with 1-week intervals among them. The students were asked to read a standard passage and the readings were taken 30, 120, and 195 minutes after ingestion of the drug. Of the four measures extracted by the spectral analysis, the mean fundamental frequency of the voice yielded the clearest results; the results of the other three vocal measures were apparently nonsignificant or redundant (with one exception to be raised below).

The analysis yielded an interaction of the drugs with time such that the drugs induced a lower fundamental frequency than did the placebo but only for the first two time points, suggesting that the relaxing effects of the drugs disappeared after about 3 hours. One of the other measures—the proportion of total energy below 500 Hz—yielded an interaction indicating that the effects of the drugs were influenced by the subjects' initial levels of depression.

The results suggest that fundamental frequency, an acoustic property of the voice, is capable of reflecting the effects of antidepressants and may, therefore, have diagnostic utility. Although the study was well designed, it may be worth noting again that the subjects were not clinically depressed and it is not clear that the results can be generalized to depressed patients. The investigators do mention, however, that the results were similar to those they obtained in a study of depressed patients they conducted with several other colleagues.

Two reports published by Jaffe and his associates (Jaffe, Dahlberg, Luria, et al., 1972; Jaffe, Dahlberg, Luria, et al., 1973) examined the influence of LSD-25 and dextroamphetamine on the speech rhythms of monologues and dialogues, respectively. The monologues were the same 5-minute speech samples used by Natale and his associates in the content-analytic studies described in the previous section. The dialogues were from the same project that produced the monologues (Mechaneck et al., 1968), but only one dialogue from each drug condition was used for each patient, that dialogue from the patient's second encounter with the drug condition. The monologues were obtained immediately following the ingestion of the drug or placebo and at about $2\frac{1}{4}$ hours later. The monologues were analyzed in terms of their mean pause and mean vocalization times, i.e., their average durations of pauses and vocalizations. Separate statistical analyses were conducted for the first and second sets of monologues and for the differences between them. The results indicated that only the average pause durations discriminated between the two drugs and between each of the drugs and the placebo and only, as had been expected, for the second set of monologues. That is, by comparison with the effects of the placebo, LSD increased and dextroamphetamine decreased the average pause durations.

The statistical analyses of the much longer dialogues yielded essentially similar results. The average duration of the pauses in the dextroamphetamine condition was significantly shorter than that in either the placebo or LSD condition. Although the pauses in the LSD condition were, on the average, longer than those in the placebo condition, the differences were not significant. Both of these studies (Jaffe et al., 1972, 1973) used all of the 7 patients in the project and their results are more conclusive than are those of the content analyses described previously. They suggest that relatively small doses of LSD and dextroamphetamine have similar effects on monologues and psychoanalytic dialogues (which, depending upon the analyst, may not differ much from monologues). They also suggest that the silences of speech are more susceptible to the influence of psychotomimetics than are its sounds (vocalizations). The fact that the two psychotomimetics differentially affected the silences requires some explanation, however. Jaffe et al. (1972) proposed that the longer pauses induced by LSD are a function of the simultaneous but competing emotions that LSD, unlike dextroamphetamine, arouses. If the explanation is viable, it implies that the two drugs have differential cognitive and/or emotional consequences that are, at least, partially reflected by the pause durations.

The data of the project were again used by Natale and his colleagues (Natale, Dahlberg, and Jaffe, 1979b) to explore the effects of the psychotomimetics on the degree to which the patient-therapist pairs match the average durations of their "phrases." A phrase was defined as the combination of vocalization plus the pause that follows it. The second, fourth, and sixth sessions from each drug condition (LSD, dextroamphetamine, and placebo) were analyzed for each of the 7 patients. The results appear to indicate that increased matching occurred during the psychoanalytic dialogues of the second and fourth dextroamphetamine sessions and the second LSD sessions but not during any of the placebo sessions. The investigators invoke the notion of tolerance development to account for the lack of matching in the sixth dextroamphetamine session and in the fourth and sixth LSD sessions. The study also purported to demonstrate that little or no matching of the separate vocalization and pause durations occurred. Natale, Dahlberg, and Jaffe (1979b) then concluded that psychotomimetics somehow induce the matching of phrases but not of its component parameters. They also concluded that LSD and dextroamphetamine "sensitize the patient and therapist to each other's phrase rhythm" (p. 50).

It is not clear why all the sessions in each of the drug conditions were not analyzed. It is also not clear what the meaning of "sensitize" is, as used by the investigators, or how the drugs, ingested only by the patients, could "sensitize" the therapist. Nor is it clear, given the small sample size (the *df* for each *r* was 5) and thus the potential unreliability of its analyses, that tolerance can be invoked as the most plausible explanation of the failure to obtain a significant correlation coefficient. It is clear, however, that the authors' interpretations and conclusions must be viewed with considerable caution. On the other hand, the results are quite provocative and the issues involved clearly warrant further investigation.

Katz, Waskow, and Olsson (1968) examined the effects of LSD and amphetamine on two direct speech measures, productivity and rate of articulation, and on ratings of vocal qualities made about filtered speech samples in terms of a number of bipolar scales. The investigators also used other dependent variables, most of which are not relevant here. Among these variables, however, were the subjects' responses to a special subjective drug-effects questionnaire. The importance of these responses is that they seemed to determine the behavior of the subjects on the other measures. On the basis of their responses to the questionnaire in the LSD condition, the subjects were divided into three groups: mildly euphoric, dysphoric, and ambivalent. Questionnaire responses in the amphetamine condition yielded two groups: euphoric and dysphoric. The LSD-ambivalent and -dysphoric groups differed significantly in terms of the rate and productivity of their speech, but they did so both before and after ingesting the drug. The LSD-euphoric and amphetamine-euphoric subjects obtained rate and productivity scores that fell between those of the ambivalent and dysphoric groups.

One difficulty with these findings is that they are based upon very small subject samples: the total number of subjects was 69, but dividing them in terms of their questionnaire scores yielded groups with *N*s ranging between 4 and 9. The important point of the study, however, is its attempt to demonstrate that an individual's subjective response to a psychoactive drug may at least partially dictate his or her vocal behavior.

Another study of the effects of d-amphetamine on speech was conducted by Stitzer, Griffiths, and Liebson (1978). The study involved two experiments and four subjects participated in each. The primary dependent variable in each experiment was the "quantity of human verbal output" or talkativeness. The participants were instructed to talk while under the influence of from 5 to 20 mg of d-amphetamine. Those in the second experiment were rewarded for talking by points received on a fixed interval schedule. The analyses of the data were performed per subject. The results indicate that, in each of the experiments, 3 of the 4 subjects spoke more after having received d-amphetamine than after having received a placebo. Moreover, the effect of the d-amphetamine seemed, in general, to be dose related. The participants in these experiments, however, engaged in monologues. The question of how d-amphetamine affects speech that occurs within the context of dialogues was examined in another study (Griffiths, Stitzer, Corker, et al., 1977) that also involved two experiments but only the second is relevant here. In it, 11 subjects engaged in repeated 60-minute verbal interactions. Only 7 of the subjects received d-amphetamine and their conversational partners were always subjects who received a placebo. The 7 subjects, however, never received the drug on two consecutive days of interaction; on those occasions, as well as others, they received a placebo. The results again seem to indicate dose-related increases in amount of speech for 5 of the 7 subjects. (No statistical comparisons appear to have been made.) There were also marked differences among the average amounts of speech of the subjects. Interestingly, only one of the partners showed increases in speaking time that were related to the drug-induced increases of the participant with whom he interacted.

The two studies indicate that d-amphetamine increases the amount of speech emitted in monologues and dialogues. These studies, together with those of Jaffe et al. (1972, 1973) do seem to suggest that amphetamine does affect a number of coverbal aspects of speech behavior. It might be noted, in passing, that amphetamine also enhances the sequential organization of meaningful information in memory (Weingartner, Rappaport, Buchsbaum, et al., 1980; Reuss, Silberman, Post, et al., 1979), an effect that seems to be related to the drug's stimulation of catecholamine activity in the CNS. It is interesting to wonder whether the drug's effects on speech are also a function of such stimulation.

Stitzer, Griffiths, Bigelow, et al. (in press) also examined the effects on speech of ethanol, secobarbital and chlorpromazine. Eighteen subjects participated but only two were given more than one drug. The interactive sessions were 60 minutes long and conducted 5 days per week for each pair of participants. In this study the effects of different doses on amount of speech were statistically evaluated. The results indicate that the speech of 3 of the 4 subjects given ethanol exhibited dose-related linear increases. Secobarbital elicited dose-related linear increases in amount of speech for 5 of the 6 subjects who ingested it. Finally, chlorpromazine produced dose-related decreases in amount of speech for all 4 of the participants who were given it. Again, unfortunately, the small number of subjects makes it difficult to assess the generalizability of the findings. Nevertheless, the study raises at least one interesting question concerning the similarity of the responses elicited by ethanol, secobarbital, and amphetamine. Given that the responses to the three drugs are not identical, is there any way of distinguishing among them and, thus, distinguishing among the drugs? For example, although the amount of speech (in number of seconds) increases with increasing dose levels of the drug, are the sound-silence patterns similar? Jaffe et al. (1972, 1973) found that amphetamine seemed to decrease pause (silence) durations in monologues and dialogues. Do ethanol and secobarbital do the same? If coverbal behavior is to be used to characterize different drugs, it may be that a finer-grained analysis of the speech is necessary. Indeed, it may be that a combination of coverbal parameters is needed to distinguish among drugs.

The effects of $\Delta^9$ tetrahydrocannabinol on speech were explored by Zeidenberg, Clark, Jaffe, et al. (1973) in a preliminary study in which only four subjects participated. The subjects were always given the placebo first, after which they were observed, interviewed, and tested. They were then given 15 mg of $\Delta^9$ tetrahydrocannabinol and tested again as soon as they began to experience the effects of the drug (about 1 to 1½ hours after ingestion). A third round of testing began after the drug effects had largely abated.

The study examined the effects of the drug on three measures of speech, derived from 5 minute, extemporaneous speech samples: the average durations of pauses, vowels, and phrases. Although the authors interpreted the results in terms of the decisions, they assumed to underly the speech behaviors measured, inspection of the results appeared to indicate that the 4 subjects increased the durations of their pauses, prolonged the durations of their vowels, and decreased the number of vowels they used per phrase. The authors suggested that the results reflect increased difficulty in information processing.

At times, drug reports have been published in which speech is important for its own sake. Such instances have usually been concerned with speech that has been adversely affected by some disease process or by a particular drug treatment. One example describes a study that (Nakano, Zubick, and Tyler, 1973) explored the effectiveness of levodopa in mitigating the phonation and articulation problems of Parkinsonian speech. Levodopa is the amino acid precursor of dopamine and is an exceedingly effective treatment for the symptoms of Parkinson's disease. The study used a double-blind procedure with 18 men and women hospitalized with Parkinson's syndrome. Levodopa was compared with lactose (the placebo) and procyclidine hydrochloride, and all three treatments were administered to every patient. Each patient also took a speech intelligibility test prior to medication and at the completion of each drug trial. The patients, investigators, and 10 untrained listeners independently ranked the recorded speech in order of preference, although the report does not clarify the basis for deciding upon preference. The statistical analysis indicated that levodopa benefitted Parkinsonian speech significantly more than did the placebo, whereas the effects of the placebo and procyclidine did not differ. Moreover, although all 18 of the patients preferred the speech sample obtained after levodopa treatment, only 14 of them were helped by levodopa alone.

Unfortunately, the investigators did not analyze the specific articulatory aberrations beneficially affected by levodopa. The increased intelligibility of the speech seemed to be a function of the decreased labial movements induced by the levodopa, however, and not a direct effect of the drug.

Solomon and Vickers (1975) have reported a case of dysarthria, or slurred speech, that occurred as a function of lithium carbonate treatment. The degree of dysarthria seemed to increase with increases in the serum level of the lithium ion, but by itself did not indicate toxicity. A number of other investigators (Krakower, 1978; Shopsin, Johnson, and Gershon, 1970) have noted that a transient aphasia sometimes occurs in response to toxic and nontoxic concentrations of the lithium ion.

An interesting report that appeared recently (Schatzberg, Cole, and Blumer, 1978) described 5 patients who developed "speech blockage" as a side effect of treatment with tricyclic antidepressants. The authors explain the blockage as a "delay in thinking and speech" and claim that the patients perceived it as "a difficulty in expressing the word or thought and as a halt in their normal speech patterns" (p. 600). Behaviorally, the blockage appeared as an increase in the durations of the patients' pauses, and was relieved after a decrease in the tricyclic dosage. The authors suggest that the symptom is a direct effect of a tricyclic-induced, central anticholinergic effect on higher cortical functions or the result of a decrease in the cholinergic activity that accompanies a tricyclic-related increase of noradrenergic activity.

It seems clear that none of the studies reviewed in this section represents much more than a suggestive beginning. Possibly the most adequate of the studies, that by Helfrich and Scherer (1977), needs to be replicated with patient samples. The studies by Jaffe and Natale and their associates used as subjects all the patients involved in the original project but not all the available data. Why such a strategy was adopted is as unclear with respect to these studies as it was for the content-analytic studies that were conducted by Natale, Dahlberg, and Jaffe (1978, 1979) and reviewed in the previous section. One consequence of the strategy is that the results of the study permit no reliable conclusions.

The studies by Stitzer and her associates (Griffiths, Stitzer, Corker, et al., 1977; Stitzer, Griffiths, Liebson, 1978; Stitzer, Griffiths, Bigelow, et al., in press) are quite sophisticated. They indicate that certain psychoactive drugs do affect coverbal behavior in specific ways. However, the primary variable they examine—the cumulative amount of speech uttered—is a relatively gross measure, and it is to be hoped that other coverbal characteristics will also be studied.

The Katz, Waskow, and Olsson (1968) study seems to suggest that an individual's subjective (perhaps affective) responses to a drug may importantly determine his or her vocal behavior while under the influence of the drug, but again the results need replication before they can be taken seriously.

The case studies, on the other hand, are clearly meant to hint at some directions for further research.

### POSSIBLE DIRECTIONS OF FURTHER RESEARCH

It seems fair to say that, mostly because of methodological deficiencies, few of the studies reviewed have tested adequately the usefulness of speech as a behavior capable of reflecting alterations in brain state as a function of psychoactive drugs. It still seems quite possible that speech can provide indices for the detection and measurement of such alterations. On the other hand, studies of the relations between speech and drugs might more profitably take two directions. One is concerned with the psychobiology of speech; the other with the use of speech to monitor the effects of drugs. This section, then, describes and proposes, albeit in a sketchy form, some productive strategies for examining the psychobiology of speech and for using speech behaviors to mirror drug-altered brain functioning.

### Psychobiology of Speech

Relatively little is known about the psychobiology of speech. The new tools that are now available for both reversibly altering and exploring the CNS provide the investigator primarily interested in speech with exciting opportunities for defining the psychobiological underpinnings of speech and speech-related functions. At the same time, the neuroscientist (neuroanatomist, neuropharmacologist, neurophysiologist, etc.) cannot define brain-behavior relationships adequately without access to detailed, quantifiable, and relevant behavioral events with which to relate those measurements that describe biological events in brain.

The study of the psychobiology of speech and related functions has had a long history. It has almost exclusively involved clinical studies of the disruption of various aspects of speech functioning in relation to an inferred, and sometimes documented, lesion system in brain. In fact, one of the hallmarks in the study of brain-behavior relationships dates back to over 100 years ago, when Broca first related lateralized lesions of the cortex to disruptions in the production of speech. Since that time, many of the details of speech behavior (e.g., aspects of auditory and auditory-pattern processing, auditory integration of signals, production, reception) have been investigated in patients with lesions of the CNS and, occasionally, in neurologically unimpaired individuals. Much has been learned about the neuroanatomy of aphasia, components of the motor expression of speech, the neuropathology of dyslexia, dyspraxia, and dysastria, each of which is reflected by some form of speech disturbance.

But despite current sophistication in mapping the topography and structure of brain, it remains difficult to define the boundaries of a lesion. There are, for example, fiber tracts that lead to or from impaired areas that may involve a wide network of brain regions beyond the obvious site of the lesion. Moreover, speech disruption in neuropathologically impaired individuals does not occur in a behavioral vacuum. Pre-impairment expectations of the self and others, the psychological responses to impairment, and unique individual histories of behavior all contribute—to a degree not easy to evaluate—to the influence of a brain insult upon the alteration of a function as important as speech.

It is possible, however, to explore the neural mechanisms of speech by the use of drugs, inasmuch as they allow for reversible brain alterations and for the measurement of actual brain responses to particular drug manipulations. In the same way that investigators of the neuropathology of speech have tried to relate alterations in the production and appreciation (comprehension) of speech to the site of the suspect lesion, it is possible to use drugs to alter specific neurotransmitters in brain and try to identify the changes in speech behavior that accompany the alterations.

It may also be possible to use drugs in a treatment-oriented context for exploring the psychobiology of speech. For example, can various forms of aphasia be transiently produced and/or altered by the use of drugs, and what does such an operation reveal not only about the neuroanatomical locus of language representation in brain, but also about its neurochemical correlates? The distinctions among various forms of disruptions in speech, such as those associated with Giles de la Tourettes Syndrome, aphasias, and dysarthrias, may be better understood by attempting to alter the disruptions with different drugs. Are there any situations in which it might be ethically possible to use drugs to model the disruptive speech in unimpaired individuals? The modeling may well help to clarify the nature of the neurochemical and neuroanatomical involvement in such possibilities as: (1) alterations in language comprehension; (2) changes in the appreciation of semantic rather than syntactic structure; (3) alterations in the accessibility of those semantic structures needed for naming or recovering words; and (4) changes in the temporal structure of speech.

## Speech and the Monitoring of Drug Effects

The logic of the usefulness of speech as a monitor of drug activity rests not only upon intuitive and experiential grounds, but also upon the fact that speech is the behavior most able to flexibly express a host of diverse human states. This direction of research capitalizes on the presumed sensitivity of speech and treats its differentiated structures as a system within which it may be possible to delineate discrete drug-induced alterations in brain function. It is a direction that represents the logical and related inverse of the study of the psychobiology of speech.

One of the ways of using speech as a measure of drug activity is to treat some component of speech behavior as if it were a simple operant (voluntary, unitary) response, the probability or rate of which could be altered as a function of drug-induced changes in brain activity. The rationale of such a strategy is that it enables the design of human psychopharmacological studies that resemble animal studies: some operant response, that is either part of the animal's repertoire or can be trained to be part of it, is used as a target behavior with which to track drug responsivity. Thus, the researcher might use bar press, latency of shock avoidance, maze running, etc., under different drug conditions. The behavior is used to map a dose-response curve that could define the psychoactivity of the drug in brain. Rarely is the particular behavior chosen of prime interest in such an investigation. The behavior is used as a fair example of possible behaviors that could be "applied" to measure the intensity of the drug response.

Inasmuch as speech is such a frequently occurring and clearly important behavior, and because components of it can be measured with relative ease, it has been used as if it were a simple operant to define the responses of certain drugs in man. Such a use is illustrated by some of the studies reviewed earlier that were concerned with the effects of amphetamine. For example, Stitzer and her associates (Griffiths, Stitzer, and Corker, 1977; Stitzer, Griffiths and Liebson, 1978) found that amphetamine increases the amount of speech uttered, and their data do seem to indicate a dose-response relationship. The reports by Jaffe and his colleagues (Jaffe et al., 1972, 1973) suggest that amphetamine decreases pause durations and, although they did not test the possibility, it may be that an examination of average pause durations at different dosage levels would yield a descending dose-response curve.

Regarding the objective components of speech as a class of operants may be quite helpful for delineating dose-response relationships and, perhaps, even for discriminating among certain drugs, although it might be argued that other motoric behaviors (e.g., finger tapping) may be found equally helpful. Clearly, however, the objective components—pauses, number of words, intensity levels, etc.—cannot easily be considered equivalent either in their sensitivity or their "meaning" in mapping the effects of drugs on brain. It is the interrelationships among these components that are likely to provide a potentially much richer framework for describing how drugs alter brain functioning. For example, it seems probable that both scopolamine and alcohol would affect the frequencies of such speech characteristics as number of speaking turns and misarticulations, and the durations of pauses and switching pauses. These measures may, in fact, be able to reflect even small changes in the dose levels of the drugs or sensitively describe their threshold values. It is highly unlikely, however, that any one of the measures can alone differentiate the determinants of disruption induced by scopolamine from those underlying the disruption induced by alcohol. It is unlikely, in other words, that a single speech measure can distinguish between the mechanisms involved in the actions of scopolamine and alcohol. On the other hand, it may well be that the speech of an individual who has received scopolamine is *structurally* different from, i.e., involves a *pattern* of objective components that is different from that of speech emitted by a person who has received alcohol. It may be that the paralinguistic and linguistic structures of speech, codified in terms of objective indices, can distinguish among the neural mechanisms of different drugs and, at the same time, provide the subtle behavioral distinctions that can be used to identify the drugs.

Unfortunately, not many investigations involving speech characteristics have utilized the type of pattern analysis suggested here.
Among those that have, however, several are clearly suggestive. For
example, it has been shown that neither the type-token ratio (a measure of vocabulary diversity) nor the speech disturbance ratio (an index of normally occurring disruptions in the flow of speech) separately
differentiates schizophrenic from nonpsychiatric patients (Feldstein,
1962; Feldstein and Jaffe, 1962a). It was also found, however, that the
two measures were significantly correlated in the speech of the nonpsychiatric patients but not in the speech of the schizophrenic patients (Feldstein and Jaffe, 1962b). In addition, the same study found
a significant relationship between the speech disturbance ratio and
number of words uttered, but again only in the speech of the nonpsychiatric patients. Another study of schizophrenic patients (Glaister,
Feldstein, and Pollack, 1980) discovered a relationship between degree
of psychopathology and a measure of vocal activity that combines durations of vocalizations and pauses in such a way that it is not the durations themselves that are important but the differences between
them. Still another study compared seven simulated affective vocal
expressions in terms of a profile of four indices, three of which were
speech disturbances, percent pause time, and fluctuations in vocal intensity. In describing the findings, the report points out that: "The
greater discriminative power of the profile [pattern] analysis, compared with the individual analysis, is particularly well demonstrated
by . . . [the fact that] . . . the profiles of sadness and depression differ
whereas the two affects were not differentiated by any of the individual measures" (Feldstein, 1964, p. 204).

It only remains to point out that nothing will be learned from either of the directions discussed unless the studies that pursue them
are methodologically adequate. The studies must have enough subjects to allow the results to be generalized. The studies must incorpo-
rate sufficient controls for extraneous variables so that there is at
least the possibility of unambiguously interpreting the results. The dependent variables of the studies—their measures—should be objective, empirically defined, and appropriate, and they should have
demonstrated reliability. Finally, the statistical analyses of the studies must match the sophistication, and often complexity, of their designs. No competent investigator who has attempted clinical research
with humans in vivo can fail to appreciate the almost unbelievable
constraints that operate to impede its progress (Feldstein, 1979). Little
of value will be learned, however, unless the constraints are challenged and overcome.

REFERENCES

Abramson, H. A. (Ed.), *The use of LSD in psychotherapy: Transactions of a conference on d-lysergic acid diethylamine (LSD-25).* New York: Joshua Macy, Jr., Foundation, 1959.

Barchas, J., Akil, H., Elliott, et al. Behavioral neurochemistry: Neuroregulators and behavioral states. *Science,* 1978, *200,* 964–973.

Bell, D. S. The experimental reproduction of amphetamine psychosis. *Archives of General Psychiatry,* 1973, *29,* 35–40.

Berelson, B. *Content analysis in communication research.* Glencoe, Illinois: Free Press, 1952.

Berger, P. A., Elliott, G. R., Barchas, J. D. Neuroregulators and schizophrenia. In M. A. Lipton, A. DiMascio, K. F. Killam (Eds.), *Psychopharmacology: A generation of progress.* New York: Raven, 1978. pp. 1071–1082.

Caine, E. D., Weingartner, H., Ludlow, C. L., et al. Qualitative analysis of scopolamine-induced amnesia. *Archives of Neurology,* in press.

Cassell, E. J. Skopek, L. Language as a tool in medicine. *Journal of Medical Education,* in press.

Chandler, A. L., Hartman, M. A. Lysergic acid diethylamine as a facilitative agent in psychotherapy. *Archives of General Psychiatry,* 1960, *2,* 286–299.

Cheek, F. E., Amarel, M. Some techniques for the measurement of changes in verbal communication. In K. Salzinger & S. Salzinger (Eds.), *Research in verbal behavior and some neurophysiological implications.* New York: Academic Press, 1967, pp. 327–344.

Crockett, D., Klonoff, H., & Clark, C. The effects of marijuana on verbalization and thought processes. *Journal of Personality Assessment,* 1976, *40,* 6.

Dahlberg, C. C. LSD as an aid to psychoanalytic treatment. In J. H. Masserman (Ed.), *Science and psychoanalysis* (Vol 6). New York: Grune & Stratton, 1964, pp. 255–266.

Davitz, J. R. (Ed.), *The communication of emotional meaning.* New York: McGraw-Hill, 1964.

Feldstein, S. The relationship of interpersonal involvement and affectiveness of content to the verbal communication of schizophrenic patients. *Journal of Abnormal and Social Psychology,* 1962, *64,* 29–45.

Feldstein, S. Vocal patterning of emotional expression. In J. H. Masserman (Ed.), *Science and psychoanalysis* (Vol. 7). New York: Grune & Stratton, 1964, 193–208.

Feldstein, S. The nitty gritty issues of psychiatric research. *Career Directions,* 1979, *6*(3), 2–12.

Feldstein, S., Jaffe, J. Vocabulary diversity of schizophrenics and normals. *Journal of Speech and Hearing Research,* 1962a, *5,* 76–78.

Feldstein, S., Jaffe, J. A note about speech disturbances and vocabulary diversity. *Journal of Communication,* 1962b, *12,* 166–170.

Glaister, J., Feldstein, S., Pollack, H. Chronographic speech patterns of acutely psychotic patients: A preliminary note. *Journal of Nervous and Mental Disease,* 1980, *168,* 219–223.

Gottschalk, L. A. Theory and application of a verbal method of measuring transient psychologic states. In K. Salzinger and S. Salzinger (Eds.), *Research in verbal behavior and some neurophysiological implications.* New York: Academic Press, 1967, pp. 299–324.

Gottschalk, L. A., Bates, D. E., Waskow, I. E., et al. Effect of amphetamine or chlorpromazine on achievement strivings scores derived from content analysis of speech. *Comprehensive Psychiatry,* 1971, *12,* 430–436.

Gottschalk, L. A., Gleser, G. C. *The measurement of psychological states through the content analysis of verbal behavior.* Los Angeles: University of California, 1969.

Gottschalk, L. A., Elliott, H. W., Bates, D. E., et al. Content analysis of speech samples to determine effect of lorazepam on anxiety. *Clinical Pharmacology and Therapeutics,* 1972, *13,* 323–328.

Griffiths, R., Stitzer, M., Corker, K., et al. Drug-produced changes in human social behavior: Facilitation by d-amphetamine. *Pharmacology, Biochemistry and Behavior,* 1977, *7,* 365–372.

Groves, P. M., Rebec, G. V. Biochemistry and behavior: Some control actions of amphetamine and antipsychotic drugs. In M. R. Rosenzweig and L. W. Porter (Eds.), *Annual review of psychology, Vol. 27,* Palo Alto, California: Annual Reviews, 1976, pp. 91–128.

Haas, A. Male and female spoken language differences: Stereotypes and evidence. *Psychological Bulletin,* 1979, *86,* 616–626.

Helfrich, H., Scherer, K. R. *Experimental assessment of antidepressant drug effects using spectral analysis of voice.* Paper read at the Acoustical Society of America, Miami Beach, December, 1977.

Honigfeld, G. Cloze analysis in the evaluation of central determinants of comprehensibility. *Research in Verbal Behavior,* 1967.

Jaffe, J. Conversation chronography and the prediction of blood plasma levels. Unpublished manuscript, Department of Psychiatry, College of Physicians and Surgeons, Columbia University, 1980.

Jaffe, J., Dahlberg, C., Luria, J., et al. Speech rhythms in patient monologues: The influence of LSD-25 and dextroamphetamine. *Biological Psychiatry,* 1972, *4,* 243–246.

Jaffe, J., Dahlberg, C., Luria, J., et al. Effects of LSD-25 and dextroamphetamine on speech rhythms in psychotherapy dialogues. *Biological Psychiatry,* 1973, *6,* 93–96.

Jaffe, J., Feldstein, S. *Rhythms of dialogue.* New York: Academic Press, 1970.

Katz, M., Waskow, I. E., Olsson, J. Characterizing the psychological state produced by LSD. *Journal of Abnormal Psychology,* 1968, *73,* 1–14.

Krakower, J. M. Transient aphasia with lithium toxicity. *Psychosomatics,* 1978, 25–26.

Levy, R. The effect of chlorpromazine on sentence structure of schizophrenic patients. *Psychopharmacologia,* 1968, *13,* 426–432.

Lipton, M. A., DiMascio, A., Killam, K. F. (Eds.), *Psychopharmacology—A generation of progress.* New York: Raven Press, 1978.

Luria, A. R. *The role of speech in the regulation of normal and abnormal behavior.* London: Pergamon, 1961.

Luria, A. R. *Higher cortical functions in man.* London: Tavistock, 1966.

Mechaneck, R., Feldstein, S., Dahlberg, C. C., et al. Experimental investigation of LSD as a psychotherapeutic adjunct. *Comprehensive Psychiatry,* 1968, *9,* 490–498.

Nakano, K. K., Zubick, H., Tyler, H. R. Speech defects of Parkinsonian patients. *Neurology,* 1973, *23,* 865–870.

Natale, M., Dahlberg, C. C., Jaffe, J. Effects of psychotomimetics (LSD and dextroamphetamine) on the use of primary- and secondary-process language. *Journal of Consulting and Clinical Psychology,* 1978, *46,* 352–353.

Natale, M., Dahlberg, C. C., Jaffe, J. The effects of LSD-25 and dextroamphetamine on the use of defensive language. *Journal of Clinical Psychology,* 1979a, *35,* 250–254.

Natale, M., Dahlberg, C. C., Jaffe, J. The effect of psychotomimetics on therapist-patient matching of speech "rhythms." *Journal of Communication Disorders,* 1979b, *12,* 45–52.

Natale, M., Kowitt, M., Dahlberg, C. C., et al. Effect of psychotomimetics (LSD and dextroamphetamine) on the use of figurative language during psychoanalysis. *Journal of Consulting and Clinical Psychology,* 1978, *46,* 1579–1580.

Quinn, P. T., Peachey, C. Stuttering: An investigation of haloperidol. *Medical Journal of Australia,* 1973, *2,* 809–811.

Reuss, V., I., Silberman, E., Post, R. M., et al. D-amphetamine: Effects on memory in a depressed population. *Biological Psychiatry,* 1979, *14,* 345–356.

Rommetvert, R. *Words, meanings, and messages: Theory and experiments in psycholinguistics.* New York: Academic, 1968.

Sacher, E. J., Gruen, P. H., Altman, N., et al. Prolactin responses to neuroleptic drugs: An approach to the study of brain dopamine blockage in humans. In E. Usdin, D. A. Hamberg, and J. D. Barchas (Eds.), *Neuroregulators and psychiatric disorders.* New York: Oxford, 1977, pp. 242–249.

Salzinger, K. Group discussion. In K. Salzinger and A. Salzinger (Eds.), *Research in verbal behavior and some neurophysiological implications.* New York: Academic Press, 1967, pp. 353–354.

Schatzberg, A. F., Cole, J. O., Blumer, D. P. Speech blockage: A tricyclic side effect. *American Journal of Psychiatry,* 1978, *135,* 600–601.

Scherer, K. R. Acoustic concomitants of emotional dimensions: Judging affect from synthesized tone sequences. In S. Weitz (Ed.), *Nonverbal communication.* New York: Oxford University Press, 1974, pp. 105–111.

Scherer, K. R., Scherer, U., Rosenthal, R., et al. Differential attribution of personality based on multichannel presentation of verbal and nonverbal cues. *Psychological Research,* 1977, *39,* 221–247.

Siegman, A. W. Cognition and hesitation in speech. In A. W. Siegman and S. Feldstein (Eds.), *Of speech and time: Temporal speech patterns in interpersonal contexts.* Hillsdale, N.J.: Erlbaum Associates, 1979, pp. 151–178.

Shopsin, B., Johnson, G., Gershon, S. Neurotoxicity with lithium: Differential drug responsiveness. *International Pharmacopsychiatry,* 1970, *5,* 170–182.

Sitaram, N., Weingartner, H., Gillin, J. C. Human serial learning: Enhancement with arecoline and choline and impairment with scopolamine correlate with performance on placebo. *Science,* 1978, *201,* 274–276.

Snyder, S. H. The dopamine hypothesis of schizophrenia: Focus on the dopamine receptor. *American Journal of Psychiatry,* 1976, *133,* 197–202.

Snyder, S., Richelson, E., Weingartner, H., et al. Psychotropic methoxyamphetamines: Structure and activity in man. In E. Costa, S. Garrattini (Eds.), *Amphetamines and related compounds.* New York: Raven Press, 1970, pp. 905–928.

Solomon, K., Vickers, R. Dysarthria resulting from lithium carbonate: A case report. *Journal of the American Medican Association,* 1975, *231,* 280.

Starkweather, J. A. Vocal behavior as an information channel of speaker status. In K. Salzinger, S. Salzinger (Eds.), *Research in verbal behavior and some neurophysiological implications.* New York: Academic Press, 1967, pp. 253–262.

Stillman, R. C., Welkowitz, O., Weingartner, H., et al. Marijuana: Differential effects on right and left hemisphere functions in man. *Life Sciences,* 1977, *21*(12), 1793–1800.

Stitzer, M. L., Griffiths, R. R., Bigelow, G. E., et al. Comparison of ethanol, secobarbital and chlorpromazine on human speaking in a dyadic social interaction situation, *Pharmacology, Biochemistry, and Behavior,* in press.

Stitzer, M., Griffiths, R., Liebson, I. Effects of d-amphetamine on speaking in isolated humans. *Pharmacology Biochemistry and Behavior,* 1978, *9,* 57–63.

Taylor, W. L. "Cloze procedure": A new tool for measuring readability. *Journalism Quarterly,* 1953, *30,* 415–433.

Volavka, J., Dornbush, R., Feldstein, S., et al. Marijuana, EEG, and behavior. *Annals of the New York Academy of Sciences,* 1971, *191,* 206–215.

Waskow, I. E. The effects of drugs on speech: A review. In K. Salzinger and S. Salzinger (Eds.), *Research in verbal behavior and some neurophysiological implications.* New York: Academic Press, 1967, pp. 356–381.

Weingartner, H., Rapaport, J. L., Buchsbaum, M. S., et al. Cognitive processes in normal and hyperactive children and their response to amphetamine treatment. *Journal of Abnormal Psychology,* 1980, *89,* 25–37.

Weintraub, W., Aronson, H. The application of verbal behavior analysis to the study of psychological defense mechanisms. II: Speech pattern associated with impulsive behavior. *Journal of Nervous and Mental Disease,* 1964, *139,* 75–82.

Yaryura-Tobias, J. A., Diamond, B., and Merlis, S. Verbal communication with L-Dopa treatment. *Nature,* 1971, *234,* 224–225.

Zeidenberg, P., Clark, W. C., Jaffe, J., et al. Effect of oral administration of $\Delta^9$ tetrahydrocannabinol on memory, speech, and perception of thermal stimulation. Results with four normal volunteer subjects. Preliminary report. *Comprehensive Psychiatry,* 1973, *14,* 549–556.

# Index

Absolute intensity, measurement
  of, 97
Acetylcholine, *see also* Indolea-
    mines
  blockade, 373
  as neurotransmitter, 372
Acoustic speech analysis, *see also*
    Speech analysis
  analog instrumentation for,
    79–101
  computer systems and, 105–109
  description of, 361–362
  spectrograms of, 10, 40, 91–96,
    335–338
Acoustic speech signal
  raw material of, 9
  source and filter in, 40
Acoustic stereotypes, in schizophre-
    nia, 265
Adaptive behavior, emotional
    states and, 193–194
Aerodynamic-myoelastic theory, 66
Affect, *see also* Affect vocalization;
    Depression; Schizophrenia
  acoustic effect in depression,
    364–365
  acoustic effect of flat affect, 365

acoustic encoding of, 363–364
acoustic effect in schizophrenia,
  364–365
behavioral expression of, 360
defined, 360
feeling versus, 360
flat or blunt, 360
inappropriate, 360
and rate of speech, 366
vocalization in animals, 196–199
Affective disorders, 267–274, *see
    also* Depression; Involution de-
    pression; Manic depressive ill-
    ness
  biochemical models, 269
  clinical symptoms of, 267–268
  defined, 267–270, 360
  diagnostic classifications, 269
  flat affect and depression, 365
  neurotransmitters in, 269–270
  speech studies in, 270–274
  voice in mood disorders, 365
Affect vocalization, *see also* Animal
    vocalization
  acoustic features of, 199–200
  in animals and man, 196–201
  human speech and, 200

Aggression, *see also* Animal vocalizations
  vocal expression of, 46
Air loss
  in psychiatric patients, 275
  in psychoses, 277
Air-to-ground communications, stress/danger reporting in, 175
Alcohol, *see* Ethanol
Alcohol delirium, language destruction in, 351
All-pole model, 108
Alveolar ridge, 8
American Psychiatric Association, 244
Amphetamines, *see also* Psychoactive drugs
  chronic use and cognition, 379
  speech and, 375, 378, 382–384
Analog instrumentation, for acoustic speech analysis, 70–101, 105
Analog-to-digital converter, 106
Animal vocalizations, *see also* Emotions
  acoustic features of, 197–198
  aggression, 46, 197
  comparison with human, 46–47, 200
  danger calls, 197
  defense calls, 197
  dominance, 197
  fright/fear, 197
  hostility, 197
  submission/deference, 46, 197
  surrender, 46–47
Antidepressants, *see also* Psychoactive drugs; *specific drugs by name* Tricyclic antidepressants;
  and fundamental frequency, 382
  and speech blockage, 387
Antipsychotic drugs, *see also* Psychoactive drugs
  action of, 262, 373
  chlorpromazine, 385–386, 378
  and dopamine, 262, 373

and Parkinsonian syndrome, 262, 373
  and prolactin response, 373
Antisocial personality, and differential diagnosis, 243–246
Aphasia, autism and, 293–294
Arecoline, 373, *see also* Scopolamine
Arousal, *see* Stress
Articulation, *see also* coarticulation; encodedness; latitudinal axis settings; longitudinal axis settings; velopharyngeal settings
  of consonants, 15, 17
  as features in phonetics, 6
  relationship between sound, 45
  of sounds, 7
  of syllables, 18
  vocal organs involved in, 8
  of vowels, 15, 17
Articulation rate, 124, *see also* Temporal features
Articulation-sound relationship, 45
Articulatory phonetics, 6
Ausdruckspsychologie, 124
Autism, *see also* Childhood psychosis
  aphasia and, 293–294
  babbling in, 295–296
  bizarre language in, 289
  cortical dysfunction in, 313
  diagnostic categories other than speech or language in, 292–295
  dullness and singsong quality of speech in, 299
  echolalia in, 301–304
  hemispheric defect in, 313
  hyperlexia in, 309–310
  inner speech of, 298
  language deficit diagnosis in, 290–292
  language therapy in, 307–309
  language use in, 295–299
  left ear advantage in, 314
  literalness in, 289, 299
  mental retardation in, 293

musical abilities and, 300, 309, 311–312
neurophysiological studies in, 312–315
phonological development in, 295–296
pragmatics of speech in, 304–307
prosodic deficits in, 299–301
reinforcement learning paradigms in, 316
sound development in, 295–296
speech acquisition in, 290
speech and language characteristics in, 288–295
syntactic and semantic studies in, 297–299
Autonomic nervous system, *see also* Emotions; Stress
activity, arousal, and acoustic patterns, 205–206, 211–212
emotions and autonomic arousal, 182, 192–193, 221–223
emotions and specificity, 172–193
ergotropic system and action, 193
fight or flight, 193, 254
parasympathetic arousal and grief, 222–223
respiratory and muscular changes and speech, 173–174, 182, 222–223
stress and autonomic arousal, 172
stress and physiological correlates, 173–174
stress and specificity, 176–177
sympathetic arousal and anger, 222–223
sympathetic arousal and speech effects, 42

Balance hypothesis, 262, *see also* Neurotransmitters
Barbiturates, *see also* Psychoactive drugs; Secobarbital

site of action, 372
and speech, 385–386
Behavior, personality and, 118, *see also* Speech behavior
Benzodiazepine, 268, 379, *see also* Lorazepam
Beta-endorphin, 372, *see also* Neurotransmitters
Bilabial closure, 8
Biogenic amine hypothesis, *see also* Affective disorders; Neurotransmitters; Schizophrenia;
of affective disorders, 269
of schizophrenia, 262
Bipolar disorder; *see* Manic depressive illness
Borderline personality, and differential diagnosis, 243–246
Breathiness, physiology of, 68

California Psychological Inventory, 125, *see also* Psychometric tests
Carrier signal, speech signal and, 40
Catatonia, *see also* Schizophrenia
excited state, speech in, 352
stupor, 331
Catecholamines, *see also* Neurotransmitters
in affective disorders, 269
dopamine, 262
hypothesis of, 269
norepinephrine, 262, 269, 372
in schizophrenia, 262
Central nervous system
lesions of, 389
psychoactive drugs and, 371–372
Childhood psychosis, 258–260, *see also* Autism
central regulatory deficit in, 260
classification of, 258–259
defined, 285
echolalia in, 301–304

Childhood psychosis (continued)
  etiological considerations in,
    259–260
  language disorders in, 285–316
  language therapy in, 307–309
  neuropathological studies in,
    286–287, 314
  onset of, 286
  personality characteristics of,
    286
  speech-related characteristics of,
    260, 287–307
Childhood schizophrenia, 258–259,
  see also Schizophrenia
Chlorpromazine, 385–386, see also
  Antipsychotic drugs
Client Vocal Quality System,
  154–157
  clinical descriptions in, 155
  individual difference in, 159–161
  interrater reliability in, 157
Close rounding, of lips, 62
Cloze procedure, in content analysis, 380
Coarticulation, 11
Cognitive ability, hyperlexia and,
  310
Cognitive processing, 163–164
Colorful-dull rating, in FISC,
  143–145
Communication
  emotional expression and,
    194–195
  identity characteristics in, 51
  in schizophrenia, 332–341
  speech behavior as, 5–29
Compound phonatory settings, 69
Computer systems, acoustic analy-
  sis and, 100–101, 105–109
Consciousness, of emotional states,
  195–196, see also Affect
Consonants, see Articulation
Consonant-vowel, defined, 18
Content, of speech, 380
Coverbal aspects of speech, 308, see
  also Extralinguistic features;
  Nonlinguistic domain; Nonlin-

guistic features; Paralinguistic
  features; Speech
blood plasma level of imipramine, 381
defined, 381
drugs and, 381–388
levodopa, 386–387
lithium, 387
LSD, dextroamphetamine,
  382–385
marijuana, 386
seconal, ethanol and chlorpromazine, 385–386
tricyclic antidepressants, 382
CPI, see California Psychological
  Inventory
Creaky voice, 66–69, see also Phonatory settings of the larynx
CVQ, see Client Vocal Quality System

Danger, stress and, 174–176
Dark-light rating, in FISC, 143–147
Deference, signaling of, 46, see also
  Animal vocalizations
Delicate-empty rating, in FISC,
  143–147
Dementia
  differentiated from schizophre-
    nia, 354
  speech in, 356
  speech in Korsakoff syndrome,
    354
Dementia praecox, 261, 329, see
  also Schizophrenia
Denasal quality, 65, see also Velopharyngeal settings
Depression, 267–274, see also Affective disorders; Involutional depression; Manic depressive
  illness
in affective disorder, 267
biochemical model of, 269–270
comparisons of speech to schizophrenia, 277–278, 363–365
flat affect and, 365

fundamental frequency in, 277
involutional, 272–273
language destruction in, 351–352
language reduction in, 353–355
multiple usage of term, 267
in other syndromes, 267
power spectra in, 272, 274, 277
primary versus secondary, 267
rate of speech in, 277–278
severity and speech in, 270–271
sighing quality in, 353–354
symptoms of, 270–272
treatment effect and speech in,
    271–272
unipolar disorder, 269
voice character and quality in,
    270
Dextroamphetamine, speech and,
    370, 382–383, see also Psycho-
    active drugs
DFT, see Discrete Fourier Trans-
    form
Diagnostic classifications
Diagnostic and Statistical Man-
    ual (DSM III), 244, 249, 330
Research Diagnostic Criteria
    (RDC), 246, 365
Dialogical-monological rating, in
    FISC, 144–147
Dichotic listening, 313, see also Au-
    tism
Digital filtering, 106–107
Discrete Fourier Transform, 107
Disease models and psychosis,
    253–256, see also Neurotrans-
    mitters
genetic-environmental interac-
    tion, 256
genetic-metabolic concepts, 255
heterogeneity, 255
multifactorial concepts, 254
psychologic concepts, 254
psychosomatic concepts, 254
unifactorial concept, 253
Distal cues, 130
Distinctive features, system of,
    15–16

Dominance, see also Animal vocal-
    izations
fundamental frequency and, 125
voice quality and, 126
Dopamine, see also Catechola-
    mines; Neurotransmitters
in balance hypothesis, 262
blockade, 373
hypothesis, 262
and Parkinsonian syndrome, 373
in schizophrenia, 262
Drawl, message in, 46
Drug effects
monitoring of, 390–392
speech inevaluation of, 369–392
Duration patterns, perceptual cue
    in, 20
reflecting mood, 20
reflecting speech rate, 20

Echolalia
in autism, 301–304
communicative potential of,
    302–303
pragmatics of, 304
Ego, personality and, 116
Emotion(s), see also Emotional
    states
acoustic correlates of, 201–206
defined, 360
identifying of, 25–26
listener identification and, 208,
    211, 224, 227
nature and functions of, 189–191
recognition of from speech,
    207–214
spectrogram examination in
    identification of, 228–231
voice changes in, 42
vocal indicators of, 202–203, 206
Emotional arousal, see also Stress
speech encoding of, 362
speech production and, 173–174
Emotional experiences, bodily reac-
    tions in, 221–223

Emotional expression, communication and, 194–195

Emotional-intellectual rating, in FISC, 144–147

Emotional states, *see also* Autonomic nervous system; Emotion(s)
acoustic parameters of tone sequences relating to, 213
adaptive behavior and, 193–194
components of, 191–196
consciousness of, 195–196
Fairbanks and Hoaglin study of, 225
Fairbanks and Pronovost study of, 224–225
laboratory production of vocal expression in, 201–204
physiology in, 222–223
in preparing organism for action, 192–193
quantitative measures of $F_0$ in, 232–233
real-life, 235–238
selected studies in, 233–238
speech and, 189–214
speech intensity in, 233–234
speech rate in, 228
vocal correlates of, 221–239
Williams and Stevens study of, 225–235

Emphasis, *see also* Stress pattern
in childhood psychosis, 260, 289, 299
in dementia, 356
in depression, 266, 273
described, 361
in flat affect, 363–364
in hypomania, 352
in mania, 274
normal, 364–365
measurement of, 361
in schizophrenia, 263
and stress pattern, 19
and voice onset, 24

Encodedness, 11–12, 19

Endogenous depression, *see* Affective disorders; Depression; Involutional depression

Energy pattern, 12

Ergotropic "action" system, 193, *see also* Autonomic nervous system

Ethanol, *see also* Psychoactive drugs
speech and, 351, 385

Ethology, *see* Animal vocalizations

"Expressive Contact" pattern, 166

Expressive strength, in FISC, 142

Externalizing style, 162

Externalizing tone, 162

Externalizing voice, 158–161

Extralinguistic features, 52–53, *see also* Nonlinguistic features; Paralinguistic features

Extraversion, *see also* Personality
and fundamental frequency, 125, 126
and intensity, 126
and silent pauses, 127
and voice quality, 126
voice and speech markers of, 128–131

$F_0$, *see* Fundamental frequency

Fährmann Inventory of Speech Characteristics, 137–148
administration and scoring of, 139–142
background of, 138–139
dimensions of, 142–147
interlistener agreement in, 145–147
potential applications of, 147–148
rating form in, 140
ratings distribution in, 145–147
Type A behavior and, 148

Fairbanks and Hoaglin Study, of

emotional states, 225
Fairbanks and Pronovost Study, of
   emotional states, 224–225
Falsetto
   creaky or whispery, 69
   hysterical, 57
   laryngeal mechanisms for, 67
Fast Fourier Transform, 107
Feeling, see also Affect; Conscious-
   ness
   defined, 360
   subjective awareness of, 195–196
Feeling tone, see also Affect; Mood
   defined, 360
FES, see Fundamental Extraction
   System
FFD, see Fundamental Frequency
   Deviation
FFI-8, see Fundamental Frequency
   Indicator
FFT, see Fast Fourier Transform
Filter
   in acoustic speech signal, 40
   information present in, 43–44
   vocal tract and, 55
FISC, see Fährmann Inventory of
   Speech Characteristics
Fixed operations, in communication behavior, 23
Flat affect, 360, see also Affect
   depression and, 365
   in schizophrenia, 365
   speech encoding and, 363–364
Flow, in FISC, 143–147
Focused style, 157–160
Focused voice, 157–160
Forensic psychiatric evaluations,
   voice quality in, 143–149
Formants, see also Spectrogram
   of consonants and vowels, 15
   jaw opening and, 64
   neutral setting in, 59
   in schizophrenic speech, 337
   in spectrograms, 10, 40
   variability of, in phonetic settings,
   57–66

Formulaic expressions, 22
Fourier transforms, 107
Frequency, fundamental, see Fundamental frequency analysis;
   Fundamental frequency deviation
Frequency analysis system, 83–89
Frequency measurement, electronic, 82–83
Frye v. United States, 249
Fundamental Extraction Subsystem, 83
Fundamental frequency analysis,
   80–89; see also Fundamental
   frequency contours; Intonation; Pitch contour; Pitch level;
   Pitch range;
   in animals, 197–198
   and arousal (stress), 125, 174,
   179, 181
   in deception, 362–363
   in depression, 271, 273
   and dominance, 125
   in emotions, 205, 225, 232–233,
   235–236
   and extraversion, 129
   in flat affect and stress, 276
   normal values, 41
   and personality traits, 125, 181
   and physiology, 174
   in pilot emergencies, 175, 235,
   238
   in psychiatric patients, 275
   in schizophrenia, 263–264,
   265–266, 277
   and sex differences, 125
Fundamental frequency contours,
   see also Intonation; Pitch contour; Pitch range
   in animals, 198
   in emotional states, 225,
   231–232, 235
   in pilot emergencies, 175
Fundamental Frequency Deviation,
   see also Fundamental frequency analysis

Fundamental Frequency
  Deviation *(continued)*
  psychotic population and,
    275–277
  in schizophrenia, 263–264
Fundamental Frequency Indicator,
    83–88
  readout from, 86–87
  system block diagram for, 85
Fundamental Frequency Level, *see
    also* Fundamental frequency
    analysis
  psychiatric population and, 275–277
  in schizophrenia, 265

General Radio Spectrum Analyz-
    er, 93
General Radio Wave Analyzer, 91
Generative grammar, 26
Genetic-environmental interaction
    concepts, 256
Germ theory of disease, 253–254
Giles de la Tourette syndrome, 390
Glottal pulse shape, 42, 59
Glottis, diagram of, 8
Gottscalk-Gleser scales, 377–378,
    380, *see also* Psychometric
    tests

Hard palate, diagram of, 8
Harsh creaky voice, 69
Harsh falsetto, 69
Harshness, physiology of, 68
Hemispheric function in autism,
    313, *see also* Autism
*Hindenburg* disaster, radio descrip-
    tion of, 42, 221
  spectrograms of, 235–237
Hoarseness
  emotion and, 42
  sexual identification problems
    and, 248
  in voice description, 56
Hospitalized adolescents, deviation
    in, 275–276

Huskiness, *see also* Phonatory set-
    tings of the larynx
  emotion and, 42
  in voice description, 56
Hyperlexia, in autism, 309–311
Hypomanic excitation, speech in,
    352
Hysterical falsetto, 57

Imagery, normal emphasis and,
    364
Imipramine, 382, *see also* Tricyclic
    antidepressants
Imitation, in language acquisition,
    302
Indoleamines, *see also* Neuros-
    transmitters
  acetylcholine, 372–373
  in affective disorders, 269
  hypothesis of, 269
  serotonin, 269, 372
Instantaneous spectrometer, 91–92
Intensity, *see also* Loudness
  and emotions, 205, 233–234
  measurement of, 97–98
International Phonetic Alphabet, 9
Intonation, *see also* Emphasis;
    Pitch contours; Stress pattern
  in childhood psychosis, 260, 299,
    301
  dual function of, 25
  in FISC, 144, 147
  in hypomania, 352
  in psychoses, 277
  in schizophrenia, 264
  stress and, 19
  as suprasegmental, 19
Introversion, *see also* Extroversion;
    Personality
  and breathiness, 126
  and fundamental frequency, 126
  and voice quality, 126
Involutional depression, 272–273,
    *see also* Affective Disorders;
    Depression

clinical symptoms, 267–268, 272
speech studies in, 272–273,
277–278

Jaw, articulatory versatility of, 64
Jaw opening, formants and, 64
Jitter
  in depression, 279
  normal range of, 59
  in schizophrenia, 264
Jitter extraction system
  block diagram of, 90
  computer and, 89–90

Kay Elemetrics Sona-Graph, 95
Kay Elemetrics Visi-Pitch **6087**, 88
Korsakoff's syndrome, *see also* Dementia
  speech in,354

Labial protrusion, 60
Labiodentalized setting, 60–61
Language, *see also* Speech; Voice
  abilities and abnormalities of interest in, 309–315
  content in, 380
  musical abilities and, 300, 309, 311–312
  neoformation in, 355
Language acquisition, imitation in, 302
Language competence, 27
Language deficits, in autism diagnosis and prognosis, 290–292
Language destruction, case studies in, 351–353
Language disorders, in childhood psychosis, 285–316
Language dwindling, 353
Language neoformation, Spoerri's theory of, 355
Language reduction, case studies in, 353–355

Language therapy, in autism, 307–309
Language/thought disturbances, in schizophrenia, 245
Language use, in autistic children, 305–309
Laryngeal settings, in normal voice quality, 70
Laryngopharyngalized voice, 63
Larynx
  constricted, 43
  lowered, 43, 61
  phonatory settings of, 66
  raised, 43, 61
Larynx pulse shape, 42, 59, *see also* Glottal pulse
Latitudunal axis settings
  acoustic effects and characteristics of, 62–64
  articulatory positions of, 63–64
  labial, 62
  lingual tip/blade, 62–64
  tongue-body, and categories of, 62–64
  mandibular, 64
  table of, 70
Lax voice, contrasting characteristics of, 71
Levodopa, speech and, 387, *see also* Psychoactive drugs
Lexicon
  defined, 7
  properties of, 27
Limited vocal style, 159–161
Linear prediction, in digital speech processing, 107–108
Linguistic content, *see also* Autism; Language; Linguistic domain; Schizophrenia
  chlorpromazine and, 378–379
  defined, 39, 380–381
  drugs and, 375–381
  Lorazepam and, 379
  LSD, dextroamphetamine and, 375–376, 379
  marijuana, 376–377

Linguistic domain
    defined, 9, 39, 52–53
    consonant in, 18
Linguistic phenomena, unique,
    355–356
Linguistic phonetics, 9–18
    defined, 6
Linguistic structure, 26–27
Lips, setting of, 62
Lisping, narcissism and, 248
Lithium carbonate, *see also* Psy-
    choactive drugs
    speech and, 387
Lofepramine, 382, *see also* Tricyclic
    antidepressants
Longitudinal axis settings, 60–62
    acoustics effects and characteris-
        tics of, 60–62
    articulatory positions of, 60–61
    labial, 60–61
    laryngeal, 60–61
    table of, 70
Longitudinal tension, defined, 66,
    *see also* Phonatory setting of
    the larynx
Long-term spectral analysis, 93–94,
    *see also* Spectral analysis
Lorazepam, 379, *see also* Psychoac-
    tive drugs
Loudness (volume), *see also* Intensi-
    ty
    in childhood psychosis, 260, 289,
        299–301
    in depression, 271, 273
    in emotions, 206
    in FISC, 141–143
    in paranoid schizophrenia, 353
    variation in FISC, 141–143
LSD, *see also* Psychoactive drugs
    speech and, 375–376, 382–384
LTS, *see* Long-term spectral analy-
    sis

Major depression, *see* Affective dis-
    orders; Depression; Involution-
    al depression

Manic depressive illness, 273–274
    biochemical model of, 269–270
    clinical symptoms, 273
    speech studies in, 274
Marijuana, *see also* Psychoactive
    drugs; Tetrahydracannabinol
    speech and, 376–377, 382–383
Meaning, *see also* Morphemes
    patterns, of, 26–29
    sounds and, 6
Medial compression, defined, 66,
    *see also* Phonatory settings
Melody, *see also* Prosody
    in childhood psychosis, 289–299
    in depression, 353
    in Korsakoff's syndrome, 354
    in schizophrenia, 263–264
Mental attitudes, physical events
    and, 8
Mental retardation, echolalia and,
    302
Metabolic disease, concept of, 255
"Method" acting, emotional studies
    in, 226
Modal register, 66, *see also* Phona-
    tory settings of the larynx
Modal voice, 66
Mood, *see also* Affect
    defined, 360
    in depression, 267–268
    speech encoding of, 365–366
Morphemes
    defined, 6
    "rules" of, 26
Musical abilities, *see also* Autism
    language and, 300, 309, 311–312
    neurophysiological studies and,
        312–315
Myopathic dysphonia, 57

Nasal cavity, drawing of, 8
Nasality, 65, *see also* Velopharyn-
    geal settings
Neologisms, in schizophrenic
    speech, 331, 345, 355
Neuroleptic drugs, 373, *see also*

Antidepressants; Antipsychotic drugs; Psychoactive drugs
Neurologic integrity, speech production and, 256–257
Neuromodulators, 372, see also Neuroregulators
Neurophysiological studies, autism and, 312–315
Neuroregulators, 372, see also Neuromodulators;Neurotransmitters
Neurotransmitters, 371–374, see also Affective disorders;Catecholamines; Indoleamines; Schizophrenia
  balance hypothesis, 262
  beta-endorphin, 372
  biogenic amine hypothesis, 262, 269
  catecholamine hypothesis, 262
  dopamine hypothesis, 262
  indoleamine hypothesis, 269
  iproniazid effect on, 269
  one gene-one enzyme concept, 266
  reserpine effect on, 269
  transmethylation hypothesis, 262
Neutral setting, in voice quality, 58–59
Neutral velic scale, 65
Nonlinguistic domain, 9, 23–26, see also Emotions; Nonlinguistic features; Nonverbal communication; Personality
  acoustic data and, 9
  attitudes, emotions in, 24–26
  biology, psychology, and sociology in, 25
  defined, 9, 52–53
  information in, 9, 39, 51
  prosody and paralinguistic features in, 19–20, 52–53
  syprasegmentals in, 19
  vowel in, 18
Nonlinguistic features, 19, 39–47, see also Coverbal aspects of speech; Emotion; Extralinguistic features; Nonlinguistic domain; Paralinguistic features; Personality
  anatomy and, 43
  attitudes, emotions and, 46–47
  cognitive processing and, 43
  fixed speaker characteristics and, 43
  laryngeal paralysis and, 41
  laryngeal tumor and, 41
  neurological disorders and, 42
  pronunciation and, 44–45
  racial characteristics and, 44
  sex-related variation in, 41, 43
  stress emotions and, 42, see also Emotions; Stress
Nonlinguistic messages, in parallel transmission, 46
Nonverbal communication, see also Coverbal aspects of speech; Nonlinguistic domain; Nonlinguistic features
  channels of, 258
  concepts of research in, 258
  diagnosis and, 244–245
  incongruency between verbal and, 246, 258, 331
Norepinephrine, see also Neurotransmitters
  in depression, 269
  as neurotransmitter, 372
  in schizophrenia, 262
Normal voice, 51–74
  phonetic setting labels for. 70
  preliminary analytic concepts in, 52–56

Open rounding, of lips, 62
Optical oscillograph, in speech analysis, 81–82
Organic factors, phonetic description and, 71–73
Organic psychoses, Spoerri's description of speech in, 354, see also Dementia

Oscillograph, in acoustic speech analysis, 81–81

Palatalized voice, 63
Palate, drawing of, 8, 12
Palato-alveolarization, 64
Paralinguistic features, 19–20, 52–53, see also Inonation; Nonlinguistic features; Suprasegmental features
Parallel transmission, nonlinguistic messages in, 46–47
Paranoid schizophrenia, see also Schizophrenia
speech pathology in, 331
Spoerri's description of speech in, 352–353
Paraphonia, in schizophrenia, 339
Parasympathetic nervous system, see Autonomic nervous system
Parkinsonian syndrome, see Antipsychotic drugs
Parkinson's disease, see also Levodopa
and balance hypothesis, 262
Levodopa and speech, 386–387
placebo, and speech, 387
procyclidine hydrochloride and speech, 387
Pathological speech, acquisition of in schzophrenia, 341–343
Pauses, see also Prosody; Temporal features; Rhythm;
in depression, 353, 365
in emotions, 225
in flat affect, 365
in mania, 274
in schizophrenia, 264, 354, 365
silent, 123, 127
silent hesitation, 123, 127
silent periods, 123
Personality, see also Extroversion, Introversion
behavior and, 118–119
Brunswikian lens model of, 130–132

concept of, 115–117
individual differences in, 117, 181–182
self-fulfilling prophecy in, 221–222
self-preservation and, 121
speech behavior and, 119–122
vocal parameters of, 25
Personality differences, 117
stress and, 181–182
Pervasive developmental disorders, see Autism; Childhood psychosis
Pharyngalized voice, 63
Pharynx, drawing of, 8
Phase, in FISC, 143–147
Phonation-time ratio, see also Temporal features
in depression, 277–278
in normal, 277–278
in schizophrenia, 277–278
Phonation types, 66–67
Phonatory settings of the larynx, 66–69
acoustic effects and characteristics of, 66–69
of adductive tension, 66
articulatory positions of, 66–69
breathiness, and compound phonation types, 66–70
creak, 66–68
falsetto, 66–67
harshness, and compound phonation type, 66–70
of medial compression, 66
of modal voice, 66
whisper, 66–67
table of, 70
Phoneme
defined, 6
illustrations of, 16–18
Phonemic segments, extraction of, 15
Phonetic description
articulatory parameters in, 14
organic factors and, 71–73
Phonetic features, 6, 14–16

Phonetics
    articulatory, 6
    distinctive features in, 15–16
    psychotherapeutic application of, 248
Phonetic setting, overall muscular tension in, 7–71
Phonetic transcript, 9
Phonology, defined, 7
Phrase-size units, in speech production, 21
Physical events, mental activities and, 8
Pitch
    defined, 80
    "natural" level of, 41
    perception of, 80–81
Pitch contours, see also Fundamental frequency contours; Fundamental frequency levels; Pitch range
    in attitude and emotion, 19–20
    and emotions, 213–231
    in schizophrenia, 354
    in sentence structure, 19–20
Pitch level, see also Fundamental frequency analysis; Fundamental frequency contours; Pitch Range
    in childhood psychosis, 260
    in depression, 271, 273
    and emotion, 206, 213
    in schizophrenia, 264
Pitch range, see also Fundamental frequency analysis; Pitch contours; Pitch level
    in childhood psychosis, 260, 299–301
    in depression, 270
    and emotions, 206, 213
    in mania, 274
Pitch perturbation, see Jitter
Pragmatic deficits, 306–307
Pragmatics, in autistic language, 304–307
Precision, in FISC, 144–147
Primary depression, 269, see also

Affective disorders; Depression; Involutional depression
Princeton Applied Research Real-Time Spectrum Analyzer, 92–93
Private meanings, 28
Process diagnosis, vocal style and, 163
Procyclidine hydrochloride, 387, see also Parkinson's disease
Prolactin response, 373, see also Antipsychotic drugs
Pronunciation, variations in, 44–45
Prosodic deficits, in autism, 299–301
Prosodic features, 19–20, see also Intonation; Temporal features
Proverb Interpretation Test, 245, see also Psychometric tests
PSE, see Psychological Stress Evaluator
Psychiatric disorders, clinical manifestation of, 275
Psychiatric evaluations, voice relevance in, 243–249
Psychiatric populations
    comparative studies in, 277–279
    mixed psychotic population studies and speech, 275–276
    speech and voice studies in, 253–281
    treatment and power spectrum analysis in, 276
Psychoactive drugs, 369–396 see also Antidepressants; Antipsychotic drugs; Specific drugs by name
    action of, 373
    antipsychotic drugs, 385–386
    Chlorpromazine, 378, 385–386
    CNS and, 371–372
    Dextroamphetamines, 375, 378, 382–384
    Effects on speech, 375–386
    Ethanol, 385–386
    and hemispheric specificity, 374
    Imipramine, 381

Psychoactive drugs *(continued)*
  Levodopa, 386
  Lithium, 387
  Lorazepam, 379
  LSD-25, 375–376, 382–383
  Marijuana, 376–378, 386
  and neurotransmitters, 373
  in psychiatry, 253
  scopolamine, 373–374
  site of action of, 371–374
  speech content and, 375–381
Psychological Stress Evaluator,
    174–178
Psychometric tests
  Chomsky transformational anal-
    ysis, 297
  Client Vocal Quality System
    (CVQ), 154–159
  Cloze procedure, 376, 380
  Gottschalk-Gleser scales,
    376–378
  Illinois Test of Psycholinguistic
    Ability (ITPA), 294
  Proverb Interpretation test, 245
  Seashore musical test, 300–301,
    342
  Subordination index, 378
  Thematic Appreception Test
    (TAT), 377
  Vigotsky Block Sorting test, 245
  Wechsler Adult Intelligence
    Scale (WAIS), 313
  Wechsler Intelligence Scale for
    Children (WISC), 313
Psychopathological populations,
    psychiatric studies of, 280–281
Psychopathology, speech behavior
    and, 246–249
Psychopharmacology, speech and,
    369–392
*Psychopharmacology* (Barchas et
    al.) 262, 270
Psychoses, speech and, 257–258
Psychosomatic concept of disease,
    254, *see also* Disease models
    and psychosis

Psychotherapy outcome, vocal style
    and, 157–161
Psychotherapy process
  clinical applications of, 162–163
  cognitive processing and,
    163–164
  future directions in, 165–166
  speech production and, 163–164
  verbal behavior patterns and,
    153–154
  vocal style and, 151–166
Psychotherapy research, at Univer-
    sity of Chicago, 152–154
Psychotic depression, *see* Affective
    disorders; Depression; Involu-
    tional depression
Psychotic speech, Spoerri's descrip-
    tion of, 349–357
Psychotic syndromes, heterogene-
    ity of, 255
Psychotropic drugs, *see also* Benzo-
    diazepine; Psychoactive drugs;
    Neuroleptics
  in agitation, 268
  in anxiety, 268
  in psychomotor retardation, 268
Purdue Pitch Meter, 88
Pursed-lips position, 62


Quasilinguistic interjections, 199


Real-life emotional situations, vo-
    cal correlates in, 235–238
Real-time spectrometers, 92
Regularity, in FISC, 143–147
Reserpine, 269, *see also* Neuro-
    transmitters
Retroflex setting, 64
Rhythm, *see also* Temporal fea-
    tures
  in affective disorders, 366
  in childhood psychosis, 260, 289,
    299
  in Korsakoff's syndrome, 354
  in schizophrenia, 263–264

Schizophrenia, 260–266, 329–345
  acoustic stereotypes in, 265
  acute and chronic, 261
  affect disturbance in, 360
  antipodal speech effects in, 266
  "artificial language" of, 331, 355
  biochemical models of, 262–263
  clinical symptoms of, 260–261
  communication in, 332–341
  comparative studies in, 277
  definitions of, 260, 329–330
  depression and, 353–354
  discrimination studies in, 263–264
  "driven-restricted" quality of
    speech in, 354–355
  flat affect in, 363–365
  fundamental frequency level in,
    263–265
  inner speech and, 343–345
  jitter in, 264
  Langfeldt hypothesis of, 261
  language/thought disturbance
    in, 245
  listener identification of, 263
  medication effect in, 266
  nature vs. nurture in, 261
  neologisms in, 331
  neurochemical imbalance in, 330
  paranoid, speech in, 352–353
  paraphonia in, 339
  pathological speech acquisition
    in, 341–343
  patient's speaking voice in,
    338–341
  primary and secondary distur-
    bances in, 331–332
  psychiatric illnesses associated
    with, 329–345
  research diagnostic criteria and,
    245
  severity prognosis and speech in,
    265–266
  speech and, 329–345
  speech deviations in, 339
  Spoerri's descriptions of speech
    in, 352–355

stress hypothesis of, 261
treatment effects and speech in,
    265
vocal regulatory phenomena in,
    264–265
voice character and quality in,
    263
voice deviation in, 264
Schizophrenic speech
  acquisition of, 341–343
  disturbances of, 331–332
  hallucinating and, 344
  "inner," 343–345
  neologisms in, 331–345
  spectrograms of, 335–338
  studies of, 333–338
Schmitt trigger circuit, 83
Scopolamine, 373–374, see also Psy-
    choactive drugs
Seashore Test of Musical Abilities,
    300, see also Psychometric tests
Secobarbital, see also Barbiturates;
    Psychoactive drugs
  speech and, 385–386
Secondary depression, 269, see also
    Depression
Segmental phenomena, vs. supra-
    segmental, 19
Self-fulfilling prophecy, in person-
    ality dispositions, 121–122
Self-presentation, personality and,
    121
Semantic patterns, defined, 7
Sepulchral voice, as descriptive la-
    bel, 57
Serotonin, see also Indoleamines
  in depression, 269
  as neurotransmitter, 372
Settings
  labiodentalized, 60
  of larynx, 61
  latitudinal, 62–64
  phonetic, 70–71
  in voice quality, 54, 57–71
SFF, see Speaking Fundamental
    Frequency

Shadowing, 21, 22
Shimmer, 59
Sighing quality
  in depression, 353–354
  in voice, 68–69
Silent hesitation pauses, 123, 127,
  see also Pauses; Temporal fea-
  tures
Slurred pronunciations, 44
Socioeconomic stereotypes, 25
Sona-Graph spectrometer, 95–96
Sound-articulation relationship,
  45–46
Sound change, pronunciation and,
  44–45
Sound pressure level, intensity
  and, 97, see also Intensity
Sounds, meaning and, 6
Speaker, pitch level of, 41
Speaker identification, voice in, 39
Speaking Fundamental Frequency,
  see also Fundamental Frequency Deviation
  analysis of, 80–89
  measurement of, 81–83
  pitch perception and, 80–81
Spectral analysis, 90–96
  in animals, 197
  in arousal (stress), 183
  in depression, 271, 273–274,
  276–277, 341
  and emotions, 234
  instantaneous, 91–93
  long term, 93-94
  in psychiatric patients, 276
  in schizophrenia, 265, 277, 341
Spectral envelope, 12
Spectrogram, see also Spectrometer
  continuous and discontinuous elements in, 10–14
  of emotional states, 229–231,
  235–236
  formants in, 40
  pronounciation differences in, 13
  of schizophrenic speech, 335–338
Spectrometer
  real-time, 92

in speech analysis, 91–93
time-frequency-amplitude type,
  94–96
Speech, see also Language; Speech
  behavior; Voice
  affect disturbances and, 359–367
  affect vocalizations and, 200
  amphetamines and, 383–385
  articulation rate in, 124
  basic features of, 80
  carrier nature of, 40
  content of, 380
  coverbal aspects of, 381–388
  dextroamphetamine and,
  382–383
  Digitation and, 106
  drug monitoring and, 390–392
  emotional states and, 189–214
  ethanol and, 351, 385
  fluency aspects of, 123–127
  fundamental frequency of,
  80–89, 125–126, 231–233,
  263–265, 275–277
  in genetic and metabolic diseases, 257
  identity characteristics in, 51
  inherent information in, 40–44
  levodopa and, 387
  LSD and, 375–376, 382–384
  multidimensional nature of,
  256–258
  noise threshold and, 362
  nonlinguistic components of,
  39–47
  nonverbal communication and,
  258
  perceptual organization of, 22
  personality correlates in,
  124–127
  psychobiology of, 388–390
  psychopharmacology and,
  369–392
  psychophysiologic dimensions of,
  257
  psychoses and, 257–258
  recognition of emotions from,
  207–214

schizophrenia and, 329–345
silent hestiation pauses in,
123–124
silent periods in, 123
sounds of, 7–8
teeth defects and, 43
temporal features of, 9, 80, *see
also* Temporal features
vocal aspects of, 122–126
Speech acquisition, in schizophrenia, 341–343
Speech acts, 28
Speech analysis
acoustic, *see* Acoustic speech
analysis
computers in, 100–101
FISC in, 137–138
instrumental approaches to, 80
intensity analysis in, 97–98
optical oscillograph in, 81–82
spectrography in, 90–96,
229–230, 335–338
temporal measures in, 98–100
vocal jitter, 89–90
wave composition in, 90–96
Speech behavior
biophysical factors in, 119–120
as communication process, 5–29
functional efficiency and,
120–121
personality and, 115–132
physiological factors in, 120
psychopathology and, 246–249
self-presentation in, 121
silent pauses in, 127
sounds and meaning in, 6–8
vocal intensity in, 126
voice quality and, *see* Voice quality
Speech bursts, pressure level of, 98
Speech characteristics, in childhood psychoses, 289–309
Speech content, psychoactive drugs
and, 375–381
Speech cues, nature and measurement of, 122–124
Speech discontinuities, 127

Speech dynamics, in FIXC,
144–147
Speech intensity, measurement of,
97–98
Speech perception, 20–23
hierarchy in, 22
Speech performance, syntactic rule
processing in, 27
Speech production, 20–23
biophysical factors in, 19–20
emotional arousal and, 173–174
neurologic integrity and,
256–257
Speech production
stress and, 171–174
vocal cues and, 163–164
Speech rate, 123–124,*see also* Temporal features
Speech recognition, 39
Speech signal
acoustic, 6, 9, 40, 55
changed properties in, 107
TED vector in, 99–100
Speech spectrum, long-term analysis of, 93–94
Speech studies, in psychiatric populations, 253–281
Speech tempo, 123–124, *see also*
Temporal features
Spoerri research methods, 350
characteristic features of, 356
Squirrel monkey, vocalization in,
187
State and trait, 125, *see also* Emotional states; Personality
Strategies, in speech communicative behavior, 23
Stress, *see also* Autonomic nervous
system; Emotions
achievement and, 178–179
and autonomic arousal, 172
deception studies in, 177–178
definitions of, 171–172
evidence on vocal indicators of,
179–182
intonation and, 19
laboratory induction of, 176–182

Stress *(continued)*
    nature of, 171–172
    personality differences in,
        181–182
    physiological correlates of,
        173–174
    real-life studies of, 174–175
    speech production and, 171–174
    as suprasegmental phenomenon,
        19
    sympathetic arousal and, 173
    vocal indicators of, 116
Stress pattern, *see also* Emphasis;
        Intonation
    in emphasis, 19
    intonation and, 19
    in linguistic contrast, 19
    as suprasegmental, 19
Submission, *see also* Animal vocal-
        izations
    and deference, 46
    and fundamental frequency, 126
    and vocal intensity, 126
Substance use disorders, speech in,
        *see* Alcohol; Amphetamines;
        LSD; Marijuana
Superego, personality and, 116
Supralaryngeal settings, in normal
        voice quality, 70
Suprasegmental phenomena, stress
        and intonation as, 19, *see also*
        nonlinguistic features
Syllabic nucleus, 18
Syllabic rate variation, in FISC,
        144–147
Syllable, construction of, 18
Sympathetic arousal, stress and,
        173, *see also* Autonomic ner-
        vous system
Sympathetic nervous system, *see*
        Autonomic nervous system
Synapse, 371–373, *see also* Psycho-
        active drugs
Syntactic rule processing, in
        speech performance, 27
Syntax, defined, 7

Tardive dyskinesia, 262
TED vector technique, 99–100, *see
        also* Temporal features
Teeth defects, speech and, 43
Temporal features, *see also* Pauses;
        Phonation time ratio; Rhythm
    in affective disorders, 366
    in alcoholic delirium, 351
    in childhood psychosis, 260
    in depression, 270–271, 277–278,
        351–353
    in emotions, 206, 213, 225, 228
    in hypomania, 352
    in mania, 274, 366
    measurement of, 98–100
    in psychiatric patients, 276
    rate, 9, 123–124
    in schizophrenia, 264–266,
        277–278, 332, 354
Tense voice, local components of,
        71
Tension, in FISC, 144–147
Δ Tetrahydracannabinol, speech
        and, 379, 386 *see also* Marijua-
        na
T-F-A spectrometry, *see* Time-fre-
        quency-amplitude spectrom-
        etry
Thematic Apperception Test, 377
Timbre
    in autism, 299
    in depression, 353
    in FISC, 143
    in schizophrenia, 263, 354
Time-frequency-amplitude spec-
        trometry, 94–96
Tip/blade system, in tongue-body
        settings, 63–64
Tip-of-the-tongue phenomenon, 27
Tone of voice, paralinguistic fea-
        tures of, 52–53
Tongue body, tip/blade system and,
        63, *see also* Latitudinal axis
        settings
Total quality level, in FISC,
        145–147

Transformational analysis, Chomsky-based, 297
Transmethylation hypothesis, 262 see also Neurotransmitters; Schizophrenia
Tricyclic antidepressants, see also Psychoactive drugs; Specific drugs by name
  Impiramine, 381–382
  Lofepramine, 382
  speech blockage and, 287
Trophotropic "rest" system, 193, see also Autonomic nervous system
"Turn taking," signals for, 24
Type A behavior, coronary heart disease and, 148

Unipolar disorder, 269, see also Affective disorders; Depression
Unique linguistic phenomena, Spoerri's description of, 355–356
Utterance, see also Speech; Vocalization
  linguistic content of, 39
  pragmatic effects of, 28
Uvula, drawing of, 8

Variant surfaces, 11
Velarized voice, 12, 63
Velopharyngeal settings, 65–66
  acoustic effects and characteristics of, 65–66
  articulatory positions of, 65
  denasality, 65
  nasality, 65–66
  table of, 70
Velum
  drawing of, 8
  movement of, 65
Ventricular voice, 68
Verbal speech, 381

Verbal urgency, in FISC, 142–147
Verbigeration, 356
Vigotsky Block Scoring Test, 245, see also Psychometric tests
Vocal behavior patterns, in psychotherapy research, 153–154, see also Speech behavior
Vocal cords
  characteristics of, 40–42
  vibration rate for, 40–41
Vocal cues, 163–164
Vocalic-consonantal rating, in FISC, 144–147
Vocal intensity, 126
Vocal jitter, see Jitter; Jitter extraction systems
Vocal organs, diagram of, 8
Vocal patterns
  discriminable aspects of, 155–156
  summary of, 158
Vocal pitch, in FISC, 142–147, see also Fundamental frequency analysis; Pitch
Vocal quality, see Voice quality
Vocal signals, quasiperiodic nature of, 89
Vocal stereotypes, 25
Vocal style
  clinical applications of, 162–163
  externalizing, 158–161
  focused, 157–161
  limited, 159–161
  moment-to-moment variations in, 161–162
  process diagnosis and, 163
  psychotherapy for, 151–166
Vocal tract
  filter system of, 55
  ideal and actual, positions in, 12
  longitudinal settings in, 60–62
Voice
  acoustical features of, 361–362
  basic features of, 80
  creaky, 66–69
  descriptive labels in, 56–57
  extraversion in, 128–131

Voice *(continued)*
  introversion-extraversion dimension and, 128–129
  normal, *see* Normal voice
  organic versus phonetic factors in, 54
  speaker identification from, 39
  tone of, 52–53
  voluntary modifications of, 44–47
Voice changes, emotion and, 42, *see also* Emotions
Voice character, in manic-depressive illness, 274, *see also* Affective disorders; Schizophrenia; Voice quality
Voice deviation, in schizophrenia, 264, *see also* Affective disorders
Voice dynamics, 55
Voice frequency, measurement of, 82–83, *see also* Fundamental Frequency Analysis
*Voice of neurosis, The* (Moses), 151
Voice quality
  anatomy in, 58
  compatibility principle in, 58
  in depression, 270
  in forensic psychiatric evaluations, 243–249
  harshness and, 68
  in involutional depression, 272
  in mania, 274
  phonetic settings in, 57–71
  in schizophrenia, 263
  speech behavior and, 126

  versus voice synamics, 55
Voice recognition, 53
Voice settings
  defined, 54
  longitudinal, 60–62
  neutral, 58–59
Voice/speech intensity information, 80
Voice studies, in psychiatric population, 253–281
Voice terminology, standardization of, 56–57
Voice-voiceless distinctions, in consonant chart, 17
Voicing, onset of, 14, 24
Volume, *see* Loudness
Vowels, *see* Articulation

Warm-cold rating, in FISC, 143–147
Wave composition, in speech analysis, 90–95
Wechsler Adult Intelligence Scale, 313, *see also* Psychometric tests
Wechsler Intelligence Scale for Children, 313, *see also* Psychometric tests
Whisper
  harsh, 69
  physiology of, 67
Whispering creaky voice, 69
Whispering falsetto, 69
Williams and Stevens study of emotional states, 225–235